FORM

MU00989934

Forms of Empire shows how the modern state's anguished relationship to violence pushed writers to expand the capacities of literary form. The Victorian era is often imagined as an 'age of equipoise,' but the period between 1837 and 1901 included more than 200 separate wars. What is the difference, though, between peace and war? The much-vaunted equipoise of the nineteenth-century state depended on physical force to guarantee it. But the sovereign violence hidden in the shadows of all law shuddered most visibly into being at the edges of law's reach, in the Empire, where emergency was the rule and death perversely routinized. George Eliot, Charles Dickens, Wilkie Collins, A. C. Swinburne, H. Rider Haggard, and Robert Louis Stevenson, among others, all generated new formal techniques to account for the sometimes sickening interplay between order and force in their liberal Empire. In contrast to the progressive idealism we have inherited from the Victorians, these writers moved beyond embarrassment and denial in the face of modernity's uncanny relation to killing. They sought aesthetic effects—free indirect discourse, lyric tension, and the idea of literary 'character' itself—able to render thinkable the conceptual vertigoes of liberal violence. In so doing, they touched to the dark core of our post-Victorian modernity. Archival work, literary analyses, and a theoretical framework that troubles the distinction between 'historicist' and 'formalist' approaches helps this book link the Victorian period to the present and articulate a forceful vision of why literary thinking matters now.

Nathan K. Hensley is Associate Professor of English at Georgetown University. His writing has appeared in *Victorian Studies, Novel: A Forum on Fiction, Genre, The Los Angeles Review of Books,* and other venues. He is co-editor of *Ecological Form: System and Aesthetics in the Age of Empire.*

Forms of Empire

The Poetics of Victorian Sovereignty

NATHAN K. HENSLEY

OXFORD
UNIVERSITY PRESS

OXFORD
UNIVERSITY PRESS

Great Clarendon Street, Oxford, OX2 6DP,
United Kingdom

Oxford University Press is a department of the University of Oxford.
It furthers the University's objective of excellence in research, scholarship,
and education by publishing worldwide. Oxford is a registered trade mark of
Oxford University Press in the UK and in certain other countries

First published 2016
First published in paperback 2018

Published in the United States of America by Oxford University Press
198 Madison Avenue, New York, NY 10016, United States of America

British Library Cataloguing in Publication Data
Data available

Library of Congress Cataloging in Publication Data
Data available

ISBN 978–0–19–879245–1 (Hbk.)
ISBN 978–0–19–883074–0 (Pbk.)

Acknowledgments

Like anything else that comes into the world looking new, this book would not have existed but for an almost infinite series of past events: in this case, good deeds, generous turns, and material acts of support accumulated over decades. These debts are profound and nothing in typeface can ever be adequate to them. But it is a pleasure to at least try, by a kind of telegraphic compression, to acknowledge the measures of generosity concealed in the finished form of this book.

I begin with money. Key support for this project came from grants, summer support, and a junior faculty leave from Georgetown University. From Macalester College I received help in the shape of a Janet Wallace Scholarly Activities Grant. A much earlier version of this project was supported as a dissertation by Duke University and the American Council of Learned Societies; even earlier, the University of Notre Dame funded my graduate work. In my first, hesitant years trying to sort out how an academic life might proceed, the Dorothy Atkinson Evans Fellowship at Vassar College gave important assistance. And my aunt, Barbara Hensley, helped out at a moment when I really needed it.

My life's lucky plot has put me into contact with many friends, colleagues, and interlocutors without whose counsel I couldn't have continued. Thomas S. Davis has been a trusted collaborator since the earliest days, and the stamp of our ongoing conversation is I hope evident on many of these pages. Max Brzezinski, Sarah Lincoln, Scott Selisker, Philip Steer, and Tim Wientzen have also commented on these ideas in many forms, over many years; to the extent that those ideas make any sense, these friends have helped make them do so. I'm grateful, too, for the insight and encouragement conveyed in various ways by Jessica Berman, Gordon Bigelow, Tyler Bradway, Calina Ciobanu, Deborah Denenholz Morse, Daniel DeWispelare, Jed Esty, Erin Fehskens, Anna Gibson, Lauren Goodlad, Aaron Greenwald, Molly Clark Hillard, Neil Hultgren, Azeen Khan, Bill Knight, Kristin Mahoney, Kyle McAuley, John McGowan, Elsie Michie, Daniel Novak, Matthew J. Phillips, Paul Saint-Amour, and Stefan Waldschmidt. At a key time, a group of then-junior Victorianists met at Devin Griffiths' house to read a chapter: I thank him and them, and Benjamin Morgan for organizing us. Another group convened in Charlottesville to talk method, and I am grateful to Rita Felski for gathering us there. Searching feedback from audiences at Binghamton,

Duquesne, George Washington, Ohio State, Penn, the Rutgers British Studies Center, and the University of Toronto helped make this book stronger. At Macalester I found a bracing and supportive intellectual milieu, and learned from Neil Chudgar, Jim Dawes, Daylanne English, Marlon James, Theresa Krier, and Robert Warde. Over the past several years I've been invigorated by the community in the Georgetown English department, a peerless place to work. I thank especially Caetlin Benson-Allott, Ashley Cohen, Jennifer Natalya Fink, Carolyn Forché, Lindsay Kaplan, Sarah McNamer, Ricardo Ortiz, Cóilín Parsons, Seth Perlow, John Pfordresher, Sam Pinto, Libbie Rifkin, Nicole Rizzuto, Henry Schwarz, Christine So, and Kathryn Temple. Dan Shore has been a sharp interlocutor on many projects including this one; Brian Hochman an imaginative reader and co-conspirator. Mark McMorris read drafts with dynamic generosity. Patrick O'Malley and Duncan Wu have been inspiring mentors.

Literature would have meant little to me without my teachers, and to them I owe a special debt. Thanks go to Mark Amodio, Brother James Joost, FSC, and Paul Russell. At Notre Dame I had daunting models in Joseph Buttigieg, Kevin Hart, Greg Kucich, and Sara Maurer. At Duke I began accumulating the profound debts I owe to Ian Baucom, Michael V. Moses, and the late Srinivas Aravamudan. I thank also Cathy Davidson, Tom Ferraro, Rob Mitchell, Thomas Pfau, Charlotte Sussman, and Priscilla Wald. Nancy Armstrong has pushed and aided me for many years. In South Bend, Durham, and points beyond, my scholarly life has been shaped most by Kathy A. Psomiades, whose intellectual DNA—source code and parent of my own—is I hope productively mutated in this book.

For help in giving direction to my wanderings among old material, I thank the expert archivists at the Alkazi Foundation for the Arts; the British Library; the Canadian Centre for Architecture; the National Archives of the United Kingdom; the Harry Ransom Center; the David M. Rubenstein Rare Book and Manuscript Library at Duke University; and, at Georgetown, the Booth Family Center for Special Collections. The creativity and diligence of Jeesun Choi, Alex Myers, Annalisa Adams, Marielle Hampe, and John James have been invaluable over the long career of this manuscript. I am grateful to the staff at Oxford University Press—Jacqueline Baker, Ellie Collins, and Sarah Barrett especially—for their work on my behalf. My students at Duke, Macalester, and Georgetown have helped these ideas come into the world, and are in that sense co-authors. All errors are, obviously, my own.

Insofar as it freezes into portable shape much of my academic life so far, this book is a testament to the influence of my parents, Dr. Paula Solomon and Jeffrey Hensley, who taught us all to persist and to imagine and to try our best. Together with my siblings, Jennifer Hensley and William Hensley, my family's support has been invaluable. My closest collaborator in life and work is Anne O'Neil-Henry, whose intelligence and unending humor make everything around her spring to life: I owe her more than can fit into these words. June and Irene Hensley show every day how newness comes into the world. They can't read much of it yet, but this book is theirs.

Some parts of the Introduction and Chapter 2 are reprinted by permission of the Indiana University Press, and were originally printed in Victorian Studies, *Volume 56 Number 1 and Volume 54 Number 4, respectively. Earlier parts of Chapter 4 originally appeared in* Novel: A Forum on Fiction, *Volume 45, Number 2.*

A note about citations. All quotations from John Stuart Mill have been standardized using the *Online Library of Liberty's* digital version of *The Collected Works of John Stuart Mill*, ed. J.M. Robson (Toronto: University of Toronto Press, London: Routledge and Kegan Paul, 1963–91), 33 vols.

Because this online tool is searchable both within each volume and across the set, I have indicated for each citation only the volume number, observing the minimalist format, e.g., (*CW* IV). Readers can access the full resource at http://oll.libertyfund.org/titles/mill-collected-works-of-john-stuart-mill-in-33-vols.

Contents

List of Figures

Introduction

Reading Endless War

Bombay 13. Mutiny all but universal in Bengal and Northwest. Nearly 30000 men disappeared from army within last few weeks. Town Delhi still in mutineers possession but all heights in our hand punjab quiet. Steamer Erin totaly wrecked. No lives lost. General Govern and Governors at their seats.

—Telegram to East India Office, 12 July 1857, 4.35 p.m.
(British Library L/Mil/5/514, p. 3)

MUTINY ALL BUT UNIVERSAL

The sporadically capitalized and badly punctuated text above gives a snapshot of a colonial sovereignty crisis in slow burn. Time-stamped with perfect specificity ("4.35 pm"), the unpublished telegram was transmitted some five months into the greatest threat to British rule in the nineteenth century: the two-year long revolt in India, during which peasants, towns-people, and some 130,000 Indian soldiers took arms en masse against British power. Debate continues about the causes and scope of this spectacular insubordination. What is clear is that the amorphous anticolonial struggle that Karl Marx (1857), in his dispatches to the *New York Tribune*, called "the revolt in India" was felt by many in England as a substantive challenge to its global rule: a "great crisis in our national history" and "our greatest and most fearful disaster," as contemporaries observed (quoted in Herbert 2009: 2).[1] To Indians it proved yet more disastrous, since in rectifying this temporary interruption of its imperium—in re-establishing colonial law—England gave no quarter. Writes historian C. A. Bayly: "[T]ens of thousands of soldiers and village guerrillas were hanged, shot, or blown from guns" (1990: 194), the last technique referring to the chaining of a live body over a cannon and then firing.

This book is about the uncanny persistence of violence in a globalized liberal society. It tracks a handful of nineteenth-century poets, novelists, and political theorists as they stretched the boundaries of their thinking to account for the seeming paradox by which a project of universal modernization could unfold hand in hand with generalized killing. "It was in the Victorian era," says jingoist historian Byron Farwell, "that continual warfare became an accepted way of life" (1972: 1). This statement finds complication in recent work showing how other periods—the seventeenth century, the Romantic era, the twentieth century—might claim this dubious honor too.[2] But as Farwell notes with proud amazement, the years between 1837 and 1901 were characterized not just by salutary social progress, widening democracy, or mechanized enlightenment but also by ongoing war: extrajudicial killing as everyday life.

There were at least 228 separate armed conflicts during the period, at least one in every year of Queen Victoria's reign; usually more. Eight, for example, in 1854. These included declared wars like the Crimean and the Boer Wars, but also asymmetrical conflicts, punitive campaigns, rebellions put down by sword and musket and Maxim gun. Fought at different scales, against diverse enemies, and in response to widely various local conditions, these "savage wars of peace," as Rudyard Kipling called them late in the century (l. 9), were waged against human bodies either marked as enemies or cast out from all legal standing, and thus without even the minimal legal protection conferred by enmity. When I transcribed these wars from Farwell's book into Microsoft Excel, the list ran to six full pages. The disconcerting profusion of this killing suggests that the images we take to characterize the world's first liberal empire should include not just the middle-class hearth or the democratic ballot box but the war zones and boneyards of England's global periphery, where mutiny, and its suppression, were all but universal.

Emancipation and death advanced together. But what narrative forms could capture this fundamental paradox of liberal empire? What language could be adequate to the *Pax Victoriana*'s endless war? And what strategies of representation might transmit the disturbing fact that peacekeeping and warmaking were not separate ideas, but two aspects of sovereign power as such? There is little room for such reflection in the halting, bureaucratic idiom of the telegraphic communiqué cited in the epigram that opened this Introduction. And yet it, too, has form; it too models thought. Its clipped syntax adapts itself to the conventions of military telegraphy, unwritten rules of genre shaped by the argot of imperial administration no less than by the expense of transcontinental electronic signaling. Compressed into a kind of stylized poetry, the document, like all pieces of writing, conveys conceptuality and formalizes a theory of the world. The picture this one paints is an official one: it tells a story not of harm inflicted or occupation contested but of order restored, political ownership transferred back to "our hand." The telegram's narrative sequence turns on two "buts": "Mutiny all but universal. [...] Nearly 30000 men disappeared from army within last few weeks. Town Delhi still in mutineers possession but all heights in our hand punjab [*sic*] quiet." Comprehensive desertion, lost towns, even maritime wreckage ("Steamer Erin totaly [*sic*] wrecked"): this defeat and chaos give way at last to what is, in the context, a happy ending. No "lives [are] lost" in the wreck of the Erin, the document reports, and stability is, at last, re-established: "General[s] Govern and Governors [are] at their seats." Tested, contravened, disrupted: by the end of this telegram law nevertheless reigns.

However striking as an epitome of the so-called Mutiny, this tidy story of legal reordering can only ring with irony for later readers, given that it was sent just three days before the infamous "Massacre at Cawnpore" (Kanpur), in which Indian forces led by Nana Sahib killed 120 white women and children before throwing their hacked remains into a well.[3] Still, despite the local effectiveness of the Indian resistance—appalling as it appeared to British observers—in the fullness of time colonial law *was* restored. Brutal reprisals re-established British pre-eminence on the sub-continent, a military control that the 1858 Government of India Act translated into legal statute. "This great convulsion has been fraught with much instruction," summarized *Bentley's Miscellany*. "It has taught us the necessity of a radical change in our whole system of government, and the propriety of an immediate assertion, throughout India, of the sovereignty of the British Crown" (Tremenheere 1858: 123).

The term "sovereignty" describes both lawful order and the violence necessary to sustain it. This doubleness means that the sovereignty concept, and the relationship between law and force more broadly, generated productive disorientations for orthodox Victorian thought. Even to some of the mid-Victorian era's most acute observers, the persistence of physical violence in their advanced stage of modernity defied explanation. Progressive models could not admit that a modernity that was by definition pacific could also be an ongoing war. Just three years after the Mutiny's definitive suppression and in a year in which, by Farwell's count, England prosecuted nine separate wars, John Stuart Mill opened what would become a founding document of political liberalism, *The Subjection of Women* (1861, pub. 1869), with the assertion that rule by force already "seem[ed] to be entirely abandoned as the regulating principle of the world's affairs" (*CW* XXI). A decade later, political writer Walter Bagehot claimed that the brute coercion of past ages had now given way to an "Age of Discussion" (1872: 156), while Herbert Spencer in 1874 explained that the "industrial life" of modernity had made "militant life" a relic of earlier times (1874: 556–60). Even when this widespread belief in the pacifying potential of

Victorian modernity was contested or its alleged desirability challenged—as it was by several authors in these pages, including Thomas Carlyle and James Fitzjames Stephen—the presumption was broadly accepted across social classes, political affiliations, and ideological lines that, over time, a primitive force would give way to a more civilized peace.

The mid-Victorian era's most powerful visions of human progress toward the rule of law were articulated by thinkers like Mill, Spencer, and Henry Maine, all of whom understood time to unfold in an upward, orderly plot that would culminate in a future in which violence might be eradicated forever. As "status" was succeeded by "contract" (in Maine's terms), and a historical phase characterized by vertical relations between ruler and ruled gave way to the horizontal relationship among equals characterizing the modern state's reciprocal sovereignty, law and commerce would replace despotism and war. As I show in Chapter 1, this fiction of the Victorian era's almost but never fully realized social equilibrium, even while questioned during the Victorian period itself, was recycled by scholars at the disciplinary advent of Victorian Studies. Those Cold War intellectuals reiterated the core assumptions of their objects of study to describe the previous century's middle decades as an "age of improvement" and "age of equipoise," thus inaugurating a still-active critical tendency, both within and outside the field of Victorian Studies, to see liberal societies not just as "unfinished projects" but as opposed in some fundamental way to violence as such. "It is curious," Farwell notes with charming candor, "that no complete list [yet] exists of the Victorian wars" (1972: 364). Farwell's wonderment measures how fully the vexing fact of modern violence has haunted Victorian Studies since its inception.[4]

Then as now, the persistence of killing and coercion in a modernity defined by protection and consent can be explained by the fact, increasingly irrefutable as the *Pax Victoriana* ground on, that liberal orders no less than illiberal ones rely on force to guarantee law.[5] Max Weber summarized a long tradition of sovereignty theory when he noted, in 1919, that law is nothing other than the effective monopoly on force, while for Walter Benjamin, writing in the same period, all law, even that experienced as peace, is "necessarily and intimately bound" to violence (1978: 295). Maine himself, in his *Lectures on the Early History of Institutions* (1888, first published 1874), observed the same thing, paraphrasing John Austin's thesis about the inseparability of force and legal order in a chapter entitled "Sovereignty." There Maine recounts Austin's division of this function into three modes—rule by one (monarchy), rule by several (oligarchy), and rule by many (democracy)—to explain that what "all the forms of Sovereignty have in common is the power [. . .] to put compulsion without limit on subjects or fellow-subjects" (1888: 350).

Austin's *The Province of Jurisprudence Determined* (1832) and *Lectures on Jurisprudence* (1869) had already framed his Hobbesian thesis that law was "essentially a command for compliance backed by a threat of harm" (Hussain 2003: 37). Maine's local concern is to redirect Austin's emphasis on force by noting that not just the threat of death but also custom and "habitual obedience" (1888: 353) ensure order.

But what Maine puts his finger on is the potentially devastating fact that any order of worldly legality is finally guaranteed by "compulsion without limit" (1888: 350): a total violence that is extra-legal, because pre-legal, and that does not so much conform to law as define the law as such. Sovereign power "is, you will understand, always a question of fact. It is never a question of law or morals" (p. 351). To Austin's foundational statement of positivist jurisprudence—his command theory of legality—Maine adds a historical narrative. He explains that, as history advances from a premodernity based on custom into a civilization based on legal statute, "[t]he force at the back of law comes [...] to be purely coercive force" (p. 393). Now divorced from superstition and vested in institutions rather than the whims of despots, modern violence is shot through, Maine says, with "indifferency," "inexorableness," and "generality" (p. 393). The Indian Revolt was just one indication of how, when the pressures of global rule buckled normal procedure into crisis, the brute coercion "at the back of law" could shudder most violently to its front. If it was true that, as historian W. L. Kostal notes, the mid-Victorian intelligentsia shared "a deeply ingrained deference to the forms of law" (2005: 8), Farwell's list of little wars underscores that the Victorian state responsible for expanding parliamentary democracy, extending personal rights, and establishing the contract as the main form of relation among men—"law" was the byword for these linked achievements—brought the world to order with hands stained in blood.

It was in the Empire, in other words, that Victorian progressive idealism came up against the most disorienting challenges to its core conceptual assumptions. *Forms of Empire* focuses on these moments of friction to show how certain nineteenth-century thinkers turned to the resources of literary form to negotiate what I treat as the central impasse of Victorian modernity: the curious intimacy between legality and harm. As I work to show, the question of how this intimacy was to take concrete shape—how sovereign violence would be distributed and on whose bodies its touch would fall—depended on mechanisms of exclusion that separated the discounted from the counted, the vulnerable from the protected. These cleavages in the social field had grave consequences for the non-voting subjects outside law's perimeter of belonging. Even in a British Empire prone to self-congratulation for its noble treatment of subject races, zones where emergency, abandonment, and death became routine were where liberal modernity's "constitutive outside" became visible (Gunn and Vernon 2011: 10).[6]

It bears stating that while this book is centrally concerned to chart a material and conceptual problem radicalized in the colonial encounter, the following chapters are not in the usual sense "about" the Empire at all, if by "about" we mean that it tracks details of imperial policy, summarizes England's overseas activity, or recounts parliamentary debates on "the Empire question." And while the book's second half deals with revolts by peasants and ex-slaves in Jamaica (1865) and by the Zulu nation in Southern Africa (1877–85), I do not provide a comprehensive overview of the era's proliferating emergencies, insurrections, or so-called small wars.[7] Nor yet does the book offer a survey of literary works featuring imperial locations or plots that engage directly with colonial policy. Macaulay, *The Moonstone*, Kipling, Conrad: these and other monuments of the "Victorian Literature and Empire" syllabus have earned their canonical status in that domain by virtue of their engagement with imperial issues at the level of plot, subject matter, and incident. Rather than in such representational content, the Empire's tattered margins figure here as the limit case for metropolitan thought and, as such, a trigger for innovation at the level of form.

An argumentative corollary to this book's largely metropolitan archive is the claim, implicit in what follows, that the Victorian state's structurally unfinishable war against uprising natives, antagonistic regimes, and other enemies of universal principles is best understood not as one topic within the broader field of Victorian studies, but as the general fact subtending the entirety of domestic life and therefore cultural production in the period. As historians P. J. Cain and A. G. Hopkins note, in an observation that reaffirms an earlier insight of Edward Said, imperialism was not "an adjunct to British history [. . .] but an integral part of the configuration of British society, which it both reinforced and expressed" (2001: 56). In this sense every artifact of Victorian culture is an artifact of Empire.

No doubt the Victorian Empire meant far more than killing: as criticism in recent decades has shown, it meant sexual encounters and accommodations across race and class lines; complex affective and political reorientations between rulers and ruled; linguistic experiments and cultural hybridization; routinized traumas large and small, archived into the muscle memories of individual bodies; and, perhaps most importantly, the complex, embodied processes of adaptation and creativity that living in a global society demands. This book's focus on legal violence seeks not to exclude those stories about Empire but to augment them. For the mostly London-based thinkers I examine here, Empire was the conceptual and physical space where visions of peaceful improvement and social equilibrium pushed uneasily, even impossibly, against the material fact of the "compulsion without limit" guaranteeing those projects. What Maine intuited in his chapters on sovereignty was that perpetual peace and perpetual war were but two phases of the force entangled forever with the notion of law itself. The writers I treat here required all the resources of literary form to comprehend how the world's first liberal democracy might have the threat of death coiled at its very heart.

A word is in order about the terms "liberal" and "modernity," place-holders I use advisedly, since one aim of this book is to restore to those suspiciously capacious terms the complexity and historical dynamism they conceal. As Simon Gunn and James Vernon point out, in the interdisciplinary field of British Studies, "few terms are as promiscuously used as *liberalism* and *modernity*" (2011: 1, emphasis original). Building on work by Andrew Sartori, Duncan Bell, and others, Lauren Goodlad has recently noted that liberalism in particular has tempted scholars to hypostasize an internally disparate and often self-critical set of positions into an oversimplified straw man, a synthetic "liberal theory" or, still worse, a monolithic "'logic', 'impulse' or 'urge'" available for our later, allegedly more enlightened critique (quoted in Goodlad 2015b: 4).[8] As I show, the tendency of criticism to moralize on an (oversimplified) past itself replays the procedures of the Victorian progressive idealism whose internal crises I work here to track. In fact neither liberalism nor Empire obeyed laws of behavior that were given in advance; still less were they simplistic or univocal ideological constructions. As will become clear in the chapters to come, I draw on recent work that has underscored how the term "liberal" has yoked together diverse theoretical outlooks and political projects, and seek to advance recent scholarship, such as that by Sukanya Banerjee, Goodlad, and Sartori, that troubles any comfortable sense that we have disentangled ourselves from the mixed legacies of that internally diverse tradition.[9] One goal of this study, then, is to account for the internal dynamism of thought-forms too often treated by self-congratulatory modern critics as inert or self-evident; another is to locate in those prior forms raw materials that might help us rethink and thus remake the present.[10]

Since *Forms of Empire* aims most of all to account for the conceptually productive work of literary presentation, it is not conceived primarily as a revision to the now considerable literature on the subject of Victorian liberalism. Still, it does track key facets of what has come to be called liberal society—bureaucratic statecraft, "free" trade and capitalist exchange, and concomitant structures of citizenship and public life—in their processes of emergence, institutionalization, and contestation. As Goodlad notes, "discussing liberalism and its limits could [...] involve an almost infinite parsing of liberal debates, paradoxes, and anxieties" (Goodlad 2015: 43). Rather than attempt such a parsing, I focus on what I take to be Victorian liberalism's most salient and consequential strain: the progressivist idealism and voluntarist rationalism that are typified, in these pages, by thinkers like Mill, Spencer, John Morley, and (less exactly) George Eliot. It is the thought of these and related writers that has, I suggest, most fully come to structure our political and methodological commonsense. As Anna Maria Jones (2007), Kathy Psomiades (2013), Zach Samalin (2015), and others have helped us see, we are still Victorian—perhaps never more so than when we critique the Victorians. Attending to this interpenetration of object and method helps *Forms of Empire* trouble any too-comfortable distinctions between ideology and theory, them and us. One result is that while I touch on micropolitical debates within the British parliamentary system and even, at moments, on the Liberal Party itself, the term "liberal" appears here most often, when it does appear, to denote the suite of conceptual presuppositions that still underwrite authorized forms of political and social life in our post-Victorian modernity. These unspoken conventions include (1) individualistic, voluntarist models of human identity and agency; (2) an implicitly progressive model of historical time; and perhaps most important for my purposes, (3) the logical or properly conceptual foundations on which, I argue, those features depend.[11]

As I explain in the book's first half, orthodox bourgeois thinking—that is, our own—operates according to the classical logic whose most prominent features are the principles of non-contradiction and identity. In force at least since Aristotle, these basic ground rules of concept-making hold that nothing can be itself and its negation simultaneously; that everything is only itself and nothing else; and that every proposition is either true or false, and cannot be both (see Gottlieb 2014). Once slotted into the developmental timescale supplied by nineteenth-century historical thinking in fields as diverse as evolutionary biology, political theory, and legal history, these seemingly non-controversial assumptions meant that antonyms like "war" and "peace," "coercion" and "consent," and "anomie" and "law," among others, sat at opposite ends of a historical sequence. As we will see over the course of this book, that effort prophylactically to separate opposite terms along a temporalized axis of value proved disorientingly inadequate to the lived facts of Victorian liberal empire.

For those Victorian thinkers most fervently committed to the principles of nondialectical logic, the inadequacy of this conceptual system in the face of the state's violent imperative to preserve itself—visible most acutely at moments of emergency, crisis, and war—produced a kind of sublime vertigo, even paralysis. The dizzying confusion that resulted when progressive idealism confronted state violence is particularly vivid in case of the Jamaica Committee, which Chapter 3 explores in detail. Led by Mill, this band of ethically minded men was a who's who of advanced liberals of the period, and included John Bright, Charles Darwin, Thomas Huxley, Spencer, and John Morley, the liberal intellectual and critic of Swinburne's poetry. Committed to upholding what Mill called "the authority and majesty of law" (*CW* XXVIII), these men tried desperately and with honorable conviction over a period of years to have Governor Eyre judged a murderer for his execution of 439 black peasants under martial law in 1865. But what Mill and his right-minded fellow Committee members learned, over and over again, was that such murder was not murder at all, but the law's self-authorizing force made manifest. (Governor Eyre was acquitted three separate times and a further civil suit was also dismisssed.) As Kostal notes laconically in his definitive history of the case, the Committee's "faith" in a universal and peaceful rule of law "proved misplaced" (2005: 482). What I show is that Mill's classical rather than dialectical logical system, and his idealist rather than materialist understanding of legality—terms I explore in more detail below—meant that he, and others sharing his core assumptions, could only oscillate between embarrassment and denial in the face of physical brutality's uncanny persistence in the Age of Discussion. For the ethically uncompromising Mill, this conceptual and political crisis generated "intense shame" (Kostal 2005: 461).

Often in contrast to such sensitive but ill-equipped analysts, other authors I focus on in the following chapters—George Eliot, Wilkie Collins, A. C. Swinburne, H. Rider Haggard, and Robert Louis Stevenson among them—tested the boundaries of the liberal idealism that has become our common sense; they labored to devise figural and therefore conceptual languages adequate to what many of them viewed as their era's constitutive antinomy: the intimate, scandalous intertwinement of violence and law. Often these writers' responses to modern legality's intractable brutality were expressed in non-propositional or non-ideational terms, as hint, evocation, enactment, or textual performance. More often their answers took the shape not of answers at all but of new questions: fresh problems, ambitious experiments, newly haunting formal paradoxes. In the case of the seemingly mysterious metaphysics of martial law so brutally manifested in Jamaica, it was Swinburne, I suggest, who best measured the situation: he stretched the capacities of the lyric poem to freeze excess and regulation together into a single presentation. The hymns to unbridled violence in *Poems and Ballads* (1866a) unfold within a grid of seemingly restraining meter, giving both control and surplus equal and irresolvable priority on the page. As this example suggests, the works examined most closely in the following chapters—lyric poems, realist novels, sensation fictions, and adventure romances—constitute highly mediated engagements with the limit condition of the liberal state, and so bear witness in slantwise fashion to the violence animating modern democracy. By attending to these works according to the dispensation of care I explain later in this Introduction, we reconstruct the story of how certain Victorian thinkers reached the edges of their era's conceptual vocabulary, expanding the possibilities of form to document what they treat as the key contradiction of political modernity: that war and peace were not opposite terms so much as two names for the same thing.

To a twenty-first-century criticism raised on postcolonial theory and ideology critique, the dialectic of nineteenth-century enlightenment just rehearsed will hardly be news, and is not announced as news here. Even beyond the work in postcolonial studies long associated with the critique of imperialism, influential studies in history and political theory have lately evaluated the vast injuries necessary to sustain England's project of global liberation.[12] Recent historical experience has made this once-polemical assertion about liberal empire a matter of everyday observation. Uday Singh Mehta's pathbreaking *Liberalism and Empire* (1999) generated some of its considerable power by exploiting the apparent tension between its title nouns; the implication was that these two things— liberalism and empire—did not match.[13] In no small part in response to the force of Mehta's argument, but also likely aided by recent years' exposure to the warmaking capacity of liberal democracies, the field has shifted such that Gunn and Vernon could explain that nineteenth-century liberalism "was not just a matter of rights steadily extended to wider populations; its existence was premised on strategic forms of suppression and segregation" (2011: 10). Thus has criticism come to understand an accidental relationship as a necessary one: liberalism does not just permit exclusion but is "premised" on it.

Such claims rest on a tactically narrowed conception of liberalism. But progressive idealism's neutral comportment with and positive work in service of domination, like its demonstrated flexibility in the face of political and economic imperatives, should alert us to the fact that we have yet to outlive the questions of legality and violence organizing this book. Yet even the most engaged cultural and political criticism in our moment continues to prove vulnerable to the lure of progressive schemes. Despite a robust debate aimed at querying just this methodological procedure, criticism continues to cast nineteenth-century texts as violent, racist, or otherwise blinkered others to our implicitly more enlightened ideational projects: they have ideology while we have theory.[14] And while mass cultural products from an era awash in illiberal sentiment may seem to call out for critical judgment now—Haggard's romances have been one site where this temptation has been all but impossible to resist—the tendency to see historical texts as naïvely ideological and our own criticism as heroically critical recapitulates the idealist progressivism that it is our business to understand in its process of unfolding. In this case, the methods of ideology critique unwittingly replicate the status-to-contract, naïve-to-sentimental narratives emerging in the late 1850s that I survey in Chapter 1.

This Introduction will have more to say about methods of political reading and their place in the contemporary academy. Here I will note that our belated engagement with the tangled dilemmas of Victorian imperialism is further complicated by a confusion about what constitutes "imperialism" in the first place, and whether this phenomenon is best construed in cultural or political-economic terms. Where cultural theories focus on imperialism as an ensemble of social forms, racial ideologies, and cultural attitudes, materialist analyses of the kind pursued in this book presume instead the priority of economic and political factors, themselves complex and often self-contradictory, in driving the capture of territory and the penetration of markets in the British Empire's expansive global network. Where a culturalist approach might focus on racial stereotypes in Haggard's romances, say, or depictions of Irishmen as savages in the British press, the point of view I test here would construe such racism and cultural jingoism—however virulent—as secondary effects of the material interests and geopolitical imperatives driving England's expansion abroad. It follows that where culturalist models might understand a heightened respect for difference or commitment to intercultural tolerance as the opposites of, and therefore antidotes to, empire as such, the Victorian case helps us see what recent experience ratifies, which is that values like tolerance and racial understanding are better seen as two tools used by imperial states—from an arsenal of many others—to maintain hegemony in a global system.[15] My emphasis on world-systemic configurations and on an (always differently contested) British hegemony follows recent work by John Darwin, James Belich, Cain and Hopkins, Giovanni Arrighi, and others in construing "imperial power" to name the dynamic ensemble of formal and informal relations that changed shape, shifted character, and mostly expanded across the *longue durée* of Britain's world leadership.[16] I part from world-systems approaches by locating the main stakes for systemic analysis in the irreducibly particular "broken and abused bodies[,] almost invariably black or brown" that globally scaled analyses like Darwin's too often confine to the margins, if they note them at all (Bell 2015: 3).[17]

At issue in this methodological decision is the distinction between cultural and political-economic forms of power, but also the definition of "power" itself. My answer departs from the conventional one in literary studies, since the form of empire I focus on in the following pages is not a primarily a discursive construction or effect of language—that is, a matter of cultural representation—but material force exerted on human bodies. Where work by Dipesh Chakrabarty, Catherine Hall, and Mehta himself has refined our understanding of how liberal ideology excluded colonial subjects from representation in the narrative of history, a conception of power as sovereignty enables us to view exclusion less as a representational than a juridical problem, as certain bodies were marked for life and others for death in a globalized sphere of political decision. So even as I acknowledge, with Raymond Williams, the complex traffic between the allegedly separate spheres of culture and politics, and seek here to add to our understanding of that relation, this book aims to wrest the term "power" from its designation as a Foucauldian field of discursive or representational possibility, reconceiving it instead as the capacity to inflict somatic harm.

In her important recent book, *The Victorian Geopolitical Aesthetic* (2015b), Goodlad defines sovereignty as "a multivalent term used to stand for the political ideal of individual, local, and national self-governance" (p. 8). Later the term describes "a juridical concept of rule" (p. 47), status as a head of state (p. 41), and "the sovereign individual" (p. 40). This definitional latitude enables Goodlad to track what she calls the "manifold intersections" among ethics, politics, and realist literary texts in England's imperial world system (p. 23). By contrast, I follow Maine in construing this term more narrowly as the law's authority to determine life and death. To advance this engagement, I draw on thinking about sovereignty and biopolitics by now-canonical analysts of liberal violence like Giorgio Agamben, Carl Schmitt, and Foucault himself, who in his late-career lectures brought to the fore this very tension in the definition of power. Tracking the sovereignty concept from premodernity to the twentieth century in his lectures of 1976—the year that volume 1 of *The History of Sexuality* was published and the year I was born—Foucault explains that "power" names not a prohibitive or regulative function but the positive capacity to create and police divisions in the population. Understood as "the implementation and deployment of a relationship of force," power is most manifest, he notes, in the capacity to make war (2003: 15).[18]

The notion that power speaks its presence most clearly in the act of killing suggests that while imperial power takes many forms—economic coercion, cultural reinscription, and sexualized inequality on major and minor scales—the paradigmatic form of empire, although far from the only one, is military violence. It also means that, whether our attention falls on violent episodes of emergency and asymmetrical conflict like the Indian Mutiny or on the sublimated, potential violence of metropolitan peacetime, "we are always writing the history of the same war, even when we are writing the history of peace and its institutions" (Foucault 2003: 16). Peace itself, Foucault says, is merely a "silent war" (p. 16). This book acknowledges the power of Foucault's provocative epigram and, in certain ways, seeks to historicize and develop it. Yet *bons mots* like this seek the status of maxims or reified slogans, and in so doing produce a twofold critical temptation this book works to avoid.

One temptation is to fold different degrees and genres of violence together, such that peacetime's violence *in potentia* is construed as somehow equivalent to the physical injuries actuated in what we would be forgiven for calling real warfare. The second temptation is to conflate diverse historical moments—diachronic processes of unfolding and contestation—into a single, eternal antagonism: modernity as an endless combat. Indeed this is how Foucault's treatment, however historicizing in its own right, has often been deployed.[19] By contrast, this book seeks to prise apart the departicularizing equation between *epistemic violence* and the somatic kind—an equation that has structured work in culturalist postcolonial studies since the 1980s—even as it works against metaphysicalizing gestures appropriate to the bumper-sticker claims that would see sovereignty as a transhistorical mechanism or timeless dynamic in some fetishized sphere of "the political."[20] Instead *Forms of Empire* tracks the thought of Victorians themselves, as they reworked ideas about martial law, legal emergency, and state killing for the era of bureaucratic democracy and translated those engagements into form.

FROM REFLECTION TO MEDIATION

The document that opened this Introduction is a very literal form of empire: a template for telegraphic transcription. As Figure 0.1 shows, its available boxes and blank lines were filled out in thick pencil and looping handwriting by a now-anonymous administrator and circulated in the midst of a colonial emergency. A handwritten remediation of an electronic signal, this form is held, with many others like it, among the India Office Select Materials of the British Library: just one piece of paperwork in a vast archive of imperial information, now anonymous among sheaves of watermarked papers, "true copies," and packets of onionskin documents tied with red string. These relics of the British response to the 1857 uprising are material and technological in an important sense, since they record not just the information that was conveyed from Agra to Bombay to Trieste to London (for example)—the mere communicative content, interesting though it may be—but also the forms through which that content was conveyed: the complex codes and shaping protocols that both constrained and enabled that transmission.

Humans work both within and outside of these shaping protocols, rupturing old forms to create new ones. This dialectic of newness and convention is the structuring condition of all expression. The conventions that organize the occasion of writing in other words restrict expression but also make it possible in the first place; these restrictively enabling rules of genre are institutional, political, and technological, but also literary and social. They are felt with particular force in the case of institutional documents like telegraphs, since in those cases several powerfully enforced shaping regimes might be operative simultaneously. A normal blank form, printed on paper and circulated in bureaucracies like Dickens' Circumlocution Office or the East India Office, already establishes comparatively rigid possibilities for discourse (write date here, write name here).[21] But the laws of genre are doubly firm when a genre's enabling constraints have to do with the capacity of another physical medium—in this case early electronic signaling. When this already complex array of limiting factors is filtered through the highly idiosyncratic social practices of telegraphic clerks, who are not only operating within the social and verbal conventions of professional hierarchy but also re-mediating oral orders (or written ones) up and down that hierarchical ladder into yet another ciphered idiom—in this case electronic coding—and at each phase altering minutely the content of the dispatches they are supposedly only transcribing, what emerges is a drama of delimitation and rupture at micro-scale.

Another Mutiny telegram, sent from Calcutta to "General J. Outram KCB" and received 18 August [1857] (see Fig. 0.2), is transcribed in fountain pen onto a pre-printed form marked with the date 1856. But the clerk has written a "7" over the "6" to correct the date (MSS Eur C124/21). The clerk was, of course, simply reusing an old form in order (most likely) to save paper, albeit at a moment of unexampled political and communicative crisis. The point is that such everyday ruptures of convention show, at numbingly mundane scale, how human actors work in dynamic tension with even the most codified rules of medium and format, stretching the constraints of the sayable. In tension with prescribed regulations and available templates, novelty enters the world. In that sense, this and other dispatches from the frontier of the Empire's merciless counterinsurgency are complex records of constraint and adaptation, conformity and freedom, in which technological apparatus, verbal and visual genre, and institutional conventions commingle with human will to shape

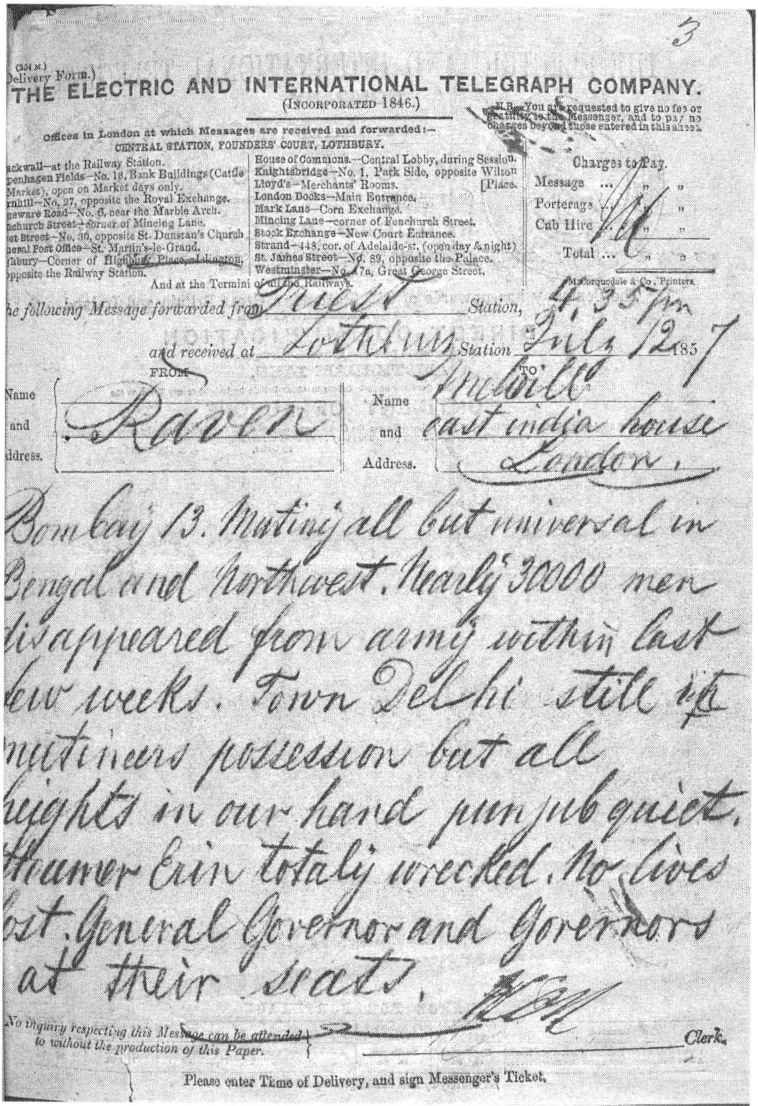
(334 M.)
Delivery Form.)
THE ELECTRIC AND INTERNATIONAL TELEGRAPH COMPANY.
(Incorporated 1846.)

N.B.—You are requested to give no fee or gratuity to the Messenger, and to pay no charges beyond those entered in this sheet.

Offices in London at which Messages are received and forwarded:—
CENTRAL STATION, FOUNDERS' COURT, LOTHBURY.

ackwall—at the Railway Station.
penhagen Fields—No. 18, Bank Buildings (Cattle Market); open on Market days only.
rnhill—No. 27, opposite the Royal Exchange.
geware Road—No. 6, near the Marble Arch.
nchurch Street—corner of Mincing Lane.
et Street—No. 30, opposite St. Dunstan's Church.
neral Post Office—St. Martin's-le-Grand.
lbury—Corner of Highbury Place, Islington, opposite the Railway Station.

House of Commons.—Central Lobby, during Session.
Knightsbridge—No. 1, Park Side, opposite Wilton [Place.
Lloyd's—Merchants' Rooms.
London Docks—Main Entrance.
Mark Lane—Corn Exchange.
Mincing Lane—corner of Fenchurch Street.
Stock Exchange—New Court Entrance.
Strand—448, cor. of Adelaide-st. (open day & night)
St. James Street—No. 89, opposite the Palace.
Westminster—No. 17a, Great George Street.

And at the Termini of all the Railways.

Charges to Pay.
Message ... „ „
Porterage ... „ „
Cab Hire ... „ „
Total ... „ „

McCorquodale & Co., Printers.

he following Message forwarded from Triest Station, 4.35 pm
and received at Lothbury Station July 12 1857

FROM
Name and Address. Raven

TO
Name and Address. Melvill east india house London.

Bombay 13. Mutiny all but universal in Bengal and Northwest. Nearly 30000 men disappeared from army within last few weeks. Town Delhi still in mutineers possession but all heights in our hand punjab quiet. Steamer Erin totaly wrecked. No lives lost. General Governor and Governors at their seats.

No inquiry respecting this Message can be attended to without the production of this Paper.

Clerk.

Please enter Time of Delivery, and sign Messenger's Ticket.

Fig. 0.1. "Mutiny all but universal." Telegram of 12 July 1857 to Sir James Melvill, Chief Secretary of the East India Office. © The British Library Board, L/MIL/5/514, p. 3.

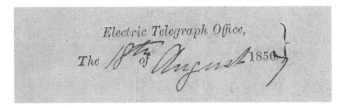

Fig. 0.2. Telegram from Col. Sanderson (quartermaster) to Gen. Sir J. Outram, KCB. Received 18 August (185[7]); correction of a 7 over the 6. © The British Library Board, MSS Eur C124/21/ (detail).

communication into highly stylized, I will say poetic, presentations. From this angle, the compressed communications just discussed only display with particular economy what is true of any textual performance, no matter its stated occasion or ostensible relation to the category of the literary. This book focuses on moments in such textual performances when convention is stretched and protocol disturbed: moments, I mean, when writing works against its conditions of emergence to push toward some way of thinking the new.[22]

These bits of Mutiny ephemera traced an incredible physical itinerary. The second communiqué was a tactical message that originated in Calcutta and terminated in the field at Dinapore (Danapur), only later to be archived in a London reading room. But campaign updates like the one that declared "Mutiny all but universal" originated at field offices in India; traveled to the Middle East on copper wires owned by private entities (the "Submarine Telegraph Company," the "Electric and International Telegraph Company"); moved from there through various mid-European waypoints; were forwarded via any number of intermediary stations and almost numberless mechanical and human agencies, often being recopied in the process; and arrived finally at the hand of Sir James Melvill, then Secretary of the East India Office, at the Company's headquarters on Leadenhall Street. The journey of these compressed tidings of insurrection thus sketches in miniature some version of the Victorian world system at mid-century. It draws together periphery, semi-periphery, and core into a single narrative, while also linking public and private interests, multiple types and scales of actors, and almost unthinkably disparate social and political spaces—including the researcher's archive. The particular material networks congealed into the imperial communications I have cited can, by synecdoche, stand to evoke the Victorian world system more generally, even while they suggest that any account of imperial law and the violence sustaining it must confront the issue of mediation: that is, the physical channels and formal codes through which information is transmitted and, in that act of transmission, inevitably changed.

To account for mediation in this sense—as formal protocol and techno-logical patterning—is to account for the imbrication of medium and message with superadded attention to genre. But in the history of criticism "mediation" also refers to the processes of reconfiguration by which cultural products refract the historical moments that produced them. In the essays entitled "Determination" and "From Reflection to Mediation" in *Marxism and Literature*, Raymond Williams addresses the challenge, in any materialist criticism, of connecting the figural or cultural realm to the more fundamental or concrete sphere of material social processes. Describing the different models available for imagining this relationship of deter-mination, he explains that the paradigm of *reflection* imagines culture as a mirror of the world; it posits an allegorical or otherwise direct "corres-pondence" between "levels" (1977: 76)—a homology, for example, or isomorphism between historical and cultural forms.[23] To the contrary, the term "mediation," Williams writes, "indicates an active and substantial process," "an indirect connection" (pp. 99, 98).

John Guillory (2010) has taken Williams' essay as a starting point to argue that ideology critique and discourse analysis undertaken by the New Historicism and Foucauldian cultural studies, respectively, rely on the metaphor of representation to flatten the mediating work a text is able to accomplish. As Guillory notes, if a text is understood merely to "represent," i.e. to reflect, to express, or to symptomatize its moment rather than to reconfigure it productively, and in historically specifiable ways, then that text can only be understood to do so ideologically. A commitment to the category of representation, in other words, guarantees that texts can only represent their moments in interested or bad ways, a fact that turns the work of reading into an injunction to discover just these (inevitable) distances between "reality" and its "representation"—an injunction that has arguably structured politically engaged Victorianist criticism since the 1980s. I conceive this book's insistence on the conceptually generative translations accomplished by Victorian form as parting from such approaches. Instead of focusing on alleged ideological distortions or unwit-ting betrayals, a shift to mediation enables this book to take stock of productive reconfigurations and critical recoding operations—that is, acts of thinking—texts themselves perform.[24]

So while I occasionally discuss other examples of *forms* in the sense of standardized documents, my main concern is with form, singular, in the sense of structural patterns and organizational modes: that is, with the various shapes language takes when subjected to the intense and distorting pressures of England's project of global rule. Caroline Levine has recently proposed "affordances," a term transplanted from design theory, to describe what a particular shape or design can do: "the potential uses or actions latent in materials and designs" (2015: 6). With Levine and others, I conceive "form" as an enabling constraint while emphasizing the productivity, not the restriction, of that dual understanding. In the context of my argument, such a view helps me show how the particular capacities of literary technologies like the heroic couplet (Chapter 3), novelistic denarration (Chapter 1), and the category of action itself (Chapter 4) enable these and other literary effects to accomplish conceptual operations that other modes of formalizing knowledge cannot. Insofar as they reconfigure conceptual content in ways unique to themselves, these formal strategies are productively viewed, I suggest, as technologies of mediation. No doubt the effort to treat aspects of literary style as media technologies departs from the widespread tendency in the fields of media studies and book history to treat mediation and technology as matters of merely physical equipment. But as Mary Poovey and Lisa Gitelman among others have noted, media history and the history of forms and genres must be told together (see Poovey 2008; Gitelman 2014: 10).[25]

Over the course of its four chapters, this book examines material artifacts drawn from archives in the U.S. and England: diplomatic cables transcribed in wobbly pencil like those reproduced above, government reports sent by packet ship, handwritten drafts mailed to publishers in haste, and extravagant cancellations on poetic manuscripts meant to mimic the lashing of whips. But the technologies I focus on most— from the Greek τέχνη, "art" or "craft"—are literary, in the sense of patterns, techniques, or organizational modes; each of these, I argue, differently reconfigures the structuring conceptual impasse of liberal modernity. In this context, "form" works not as a marker of transhistorical value or koanterm for a neo-Romantic ideology of the aesthetic. Instead "form" marks, for me, the capacity of literary ensembles to set ideas into motion in ways particular to their suite of affordances—ways that, by definition, other modes of presentation cannot. As Levine notes, "[e]very literary form [. . .] generates its own, separate logic" (2015: 10).

Garrett Stewart has eloquently called for "novel criticism as media study" (2009: 220–38). His proposal, shared widely across a discipline eager to justify its existence to presentist administrators eager to cut costs, is to reinvigorate literary studies by arraying it beneath an umbrella supplied by the seemingly more relevant field of media studies. But this relation of priority might well be switched around, and one aim of this book is to invert the tendency of literary studies to look to other disciplinary languages to justify itself, and instead insist on the capacity for what is called "literary method" to make claims of political and historical import now. In the context of this effort to reclaim for literary study the consideration of the formal "devices, structures, [and] practices" too often imagined as the domain of media study (Gitelman 2014: 10), it bears repeating that labels in this book like "form," "literature," and "literary" do not stand as markers of value. Nor, despite appearances, do they indicate that a stable category called "literature" even exists. As Chapter 4 shows in reference to William Dean Howells' sponsorship of Henry James, the process by which "literary form" was sheared off from mass culture and frozen into an ageless marker of value is itself an episode in the history of liberal violence during this period. Sustained close attention to particular textual objects serves here to emphasize not their timeless humanistic value or ennobling beauty but their capacity—and the capacity of all cultural objects—to generate concepts in excess of the ideological inputs that produced them. I use the term "poetics" to name this creative, even critical capacity of Victorian form. Yet as the photographs I turn to now demonstrate, an investment in what I am calling literary presentation need not be "literary" in any narrow way at all. Telegraphic messages, wet collodion albumen prints, lyric poetry, the realist novel: each of these and other instances of Victorian form has its own capacities and affordances, its own particular way of organizing thought that other modes do not have. All are, in that sense, poetic.

The word "poetry" derives from *poiesis* (ποίησις), an act of making or doing. Taken in its broadest sense to mean human creativity and acts of aesthetic making, poetry is an action that reorganizes the world. Emphasizing form as an active faculty of knowledge-making avoids the methodological dead end by which historical texts are cast as symptoms of a cultural or political condition that later literary critics, empowered by historical remove, might diagnose in a heroic mode. This means that I part from even those modes of sensitive political formalism, like Fredric Jameson's, that hold aesthetic form to respond to, symptomatize, or otherwise figure geopolitical dynamics beyond their power consciously to apprehend.[26] It is worth noting that not a few of the texts examined here, most iconically *The Strange Case of Dr. Jekyll and Mr. Hyde* (Chapter 4), prominently feature patients experiencing symptoms and characters who diagnose them—often mistakenly. I follow such hints to view historical texts as containing within their figural systems a commentary on the methodological value of symptoms and diagnoses. To show how such reflexivity might work, I turn now to a media technology everyone knows is a media technology, early war photography. This helps highlight in reverse fashion how the more obviously literary presentations I read in the following chapters rework and even, in some cases, diagnose the conceptual antinomies of liberal imperialism. The cryptic war photography of Felice Beato (1832–1909) helps show how, not modern critics, but historical objects themselves might perform such conceptual work. As they transfigure their moments into complex ensembles of conformity and resistance—works of literature—they register the fundamental contradiction of liberal imperialism while testing in advance the frameworks of interpretation we bring to bear on them.

UNBURIAL GROUNDS

What would happen to our habits of reading if we saw Victorian texts as actively reconfiguring their moments, rather than "reflecting" them, "reproducing" them, "engaging" them, or doing something else to recapitulate the metaphors of symptoms and diagnoses, blindness and insight, surface and depth, that still structure our understanding of hermeneutic method? To test this question would be to imagine Victorian objects as particular kinds of subjects: dynamic agents of thought, speakers from the grave, commenting on their historical conditions of emergence and, in the images I turn to now, exposing in advance the inadequacy of the models of reading we might use to explicate them. Such emancipated objects would become agents of theoretical activity, endowed by us, their readers, with the power to perform conceptual work that we, as later witnesses, receive and document under a dispensation of care.

This book's wager is that such a procedure might preserve an affect of enchantment with historical texts while refusing to abandon the project of critique; remain (in the psychoanalytic terms Eve Sedgwick made famous) paranoid about the obscene fact of the Victorian endless war while reading the objects mediating that fact with reparative care. In looking at the brutal photographs of Victorian "small wars" Beato made at mid-century, this means caring both intrinsically, for the artifacts under study in the reading event, and extrinsically, outside the scene of reading, for the human bodies that have been abandoned, killed, or otherwise cast out from the Victorian era's globalized system of belonging. Beato's images organize an encounter between scenes of such catastrophic exclusion and our readerly practice. In framing for judgment burned, hanged, and unburied bodies from Victorian endless war, these objects highlight the importance of care in both senses just described. They also disclose with special urgency what we assent to when we abandon critique.

The first depicts the bombardment of Shimonoseki, a tiny and (to us) forgotten operation on the southwest seacoast of Japan, 1864. In *Queen Victoria's Little Wars*, Farwell groups this with similar episodes into a single entry (1972: 364–72). Merely a fraction of a "little war," this operation sought to open a route for international trade through the Japanese islands, and "proved a turning point [. . .] in Japanese history" (Norman 2000: 64), since it defeated the Chōshū clan, a precapitalist social group that had to this point resisted incorporation into the progressively universalizing world market (Fig. 0.3).

Like all of Beato's documentary pictures, this one is obsessively con-structed. Tilted upward to face the water, the five captured cannon create a diagonal structural line that links with the downward-sloping hill some-where beyond the picture's left edge. The resulting triangular form embraces the presumed focal point, a half-limp Union Jack. This national emblem has been made ghostly by a long exposure, which inscribes duration into an apparently synchronic instant and marks the image as a process, not a thing. Like all skies photographed using the blue-sensitive wet collodion process, the one behind this dazed victory party is overex-posed and thus vacant. Almost invisibly, a plume of smoke dissipates. As in the first stanza of William Wordsworth's "Tintern Abbey," which describes "wreathes of smoke / Sent up, in silence, from among the

Fig. 0.3. Felice Beato, "British Naval Landing Party at the Maedamura Battery, Shimonoseki" (*La 2ème Batterie de Matamoura*), 1864, albumen silver print, courtesy of the J. Paul Getty Museum, Los Angeles. Partial gift from the Wilson Centre for Photography.

trees," the mute smoke here offers what Wordsworth called "uncertain notice": it is a signifer whose referent cannot be directly ascertained (2000: ll. 18–19, 20). But where Wordsworth drew from a storehouse of tropes for poetic autonomy to imagine "vagrant dwellers" and "some Hermit" as the referents for his vaporous sign (ll. 21, 22), we know from the cannon and the soldiers and the date that a village full of Japanese peasants has been burned.

Beato's trailing smoke has a methodological pedigree. In readings by Jerome McGann and Marjorie Levinson that have come to epitomize the suspicious reading practices of the New Historicism, the wreaths of smoke in "Tintern Abbey" stood as key evidence in the case against the romantic strategy of evasion. For Levinson and a generation of later symptomatic readers, Wordsworth's smoke typified not just how the poet turns impoverished refugees into figures for imagination (campfires of homeless people made the smoke), but also how all literary texts occlude their traumatic historical contexts—the "war, revolution, poverty, diaspora, terror, and so on" that Alan Liu describes in a reflection on his own former reading practices (2008: 260). Like Steven Best and Sharon Marcus, Liu indicates that the New Historicist's injunction to counter the obscuring moves of heroic poets required its own kind of heroism, namely the principled acts of decryption that would unbury the "significant truths" lurking beneath the surface the text (Best and Marcus 2009: 4). Conspicuous absences like the burning of villages in the name of progress would be illuminated through the critic's act of heroic digging.

"Landing Party" testifies to the inadequacy of these mixed metaphors. To begin, the physical affordances of this flat print push the now ethically charged categories of background and foreground together, even while seeming to depend on their distance. The image's apparently manifest surface—the patriotic "party" celebrating victory over an archaic tribe—and its seemingly latent depth—the violent, obscured underside of modernization—exist on the same "level," a material arrangement of flatness that only makes physical the finally undecideable relationship between surface and depth that Paul de Man among others suggests characterizes any verbal text (1979: 12).

The epistemological difficulties of this problematic—which also drives detective fiction—are as evident in Beato's image as in McGann's reading of "Tintern Abbey," which must claim that the allegedly absent poverty and terror are never "entirely displaced" (1983: 85–6). The reading I am offering seeks neither to uncover an obscured historical violence nor to ascribe that unmasking to the image itself. I am suggesting instead that the photograph should be seen to transform those very spatial (and ethical) figures of reading into its subject, turning "unmasking" itself into a conceptual problem. What the image shows, from this curatorial angle (from the Latin *curare*, "to care, to take care of "), is neither a victory party nor a brutal act of asymmetrical war so much as the operation of transcoding by which brute violence might appear as something called victory: a landing party, as the caption has it. The only thing this object makes manifest or unmasks, I mean, is the inadequacy of existing readerly metaphors to understand the conceptual work the image itself performs.

Beato's work has only recently begun to receive critical attention, and a full account of his life has only in 2010 been definitively pieced together.[27] Born in Venice in the year of the first Reform Bill (1832), Beato became a subject to the British crown on Corfu, then a British protectorate. He moved as a teenager to Constantinople, where he learned the wet collodion albumen processes and the ins and outs of professional photography. Filling in for and then displacing his mentor James Robertson, who had been assigned to replace Roger Fenton in the Crimea (Lacoste 2010: 184), Beato made some 150 images there; created tourist albums of the Holy Land; took brutal documentary photographs of the Opium Wars, in China; and in February 1858, just after the final British reoccupation of Lucknow, went to India, where as Zahid Chaudhary (2012) has shown he produced the most ambiguous and devastating images of the Mutiny we have. Amidst these appointments Beato photographed battlefields and towns and native peoples in India and China; traveled to Japan, where he made (and lost) fortunes as a speculator; and documented England's counterinsurgency in the Sudan (1885). He did piecework for the American army as well, photographing operations in Asia in between excursions to, for example, Korea, where he took the first photographs of that nation for the West. He wound up in Burma, selling furniture and curios to tourists. Even there he made photos for his catalogs, sparse and melancholy studies whose captions read like names from a haunted archive: "View of Swords," "View of Sideboard," "View of a Chair."

Beato was a technical innovator too, a pioneer in what were then new media: he developed novel modes of transporting chemicals, perfected formulas for mixing them, and claimed to have reduced exposure time by half, to four seconds. In 1880 he was called as an expert to the London Photographic Association. He was the first person to photograph enemy war dead, which he did during the Second Opium War (1856–60), beating the American Civil War photographer Matthew Brady by nearly a decade with photographs that depict "scenes of abject, unredeemed victimization, bleached by light, [that] are reminiscent of Goya's *Disasters of War*" (Ritchin 2010: 121). Employed as an embedded photographer and working freelance, operating under, alongside, and outside the supervision of the British state throughout the Victorian era's permanent war,

Beato as much as anyone helped mediate his era's structuring violence to a burgeoning British image culture. Yet his provisional and instrumental relation to his work—he was a hustler above all, working between art and commerce as a subject to an Empire in which he had no vote—means that even efforts to ground readings in authorial intention can only produce new questions: despite our almost reflexive efforts to do so, we simply cannot ascribe a definitive purpose to his work.[28]

In keeping with the ample silence of many of Beato's war images—their capacity to speak without offering a thesis, or to signify while defying mere description—his images of the so-called Mutiny seem to signify both too much and not enough; they go further to build the problem of reading them into their own content. Beato arrived in the subcontinent in time to photograph the aftermath of the key episodes in Britain's brutal counter-insurgency, that prolonged and unremitting campaign of terror aimed at returning "all heights in our hand" and making "punjab quiet." The mechanisms for securing this quiet required the full spectrum of what Maine called sovereignty's "compulsion without limit." In Sedgwick's terms, should we be paranoid or reparative when confronted with this history?

One of the many stunning images Beato made in India seems to build this question into its very form, forcing us to decide what we see and to take sides on the politically and ethically consequential decision of how to read it (Fig. 0.4). The albumen print shows two dead fighters dangling like wraiths against another evacuated sky. One is hooded. Alternating with disturbing beauty between dark and light values, hired native soldiers gather around the central scene of lynching. Just one man's face is visible; we can't make out his expression. We don't know what he sees. The photograph in this way refuses to complete the circuit of interpretation built into its design. Rather than showing a brutal act of sovereign killing or a triumphant scene of order restored, this image shows implicated witnesses reading that ambiguous thing. The caption calls it "The Hanging of Two Rebels," but what the photo depicts is not a hanging but a hanging being watched.

Discussing a strikingly similar image—the now iconic photo of Thomas Shipp and Abraham Smith dangling from a tree in Marion, Indiana (1930)—Shawn Michelle Smith has noted that lynching photographs, like all photographic images, do not work as evidence in any straightforward way. Smith explains that the lynching photo of Shipp and Smith has been used as propaganda by both white supremacists and the NAACP; the "malleability of [. . .] photographs as evidence" (2007: 37) thus refers to the fact that the evidentiary content of photographs is not *inside* the object so much as called into being by the triangulated relationships among the

Fig. 0.4. Felice Beato, "The Hanging of Two Rebels" from the Warner Album, albumen print, 1858, 210 × 266 mm. ACP: 2001.18.0001(11). The Alkazi Collection of Photography.

creator, the depicted scene and/or people, and, most crucially, the reader of the image and her institutional situation.[29] Given that Stanley Fish suggested as much of Milton's poetry in the 1970s, Smith's observation means that photos of historical violence like Beato's only make especially palpable what is true of all literary objects, namely that (in Fish's words) "[t]he objectivity of [any] text is an illusion [...] of self-sufficiency and completeness" (1980: 82). Awareness of the shaping power of readerly decisions "forces you to be aware of 'it' as a changing object—and therefore no 'object' at all" (1980: 82–3).

Smith's reoutfitting of reader-response criticism at the scene of racialized killing discloses political stakes for what can seem, in Fish, like a parlor game. For "Hanging," this means that Beato's object disables hermeneutic reading practices no less than "surface" ones, since no reading could hope to make manifest, expose, or even deconstruct this photograph's meaning—let alone describe it. The object's communicative content (its meaning) does not exist as an ontological facet of the object itself, whether "sediment[ed]" (Jameson 1981: 147) or superficial. Nor yet can it ever become specifiable in terms of what Derrida calls a text's "*voudrait dire*": the message a text *wants* to communicate in a "conscious, voluntary, intentional" fashion, even when that alleged intention is held to produce meaning in excess of itself (1997: 157–8). What does this object want to say?

We might say it wants to celebrate victory, and is thus a problematic apology for state violence deserving (paranoid) critique. Alternatively we could say that the image wants to critique the rhetoric of victory, and is thus deserving of (reparative) fetishization. Or again we might say (via Derrida) that the image wants to celebrate victory but in fact (and against its "will") critiques that very thing. (Or vice versa: it wants to critique violence but actually reaffirms it.) Still another tactic would be to simply describe it: but how? To take any such route would be to hypostasize a dynamic set of relations into a stable thing, reified into self-identity and made knowable using any one of the methods just surveyed. I am suggesting that instead of crystallizing into that standstill the photograph generates what Fish calls a "pressure for judgment," a "responsibility of deciding [. . .] transferred from the words on the page to the reader" (1980: 166). The interrupted network of reading in Beato's print replicates our predicament, as later viewers, as we, like these hired agents of a foreign state, gaze at a spectacle of military justice. Is that what we see?

The responsibility to decide that Fish describes and Derrida labels the "task of reading" (1997: 158) is thus encoded into this picture's formal construction. From the perspective I advance here, this knowing dynamism can be considered the object's defining problematic, what it is "about."[30] Beato's "Hanging," in other words, should be read as staging in advance a formal reconfiguration of exactly the challenge to interpret facing its belated readers as we, with Smith, Jameson, Derrida, and those mute executioners, watch it. The image calls us to decide what we see and refuses to provide a guarantee for that decision.

Beato's most famous photograph—and the only one to have received sustained critical attention—heightens still further the stakes of these seemingly only methodological questions. The massacre it seeks to commemorate was decisive in the British counterinsurgency. Indian fighters had retreated to the fortress at Lucknow, the city at the center of the Awadh (Oudh) region which, thanks to Henry Havelock's relief of the Residency complex there in September 1857 and Colin Campbell's second reoccupation of the city that November, had become ground zero for British mythologies of the revolt (Bayly 1990: 181). When the fortress walls were finally breached in that second liberation, Campbell sent in the Sikhs and Scots, who systematically executed some 2,000 Indians. Like other episodes of British valor, the killing at Lucknow was instantly memorialized in ballads, lithographs, eyewitness accounts, and historical overviews both popular and scholarly, nearly all of them emphasizing how (for example) "gallant Highlanders" and "daring and invincible Sikhs" "deal[t] death" to "the miscreants, the blood-stained monsters of Cawnpore" (*The Sepoy's Daughter* (1860): 440). Eyewitness Frederick Roberts recalled it more vividly:

> It was beautiful to see them going at it, regularly racing to see who should be first in. They went, and before half an hour was over, nearly 2,000 Pandies were on the ground dead or dying. I never saw such a sight. They were literally in heaps, and when I went in were a heaving mass, some dead, but most wounded and unable to get up from the crush. How so many got crowded together I can't understand. You had to walk over them to cross the court. They showed their hatred even while dying, cursed us and said: 'if we could only stand, we would kill you.'   (103–4)

Four months had elapsed before Beato returned to recreate the already legendary moment. To do so, he exhumed the corpses of dead peasants and arranged their bones on the floor of the courtyard where the killing had taken place. The resulting image is captioned with clinical specificity and ambiguous jingoism: it cites specific dates and proper names and refers to "rebels," but also to their "slaughter." It shows what Susan Sontag has called an "unburial ground" (2002: 54) (Fig. 0.5).

Only apparently chaotic, the still-startling image of tattered rags and splayed bones is in fact fastidiously constructed. For scale, Beato positioned four living peasants in carefully arranged poses of desultory boredom amid the bleaching remains. The triangular composition they form at the picture's structural center is flanked on the left by a standing man and a horse, whose movement during the exposure has again inscribed temporal process into this apparently frozen instant. Smashed wood, carefully arranged into compositional figures, works as a structural device, drawing our eye to the focal point of the photo (Fig. 0.6).

In contrast to contemporary accounts that imagined the killing at Secundra Bagh as (in Roberts' word) "beautiful," criticism has treated Beato's image with revulsion, a moral indignation I want to suspend without refuting in my evocation of it here. (Beato's image will not let us remain comfortable in either readerly affect.) As Tom Prasch notes, Sontag sees "Secundra Bagh" as a "depiction of the horrific," while Fred Ritchin describes it as representing "the grotesqueries of war" (quoted in Prasch 2012). But horrific to whom? Grotesque in relation to what? In the most sophisticated reading to date, Chaudhary refers to Beato's scene as a "phantasmagor[ia]," citing the fastidious constructedness of this image only to buttress the assumption that Beato aimed "to capture the immediacy of a historical event" (2012: 98). But this offhand nod to intention, like the

Fig. 0.5. Felice Beato, "Interior of the Secundra Bagh, after the Slaughter of 2,000 Rebels by the 93rd Highlanders and 4th Punjab Regiment. First Attack of Sir Colin Campbell in November 1857, Lucknow," 1858, albumen silver print, 26.2 × 30.2 cm. PH1982:0301:013. Collection Centre Canadien d'Architecture/Canadian Centre for Architecture, Montréal.

other critics' assumption of thesis content available for our later moral judgment, is frustrated by the image itself. As Prasch notes, any attempt to fix a meaning to it "only guesses at intentions" (2012), while Chaudhary cites the photo's "critical and reflexive engagement with itself" (2012: 99). Obsessively shaped, openly artificial, this sign of an already mediated event has been translated through any number of physical processes and formal vocabularies—the digging of the bones, the preparation of the plates, the arrangement of broken wood in keeping with the genre conventions of the eighteenth-century picturesque. Each of these mediating processes remains visible in the photo itself; these formal steps of shaping and figuration can themselves be seen as the photo's content, what it is about.

Rather than offering "immediacy," "Secundra Bagh" should be read as calling attention to just the opposite noun; it speaks most of all to its historical referent's mediacy, since direct historical communication—the

Fig. 0.6. Felice Beato, "Interior of the Secundra Bagh," detail. Collection Centre Canadien d'Architecture/Canadian Centre for Architecture, Montréal.

inert transfer of information in a documentary or representational mode—is here definitively frustrated. Surely what Jennifer Green-Lewis refers to as "the enormity of what [Victorian war] pictures do not show" (1996: 107–8) would seem misapplied to this horrendous surplus of showing. But this showing produces no thesis, speaks no truths: "it is difficult to sustain a reading of the image as a triumphal representation," Chaudhary notes, even while presuming our desire to do so (2012: 99). Is the photograph triumphal or critical? Is it, in W. J. T. Mitchell's terms, a bad object or a good one (2005: 188)? The decision rests with us, for the only meaning the image definitively contains is a reference to its construction as an image. It is, in this way, about mediation: the "after" of Beato's caption—"after the slaughter of 2,000 rebels"—is a temporal marker that is also akin to the painterly one, used for labeling imitations: the "after" Titian or "after" Poussin that signals a heavily mediated remake, the student-made mirror image that is inescapably not the original. Rather than waiting inertly for our moral judgment, the hypermediated photo Beato made at Secundra Bagh should be read as depicting its own emergence as an actively reconfigured sign of an already historical event: that is, as a trope.

Considered as an active process of critical mediation rather than an inert object awaiting our conceptual work, the boneyard at Secundra Bagh comments on just these metaphors of meaning-making; defeats hypostasizing "description"; and in the process performs the dialectical activity we would best call thinking. As the New Historicist exposure of Wordsworth's smoke-rings reminds us, symptomatic readings in a political key aim (in Jameson's words) to "detec[t] the traces" of the violence obscured by the textual artifacts of culture, "restoring to the surface" this "repressed and buried reality" (1981: 20). The critic works historically only to the extent that he brings to light, unearths, and dis-covers a previously encrypted real. Scandalously, Beato's image does all three things: here a literally buried historical violence has been disinterred: pulled from below, laid open to view, and arranged into striking pattern. In brutal detail, that is, the image uncomfortably literalizes just such a scene of decryption as Jameson imagines to constitute historical reading as such, with "decryption" standing in its full sense as both decoding and unburial. If the obscene violence of the British counterinsurgency is elsewhere disavowed or buried under layer after layer of jingoistic overwriting, it is here uncomfortably manifest.[31] Not "pandies," "wretches," "monsters," or "devils," these are simply the remains of dead human bodies, laid open to view. By concretizing the metaphors that structure the very hermeneutic protocols we might use to read it, the object called "Secundra Bagh" can be said itself to perform the act of historical interpretation Jameson assigns to the critic.

In *The Political Unconscious* Jameson famously positions the reading subject as the one able, "like Tiresias," to drink from the mysterious cup of the past (1981: 19). Yet in the earlier *Marxism and Form*, Jameson leaves room to understand that such historical work might be performed by objects themselves. Discussing Adorno, Jameson notes that the office of dialectical criticism is to create "historical tropes" (1974: 3–60): figures for totality able temporarily or provisionally to freeze into the same frame of analysis what were, before that act of reading, disconnected "worlds." Properly figured, such tropes "se[t] into contact with each other [. . .] two incommensurable realities" (1974: 189): they disclose the involvement of apparently separate sociocultural "levels," even as they expose their artificiality as constructions aimed at doing just that. "Secundra Bagh" operates as a historical trope in just this still-vital dialectical sense: for a frozen instant that it marks as such (recall the twitch of diachrony registered in the moving horse), this image puts into contact two apparently exclusive narratives—the stories of imperial lawkeeping and genocidal extermination, of a "Mutiny" and a "War for Independence," of "our" peacekeeping and "their" unredeemed death—without enabling the matter to be settled into any (self-identical) thesis or meaning.[32] Documents of civilization are also documents of barbarism: but Beato's document turns this inert cliché back into a conceptual struggle and makes this dynamism its operational activity as an image. When we determine whether and how that struggle resolves, we expose not the object's ethical and political investments but our own.

Such a reading might seem to replace other critics' moral revulsion with my fetishistic attachment. But insofar as "Secundra Bagh" turns the metaphors of decryption, penetration, violation, and unburial into its content, it also exposes the violence constituting any number of our own procedures for reading it. In so doing the image makes discomfitingly visible what Sontag in "Against Interpretation" calls the "open aggressiveness" (1967: 6) and "impious" (p. 7) tendency toward "ravishment" (p. 8) characteristic of hermeneutic approaches. "The modern style of interpretation," she notes as if describing Beato's *mise en scène*, "excavates, and as it excavates, destroys; it digs 'behind' the text, to find a sub-text which is the true one" (p. 6). What Bruno Latour refers to in a related observation as "the cruel treatment objects undergo in the hands of [. . .] *critical barbarity*" (2004: 240, emphasis original) is here elaborately performed; the photographer's relation to the bodies he has unearthed is nothing if not "cruel"; it is extravagantly "impious." To say all this is to mark distance from the model of the hero-critic who performs feats of ethical-political unmasking. But it is also to refuse to abandon the politics of engaged care underwriting that model. My claim is that the critic's act of historical reading—that impious but illuminating trope-making process— has been performed by the object itself. The object has gone further to draw attention to the constitutive perversities of this very process.

Of course, to ascribe theoretical activity to objects involves some of the oldest rhetorical moves in literature: not just *ekphrasis*, or the literary description of plastic objects, but also *prosopopoeia* (from the Greek *prósopon*, πρόσωπον, "face, person," and *poiéin*, ποιεῖν, "to make, to do"): the device by which the poet offers her ideas as the voice of something outside herself. De Man (1984) critiques this trope in Wordsworth's poetry, but my suggestion is that it might have methodological value now: it would help us keep faith with Victorian objects in their textured specificity, but also with the human bodies whose suffering such objects cannot but translate into form.

The following chapters will test how such an approach might keep faith with narrative, poetic, and other verbal texts: objects less obviously imbued with the constitutive ambiguity that commentators since Barthes have habitually located in photographs. Now we can note that each of the images arranged here actively reconfigures a scene of historical violence and exploits the capacity of form to comment on its act of critical seeing. In so doing, Beato's eloquent and unrelenting images spotlight the problematic status of decision as it relates to any act of historically implicated reading. As Derrida explains of all decisions properly so called, any decision to read this way instead of that—for example, to ascribe conceptual agency to objects prosopopoetically, as I have done here— cannot find authorization in anything beyond itself, since then it would not have been a decision at all but "the programmable application of unfolding of a calculable process" (1992: 24). Decisions in the true sense of choices without guarantees can only ever be responses to the undecide-able that take place in relation to commitments, or ends. Paranoid or reparative, then? The question is not about method so much as it is about value: a matter, in Latour's words, not of fact but of concern (2004). Whether Beato's photographs are bad objects or good ones cannot be determined except by a choice of this kind on the part of the reader, one made in reference to a category of belief or purpose—with reference, that is, to the category of ends. Responding curatorially to this pressure for judgment lets us view these photographs reparatively while maintaining a stance of critique toward the obscene violence of Victorian modernity they necessarily mediate.

Positing the conceptually productive capacities of Victorian objects like Beato's—their active mediating operations, their work as thought—helps interrupt tired discussions about photography's privileged relation to the real and reintroduces the category of form into often technocentric analysis of media. It also opens new dimensions to the sometimes narcissistically self-contained debates over reading in literary studies. The wager of such a method is that we might experiment with genres of reading that would maintain solidarity not just with nineteenth-century objects in all their textured specificity, but with those remaindered human bodies that have their own specificity, and that have been cast to the outsides and undersides—and into the jumbled bone piles—of the Victorian era's prom-ise of inclusion.[33] Situated as we are in corporate universities ready to pay for appreciation but calling out for critique, could we read this way now?

EQUIPOISE AND ELSEWHERE

This book is a way of testing a positive answer to that question. It is a long book whose chapters take shape around sometimes exorbitantly close engagements with individual objects. For reasons just explained, this book's arguments do not develop transcendentally apart from its objects of analysis but immanently through them. Put another way, this approach does not conceive "theory" as knowledge to be applied to or tested on historical objects; nor yet does it construe readings as "evidence" or support for claims external to those engagements. Instead this book's claims are crystallized in, and figured by, historical artifacts themselves, and for that reason can only emerge through a patient reading of those singular texts, a brushing along their grain. The story told by these encounters transpires chronologically and in two parts, "Equipoise" and "And Elsewhere." Together these halves move from 1857, the year of the Victorian Empire's first crisis of global sovereignty, to the period following the 1885 Berlin Conference, when a newly multilateral international system began slowly to replace a splintering British hegemony. This geopolitical or macrohistorical chronology helps ground a literary plot that begins domestically, in London, but moves, in the book's second half, to the war-torn edges of the British world system.

The first chapter, "Time and Violence in the Age of Equipoise," builds on the engagement with Victorian mediation just surveyed to address what may be the most longstanding aesthetic enigma in nineteenth-century fiction: the flood scene that closes George Eliot's novel of countryside modernization, *The Mill on the Floss* (1860). Declared a clumsy *deus ex machina* by Henry James and defended by others as a subtly realistic denouement, the deaths of Maggie and Tom Tulliver are crucial to the novel's plot but unrepresented by it. Eliot's careful prose ensures that the instant of their drowning happens out of view. In the context of temporal-political narratives about law's birth that Eliot knew intimately, the non-scene of Tom and Maggie's death becomes legible as a version of the violent but unrepresentable event from which modern legality emerged. It forms the kind of hiatus between then and now that political theory terms a revolution, and that Victorian geology (which Eliot also studied) called a catastrophe. Eliot twists the narrative schemes of her gradualist liberal colleagues to document the fundamental, law-making disruption necessary to bring a new order into being. When she uses free indirect discourse to denarrate the novel's startling and violently sacrificial finale—its catastrophe—Eliot generates an effect of form that introduces into liberalism's *Bildungsroman* of modernity a grounding violence that would be felt most acutely elsewhere, by human bodies beyond the compass of modern law's protection.

Chapter 2, "Reform Fiction's Logic of Belonging," shifts from provincial realism to metropolitan sensation fiction to show how Reform-era potboilers about the lost people like *No Name* (1863), *The Woman in White* (1860), and *Lady Audley's Secret* (1862) engage critically the mechanism of exclusion animating mass democracy. Sensation fiction is still read as an ideological machine for shoring up the bourgeois values threatened by the 1867 Reform Act. By contrast, I treat these elaborate plots of recovery as productive engagements with the most glaring theoretical challenge of their moment. Following lost people until they become counted subjects, these works transcode into plot the state's efforts to uplift particular bodies and convert them into members of a set, "citizens." Collins (1866) endorses but also mocks this political induction, while explicitly theoretical works of the same moment, J. S. Mill's *A System of Logic* (1843–73) and Karl Marx's *Capital* (1867), explain that a conceptually necessary but logically unspecifiable moment—Mill calls it a "leap"— separates the particular individual from its general category. I show that the sensation novel, the logical treatise, and the critique of political economy exploit their separate affordances to dramatize this unnameable leap. *Armadale*'s double-generational plot goes further, since it locates the origins of inductive democracy in the social death of chattel slavery, even while directing its care toward those cast out from law's avowedly universal embrace. What the lost-person plots of Collins and Dickens variously mediate, then, is how belonging and abandonment evolved as mutually dependent characteristics of life at the center of imperial modernity.

Chapter 3, "Form and Excess, Morant Bay and Swinburne," follows this logic to the colonies, to show how the Victorian era's most formally sophisticated poetry illuminates dramas of legal exclusion that justified killing 439 black peasants under martial law in Jamaica. Published at the very instant news of the 1865 Morant Bay Rebellion hit London, A. C. Swinburne's hyperformalist *Poems and Ballads* (1866) cite the Marquis de Sade and romanticize a force that could supersede all law— "a superflux of pain"—even while couching this excess within what contemporary poetic theory called "the laws of meter." I explain the political logic of Swinburne's dialectical poetry by constellating what I treat as related literary and political controversies in the late summer of 1866. Seen alongside other forms such as legal depositions, parliamentary reports, and minutes from colonial show trials, lyrics like "Anactoria" freeze sadomasochistic excess and absolute control into a single conceptual unit on the page, disclosing law's secret unity with death. In so doing they transcribe into poetic form a fact about sovereignty that even the well-meaning commentators on the "atrocities in Jamaica" (as Mill called them) could not grasp. As idealist commentators like Mill and John Morley looked on in paralyzed frustration, the poems and the legal controversy both disclosed how an extralegal excess (a superflux) might vexingly animate the legal order it seemed to contravene. In Swinburne's hands, technologies like the lyric poem and, at a smaller scale, the heroic couplet help explain how an order of law might subject to death the very bodies it claimed to protect.

Chapter 4, "The Philosophy of Romance Form," locates the origins of modern novel form in the sovereignty crises of the late Victorian state. It shows how the coterie of Andrew Lang, H. Rider Haggard, and Robert

Louis Stevenson reconceived the novelistic categories of action and event in response to the small wars blooming at the edges of a British world system in decline. While criticism has for three decades read the adventure romance as a clumsy intervention into cultural jingoism, I explain how this key subgenre of the 1880s aesthetically negotiates material changes in England's geopolitical posture. Long mocked as a racist and simpleton, Haggard was a barrister who wrote *King Solomon's Mines* (1885) with self-conscious style and a conspicuous legal vocabulary. This idiom he derived from his relationship with classical scholar and literary impresario Andrew Lang no less than from his experience prosecuting asymmetrical wars in southern Africa, where universal reason was secured with unlimited death. The man responsible for shaping Haggard's apparently shapeless prose, Lang, drew on his studies of Homeric epic to brand these eventful tales as alternatives to the character-driven "adventure[s] of interiority" (Lukács 1971: 89) that William Dean Howells was advertising as proper to a rising American world order. In light of these transatlantic "realism wars" (as Lang styled them), Haggard's mock-epics emerge as active stylistic engagements with an inter-imperial rivalry England was then losing. The most self-reflexive productions from the Lang coterie, by Stevenson, expose how atavistic violence and bourgeois civility were not opposite terms but two facets of a sovereign system in decline. As Jekyll explains of Hyde, "This, too, was myself" (2002: 58).

The book's Conclusion asks what forms might emerge to mediate our own moment of retreating hegemony and proliferating war, so similar in world-historical shape to Haggard's. Attending to these historical echoes, analogies, or resonances—all of these being tropes for a relation of simultaneous identity and difference—enables this story to close by making explicit the dual historicist wager at the heart of this book. On the one hand, *Forms of Empire* argues that caring regard for objects of the past can attune us to the particularity of the Victorian moment and its conceptual mediations; on the other, this very particularization might somehow and paradoxically affirm Victorian form as a resource for thinking in the present. Because the present scene of writing is bound necessarily to the historical period under analysis, I treat the Victorian era not as a curio box of old things, but as a workshop in which the conceptual and political categories of the present, including those deployed in this book, are under dynamic construction. Criticism has literary shape too. This book's method, I mean, is implicated in its claims about the conceptually significant work form accomplishes. The efforts at immanent critique to follow use a strategy of selection, arrangement, and juxtaposition I conceive as poetic to challenge the alleged division between historical and formalist approaches.

One of this study's assertions is that a stance of renewed enchantment toward Victorian objects need not cancel, but might instead invigorate a commitment to critical and political engagement now. This commitment means that *Forms of Empire* stands in solidarity with the human damage still accumulating in our post-Victorian modernity. But the point is that these allegiances have already been modeled by nineteenth-century literature itself.

PART I
EQUIPOISE

1

Time and Violence in the Age
of Equipoise

[T]here is a tendency to and taste for startling events in George Eliot,
which seems to crop out of the rich culture of her mind, like the
primitive rocks of an earlier world. The flood in the mill, and the
rescue of Hetty in *Adam Bede*, are instances of what we mean; they
are vestiges of a Titanic time, before the reign of peaceful gods
commenced.

—*Westminster Review*, 1860

GEOLOGICAL LIBERALISM AND SLOW TIME

The backward-looking, cataclysmic plot of George Eliot's second full-length
novel, *The Mill on the Floss* (1860), does many things, all of them well. It
describes Maggie and Tom Tulliver struggling toward adulthood in a kind of
doubled *Bildung*;[1] it shows a charming but outdated village called St. Ogg's,
and nestles it at the confluence of two grandly symbolic rivers;[2] it relates a
sequence of historical modernization and family drama that take place in
a golden past, "many years ago" (p. 11); and it features, less charmingly, a
shocking flood whose victims, killed by wooden shards and a vortex of water,
end up in graves arranged for view. "It is the epic of the human soul," wrote
the *Spectator*, "traced through childhood, development, and temptation"—
we might add catastrophe (Carroll, ed. 1971: 112).

This chapter is about time, violence, and law, and looks to show how
Eliot's description of the twilight of country life in *The Mill on the Floss*
reconfigures a political narrative common to the late 1850s and early
1860s. This story is about the advent of a political order conceived in
temporal terms. It narrates the birth of a self-consciously modern social
formation understood to be governed by "law," in which formally equal
subjects interact rationally in a theater of exchange apparently evacuated
of force. In this shared vision of political modernity's dawn—named

"liberty" by John Stuart Mill and "contract" by Henry Sumner Maine, and construed by Eliot's novel as the present—coercion by violence is understood to have been superseded, in the world's most advanced or adult nations, by discussion, reason, and the operations of equal justice. "We learn to restrain ourselves as we get older," Eliot's narrator says. "We no longer approximate in our behaviour to the mere impulsiveness of the lower animals, but conduct ourselves in every respect like members of a highly civilised society" (p. 43). Eliot's characteristic irony does not obscure the force of this historical novel's operative categories: in the story it shares with the political theory of its moment, an "old" custom is said to have already turned, by a long process of historical necessity or the short shock of revolutionary event, into a "new" peace, a modernity that "we" inhabit.

It is well known that the Victorian age generated a profusion of developmental narratives, but the years directly adjacent to 1860 proved especially productive. Interventions in natural history, biology, political theory, and comparative legal history, among other proto-disciplines, all testified to the fact that to many theorists of the period, the "now" of the late 1850s represented the very crest of time's upward motion.[3] A stable domestic state and an unquestioned global hegemony meant that England seemed to stand in a unique relationship to modernity—that is, as its very instantiation. Mill's *On Liberty* (1859) and Maine's *Ancient Law* (1861, begun late 1850s) make this narrative explicit. The story Maine and Mill tell in common, like Eliot's, charts the birth of a self-consciously modern political rationality out of the dark past of a previous age, a narrative in which peace and law supersede force and coercion. These are parables of the English liberal state's emergence, stories about how old custom transforms into modern contract, and into the peace with which this stage is held to be coextensive.

In a critique of what he calls "the trope of modernity" (2002: 40), Fredric Jameson has suggested that "modernity" signifies an unspoken conflation of political parliamentarism, philosophical individualism, and capitalist rationality. All of these registers find expression in the rational *Gesellschaft* represented by Lawyer Wakem, *The Mill on the Floss*' property-buying villain and privatizer of water rights. As the novel's very embodiment of modern times, Wakem's name suggests his function: even as it calls on us to memorialize, in a wake, the *Gemeinschaft* he helps displace, the lawyer's name signals his primary role, which is to awaken the primitive St. Ogg's into the modern rule of law.

Later historians have reproduced almost exactly the optimistic self-assessment of the English nineteenth century's middle years: twentieth-century scholars in particular isolated the previous century's middle decades

as a free-standing, synchronic moment, an "Age of Equipoise" characterized by the linked achievements of law, peace, and free trade. In the book
of that title, W. L. Burn dates the mid-century's happy balance as
extending from 1852 to 1867 (1964: 15). Asa Briggs (1955: 1), describing what he calls "high Victorian England," offers the Great Exhibition
(1851) and the Second Reform Bill (1867) as this era's bookends. Briggs
tells us that during the extending present of this period-within-a-period,
social equilibrium meant that violent events and radical disturbances
were a thing of the past—if also, for the historian with the benefit
of hindsight, the future. With law as its rule and domestic tranquility as
its achievement, the mid-century, Briggs writes, was unpunctuated by
interruptions of any kind:

> The picturesque battles of the nineteenth century fall on either side of the
> period. On the one side, there are the sharp conflicts of the 1840s, when
> contemporaries talked openly of class war and imminent revolution, and,
> on the other, there are the bitter struggles of the [1870s and] 1880s,
> when Irish nationalism molded English history and Victorian radicalism
> overlapped with twentieth century socialism. The middle years of the
> century form a great plateau bounded on each side by deep ravines and
> dangerous precipices.   (1955: 1)

It may surprise us to see the period that included the Crimean War, the
Indian Mutiny, and the Morant Bay Rebellion invoked as the very picture
of calm. But Briggs' concern here is domestic, and his investments are in
equipoise. The passage describes homeland upheaval in language that links
military violence ("sharp conflicts") with geological hazard ("dangerous
precipices"). In so doing Briggs replicates the conceptual arsenal of the
Victorians under discussion, and in the process gives voice to his own age's
preference for defused conflict and steady terrain.[4]

Briggs also favors a geological metaphor to describe the period's event-
less calm, and the "social balance" it represents (1955: 1). Here, the "great
plateau" of peace is coextensive, Briggs writes two pages later, with the
British rule of law, itself another name for what he calls the "movement of
unremitting adaptation and reform carried out without violence" during
the period (1955: 3). This characterization of British law as the very
antithesis of violence has a long pedigree, beginning at least with jurists
and political theorists of the Victorian era themselves. Briggs' account of
"Victorian People" does not mention Maggie Tulliver or the flood event
that kills her, a natural event so catastrophic that it might have been pasted
directly from the tales of rocks and hazards Eliot copied into her
commonplace books while writing the novel, including Charles Lyell's
Principles of Geology (1830, rev. 1852, 1860). (She had read Leveson

Vernon Harcourt's account of the Noachian flood, *The Doctrine of the Deluge*, in 1839.)

The Mill on the Floss anticipates the tendency of its neo-Victorian interpreters to think of political modernity in the mixed registers of time, quasi-theological catastrophe, and geology. It also shares with those accounts an understanding that these processes, understood as "history," culminate in its own, putatively peaceful moment: the stable plateau of the now, where floods and other violent interruptions belong to another, previous temporal-political order. An analysis of the figural repertoire common to Cold War liberalism and post-1990 neoliberalism is beyond the scope of this chapter. Provisionally we could note that mid-twentieth-century assessments of the mid-Victorian age, like those following the fall of the Berlin Wall, have rearticulated in secular terms the Victorian era's representation of itself as the very apogee of the modern. Insofar as this is true, turning to the Victorian source of those stories can shed light not only on the ideological conjuncture of the late 1850s but on its legacy in our own era and the critical models attempting to explain it.[5]

Like "politics," the grand movements of history have long been understood to sit among George Eliot's signal themes—they are the twin obsessions, we might say, both of her writing and of writing about her.[6] So too have studies explained Eliot's debt to the geological thinking of her moment, even focusing on the *The Mill on the Floss* to do so (Buckland 2013). By exposing the links between Eliot's second novel and other historical-political narratives from the "plateau" of the late 1850s and early 1860s, this chapter shows how Eliot's most charismatic local novel exploits the affordances of its medium to register a fundamental contradiction in the historical logic of progressive idealism; the novel goes further to use the particular capacities of literary presentation to radicalize that very contradiction. More specifically: Maine and Mill's storylines emphasize, on the one hand, a perfect disjunction between stages (as primitive "status" transforms to modern "contract"), but on the other hand couch this in terms of law's emergence after an extended past of gradual development.

This tension between *durée* and event is narratological in nature; in exhibiting it, Maine and Mill's stories evince a reluctance to conceive the *source* of the lawful stability they valorize, its origin in a violent founding event—a reluctance Eliot's story of flood and sacrifice does not share. I will be arguing, in other words, that against its contemporary theories of idealist progress, Eliot's novel tackles "the problem of law in its originary structure" (Agamben 1999: 167); it departs from its rival modernization stories to document the raw, extralegal force that authorizes any regime of legality and that remains, in potential form, after that order's founding.

After establishing the intellectual milieu into which Eliot's 1860 novel intervened, this chapter argues that Eliot's novel does three things. First, it sharpens the contradiction whereby the achieved present of English lawfulness (whether called "liberty" or "contract") can be viewed both as history's natural progression and as the result of a radical jump between stages. Second, Eliot's novel solves the tension it raises between *durée* and event by presenting, in the midst of a gradualist, organic historical model, a moment of transfigured revolutionary violence (the flood). This event effects a radical rupture in what we might, following New Critical practice, call the novel's organic order: it kills Maggie and Tom in a single, unrepresented instant of violence, and it arrives on a formal level, as *deus ex machina*, to reorder the narrative's existing codes of expectation. Third, *The Mill on the Floss*' retrospective structure accomplishes formally what is also (on the level of plot) the actual encryption of its modern order's violent origin: it buries the dead bodies of Tom and Maggie in graves that we, as later sentimental readers, stand positioned to view.[7]

Tracing *The Mill*'s complex temporal-political configuration, and charting its significance to its moment, in and around what we can call the high-water mark of the Victorian liberal empire, alters our views of Eliot's historicism and that of her age; it also provides a test case for this book's method, insofar as the chapter locates in Eliot's text not ideological enclosure but poetic innovation—a conceptual creativity that shows Eliot's novel to have outstripped in advance the critical models to date arrayed to explain it. Most important for the book's larger argument, this chapter opens a connection the following ones will examine in depth: the link between a metropolitan rule of law and that law's authorizing violence, a force that remained in potential form to re-emerge, at the edges of law's reach, as open war.

COUNTRYSIDE GRADUALISM: *THE MILL ON THE FLOSS* I

Links between the imperial system's violent outside and its allegedly pacified inside will be traced more fully in following chapters. But it is national time, not imperial war, that forms the central topic of Eliot's 1860 story of law's rise: temporality is its most recurrent and unmissable theme. Appearing in editorial asides throughout its pages, *The Mill on the Floss*' explicit descriptions of temporal process have inspired a long tradition of criticism to view the novel in terms of something called "history." Readers have noted Eliot's belief in the priority of historical

forces over individual wills (Crosby 1991, Li 2000); documented her
engagement with evolutionary thinking in its Darwinian, Spencerian,
and even Lyellian modes (Beer 1986, Paxton 1991, Buckland 2013);
and explained more particularly how *The Mill on the Floss* seems driven
by a single historical motion, a forward flow well symbolized, readers will
recall, by the sweeping currents of the rivers Ripple and Floss themselves
(Arac 1979). All these accounts note how Eliot's theory of history
imagines land, people, and politics as tied into a single course of time—
a unified, nearly geological process in which temporality accumulates, and
the present takes its place literally on top of what preceded it. "History" is
the name Eliot and her later readers give to this sedimentary wash of time.

As this description suggests, *The Mill*'s diegetic action is described not in
the language of revolution and event—of history understood as eruptions
or sudden overturnings—but in terms of the slow unfolding that characterizes Eliot's gradualist theory of social change. By the time of *Middlemarch* (1871–2), Eliot's emphasis on gradual process over instantaneous
rupture would become total, as "unhistoric acts" (p. 785) slowly accrue as
part of an effort, as Eliot wrote to her editor, John Blackwood, "to show the
gradual action of ordinary causes rather than exceptional" (Eliot 1958–78:
5.168). In *The Mill on the Floss*, the country village of St. Ogg's prefigures
Middlemarch's decelerated, anti-"exceptional" temporal-formal scheme,
with its emphasis on ordinary rather than extraordinary events: this
place has "developed," Eliot's narrator tells us, in "a long growth" that is
not unlike the growth of a plant (p. 254). Giving voice to the organicist
social historicism Eliot was in these years developing in tandem with her
colleague and love interest Herbert Spencer, *The Mill*'s narrator describes
the country village as a kind of historical shrub. This biological metaphor
stands in for another, geological language, where sedimented years and
the residue of them are legible as the "traces" marking this "spot." The
narrator reports:

> It is one of those old, old towns, which impress one as a continuation and
> outgrowth of nature as much as the nests of the bowerbirds or the winding
> galleries of the white ants: a town which carries traces of its long growth and
> history, like a millennial tree, and has sprung up and developed in the same
> spot between the river and the low hill from the time when the Roman
> legions turned their backs on it from the camp on the hill-side, and the long-
> haired sea-kings came up the river and looked with fierce, eager eyes at the
> fatness of the land. It is a town 'familiar with forgotten years.'   (pp. 123–4)

In this often-cited passage Eliot's narrator quotes the Wanderer from the
first book of Wordsworth's *Excursion* to emphasize the accumulated sense
of history in St. Ogg's, its paradoxical ability to remain "familiar" with

what it has "forgotten." Here, we are told, on this "spot," time stacks on top of itself: history accumulates, and each epoch leaves behind a "trace" that is the mark of its former presence. The physical town, the very ground it occupies, registers this extending *durée*, even if its living inhabitants do not.

Here, any event that might seem to have introduced disjunction is folded into the long, slow sedimentation of millennial time. As my own metaphors of stratification and accumulation have already suggested, this is the realm of geological history, of the long ages and layered time described in Lyell's *Principles of Geology*, the work that influentially helped extend the horizon of early Victorian thinking about time. Though James Secord has cautioned against viewing *Principles* as an isolated, revolutionary text—as an event in its own right—it was undoubtedly the most important framing of gradualist geology for Victorian lay readers, in this way fulfilling one definition of the event as something that "forces" those in its wake "to take sides, for or against" (quoted in Hallward 2003: 113). It certainly set the terms for a subfield with which Eliot was familiar at least from her earliest researches on her second novel, on "inundation" in the British Library.[8] The science of stratigraphic reading had been around since William Smith's first systematic attempt to map England's rock layers (1815)—Smith had himself only updated an earlier practice called "geognosy" (Rudwick 2008: 36)—and Georges Cuvier explored the stratigraphy around Paris in 1808. But it was Lyell's treatise that most influentially reshaped early notions of geologic time; *Principles* has become famous for refuting Cuvier's belief that a lost world had been demolished in short, violent interruptions—"*révolutions de la surface du globe*," as the title of his 1825 treatise put it. A version of Cuvier's catastrophist thesis had been articulated for Eliot in Biblical terms—and to her mind poorly—in Harcourt's *Doctrine of the Deluge* (1838), an anti-gradualist polemic whose subtitle is *Vindicating the Spiritual Account from Doubts which have been Recently Cast Upon It by Geological Speculations*. Against catastrophist models both secular and Christian, Lyell argued for a long view of an extended history, one in which apparent ruptures of historical change are contained within the grand, equalizing extension of geological continuity, epochs of gradual, "uniform" development.

Secord's emphasis is on the minor geologists arguing in Lyell's shadow,[9] but as other historians of geology have shown, once the long historicity of the earth had been posited, scientists responding to Lyell continued to argue whether geological change happened in long epochs or brief, violent events (cf. Rudwick 2008: 356–61). In this debate about geological causation, catastrophists followed Cuvier to hold that periodic, violent events (Cuvier's "revolutions") punctuated long eras of calm, forming hinges between discrete epochs, while the uniformitarian position (Lyell's) put its lot with long, slow growth. For Lyell, in other words, the momentary interruptions of historical change certainly had effects (volcanoes, earthquakes, and what he calls "aqueous causes"—floods—are his signal examples), but these forces were best interpreted as mere blips, tiny exceptions legible, just barely, in the rocky texts of England's long past. In ways that prefigure the method of reading for "sedimented" generic signals that Jameson elaborates in *The Political Unconscious*, interpretation and reading were the favored metaphors for describing geological analysis in the Victorian age; the term "stratigraphy" refers both to the transcription of sedimented geological epochs into imagery and text and to the process of reading those epochs in rocks (Secord 1986: 25; see Rudwick 2008: 35–46). For Lyell and Cuvier as for Jameson, these transfigured marks constitute the "archive" (Rudwick 2014: 82) that any modern analyst must interpret to access the past, a metaphor of history-as-layered-inscription that persists in contemporary geology and historicist method alike.[10]

The accumulated strata in Eliot's St. Ogg's—its interpretable deposits of long, slow growth—certainly appear to place it under the auspices of geological uniformitarianism and the layered time this theory imagined. As Eliot's narrator explains in the Wordsworthian passage cited above, even the apparent ruptures of imperial incursion (waged by "Roman legions" and "long-haired sea-kings") have become part of the town's process of temporal accretion. Here, traces of what might be seen as events have been flattened into the past, stripped of their evental status and written into the ground itself. At this early point in *The Mill on the Floss*, then, the novel's emphasis is on process and slow time, and Eliot's metaphors are more natural than rocks. "[L]ike a millennial tree," Eliot's narrator explains, St. Ogg's has experienced its development as an organic accretion, the adding of rings to its social trunk. The town and its inhabitants are literally a part of its physical location, a "continuation" and "outgrowth" of the earth itself—what Eliot's narrator, taking a cue from Wordsworth, calls "this spot."

Whatever its status as scientific knowledge, Lyell's theory of historical sedimentation, like Eliot's articulation of a version of it, also works as political thought: it provides a model of deep time directly useful to political theories reliant on "the land" as the guarantor for national stability. *The Mill* does not mention Edmund Burke, nor Burke's notion that English political institutions gain their stability from ties to the ground of a long national-historical tradition. Yet tropes of land and earth do organize the descriptions of spots of time in St. Ogg's, and Eliot's tale of geological forward motion does seem to imagine the British political order *c.*1859 as one (inevitable) outcome of its developmental plot (Arac 1979: 676). But as is suggested by the metaphorical substitution of "millennial tree" for rock and earth in the passage above, *The Mill* also transforms its geological metaphors into the biological ones of earth and trees, framing a series of explicit "biogenetic analogies" (Paxton 1991: 71) that place St. Ogg's residents in thrall to Eliot's developing theory of political organicism.

Eliot's 1856 program essay, "The Natural History of German Life," expounds upon the ideas of W. H. von Riehl to argue that the contemporary moment is what she calls "incarnate history," the accrual of the past realized in the present (1963: 289). In this often-discussed essay as in *The Mill on the Floss*, Eliot argues for a long view of England's political development: providing childish subjects with the voting power of rational man too early, she explains, is to play dangerously with time. As in other of her directly political texts, such as the 1868 "Address to Working Men, by Felix Holt," Eliot's purpose in "Natural History" is to argue against any hasty or revolutionary change. The short, sharp shocks of popular uprising, she argues, disturb the normal growth of the state's social body—a body understood, in Eliot's persistently biological metaphors, as a living organism.[11] What is needed before political change can safely be introduced, therefore, is time. As Eliot writes: "As a necessary preliminary to a purely rational society, you must obtain purely rational men, free from the sweet and bitter prejudices of hereditary affection and antipathy" (1963: 287). Here Eliot invokes the "prejudice" and "hereditary affection" of premodernity's inhabitants, then pits these against the disinterested rationality enjoyed by the modern subjects of her imagined audience.

Rather than judging the positive or negative aspects of this dichotomy between old prejudice and modern rationality, I want to note its temporal structure: this is a theory of time with two categories, old and new ("heredity" versus "rationality"); but the stress, here as in St. Ogg's, is on gradual process, on the slow growth of the social plant. The "Natural History" essay goes on:

> What has grown up historically can only die out historically, by the gradual operation of necessary laws. The external conditions which society has inherited from the past are but the manifestation of inherited internal conditions in the human beings who compose it; the internal conditions and the external are related to each other as the organism and its medium, and development can take place only by the gradual consentaneous development of both. (1963: 287)

With its play between individual and environment, this, like Spencer's, is a complex sociology of systems, as critics like Amanda Anderson, Nancy Paxton, and Irene Tucker have differently appreciated. Highlighting the value of equilibrium, slow motion, and something called "consentaneous" development, it is also the "central expression," as Eliot's editor writes, of her "conservatism" (Pinney, in Eliot 1963: 267).[12] The *OED* informs us that "consentaneous" means "done by common consent, unanimous, concurrent, simultaneous." But "consentaneous development," as the phrase is deployed here, describes the concord between "organism" and "medium," not between the ruled subjects and the state that rules them. Eliot's cagey rhetorical move thus invokes the very keyword of liberal contract theory at mid-century ("consent") to argue against its too-wide dispersal. Nevertheless, in "Natural History" as elsewhere in Eliot's social theory, the slow, "consentient" growth of organism and individual, seen in the *longue durée* of geological time, will engender liberal developments in the long run. Even Eliot's apparent conservatism, that is, understands that an unhurried social growth will eventually culminate in equality, commercial modernization, and even suffrage for the someday-to-be-liberated peasantry. At the moment, however, these specimens live in what Dipesh Chakrabarty calls liberalism's "not yet" (2000: 9).[13]

My concern is not to critique Eliot for subscribing to this widespread notion of uneven developmental time, a model that had in any case structured the liberal political tradition at least since Kant's "What is Enlightenment?" (1784) if not before.[14] It is rather to suggest that Eliot's historicism evinces what seems to be a contradiction at the level of structure: here we have a theory of two-stage difference (between peasant blindness and "our" insight) that also puts faith in long, Lyellian processes of geological accumulation, the growth of a Burkean "millennial tree" that will engender insight in the peasantry in due time. Catastrophism and gradualism sit uneasily together.

In fact, while *The Mill on the Floss* may be interested in documenting the "changing circumstances" of country life (Rignall 2000: 264), the landscape of the novel seems, at first glance, untouched by any historical motion at all. Blind to the ghosts in their midst, the residents of St. Ogg's believe that what Cuvier called "revolutions and catastrophes" (1825: 5)—and events as such—have been banished from their world. Their seemingly inert peasant world "goes from generation to generation," we are told, apparently without change:

> The mind of St Ogg's did not look extensively before or after. It inherited a long past without thinking of it, and had no eyes for the spirits that walked the streets. Since the centuries when St Ogg with his boat and the Virgin mother at the prow had been seen on the wide water, so many memories had been left behind, and had gradually vanished like the receding hill-tops! And the present time was like the level plain where men lose their belief in

volcanoes and earthquakes, thinking tomorrow will be as yesterday, and the giant forces that used to shake the earth are for ever laid to sleep.   (p. 126)

By describing the "memories" that have been "left behind" here, Eliot refigures the complex Wordworthian formulation of the millennial tree passage to explain that past events have been both forgotten and deposited here in residual form. By the same logic that their town can be said to be "familiar with forgotten years," the current residents of St. Ogg's are described as unaware of the tradition written into their surroundings, their "inheritance." In *The Mill on the Floss*, as in Asa Briggs' twentieth-century account, geological events emerge as the preferred figure for describing such historical-political events ("[T]he giant forces that used to shake the earth" have been "for ever laid to sleep"). Yet the passage also underscores that the residents of St. Ogg's have been lulled into what we might call a naïve uniformitarianism: they are locked into an extended geological time without the ability to read for the memories inscribed in their spot.

For the characters grafted bodily to its rhythms, this rural spot seems a serially recurring contemporary, a perpetual present. "It's just as if it were yesterday, now," Mr. Tulliver exclaims (p. 277), epitomizing the antidevelopmental temporality he falsely identifies him. Tom and his sister also think they live in an arrested development: as children they had, the narrator says, "no thought that life would ever change much for them; [. . .] and it would always be like the holidays" (p. 45). With its provincial characters believing that they wander the level plain of a continuous present, *The Mill* in this sense appears to live up to its reputation as Eliot's signal intervention into pastoral.[15] As with the shepherds and nymphs of that mode, Tom (for example) possesses "a nature which had a sort of superstitious repugnance to everything exceptional" (p. 353). Perhaps because he does not believe in interruptive events in the first place, "Anxiety about the future had never entered [his] mind" (p. 198). But this is his own oversight.

The world's apparent uniformity may be symbolized by the grinding revolutions of the mill itself, whose "unresting wheel" (p. 10) turns and turns without ever moving. But in Eliot's complex symbolic economy, the very emblem of an apparently static, eternal return is driven by the novel's central figure for progressive motion, the river. (This metaphorically charged body of water will also, of course, generate the novel's final meteorological-geological event, in the novel's closing pages.) For while Tom and Maggie may believe that they live in a static present of eternal holiday, the narrator emphasizes, abruptly, that they are wrong. "Life did change for Tom and Maggie" (p. 45), and if the other residents of St. Ogg's believe that the "giant forces that used to shake the earth" have been equalized into stability, the flood of the novel's final book will dramatically prove them wrong. Catastrophic events *do* happen in St. Ogg's, and reordering, geological ruptures—"aqueous causes," as Lyell named them—do take place. If these fold, in the long run, into the accumulating strata of an extending geological-political now, it remains the case that for at least two of the event's human witnesses the results are lethal. Tom's and Maggie's bodies will be sacrificed to the same interruptive violence that their fellow villagers believe has been forever deactivated. The "rupture with what exists" that this event effects (Badiou 2005: 24) means that in Eliot's novel, it is the figure of force itself, delivered in its most apparently natural form, that arrives to inaugurate the new world of consent. At once Biblical and scientific, this flood-event will chasten transgression and restart the clock of world-historical time.

LIBERAL TIME *c.*1859: HENRY MAINE AND JOHN STUART MILL

The amalgamated logics of geology, biology, theology, and slow time provide structure for Eliot's social theory and metaphors for her description of St. Ogg's. But "consent" is an operative term too, and it is this term that would prove the marker of modernity for Eliot and the political theorists contemporaneous with her.[16] In fact Eliot's text shares nearly all of its categories with the mid-century political theory being developed in the intellectual circles around her. The same year Eliot was drafting her story of the geological-political movement from prejudice to sympathy, her colleague at the *Westminster*, John Stuart Mill, described just this conversion as the key moment of liberal modernity. In *On Liberty*, Mill posits "the despotism of custom" as "the standing hindrance to human advancement, being in unceasing antagonism to that disposition to aim at something better than customary, which is called [...] the spirit of liberty, or that of progress or improvement" (*CW* XVIII). As Chakrabarty and Uday Singh Mehta have argued, Mill's historicism posits the "now" of improving and rational civilization against a "not yet" of what his essays (following the political nomenclature of the period) consistently name "despotism."[17] For Mill, force and physical coercion typify an older, archaic way of life ("custom"), while sympathetic rationality, contract, and a consent-based sovereignty—"liberty"—constitute its successor.

As its contemporary critics like James Fitzjames Stephen recognized, Mill's later work, in *The Subjection of Women* (1869, drafted 1860–1), should be read as an extended elaboration of the historical model announced in *On*

Liberty. Both texts are best seen as products of the post-Mutiny, pre-Reform "Age of Equipoise" plateauing between 1857 and 1861. In *Subjection*, Mill expounded on *On Liberty*'s two-stage formulation, comparing an outdated rule of custom, "a social relation grounded on force," with a new law of exchangeability ("institutions grounded on equal justice" (*CW* XXI)). Mill explains:

> We now live—that is to say, one or two of the most advanced nations of the world now live—in a state in which the law of the strongest seems to be entirely abandoned as the regulating principle of the world's affairs: nobody professes it, and, as regards most of the relations between human beings, nobody is permitted to practice it.   (*CW* XXI)

Mill's hesitating distinction between inferior nations and "us" has become infamous in postcolonial critiques of Victorian liberalism. But this distinction introduces an even more telling temporal ambiguity.

Mill cites the apparent extinction of "the law of the strongest" within advanced nations (it "seems" to be superseded), but argues here that the old way of force is not dead yet. Mill's polemic gains its own force, that is, by suggesting that the inequality characteristic an the older regime, "institutions which place right on the side of might" (1989: 124), has been historically superseded, but that it also, paradoxically, still survives. It is a holdover from an earlier stage that, while doomed in any case, must also be extinguished actively in the present. This narratological confusion, by which the text must depict as historically inevitable the outcome it also wishes performatively to effect, is characteristic of the genre I will call the liberal manifesto, but structures manifestos of all kinds: the same tension drives, for example, Marx and Engels' *Communist Manifesto* (1848, English translation 1850), a formal symmetry that underscores the affinity between liberal and Marxist historicisms I will elaborate in reference to Jameson.

In Mill's document, a conflation of historical optimism (force *will* give way to contract), triumphalism (force *has* given way to contract), and activism (it *should* give way) betrays a confusion of historical models. The strategy of this polemic is to criticize the state of English modernity by valorizing its already achieved accomplishment, showing how archaic forms persist in these high days of liberty. We live in "a state," Mill writes, where liberty mostly rules. But the term "state" is ambiguous, referring both to a social stage and a material political organization: our "state," in Mill's carefully poised uncertainty, is both our status with respect to the scale of civilization and England in 1868. Mill's language studiously blurs the distinction between temporal stages and political forms, the stage and the state.

Replicated in the later *Subjection* essay, the effort of Mill's 1859 *On Liberty* to usher in "something better than customary" by explaining that

it has already been achieved stands as the most enduring Victorian effort
to argue into being a situation whereby a rule of law characterized by
human exchangeability has superseded an older order characterized by
expropriation and violence. Eliot was familiar with Mill and knew his
work—the elder theorist served as the editor of the *Westminster Review*
just before Eliot—but also came to intellectual maturity in a milieu in
which the modernity story of progressive idealism was expressed in
diverse proto-disciplinary languages. As Nancy Paxton has shown,
Eliot was personally and intellectually intimate with Spencer in the
years leading up to *The Mill on the Floss*; Spencer's related but more
explicitly scientific theory of historical progress from superstition to
rationality had been elaborated in essays Eliot read in manuscript,
including "Progress, its Law and Cause" (1858), as well as the 1851
Social Statics. (An awkward biographical episode explains how Eliot
sought to marry Spencer in 1852 but was rebuffed.) But the theory of
law's inevitable emergence arguably most similar to Eliot's came from
another influential theorist of custom and contract active in the late
1850s, Henry Sumner Maine.

Written while Eliot was composing *The Mill*, Maine's contribution to
Victorian legal theory in *Ancient Law* (1861), like *On Liberty*, figures the
movement into the Victorian modern as a transition from compulsion to
voluntarism. But like Eliot, Maine tells this as a family story, one where
the force relations of kinship give way over time to a stage characterized by
putatively free contract. Here sexual relationships like marriages are no
longer arranged by custom but negotiated by consent. *Ancient Law*
describes the movement from then to now as the switch from the rule
of violence characterized by the *patria potestas*—the supremacy of the
father and of physical compulsion itself—to the law of liberal choice,
where individuals contract with mates in an open market of freely actualized agents. In Maine's two-step model, that is, the development that can
in one context seem like continuous development—gradually "progressive," as Maine calls it (1873: 23)—is also a radical switch, a leap from
then to now: from the world of local ties, kinship relationships, and
harvest temporalities to the world of formal equality, contractual relations,
and homogeneous, empty time—a modernity through which individuals,
not groups, move as agents. Maine names this the "movement *from Status
to Contract*" (1873: 165, emphasis original).

In this way does *Ancient Law*'s animating sociopolitical dualism conform
to a narrative of old turning into new according to what Maine, with nearly
every other intellectual of the period, called the "law of progress" (1873:
170). (The 1851 prospectus Eliot wrote to announce her editorship of the
Westminster cited "the Law of Progress" as the journal's "fundamental

principle" (1991: n.p.).) In Maine's version, "status" signals an archaically communal or tribal condition based on kinship ties and unequal relations among subjects. "Contract," on the other hand, stands as shorthand for the liberal society in which what was once a collective social body has been disaggregated. "[S]ociety in primitive times," Maine summarizes:

> was not what it is assumed to be at present, a collection of *individuals*. In fact, and in view of the men who composed it, it was *an aggregation of families*. The contrast may be most forcibly expressed by saying that the *unit* of an ancient society was the Family, of a modern society the Individual.   (1973: 121, emphasis original)

Pitting collective family groups against deracinated and, by assumption, male free agents, Maine's modernity is populated by exchangeable individual units ("men"), liberated from involuntary ties, "freed from the *patria potestas*" (Smellie, quoted in Burrow 1966: 156), and outfitted for a gender-segregated sphere of exchange in which "freedom" will name the ability to subject oneself to the open marketplace in labor. At least since Carole Pateman's *The Sexual Contract* (1988) it has been clear that such freedom arrives in name only.

Underscoring that fact, Karl Marx in *Capital* (1867) plots Maine's story in reverse, emphasizing just this switch from kinship to contract. But rather than celebrating this forward motion, Marx whisks the reader backwards from an allegedly enlightened phase of individualized freedom into the "dark[ened]" age whose relations of open exploitation Marx sometimes seems to prefer:

> Let us now transport ourselves from Robinson [Crusoe's] island, bathed in light, to medieval Europe, shrouded in darkness. Here, instead of the independent man, we find everyone dependent—serfs and lords, vassals and suzerains, laymen and clerics. Personal dependence characterizes the social relations of material production as much as it does the other spheres of life based on that production.   (Marx 1990: 170)

For Maine as for Marx, history's advance toward contractual modernity is legible across multiple of what Marx here calls "spheres of life": from individualized marriage relations and economic free agency to the political state-form that is understood to guarantee these social arrangements. None, for Maine, is granted causal status, and all these social levels— economic and sociopolitical, base and superstructure—are for Maine folded into the controlling figure of "contract," and then arrayed under the heading of law itself.

Marx would not discuss Maine's theories at length until the *Ethnological Notebooks* (1881), where with venomous energy he referred to Maine as a "blockhead" (Marx 1974: 39) even while he also, in an editor's words, "tacitly accepted" Maine's theory of status turning to contract (p. 39). Marx's own sense of modernity's power to dismantle the bonds of kinship remained for Engels to systematize in *The Origin of the Family, Private Property, and the State* (1884). This tiny genealogy can be taken as evidence of how the most perceptive minds in England engaged across disciplinary boundaries with what I will call the narratological problem of modernity in the years just before 1860. For all of these thinkers, history is the process by which progressive societies emerge into law.

Readers will remember that *The Mill on the Floss* locates kinship ties as among the central indicators of the lagging status of St. Ogg's with respect to modernity. Tom Tulliver and the other pre-contractual characters of St. Ogg's find themselves strangely tied up with blood. The novel emphasizes their thrall to kinship by repeating the key words of Maine's opposition. "There were some Dodsons less like the family than others," the narrator notes with amusement,

> that was admitted—but in so far as they were 'kin,' they were of necessity better than those who were 'no kin.' And it is remarkable that while no *individual* Dodson was satisfied with any other *individual* Dodson, each was satisfied, not only with him or her self, but with the Dodsons *collectively*.
>
> (p. 48, emphasis added)

Here as elsewhere, Eliot echoes Maine's status-to-contract narrative, in which a modern era of contractual individualism is understood to supersede and thus cancel the kinship bonds that the narrator elsewhere calls "the great fundamental fact of blood" (p. 138). In the manuscript Eliot had for "blood" originally written "kinship," further underscoring her sense that family ties synecdochally represent countryside premodernity (Eliot n.d.).

The quaint kin relations of the Dodson and Tulliver clans have long been part of the novel's famous charm, but they also mark a political distinction between the country's charming inhabitants and "us." Although Eliot would not compose her sheaf of notes and commentary on *Ancient Law* until 1869, she listed Maine's treatise with a check beside it among her "Books for Historical Studies" while she was working on *The Mill on the Floss* (1979: 57).[18] And given that Maine delivered the material from the book at the Inns of Court in 1854–8, Eliot may have heard the ideas in lecture form, and surely knew it later from the long and positive review the book received from Frederic Harrison, in the *Westminster* of 19 April 1861. In her later abstract of Maine's treatise Eliot approvingly emphasized *Ancient Law*'s central distinction, writing admiringly of Maine's differentiation between old collectivity and new individualism. In a state of status, Eliot noted, paraphrasing Maine, "kinship

[is] conceived as the sole ground of community in political functions." She elaborated in her own language: "A man was not regarded as *himself*—as an individual; his individuality was swallowed up in the group to which he belonged" (1979: 204–5, italics original). Eliot's choice of the word "swallow," along with her emphasis on "himself"—emphasizing "a man's" lost individuality—betrays her qualified preference for modern contractual relations over allegedly archaic communal ones.

The point is not that one figure influenced the other, but that both Eliot and Maine, along with others including Marx, Spencer, and Mill, responded to the conceptual challenges of the years around 1859 with a shared narrative structure. Noting this helps us appreciate how *The Mill on the Floss* echoes Maine in locating time as an issue of individuality, or what we might call self-actualization—the making actual of a free self. Besides poking gentle fun at the outdated kin relationships of the Dodsons and Tullivers (the novel makes humorous asides at the shared traits among these clan groups), Eliot's novel also works to dramatize Maggie's struggle to individuate herself in distinction from her blood associations.[19] Her ride to the gypsies, her penchant for excessive reading, and her affair with Stephen Guest, among other rebellious episodes, are all conventionally cited as moments of her asserting individual autonomy against family strictures (see Esty 2012: 59–60). It is not coincidental, I am suggesting, that Samuel Smiles' *Self Help* appeared in the year Eliot was drafting her *Mill*, the very moment in which the other Mill, John Stuart, wrote in *On Liberty* that "[o]ver himself, over his own body and mind, the individual is sovereign" (1989: 6).[20] Yet as Mill's recourse to the idiom of sovereignty suggests, Maggie's tale, seen alongside contemporary stories from the late 1850s and early 1860s, does not just narrate the birth of something called the modern subject, as Nancy Armstrong has argued (1999: 97–9). It is also, and more, the story of the birth of liberal modernity itself, and the entire political regime understood to coincide with its new contractual individualism.[21]

The place of St. Ogg's further upstream in the "onward tendency of human things" (p. 284) may be most evident in its not-yet-liberated characters: the specimens of peasant life who perfectly mimic Mill's "barbarians," Marx's benighted vassals, or the German farmers of Eliot's "Natural History" essay in their imperviousness to reason, the rule of exchange, and the modern political order. ("The idea of constitutional government," Eliot quoted von Riel as saying, "lies quite beyond the range of the German peasant's conceptions" (1963: 285).) Described in the chapter of *The Mill on the Floss* that also discusses St. Ogg's collectively, Mr. and Mrs. Glegg exemplify the distance between then and now, since they provide the very type of archaic provincialism in their ties to the land, to kin, and to custom. (Esty remarks on the "Anglo-Saxon velar stop, 'gg,'" shared by St. Ogg's and the Gleggs, their Saxon names signaling a shared archaic localism (2012: 59); Maggie's own name carries the remainders of this world inside its own phonemes (Eliot 1860: 59).) Belonging "to a generation with whom spelling was a matter of private judgment" (p. 138), both Gleggs inhabit an era ruled by "proud tradition" (p. 138), when rationalization and bureaucratic standards have yet to take hold. "It was a time," Eliot's narrator summarizes, "when ignorance was much more comfortable than at present" (p. 127).

Like the unstandardized Gleggs, Tom is an instance of the natural world rather than someone who reflects on it, pre-modernity being figured here as both a lack of cognitive remove from nature and an incurable localism. "An excellent bovine lad" (p. 185), he is unreachable by education: his tutors try in vain to educate him in the codes of bourgeois Englishness (he is studying, unsuccessfully, to become a businessman) and prove unable to instruct him out of his love for animals, guns, and armies—all coded, in Eliot's optimistic historicism, as "old." (She shared Spencer's belief that violence is fundamentally archaic, a point that will return.[22]) Not yet having achieved what Amanda Anderson extols as "modern detachment" from the spot of his upbringing (2001: 10), Tom, like the St. Ogg's to which he is rooted, remains locked in pre-modern fixity. "I'm attached to the place," he says of Dorlcote Mill (p. 414); but his imagination was "not [. . .] rapid and capacious enough" to understand it fully (p. 109). Tom is native flora and local fauna wrapped into one, a natural feature only intermittently granted the personal pronoun: "one of those lads," we are told, "that grow everywhere in England" (p. 36).

Tom's function as a bovine extension of the land, unreflectively focused on his place and on the kinship allegiances native to it, is only confirmed when he signs a blood-oath to his father, a promise, signed on the family Bible, that solidifies an anachronistic, transgenerational vendetta of status. To this archaism Maggie forms a developmental counterpoint; she is the character who is able, somehow, to grow past Tom's historical stage of natural heredity to become not an object but a subject of history. Dark-haired, individualized, and broad-minded, she has enough perspective to scold Tom for the fact that he "ha[s] not a mind large enough" to be rational (p. 360): in contrast to her colleagues among the pastures, Maggie's consciousness is in the process of learning how to engage in the broad-minded, wide-ranging liberal imagining that Bruce Robbins in 1999 called "feeling global."[23] Indeed, even in her own slack, repeatedly emphasized passivity in the boat with Stephen Guest, Maggie achieves something like an expansion of her sympathetic faculty: in the episode her own desires are revealed to be generated entirely from her "sense of others' claims" (p. 487)—an emphasis on sympathetic interchange that would be radicalized to the point of reversal in the gothic experiment of *The Lifted Veil*, which Eliot wrote during breaks from composing the *Mill*, "when my head was too stupid for more important work" (quoted in Haight 1968: 295). But where Latimer's capacity to connect with other minds figures as perverse debility, Maggie's marks her as a participant in a modern regime of interpersonal ethics, a positively charged virtue nowhere more visible than in her often-praised "tenderness for deformed things" (1860: 186).

The sympathetic idealism the novel labors to code as modern comes, too, with a geographical corollary, since the novel uses physical travel as a metaphor for sympathy's efforts at cognitive outreach. In accord with modernity's move from narrow- to broad-mindedness, from selfishness to sympathetic cosmopolitanism, the first book we hear of Maggie reading is not about pastry-making or vegetable cultivation (the preoccupations of the other female Tullivers) but European travel. She recommends a work she calls *Pug's Tour of Europe* (p. 25) to the simpleton Luke as a remedy for his too tightly focused mind, similar in its limitations to her brother's ("Why, you're like my brother Tom, Luke" (p. 34)). As she reaches out to help this blinkered soul, Maggie conjures the border-spanning logic of cognitive exchange, packaged as sympathy, that will emerge as the novel's signal content for the term "modernity." Maggie tells Luke that this book about crisscrossing Europe

> "would tell you all about the different sorts of people in the world, and if you didn't understand the reading, the pictures would help you—[. . .] There are the Dutchmen, very fat, and smoking, you know—and one sitting on a barrel."
>
> "Nay, Miss, I'n no opinion o' Dutchmen, There ben't much good i' knowin' about *them*."
>
> "But they're our fellow-creatures, Luke—we ought to know about our fellow-creatures."   (p. 33)

I will emphasize in subsequent chapters how this central lesson of idealist rationality presupposes a geography of expansion.[24] In a move Eliot's later critics often repeat, the novel shuffles promiscuously between material and ideal registers—and conflates ethics with politics—while replicating the internationalist universalism of Eliot's advanced liberal cohorts at the *Westminster*.

What is clear is that Maggie stands as the novel's proto-modern individual: her complex ethical sensibility, a "keen vibrating consciousness poised above pleasure or pain" (p. 459), reveals her to have arrived at a sympathetic state of reflection unreached by her brother or his benighted friends. Rather than being rooted to her spot, she reflects on it; unlike

Tom, who "desire[s] . . . mastery over the inferior animals" (p. 98), Maggie
wants to understand them. Hyperbolically reflective, able to connect with
other consciousnesses across temporal, spatial, and even species divisions,
Maggie bears the seeds of a future world of liberal exchange already within
her residual moment of hereditary custom.[25] In this, she is what Hegel
terms a world-historical individual, asynchronous with her now: "the
hidden Spirit knocking at the door of the present, still subterranean, still
without a contemporary existence and wishing to break out, for whom
the contemporary world is but a husk containing a different kernel from
the old" (Hegel, quoted in Lukács 1983: 39–40). As Neil Hertz (2003)
and Stewart (2009) have observed, Hegel's language of seeds and germin-
ation also structures Eliot's novel: Maggie is a "living plant-seed" who
must "make a way for [itself], often in a shattering, violent manner" (Eliot
1860: 248).

  Though the event that will burst her world into modernity is unremittingly violent, Maggie herself is anachronistically peaceful, acting in accord
with sympathy and not force. Her function as the novel's world-historical
individual is therefore most evident when she quells violence—open force
being, for Maine, Mill, and Spencer no less than their predecessors Locke
and Hobbes, the central synecdochal feature of the state of status or
custom. With restraint coded as adult and the violence of "impulse"
associated with a childlike premodernity, the episode in which Mr. Tulliver
thrashes Lawyer Wakem further clarifies that while the rule of this father
may have structured the past, it is peaceful reserve that characterizes its
historical successor. Maggie's role is not only to represent a nascent version
of this regime of exchange already alive in the present, but to shepherd its
ascendance. Here is the episode:

> The sight of the long-hated predominant man down and in his power, threw
> [Mr. Tulliver] into a frenzy of triumphant vengeance, which seemed to give
> him preternatural agility and strength. He rushed on Wakem [. . .] and
> flogged him fiercely across the back with his riding-whip. Wakem shouted
> for help, but no help came, until a woman's scream was heard, and the cry of
> "Father, father!"
>   Suddenly, Wakem felt, something had arrested Mr Tulliver's arm, for the
> flogging ceased, and the grasp of his own arm was relaxed.
>   "Get away with you—go!" said Tulliver angrily. But it was not to Wakem
> that he spoke. Slowly the lawyer rose, and, as he turned his head, saw that
> Tulliver's arms were being held by a girl.   (pp. 369–70)

The moment compresses the rise of Victorian modernity into a single
episode. With the local man cast as vengeful animal, the scene shows
that while an unthinking struggle for male "predominance" may define
Tulliver's clannish patriarchal world (Maggie's cry of "Father, father!"

emphasizes just this), his epoch is on the wane. Mr. Tulliver, the passage suggests, is one of those "certain animals" the book has already introduced, "to whom predominance is a law of life" (p. 207). By extending Daniel Hack's description of the temporal distancing accomplished in the Victorian revenge plot (2006: 279–81), where revenge is a part of the past and forgiveness characterizes the present, we can appreciate the political stakes of Maggie's attempts to restrain her father's "frenz[ied]" violence: the feminine civilization to a patriarchal savagery, the modern girl has subdued her atavistic Father, leaving the lawyer to escape unhurt. Maggie mediates between a residual patriarchal authority and the regime of law rising to succeed it.

Like other, more recent interventions into modernization theory, Eliot's poetically reconfigured political tale has added specific content to the otherwise formal distinction between then and now. What I have attempted to overlay onto the familiar fact of Maggie's asynchrony with her environment is her role as the mediator of the novel's antagonistic political temporalities—the function her character plays in negotiating between what Matthew Arnold might have called (in a twist on his 1855 phrase) two ages, one doomed to die, the other almost ready to be born. These familiar passages from *The Mill on the Floss*, in other words, help illuminate how Eliot generated her own temporal-political allegory from the historical models circulating around her in the mixed idioms of geology, legal theory, Christian doctrine, and political theory itself. For all its emphasis on the continuous, organic connection of one epoch with the last, Eliot's account also depicts the development of St. Ogg's as a process of two-step modernization between old and new. This motion hurtles country life toward a moment that Eliot herself, like the thinkers she adapted and anticipated, understood to result in the arrival of a world in which autonomous agents are able to discuss, not brawl, and contract, not enslave. With Maggie's help, history has been ushered to the brink of a modernity that has as its substance rational reflection, sympathetic exchange, and the parliamentary legality that is these mental qualities' political instantiation. "To the mind of the peasant," Eliot wrote in the "Natural History" essay, "law presents itself as the 'custom of the country'" (1991: 279)—that is, as no law at all.

The story told here is a familiar one. Suzanne Graver's still-unrivalled *George Eliot and Community* points out "analogies" between Eliot's model and the late-century sociologist Ferdinand Tonnies, whose two-stage history of *Gemeinschaft* and *Gesellschaft* describes, like Maine and Marx, how organic "community" transforms into bourgeois "society" (1984: 8).[26] Following Graver we might point to a long list of two-step codes similar to the one

Eliot elaborates. This list of before/after narratives might include not just Marx's but Max Weber's, in *The Protestant Ethic and the Spirit of Capitalism* (1904), and Friedrich Nietzsche's, in *Genealogy of Morals* (1887), which described the birth of the modern, "emancipated" individual—"*calculable, regular, necessary*"—as one "with the actual *right* to make promises" (Nietzsche 1967: 58, 59, emphasis original).[27] The status of promise-keeping as an index of political personhood will return in Chapter 4, in the context of the compromised sovereignty plot of *King Solomon's Mines*. But while Maine's story of status turning into contract and Mill's story of custom turning to liberty may be better candidates for intertextuality than Tonnies, Weber, Nietzsche, or even Marx—whom Eliot does not seem to have read in these years—I do not propose any causal or empirical relation of influence. The point is that these thinkers responded to the theoretical challenges of the so-called Age of Equipoise with a common figural repertoire, one that, I will now suggest, could not finally decide between narrative models. When and how, exactly, did modernity arrive?

In *Evolution and Society* (1966), W. L. Burrow reviews the nineteenth century's most significant theories of development, and in doing so off-handedly describes what he represents as a minor confusion in the political stories of Maine and Mill, a confusion that identifies the paradox of historical representation Eliot will work dramatically to solve. Burrow cites Mill's often-quoted lines from *On Liberty* about the suitability of despotic means in dealing with barbaric, pre-rational societies, emphasizing not the racism of this notorious formulation, but its confusion about time. Burrow explains that on the one hand, Mill, like Maine, implies a natural course of growth from savagery to civilization and thus assumes the continuity of these categories on the same evolutionary timeline. "But the whole force of his argument," Burrow continues of Mill, "rests on a rigid distinction between 'barbarism' and civilization." Burrow continues:

> It is precisely this distinction, quite as much as the evolutionary element which is also apparent, that [also] underlies much of Maine's social thought. When he wants to emphasize the fact of continuity, the similarity between "barbaric" institutions and those of the European past or even present, Maine speaks in an evolutionary, "gradualist" manner. But almost equally often he speaks in terms of a straight dichotomy—status and contract, progressive and non-progressive, barbarous and civilized. (1966: 158–9)

What Burrow notices is that a temporal confusion between gradual time and radical rupture—the geological difference between "uniformitarianism" and "catastrophism"—is written into the very heart of both of these theories. Neither Mill's 1859 narrative of custom giving way to liberty nor Maine's 1861 story of status turning into contract can decide, at narrative or conceptual level, *when*, precisely, and *how* such a shift into modernity occurs.

In all of its formulations, I mean, the status-to-contract narrative is marked by a dilemma that is finally narratological: an inability to pinpoint the *event* of rupture or switch, the *moment* of the rule of law's emergence. This problem of historical representation is not local to Victorians. In *A Singular Modernity* (2002), Fredric Jameson simultaneously analyzes and recapitulates the Victorian storylines we have been tracing. Despite arranging his entire project around a critique of searches for the breaks, ruptures, and novelties which are, he says, the symptoms of modernization narratives of all kinds, his own account resorts to just such a trope. The instant of modernity's arrival, writes Jameson, is nothing less than

> the moment of the overcoming of feudalism by capitalism, and of the aristocratic social order of castes and blood by the new bourgeois order which at least promised social and juridical equality and political democracy.
>
> (2002: 39)

As in Maine and Mill and nearly all liberal historicisms "blood" is inevitably replaced by "equality." This is the secularizing modernity story to which, as we saw, Marx also subscribes. Elsewhere in *A Singular Modernity* Jameson insists that every narrative of modernity participates in what he calls "a dialectic of the break and the period" (2002: 23): an irresolvable tension between continuity and event, gradual development and dramatic instants of change. Since this paradox attends any effort of periodization, all narratives of modernity must participate in this representational dialectic by virtue of their status as narratives. It is perhaps surprising to find, then, in the context of an argument about the necessarily figural nature of any alleged rupture, a citation in Jameson's own discourse of "the moment" in which feudalism is overturned by capitalism. This "moment," Jameson writes, stands as the "real historical event and trauma" that any subsequent narrative of modernity must inevitably recode (2002: 39).

In the context of Jameson's Marxian identification of the bourgeois mode of production as the modernity story's ultimately determining "level," it is worth recalling that it is not simply restraint, rationality, or "public spirit" (Eliot 1860: 127) that characterize *The Mill on the Floss'* vision of the now, but business. The efficient capitalist Mr. Deane "had been advancing in the world as rapidly as Mr Tulliver had been going down in it" (p. 216). And with his own plans to privatize irrigation procedures in the face of Tulliver's sense that "water was water" (p. 163), Lawyer Wakem functions as one mechanism, with Maggie, by which the dreamlike era of custom is awakened into the rule of this

Lawyer's law, and into the privatization and capitalist exchange with which it is held to be coextensive. As Esty explains, the peasants of St. Ogg's bear mute witness to "the complete reorganization of their economy" (2012: 54).

But the point is not just that Eliot, too, figured the advent of modernity in terms that are economic no less than political. Certainly the arrival of capitalism stands for Jameson (though not for Eliot) as the condition of possibility for the superstructural response he calls "the modernity effect" (2002: 41); it is the grounding narrative that any other story of transition can only metaphorize.[28] But the point is temporal, and narrative: though Jameson will later specify that one characteristic of modernity itself is "its irrepressible search for the break, for the 'first time,' for the beginning" (2002: 145) ("[T]here can be no question of deciding on any 'true' beginning of modernity as such" (p. 145)), his own story has by necessity resorted to this figure. On the one hand Jameson is arguing that "modernity" has no content, yet on the other he is offering "the rise of capitalism" as its content.

This point brings with it several corollaries. One is that Marxist historicisms are committed to recapitulate the figures and narrative structures of their dialectical twins, those of liberalism. But since I am not drawing on Jameson's 2002 story as the true story, reflexive and enabling though it is, but rather as one that shares tropes with those from the 1850s and 1860s I am discussing here, I will emphasize a second corollary. It is that despite its self-consciousness about just this problem, *A Singular Modernity*'s Marxian narrative replays the central temporal ambiguity of the modernity stories it analyzes, an ambiguity that also lies couched in liberal narratives from the mid-nineteenth century. With the book's project arguing against the very possibility of positing an identifiable moment of the modern, Jameson's citation of the "real historical event and trauma" of modernity (the *real* to the other narratives' mere recodings of it) is, like those other accounts, structurally unable to decide whether "modernity" arrives gradually, after a long process, or whether it comes in an instant of radical change, in "*the moment* of the overcoming of feudalism by capitalism."[29]

When was this moment? In Jameson's as in Mill's and Maine's stories, what is inaugurated in this narrative instant, this structurally necessary but unrepresentable switchpoint, is the modern rule of citizen-subjects, capitalism, and of procedural law itself. But this event of a radical change, this "moment of overcoming," is also conceived as the result of gradual change and an apparently inevitable historical accumulation. (Jameson cites Arno Mayer's *Persistence of the Old Regime* to describe the "incomplete modernization" even within an apparently modern Europe (2002: 141).)

Does modernity arrive gradually or in an instant? Is its narrative mode uniformitarian or catastrophist—or, somehow, both? As we have seen, Maine's text oscillates between uniformitarian gradualism and evental catastrophism. Yet in those passages that emphasize the momentary switch, Maine describes law's emergence as an instant of creative destruction—a transformation in human life akin to what Cuvier called a *révolution de la surface du globe*.

Describing what happens when one social organizing principle (the blood ties of status) gives way to another (the geographical connections of contract), Maine, here emphasizing break, not continuity, says this:

> Nor is there any of those *subversions of feeling, which we term emphatically revolutions*, so startling and so complete as the change which is accomplished when some other principle—such as that, for instance, of local contiguity— establishes itself *for the first time* as the basis of common political action.
>
> (1873: 124, emphasis added)

Like geologists before him, Maine's rhetoric describes Jameson's "moment" of change in the language of political revolution; he sharpens here the catastrophist thesis that the transition from one stage to another is felt as a systemic disruption and indeed reordering of political form: a "first time." We have seen that Maine's theory is not consistent in this emphasis on the break, but here at least the shocking transition into the now is offered in terms apparently borrowed from the Burkean lexicon of counterrevolutionary historicism (it is a "startling" "subversion of feeling," Maine says, "which we term emphatically" a "revolution").[30] Eliot, too, will construe the instant of law's arrival as an instant of violent overturning that is nonetheless unimaginable in narrative terms: a mythical zero point of modernity that takes shape as the novel's "*Deus ex Machina* of sudden death" (quoted in Rubin 1956: 18).

COUNTRYSIDE CATASTROPHISM: *THE MILL ON THE FLOSS* II

When Eliot was told, after *The Mill on the Floss*' publication, of charges by Edward Bulwer-Lytton that the novel had been ruined by its "too hasty" ending, Eliot attested that she had composed the finale in a surge of energy. The novel's last eleven pages, she said in a letter, "were written in a furor" (1958–78: 3.278), and the manuscript bears this out: her handwriting becomes more open, with ligatures now connecting words that earlier in the MS remain tidily separated (n.d.: Add MS 34025). Despite having been planned since the novel's very outset, these eleven final pages bear out the fury Eliot evinced in composing them. Critics have long been disturbed by Victorian literature's best-known geological cataclysm, with a long tradition of feminist critique identifying the flood alongside the novels of Thomas Hardy as an instance of anti-feminist female sacrifice. Readers less inclined to see novels as performing ideological recapitulation have likewise debated the flood's propriety since the first reviews appeared, calling attention to the final event as an example of Eliot's artistic failure, a breakdown in the laws of realist narration. For these critics the final overflow of the Ripple and Floss arrives out of nowhere. It is a transcendent, melodramatic event delivered from on high, like the helmet in *The Castle of Otranto*: a random occurrence from the genre of romance infiltrating this otherwise respectably probable realist novel.[31]

The final flood was so shocking to Henry James that in an often-quoted review this other member of the Great Tradition described Eliot's scandalous conclusion in terms normally reserved for political upheaval. For James, the flood represented an entirely unpredictable break in a plot that should have been governed by existing laws of continuity and expectation. The novel's final event felt imposed from the outside, James judged; it effected a suspension of the normal procedures of realist succession, rupturing the novel's laws of form. Here is James:

> The chief defect—indeed, the only serious one—in *The Mill on the Floss* is its conclusion. Such a conclusion is in itself assuredly not illegitimate, and there is nothing in the fact of the flood, to my knowledge, essentially unnatural: what I object to is its relation to the preceding part of the story. The story is told as if it were destined to have, if not a strictly happy termination, at least one within ordinary probabilities. As it stands, the *denouement* shocks the reader most painfully. Nothing has prepared him for it; the story does not move towards it; it casts no shadow before it [. . .]. But one thing is certain: a *denouement* by which Maggie should have called Stephen back would have been extremely interesting, and would have had far more in its favor than can be put to confusion by a mere exclamation of horror.   (James 1968: 32–3)

A tear in the novel's narrative fabric elicits from James the codewords that, for a conservative tradition extending from Burke, have provided the lexicon for denouncing revolutionary violence. Meaningless, brutal, "improbable," the flood is for James an unbidden disturbance of the existing system, one that "shocks the reader most painfully." It can elicit no rational response, he tells us, nothing at all beyond "confusion" and "a mere exclamation of horror." James' confrontation with this apparently unfathomable violence blurs aesthetic and political registers and in so doing opens a window onto *The Mill on the Floss*' own commitment to linking those domains together. I use James' famous language here not to weigh in on what is or is not the proper aesthetic response to Eliot's ostensibly unmanaged ending, nor yet to determine whether or not the ending is unmanaged in the first place. Rather, his reading highlights the novel's own success in melding its political and aesthetic projects, as it radicalizes to the point of formal innovation the narratological and political tension between *durée* and event at the heart of the Victorian modernity story.

What James correctly identifies is a revolution in the novel's form, a rupture in this fictional system's existing symbolic order, its "laws." This seemingly improbable and certainly horrific event functions at the level of novelistic structure as what Alain Badiou terms a "properly political" event, since it effects, in an instant, an overturning of an existing order of expectation and in so doing refigures the horizons of probability as such, thus reorienting what James referred to as the novel's "destiny." For Badiou, a properly political event is not debate within a given system of possibility but a renovation of the existing order of regularity from which we might derive expectation in the first place: it is "the prescription of a possibility in rupture with what exists" (*sic*, 2005: 24). An event in this sense reorganizes the old into the new and forms a hinge between contending political-aesthetic temporalities. We can emphasize the recurring language of abruptness, violence, and shock in James' assessment, I mean, to note that James' reading of the flood is an encrypted judgment on the problem of revolution as such: the question is whether the flood is justified by history (the "preceding part of the story"); whether this shocking reordering is "essentially unnatural"; whether it is or is "not illegitimate."

If the novel's final, world-shaking inundation asks to be read as a transcoded revolutionary event—and that is what I am arguing here—then it is true the novel has trained us to expect such a rupture. Throughout the novel, political language inflects the story of Maggie's development; readers will recall that her *Bildung* is narrated as a series of revolts, insurrections, and semi-politicized contraventions of the status quo, moments of resistance that show this child always to have been play-acting revolution. When the impulsive Maggie cuts her own hair, it is an uprising that both thrills and frightens the onlooking Tom (p. 69). The "delicious grinding snip" of the shears cuts away Maggie's long hair and leaves her momentarily free, her hair "cropped in a jagged uneven manner, but with a sense of clearness and freedom, as if she had emerged from a wood into the open plain" (p. 69). The violence has liberated her, if only momentarily. Later, when Maggie explodes to Mrs. Tulliver and the aunts, her behavior is judged an "aberration" (p. 226): "there was something portentous in this mad outbreak: she did not see how life could go on after it" (p. 226). Effected though it may be with an odd passivity, Maggie's affair with Stephen Guest is only the most damning example of what her father, in reference to her persistent insubordination, calls "this revolutionary aspect of things" (p. 111). Prefiguring Gwendolyn's conspicuous non-murder of Grandcourt in *Daniel Deronda*'s boat scene, Maggie's love-boat cruise with Stephen is a non-act with revolutionary results: after it, she thinks, "a new era had begun for her" (p. 350). The point is not just that the novel insistently deploys the language of revolution to describe these little offenses against the strictures of status (there are many more); nor simply that these mini-revolts occur against the mill-like monotony of the novel's apparently placid uniformitarian environment. The point is that these brief and aberrant acts prepare us for something more—an "event" in the philosophical sense—that will expand this motif of interruption to its "dream-like" (p. 538) conclusion, a revolution of the surface of the earth.

It comes. As the waters rise around her and the flood begins to be recognizable for what it is, Maggie commandeers a boat and, floating, finds her eye drawn to the threats encroaching around her. "What were those masses?" (p. 540), she wonders. Her remark conjures an image of the crowd as it registers shock at the size, the darkness, and the fear instilled by the destroyed machinery coming at her in rafts. "[I]n dreadful clearness," we read, "floated onwards the hurrying, threatening masses" (p. 542). Seeing these masses for the first time, "Maggie's heart began to beat in an agony of dread" (p. 540): as she and Tom cling to their own boat, their "anticipated clash" with this flotsam is avoided once (p. 540), but the forms bear down on them, and the siblings are overturned, finally, by these pieces of "wooden machinery," these floating shards of mechanization (p. 542). Eliot made tiny edits to this final sequence in the proofs stage, worrying over her word choices overnight—adding "wooden," for example, to describe the machinery (cf. Haight 321) and changing "pause" to "shudder" so as to heighten the immediate physicality of the scene (Eliot n.d.); these late alterations were unique in the compositional procedures of this book. As Eliot's prose carefully specifies, what kills Maggie and Tom is not just broken wood but the refigured violence of popular revolt, a violence rendered in terms recalling not just farm implements in the water but Chartists at the barricades. Here is their death:

> Huge fragments, clinging together in a fatal fellowship, made one wide mass across the stream.
>
> "It is coming, Maggie!" Tom said, in a deep hoarse voice, losing the oars, and clasping her.
>
> The next instant the boat was no longer seen upon the water—and the huge mass was hurrying on in hideous triumph. (p. 542)

It is instructive to compare this version of Maggie and Tom's sacrificial death with the scenes of floating refuse Eliot documented in her notebooks. There, she copied: "Many thousands of deals & baulks of large timber, with household furniture, horses, cows, staiths, came floating down & almost covered the river for some hours" (1981: 36). The novelistic version uses metaphor to charge with political resonance the organic floating refuse of the notebook indundations. "Horses" and "timber" have become a "mass" of "huge fragments" "in a fatal fellowship." Tom's voice is "hoarse," homophonically connecting him to the animal life now being erased from the world. In the novel's fatal scene, a dark crowd of machinery, a "huge mass," performs the "hideous" violence that kills the wavering Maggie and her doomed, archaic Tom.

The word "mass" is repeated four times in less than a page here, a choice that confirms the novel's association of geological flood-events with popular uprising and solidifies its metaphorical connection of death by nature with death by political revolution. Both are catastrophes. Criticism has agreed on the symbolic supercharging of this flood-event, its overdetermination in a thicket of hyper-referential language—a floodlike "drift of figuration" that Garrett Stewart sees as yet one more metaphorical meaning for the deluge itself (2009: 130). As Stewart's own lyrical account seems to recognize, Eliot's novel somehow predicts the extent to which this enigmatic violence will spur its later readers to decode it, as if building its susceptibility to metaphorical reading into its own structure: "Those heavy fragments hurrying down the Ripple," wonders Maggie, "what had they meant?" (p. 540). But whether it is construed as a psychologized weather event, an incestuous apocalypse, or (as I read it here) a transcoded popular uprising, the flood is like Maggie's haircut—a fleeting moment of shocking, irrevocable violence.

I introduced the passage by writing "here is their death," but I now want to note that the "death" itself is not presented: the instant of violence is in fact skipped over in the temporal complexities of the "moment" Eliot's text stages here. Tom warns, "It is coming, Maggie!" but there is no single referent for the "it" of his exclamation. "It" can be read as the flood, or their death, or the "mass" itself, but Eliot's prose allows for all of these: indeed the "it" may refer most of all to the violence of the event itself. After pages of past-tense narration, the ambiguous referent of Tom's utterance arrives, conspicuously, in an extending present tense ("It is coming"), a present participle followed by a series of other participial verbs, mimicking gerunds, that likewise call attention to the lengthening function of the participle's incomplete action ("loosing," "clasping"): they grammatically prolong the instant of the event. Time slows here, a moment extends, and a paragraph break vaults us from these static verbs past the event itself, skipping "it." "The next instant," the narrator tells us, all is over. The past tense returns: The boat *was* no longer seen upon the water, and the huge mass *was* hurrying on in hideous triumph.

What I want to underscore in this amazingly rendered scene is not just the recurrent and apparently deliberate language of massed bodies and revolutionary violence. Time is what is at issue here, and what Eliot's staging of the death event underscores is that the instant of violence itself—the death—eludes representation: it is not and, as event theory suggests, cannot be shown. Skipped over in a paragraph break, Eliot's conspicuous denarration of the "hideous mass'" triumphant violence bears out Stewart's sense that death-events defy mimetic depiction in prose, forcing "an absolute poesis of the word" (1984: 5); it also confirms the same critic's later analysis of the flood, which explains how Maggie's demise cannot be shown so much as inscribed as performance into syntax, "meshed with the pacing of the writing itself" (2009: 130). Prose fiction cannot inertly *depict* Maggie's death, *convey* it, or do anything else to recapitulate the metaphors that would presume a frictionless transmission of information in what Jakobson calls language's "referential" mode (1987: 66). According to philosophical definitions of the event (and to Eliot's narration here), the moment of transition between temporal-political orders—what in the scene's language would be called the "instant" that came before "the next" one—is like a point in geometric mathematics: it cannot be presented. A hinge between before and after, the moment of overturning is itself nothing: an atemporal zero-point outside of the order of calendric or ordinary time. "Even though it can always be *localized* within presentation," Badiou specifies, the event "is not, as such, presented, nor is it presentable. It is—not being—supernumerary" (2006: 178).[32]

What Eliot's non-scene thus conveys is that the creative destruction giving rise to a new regime of law evades both temporal "counting" (in Badiou's language) and representation itself. The apocalypse happens, but without registering as part of experience. It is *not being*. Or as Maggie realizes just before she is sucked into the water, "It was the transition of death, without its agony" (p. 538). In language more easily grasped than Badiou's but less poetic than Eliot's, Hannah Arendt has described what *The Mill on the Floss* more strikingly performs, namely that any revolutionary transition between one periodizing order and another exists in what Arendt calls the "hiatus between the end of the old order and the beginning of the new," "the legendary hiatus [...] between a no-longer and a not-yet" (1970: 206).[33] That this hiatus is skipped over in Eliot's beautifully written death scene—that it is represented as unrepresentable—precisely serves to confirm the scene's status as the not-present pivot between the novel's contending temporalities. It is the violent but uncountable zero-point of a new conceptual-political order, the catastrophic restarting of a world-historical clock.[34]

A longstanding and otherwise tedious dispute among formalist readers symptomatically ratifies this assessment. James' review indicated his preference for a conclusion that might fall "within ordinary probabilities." ("Nothing has prepared [the reader] for it," James complains. "[I]t casts no shadow before it.") In terms taken from the aesthetic codes of realism he himself helped naturalize, James asks for a conclusion that would be predictable, probable, that would accord with what is "destined" to happen—he asks, that is, for a conclusion that in Arendt's terms might be calendric or datable, "ordinary." Later readers like Jerome Buckley have concurred with James' evaluation of the flood as transcendent with respect to the novel's figural system. "The flood is a physical force outside the psychological framework of the action," he writes. "It has no real relation to Maggie's dilemma; it encroaches upon her melodramatically, an agent from without" (1968: 114). For Buckley as for James as for the *Westminster Review* writer quoted in the epigram above—about whom more shortly—the flood derives from beyond the novel's established order of predictability and is consequently foreign to the codes of realistic representation, an invasion from another genre: "altogether melodramatic," the *Westminster* said (Carroll, ed. 1971: 143).

Even granting the shocking nature of the ending, an opposed set of readers has countered by noting that Eliot had the flood in mind all along; it was "the part of the story that George Eliot planned first" (Haight, quoted in Eliot 1981: 168n.). There are *hints* of the flood, these critics say, clues or hermeneutic toeholds planted throughout *The Mill on the Floss'* many pages, and in light of these it is impossible to call the flood's arrival unexpected. "James was clearly wrong in one respect," one says, "since the ending is prepared for in a formal sense by various allusions and foreshadowings" (Rignall 2000: 266); for Stewart, the flood is "so metaphorically inevitable that the only way we didn't see it coming is to have repressed it in our own desire for the suspense of plot" (2009: 130). Indeed, those who have read the novel more than once find its numerous allusions to flooding, raining, catastrophe, and even drowning to be the kind of clues that trouble too-easy distinctions between "surface" and "depth," since these subtle hints seem, on second reading, painfully unsubtle—a hermeneutic predicament of which Eliot's novel seems acutely aware.[35] Yet if readers taking account of such prefiguring details must adopt defensive tones or build psychological models to protect Eliot's novel from charges of artistic failure, what they quietly ratify, even in dissent, are the codes of organicist realism that, as I show in Chapter 4, James helped institutionalize. That is because readings that inventory the "allusions and foreshadowings" that "prepar[e]" for the flood also register what I will say is a more important point about the status of the final flood with respect to the novel's representational system. In defending the organic wholeness of Eliot's novelistic world, these readers reference the very figures of accumulation, sedimentation, and development with which Eliot's novel is obsessed to argue that the event of the flood comes from "within" the novel's world rather than "without" it. Its arrival is, in Rubin's words, "a matter of time" (1956: 21). This argument suggests that the flood is immanent to the novel's order: it develops, if not predictably, then at least believably, perhaps even inevitably from elements already present within the novel's representational world, its "whole finely meshed system of prefiguration" (Rubin 1956: 21).

For Badiou an event is "supernumerary" inasmuch as it evades the count of what already exists: it is a new emergence, a not-present arrival that cannot be accounted for within the existing order (or set), but that can nevertheless be shown, retrospectively, to have been present as possibility in the elements of what Badiou calls the situation. Badiou explains that the elements actualized in the event were present in the situation *before* the occurrence of the event that made them visible. But these elements could not have been known to be such—they were not recognizable *as* elements— until after the event in which they coalesce takes place.[36] Another way of phrasing this is that events can only be seen to have been possible retrospectively: they cannot be viewed as even possible until after they have occurred, at which point they seem to have been not just possible, but inevitable. The signal temporality of the revolutionary event is therefore the future anterior, the "will have been." It *will have been* possible.

What I am driving at in this theoretical detour is that a reading of the flood underscoring its having been "prepared for" posits the flood's immanence to its "situation"; in so doing it confirms the flood as the equivalent, at the level of narrative form, to the political event in Badiou's sense. It can be seen as "inevitable" (and *has* been seen as inevitable by the critics I have mentioned), but it can only be seen as such after the event has happened—upon rereading, as it were. The event's constituent elements are present in the form of "foreshadowings" or "hints" within the system it will disrupt, but there is no way to predict how these elements will coalesce until the event itself has already occurred. Dangling in this "conditional space of catastrophe," we, along with the *Mill*'s characters, await without quite knowing we do what Paul Saint-Amour calls a "limit event," a disaster so total that it might remake the order of expectation itself (2015: 3). It is a matter of time.

Despite the inarguable fact that Eliot had planned for the flood since even before she began writing, readings of the flood as a *"Deus ex Machina* of sudden death" (quoted in Rubin 1956: 18) are worth dwelling on because they confirm the mythic violence of St. Ogg's as revolutionary in still another register. The *OED* gives *"deus ex machina"* as a "power, event, person, or thing that comes in the nick of time to solve a difficulty; providential interposition, esp. in a novel or play." Calling it "a power" and "a providential interposition," the definition underscores what the Latin term already advertises, which is that this often maligned aesthetic device operates theologically as a transcendent ordering power. A standard feature of literary romance, the *deus ex machina* denotes an unexpected arrival of a godlike, refiguring force that redraws the horizons of possibility within a fictional work's existing regime of representation. (What was once considered impossible—the genie's descent or the long-lost cousin's plot-solving arrival—is now, after it has happened, proven to have been possible.) Divine and unexpected—"It casts no shadow before it," as James noted—the *deus ex machina* changes the rules of possibility in the world of the narrative. It sets new laws. The partisans' dispute about whether the flood is immanent to the novel's organic fictional world or transcendent with respect to it confirms that it is, in fact, both at once. In Stewart's words, it is "metaphorically inevitable": a sublime zero-point on which what the novel construes as a new set of laws can be founded.[37] "Maggie's destiny," summarizes the narrator, "is at present hidden, and we must wait for it to reveal itself like the course of an unmapped river: we only know that the river is full and rapid, and that for all rivers there is the same final home" (p. 418).

In his "Critique of Violence" (*Zur Kritik der Gewalt*), Benjamin draws on his ongoing correspondence with Carl Schmitt to meditate on the sources of "law" or political order in what he calls "mythic violence." (*Gewalt*, as Derrida notes in his reading of Benjamin's text, means violence but also power, in the sense of founding or "constituting" political power.) Benjamin's essay distinguishes between three kinds of violence, which he calls law-preserving violence (or "police violence"), law-making violence ("mythic violence"), and that violence which abolishes all law, which Benjamin names "divine violence." For Benjamin, any sequence of worldly legality begins with a founding, violent event (an instant of mythic violence); this establishes a new order, one that is preserved by police, or law-preserving violence, which for Benjamin is merely the refiguration of the founding violence into potential form (the power of the foundational event can always exert itself in any moment of "peace," but does not do so at all moments). Any order that is founded, as all are, on foundational, constituting violence is subject to interruption by another, subsequent event of mythic founding in a future time, an interruption that would establish a new order in opposition to the old (the general strike is Benjamin's example).[38] By this account, all law, even that understood as "peace," is "intimately bound up" with violence (Benjamin 1978: 295). What is of interest for this reading of the moment of mythical violence (not) represented in Eliot's text is Benjamin's idea that new orders of law can be established only by an unexpected and unregulable force, a violence unconstrained by extant orders of legality.

This means that for Benjamin, mythical, founding violence is to politics what the *deus ex machina* is to fiction or drama. "Mythical violence in its archetypal form," he writes, "is a mere manifestation of the gods" (1978: 294). It is an insurgent violence that comes as if from "without" or "on high" to destroy an older sovereign order and establish a new one. The breach of orderly succession in *The Mill of the Floss*' concluding pages is, of course, lethal: it kills the book's two main characters in a vortex of water and wood in ways long read as "sacrificial." What I add to this is the point I have been arguing with reference to Mill and Maine, and to Maggie's own invocations of "consent", which is that an abrupt, unexpected violence ("What were those masses?") pivots between two epochs, in a shift that is itself both unreservedly violent and unrepresentable in temporal terms, making it a problem for a realist narration founded on protocols of expectation and "destiny" (as James termed this understanding of realist probability). Maggie's thoughts as the flood swells capture exactly how fully the flood-event has disrupted the processes of succession to this point deemed normal, in both their aesthetic and sociopolitical senses: "The whole thing had been so rapid—so dreamlike—that the threads of ordinary association were broken" (p. 538).

As Benjamin explains and as Eliot in her essays attests, this convulsive instant of lawmaking—Maggie's "transition of death, without its agony"— cannot ever be "justified," since it belongs to no previous order of law, no "thread of ordinary association."[39] What is at issue is precisely what counts as "ordinary," and by what authorizing power it has been made to appear so. The moment of founding is properly self-justifying or, in grammatical terms, performative.[40] As Benjamin, Derrida, and Eliot likewise make clear, the performative *Gewalt* that brings nothing but its own power into being—that has only itself as its foundation—"demands sacrifice" (Benjamin 1978: 297). All three note how law's foundation requires a martyr on which the self-grounding violence that would authorize a new order can exert itself. Long notorious for its anti-feminist sacrifice of Maggie, Eliot's novel instructs us to read its historical transition in just these disturbing terms. As Eliot's narrator informs us, sacrifice is the explicit price of every epochal shift, since "suffering, whether of martyr or victim [. . .] belongs to every historical advance of mankind" (p. 284).

The scene that immediately precedes the flood and foments this catastrophe is Maggie's transgressive boat trip with Stephen Guest. Like the episode with her father and Lawyer Wakem discussed above, Maggie's cruise with Stephen forces to a physical confrontation the epochal struggle between the novel's old and new temporalities, a standoff between status and contract that cannot be "solved" without the providential intervention I have just described. The episode that triggers the novel's mystical water event—its aqueous cause—is significant in Maine's terms no less than Eliot's, since it finds Stephen trying out a sequence of rhetorical tricks to persuade Maggie legally to marry him. (Maine and Eliot similarly view historical succession as a marriage plot.) The two have already spent the night in the boat together: while nothing untoward has happened (that we know of), the eyes of the community will see them as united. Maggie, Stephen is arguing, should bring "fact" into step with "law." Finally he hits a nerve:

> "Dearest," he said, in his deepest, tenderest tone, leaning towards her and putting his arm round her, "you *are* mine now—the world believes it— duty must spring up out of that now—in a few hours you will be legally mine. And those who had claims on us will submit—they will see that there was a force which declared against their claims." (p. 499)

Force and submission are the argument's key terms. Physically laying claim to his charge with "his arm round her," Stephen voices his appeals in terms Maine and Mill have already provided; he uses the archaic language of primitive coercion native to the epoch of *patria potestas*.[41] In the face of Stephen's insistent effort to force her to elope, Maggie reverts feebly to the language of contract, of consent, and of the liberal "now" in which such concepts might conceivably have validity. She responds to the arm around her and the brute force it represents by saying she does not "consent," but there is no power behind her claims:

> "O, I can't do it," she said, in a voice almost of agony —"Stephen—don't ask me—don't urge me." [...] "Dear—dear Stephen—let me go!—don't drag me into deeper remorse. My whole soul has never consented—it does not consent now." (p. 499)

To "ask" is to make a request without coercion of another sovereign individual, one that is a matter of free choice or consent; to "urge" is to use power on a subservient or non-sovereign actor, to forcibly persuade.

Though the semantic distance between the terms is small, politically they are an epoch apart: Maggie's hesitation between "ask" and "urge" names the antagonism between political temporalities now reaching its crisis. The problem is that though her "whole soul" resists, Maggie's body has already consented, floated out onto the river in the water-borne, tidal ride that will prove her undoing. This is the crisis point in the novel's historical plot, where the old language of force and of possession has come into irresolvable conflict with the new voluntarist idiom of consent, of equal relations among sovereign agents (marriage as contract, not coercion). But this emergent language does not yet have the force of law to back it up; it is a set of empty signifiers, and Maggie cannot inaugurate the new order herself. After her feeble rejection of Stephen's advance, Maggie notes that she "was not conscious of a decision as she turned away from that gloomy averted face—and walked out of the room: it was like an automatic action that fulfils a forgotten intention" (p. 500). Maggie cannot decide. Hastened here to its unsolvable crisis point, the transition between old and new will require something more material than Maggie's own thoughts to effect it.[42]

The flood follows. In its 1860 review of Eliot's first novels, the *Westminster Review* invoked all of the registers in which Eliot's own text was operating to condemn the violent arrival that kills *The Mill*'s asynchronous protagonist and, I am arguing, founds the new order of law that Eliot's text, like others in and around the moment of 1860, associates with modernity as such. Time, geology, and the narrative of an earlier world giving way to a new one organize its comments. "[T]he denouement is altogether melodramatic," the reviewer judged:

> indeed, there is a tendency to and taste for startling events in George Eliot, which seems to crop out of the rich culture of her mind, like the primitive rocks of an earlier world. The flood in the mill, and the rescue of Hetty in *Adam Bede*, are instances of what we mean; they are vestiges of a Titanic time, before the reign of peaceful gods commenced.   (Carroll, ed. 1971: 143)

By charting the violent process by which "startling events" trade the old, violent forces of status for the allegedly "peaceful gods" of liberalism, Eliot's novel proposes that a rupturing moment of mythic violence must ground any new rule of law.

If in this insight Eliot seems to anticipate the insights of more recent thinkers on law, violence, and secular modernity, she follows her contemporaries like Maine and Mill in viewing the new order thus founded as one of lawful equipoise—as an epoch characterized by what Maggie called "consent." But in distinction from narratives by Maine, Mill, and even Asa Briggs, *The Mill on the Floss* attests poetically to the intimate relationship between this new law and the violence that must bring it into being—the same violence that must remain, if in just potential form, as the law's authorizing force after its founding. My argument has tracked how Eliot exploits the affordances of prose fiction to document the unrepresentable violence nestled at the foundations of modern liberal peace. But in closing this analysis of a liberal order's violent birth, it is important to note how the mythical moment Eliot's novel poetically denarrates is itself bracketed in the novelistic time of "the past." The novel's retrospective frame turns that founding trauma into a memory that we, its later witnesses, assimilate into our own consciences, in a process of cognitive exchange that valorizes our status as residents of the very order of sentimental peace this catastrophic rupture has founded.

ON NAÏVE AND SENTIMENTAL NOVELS: SCHILLER AND THE PLEASURES OF THE PAST

Before we close the book on Eliot's violent modernization story, it is important to note how it doesn't let us. The *Mill*'s conspicuous but rarely remarked upon framing device positions its readers as modern subjects able, first, to seal into the past the events and dead subjects just depicted and then, in a second step, to convert this founding trauma into the occasion for our own ethical self-fashioning. The novel has long been celebrated as a picture of the past, an enclosed image of what has already left us. Since the earliest responses, readers have called upon pictorial metaphors to describe the novel's effects. The *Westminster* referred to "the beauty of the early pictures of mill life" (Carroll, ed. 1971: 141), a still-life effect also evident to other early readers. For the unimpressed *Dublin Review*, the novel was merely "a series of photographic studies" (Carroll, ed. 1971: 148), while the same reader who complained in the *Westminster* of the primitive rocks jutting through Eliot's imagination found something to appreciate in *The Mill*'s painterly quality, in the "numerous" "pictures" of the past the novel mounts for its readers.[43] "You can hardly stop before a single frame," he noted, "without finding food for the day's thought" (Carroll, ed. 1971: 141). "Why is it so delightful," *Blackwood's* wondered, elaborating this response to the *Mill*'s photographic or painterly effect (the language will not let us decide which), "to read what we have known and felt so well already?" (Carroll, ed. 1971: 13). Understanding how the novel can seem to present us, as if for the first time, with the naïveté and violence we have already moved past helps introduce a political reading of the novel's retrospective form. A dream, a hallucination, and a picture, *The Mill on the Floss* is also a backward-looking frame narrative, one that, after depicting the revolutionary foundation of law in a time "many years ago" (p. 11), contains this deadly story and presents it as a hypostasized or sealed image of "nature." In so doing,

Eliot's novel presents a sentimental image of a simple past and the lethal event that kills it off: the novel's readers become those modern subjects who gaze retrospectively upon the "trace[s]" and "marks" of a vanquished age, as we contemplate the textual remainders of a naïve world that, in the Schillerian terms I want to develop now, we no longer *are* but *seek*: vestiges of a lost pastoral state that we do not inhabit but regard from a position of reflective sophistication.

There is a frame, after all, around these photographic traces of country life. If Eliot's modernization tragedy in *The Mill on the Floss* is properly the story—the diegetic space of the novel that moves us, violently, from then to now—the first chapter, "Outside Dorlcote Mill," is literally that: outside, an extradiegetical casing of the story. In manuscript Eliot (n.d.) added the "Outside" to her chapter title, emphasizing just this formal remove. Inside the novel's frame, Maggie is the narrative's modern consciousness reflecting on her more natural peers, but the book's form ensures that we, too, are in position to scale what the narrator calls "the steep highway of tolerance" (p. 305) and ascend toward the reflective, peaceful rationality the novel codes as modern. ("[T]he responsibility of tolerance lies with those who have the wider vision," the narrator instructs, p. 520.) In the book's opening pages, our narrator sits in a chair but dreams he is standing on a bridge. Thus doubly distanced from past events, he finds himself awash in a reverie of nostalgia, giving what seems like physical expression to his stance as sentimental spectator:

> Ah, my arms are really benumbed. I have been pressing my elbows on the arms of my chair and dreaming that I was standing on the bridge in front of Dorlcote Mill as it looked one February afternoon many years ago. Before I dozed off, I was going to tell you what Mr and Mrs Tulliver were talking about, as they sat by the bright fire in the left-hand parlor on that very afternoon I have been dreaming of. (p. 11)

After these words the novel begins. *The Mill on the Floss* thus opens with the desensitized, indeed dozing body of the spectator-narrator, actually in an armchair but dreaming he is viewing from a bridge. It ends, as we will see, with another spectator, the reader, gazing at a tombstone. Separated two times from the direct objects of the past, the acting subject of these opening sentences is also linked to them by the sinews of an operation he here calls "dreaming" but elsewhere refers to as "remember[ing]" (p. 9). With "us" identified with this doubly distanced onlooker, the novel's retrospective structure acts as the formal machinery by which the *Mill* both depicts historical trauma and formally reflects on it, condensing this violence into a synchronic, lyric moment that we regard. In the process the novel celebrates the doubled or sentimental character of those super-empowered subjects who, like "us" and the narrator, are able to perform this reflection (see also Stewart 2009: 130–2).

In writings Eliot knew intimately,[44] "our divine Schiller," as Eliot called the German poet and theorist (1958–78, v 8, 13), framed a distinction between "naïve" and "sentimental" cognitive modes whose terms, like Maine's and Mill's, are legible throughout *The Mill on the Floss'* depiction of its premodern peasants. Schiller's neo-Kantian philosophical aesthetics, which Eliot studied "intensively" during the 1840s and 1850s (Guth 2003: 25), prefigured the mid-century story of custom transforming into law, but did so in terms of literary form and cognitive process. Schiller's 1801 "On Naïve and Sentimental Poetry" explains that existence can be divided into two temporalities, ancient and modern, but adds that these temporalities are coextensive with distinct aesthetic dispositions— one unreflective and single-minded (that is, old) and the other reflective and rational (new). For Schiller as for the early Eliot, naïve or premodern people are like other features of nature, existing as parts of their organic world, necessary to it and determined by its law, even though, like Tom or Mr. Glegg, they may be unaware of that law's character. The rational or reflective modern subject, by contrast, is he who has achieved "distance" from his surroundings and is able to use his powers of rationality to reflect critically upon them.

In a formula that would later come to structure Lukács' theory of the novel, what Schiller calls the "unity" of the peasant consciousness—his direct, unmediated participation in his world—is thus set against the self-division of the modern man. "We are free and what they are is necessary," Schiller writes (1998: 181). This distinction between mental dispositions is reflected, too, in the art native to each temporality, where naïve art is a direct expression of a unified state, while sentimental art reflects critically upon that (now lost) prelapsarian state—a distinction whose institution-alization into fictional practice I chart in Chapter 4. "[I]n the experience of sentimental poetry," Schiller clarifies, "the mind is in motion, it is tense, it pulsates between conflicting feelings, while in the case of naïve poetry it is calm, relaxed, one with itself, and perfectly satisfied" (1998: 233). Under-standing cognitive modernity as a nearly physiological state of agitation— "tense," "pulsat[ing]"—and setting it against the "calm" ignorance of the satisfied peasant, Schiller's distinction recalls our narrator's work, through-out *The Mill*, to establish a distinction between the progressive Maggie's "keen vibrating consciousness" (p. 459) and Tom's narrow familialism, or the blithe but rooted foolishness of the Dodson ladies.[45]

In keeping with the melancholic structure of pastoral outlined by William Empson, whereby complex forms of life regard simple ones under an affective dispensation of loss, Schiller's signal innovation—and the one linking his own narrative with Eliot's here—is to ascribe to this framed past not the negative valence we might expect but a positive one. In adapting the long tradition of encomia to *l'homme sauvage* extending from Rousseau, Schiller writes of the naïve man: "We laugh at him, but by the same token we still cannot help admiring him" (1998: 187). He continues in language that sheds light on *The Mill on the Floss'* narrative structure. Schiller writes:

> [I]f you can take consolation in the loss of natural *happiness*, then let its *completeness* serve as a model for your heart. If you step out of your artificial circle toward the completeness of nature, then it stands before you in its magnificent stillness, in its naïve beauty, in its childlike innocence and simplicity. Dwell at that moment on this image, cultivate this feeling [...].

Importantly, however, our sympathy with this lost epoch must have its limit:

> Do not let it occur to you any longer to want to *change places* with nature. Instead take nature up into yourself and strive to wed its unlimited advantages to your own endless prerogatives, and from the marriage of both strive to give birth to something divine. Let nature surround you like a lovely *idyll*, in which again and again you find the way back to yourself from the aberrations of art and gather the courage and new confidence about the course of life, so that the flame of the *ideal*, so easily extinguished in life's storms, is rekindled in your heart.   (Schiller 1998: 139, emphasis original)

We pity and love the past, but we do not want to change places with it. For Schiller as for Eliot, the modern hero has dialectically lapsed into a state of heroic reflection, "tak[ing] nature up into yourself." In describing the complex operation whereby a modern, expansively minded subject claims mental ownership over a lost nature, Schiller's text describes a version of the cosmopolitan rationalism Eliot and many of her later critics construe as our modern birthright.

As we've seen, for Eliot the metaphors for describing this emancipated mental state are of travel. *The Mill on the Floss'* narrator presumes that citizen-subjects like the reader no longer find their imaginations restricted to "home scene[s]," but instead roam abroad, alighting mentally upon "grove[s] of tropic palms," and the "strange ferns or splendid broad-petalled blossoms" of foreign zones (p. 45). Far from accidental, *The Mill'*s references to the British world system's leafy peripheries perform an important function in the novel's differential historical logic: no longer simply a matter of time-coded politics (custom versus law), nor just of ethical aesthetics (naïve versus sentimental), the difference between now and then here takes its final turn, emerging as the demarcation between hedgerow and tropics, between a rooted nationalism of the past and the cosmopolitan globalism of a contractual future. In Eliot's model, the chronotope of civic tolerance emerges as a time that is modern, and a space that is all over the world—but specifically, in Eliot's recurrent example, in the palm-covered expanses of the imperial periphery. "Our instructed vagrancy," the narrator says later,

> which has hardly time to linger by the hedgerows, but runs away early to the tropics and is at home with palms and banyans,—which is nourished on books of travel and stretches the theatre of its imagination to the Zambesi— can hardly get a dim notion of what an old-fashioned man like Tulliver felt for this spot, where all his memories centred and where life seemed like a familiar smooth-handled tool that the fingers clutch with loving ease.
>
> (p. 277)

The tone of this well-known passage appears to criticize our wide-ranging peregrinations. Yet the "stretched" "theatre of . . . imagination" it describes is also the precise form of cognition the novel has valorized as modern. This is the tensed sentimental lawfulness Maggie's own sacrifice has inaugurated, and in which "we" have been positioned as viewers. Feeling "at home" not in any domestic scene but in the jungles along the imperial river only just explored and documented by David Livingstone (in 1858), *The Mill* itself identifies concrete geopolitical corollaries for the cognitive cosmopolitanism it advocates, disclosing the material register secreted within its idealist theory of ethical expansion. Eliot's easy transfer between mental and physical versions of expansion—and, by extension, idealist and materialist modes of analysis—aims us toward *Forms of Empire*'s coming chapters, which track the export of law's violence to the imperial margins here troped as the very emblem of "elsewhere."

But as Schiller and Eliot equally indicate, if we remain stuck at home while in the midst of performing the sympathetic expansion Robbins calls "feeling global," we should not despair. We may be disheartened, Schiller tells us, by our awareness that the centered satisfaction of the simple life is gone. We may indeed feel the need to celebrate, even to lionize those who remain in that state of nature. But we should not look to "*change places*" with the objects we regard, Schiller says. This is impossible. Instead, the sentimental modern is enjoined to "take nature up into yourself," to "strive to wed its unlimited advantages to your own endless prerogatives" (1998: 139). Aimed at "us," the paradoxical injunction is to renounce our expansive powers, but by renouncing intensify them. Schiller's moral and aesthetic theory of flaming, ideal reflection—the sentimental self-division that is also a self-aggrandizement—articulates the modernizing moral pedagogy Eliot's novelistic structure also effects. To understand the work of Eliot's frame structure this way is to begin answering *Blackwood's* question about why, in *The Mill on the Floss*, it was so "delightful" "to read what we have known and felt so well already" (quoted in Carroll, ed. 1971: 13).

For Schiller, looking at premodernity's inhabitants produces "a unique phenomenon of a feeling," one "in which cheerful patronizing, respect, and melancholy flow together" (1998: 183). We might call it delight: in any case a similar complex of affective responses results from Eliot's sentimental pictures. The effect is not precisely nostalgic, because it does not want to recapture the lost age it depicts. Rather, as Schiller and Eliot equally suggest, the lesson is to "take up nature into" ourselves; in psychoanalytic terms, it is to introject naïveté into our own more complex mental state, this introjection serving further to aggrandize the omnivorous appetite for cognitive exchange here understood as sympathy. What the sentimental man feels when he regards the doomed past is something richer and stranger than animal delight: it is the appreciation of his own ability to inhabit temporarily the naïve position he has now superseded. This "patronizing respect" (Schiller 1998: 183) or sympathetic interchange finds us, with Eliot's narrator and Maggie herself, cognitively re-experiencing the fate of lost objects or "deformed things," apparently celebrating these benighted others through a sentimental, self-dividing operation that serves most to celebrate our capacity to perform this appreciation.

In the 1851 "Progress of the Intellect," Eliot weighs in using these terms exactly. Her syntax is complicated, her temporal logic more so. "It may be doubted," she writes,

> whether a mind which has no susceptibility to the pleasure of changing its point of view, of mastering a remote form of thought, of perceiving identity in nature under variety of manifestation—a perception which resembles *an expansion of one's own being, a pre-existence of the past*—can possess the flexibility, the ready sympathy, or the tolerance, which characterizes a truly philosophic culture.   (1963: 29, emphasis added)

With "sympathy," "flexibility," and "tolerance" standing in for our "truly philosophic" or modern culture—Mill's "liberty," Maine's "contract"— the sympathetic operation Eliot parses here calls for "an expansion of one's own being, a *pre-existence* of the past." The call, that is, is to descend into the pre-modern world of naïveté to re-experience it, as if for the first time. The most salient effect issuing from this operation is, as Eliot specifies, "pleasure."

The Mill's narrator also finds a pleasant effect attending his observation of the past's simple objects—a "romance," as he calls it, that "thrills me with a sense of poetry" (pp. 282–3). In this book's final chapter we will see how the romance mode emerges as the generic logic appropriate to the archaic, unified mode of being Lukács calls epic. Now we can see that the thrill *The Mill*'s narrator registers shares with Schiller's account the self-satisfying aim of what we could call an aesthetics of temporal sentimentalism. The paradoxically self-affirming power of this self-denying concern with others exerts its appeal for Maggie, too. When she receives her collection of books, each one full of moral instruction and chastening power, this catechism awakens in her the second-order pleasure of pleasure's denial. "[R]enunciation," the narrator reports, "seemed to her the entrance into that satisfaction which she had so long been craving in vain" (p. 303).[46]

My claim is that the novel's retrospective frame structure confirms that the powers and pleasures of observation Maggie enjoys mirror our own, as we, like *Blackwood's*, register "delight" and "patronizing respect" at the peasant specimens Eliot's novel arranges for our view. But *The Mill on the Floss* also ritually kills two of these specimens, and as we have seen it is not simply an idyllic past that we are positioned to regard as if in pastoral mode. Rather, it is the mythic sacrifice of the novel's key characters that is made spectacular. Beginning with a seated narrator dreaming of a time "one February afternoon many years ago" (p. 11), separated from the diegetic action by ellipses that Eliot, in manuscript, extended halfway across the page,[47] the novel does not end with its *deus ex machina* of sudden death. It ends by laying out for view a monument to those it has killed. Maggie and Tom lie buried together near their father, this clan group's shared grave forming the novel's final image. These are the book's last words:

> Near that brick grave there was a tomb erected very soon after the flood, for two bodies that were found in close embrace: and it was often visited at different moments by two men who both felt that their keenest joy and keenest sorrow were for ever buried there.
> [. . .]
> The tomb bore the names of Tom and Maggie Tulliver, and below the names it was written—
> 'In their death they were not divided.'   (p. 544)

We end by gazing on an epitaph. *The Mill on the Floss*' famous graveyard ending is not alone among Eliot's tomb-obsessed texts: *Middlemarch* (1874–5) ends with the "unvisited tombs" of the historical dead; two of the three *Scenes of Clerical Life* (1857) conclude with grave scenes; and the first piece of fiction Eliot ever wrote, an awkward short story called "Poetry and Prose, from the Notebook of an Eccentric," begins with a "sole mourner" staring into an open burial pit (1963: 14). Like all of these,

The Mill on the Floss' ending positions modern readers as survivors of the historical experience just documented: we are spectators above a tomb, regarding sentimentally the written traces of a historical past that has been decisively laid to rest. Why is it so delightful? Twice removed from the flood and its trauma, self-divided and sentimental, the modern spectator is asked in this final scene to incorporate the violence of the novel's founding event, *taking it up into ourselves* as the novel seals its own rupturing catastrophe into the narrative time of the past. In all this Eliot's novel enjoins us to perform the act of political-aesthetic mourning well dramatized in the historical novels of Walter Scott she so admired in her early career.[48]

Sympathy has since its foundational expression in Adam Smith's *Theory of Moral Sentiments* (1759) functioned as a discourse of pleasure-bestowing exchange. As Audrey Jaffe, Rae Greiner, and others have shown, sympathy discourse was central to the cognitive toolkit of mid-Victorian liberalism; as Jaffe explains, this conceptual innovation transformed singular human beings into units available for (cognitive) exchange, and thus played a key role in naturalizing commodity culture (2000: 8, 15).[49] Yet the sympathetic operation of "feeling another's pain" does more than individuate and depoliticize. Smithian sympathy is itself an operation of exchange, since it allows the sympathetic viewer to trade away her openly self-interested position, so as to receive the higher, less obvious, and apparently disinterested satisfaction that comes from having engaged in that act of (apparent) self-denial in the first place. By this logic, the empowered observer gains affective satisfaction from having "disin-terestedly" sympathized with the injured or—in Smith's recurrent examples—the impoverished objects of his feeling gaze. As Smith writes in the opening pages of *Theory*, upon viewing the pain of a suffering man, the sympathetic observer "derives nothing from it except the pleasure of seeing it" (1982: 9). The exchange confers "nothing [...] except": it seems to yield him nothing, but "pleasure" is the commodity that is traded for pain. Another of the books Maggie reads as part of her moral catechism is called *The Beauties of the Spectator*, a title whose ambiguous genitive leaves open the question of whether "beauty" redounds to the viewed object or subject who looks at it.[50] The answer is both, since like the novel's modern reader, Maggie sympathizes with the attractively naïve or, in Philip's case, the charmingly disabled, but solidifies her own, more sophisticated beauty in the process of this renunciative act. If Smith's theory focuses on individual moments of sympathy—on the uneven exchange between individuals in a synchronic encounter—Eliot's remedi-ation of Smithian sentimentalism is lengthened, since it positions us to regard not only a single instance of suffering (the flood) but the whole history leading up to it—validating, in the process, our own status as the historical beneficiaries of that harm.

What remains is historical trauma's ghostly after-image. The flood and its death have been turned into a text of history, the narrator tells us, a registration of past violence not dissimilar from the stratigraphic marks that Lyell called the "symbolical language, in which the earth's autobiography is written" (1860: v) now crisscrossing the spot at St. Ogg's. "Nature repairs her ravages," Eliot's narrator explains in the line directly following Maggie and Tom's death (p. 543). The implicitly male voice continues: "The desolation wrought by that flood, had left little visible trace on the face of the earth, five years after. [. . .] [T]he hills underneath [its] green vesture bear the marks of the past rending" (p. 543). After the flood, beyond the event, all we are left with is "marks," "trace[s]": the barely visible graphic remainders of foundational trauma that, like the melancholy photographic images described by Barthes (1982), mark a past presence ("it happened here") even as they confirm its current absence ("it is gone").[51] But Eliot's novel of catastrophe and progress ends with a different kind of writing, a re-quotation of its earlier inscription: "In their death they were not divided." Cited from the Bible, framed in quotes, and reproduced in typeface from a carving in stone: the now-famous final words provide the closure of the novel and the bookend of its mourning frame. In literal terms, the event and its damage have become part of the ground, literally encrypted in what Eliot's narrator earlier called "this spot." Yet in formal and psychoanalytic terms too, this violent past has been buried: the maxim operates as a code into which the entire catastrophe of the modern order's founding has been distilled and then contained: it is a formula, a cliché, a second-hand maxim that can only ever stand in for—that is, flatten into the exchangeability required for consumption— the traumatic violence just surveyed.

Literary criticism is most comfortable when it presumes a separation between "literature" and "theory." Thus do critics, even when treating a "novelist of ideas" like Eliot, continue to cite extraliterary ideas and track the effects those conceptual ensembles have on what is construed as the secondary category of literary representation. This tendency to treat literary fiction as a vessel for concepts external to itself forces even so astute a reader as Suzanne Graver to describe Eliot's ideas as "analogous" to those of Tonnies (Graver 1984: 8). But literature does not recapitulate thought; it is itself thought. In response to this I have emphasized the difference literary presentation makes: I have shown how Eliot pushes to the limits of her medium so as to ring key changes on the stories she adapts, remaking them in the very process of transmission. Since no content is conceivable without a form of transmission—no message thinkable without its medium—the conceptual improvements Eliot makes to her advanced liberal peers are only possible because of the particular affordances of prose fiction. By emphasizing these moments of creative remaking—the denarrated killing, the radicalization of narratological paradox, the containment and encryption of trauma in a bracketed past—I have treated Eliot's novel not as a site for the re-articulation of ideology nor as a relay point for Foucauldian discourse but as an agent of thinking itself. As Frederic Harrison once remarked, aside from Eliot, "no English thinker of the higher quality has ever used romance as an instrument of thought" (1885: 26). *The Mill on the Floss* is one such instrument of thought. It exploits the capacities of its form to stage, inter, and then regard from a modern vantage what is at once a gradual historical accumulation and a two-stage model of modernization, a narrative of liberal modernity punctured by the founding violence of a mythical event Eliot's novel figures as the arrival of law. Yet if Eliot's most Wordsworthian novel provides the backstory for mid-century England's domestic "equipoise," it has also described the inhabitant of this modern area as one whose mind skirts the Zambezi in sympathetic, wide-angle flights of imagination.

By thus locating Victorian legal modernity in its properly international— that is, imperial—context, *The Mill on the Floss* itself offers clues about where, how, and under what political conditions the sublimated force of liberal peace emerged as open war. But before shifting to the civilized world's outskirts, this book turns to the metropolitan core of Victorian modernity itself. There, in London, Victorian theory and fiction conceptualized modern law as a network of peaceful human interchangeability that might eventually know no horizon. Set in the very epicenter of modern exchange, urban fictions about lost, nameless, and abandoned bodies give form to the dynamics of exclusion and violence structuring what Humphry House in 1941 named "The Dickens World."

2

Reform Fiction's Logic of Belonging

Everybody to count for one, nobody for more than one.

>—John Stuart Mill quoting Jeremy Bentham,
>*Utilitarianism* (1863)

The calamity of the rightless [...] is not that they are not equal before the law, but that no law exists for them; not that they are oppressed, but that nobody wants even to oppress them.

>—Hannah Arendt, *Origins of Totalitarianism* (1951)

I have no position to lose, and no name to degrade.

>—Magdalen Vanstone, in *No Name*,
>by Wilkie Collins (1862)

BECOMING GENERAL: THE CENSUS

The officials of the 1841 Census responsible for taking account of every individual human being in England and Wales were called enumerators. But this suggestive title was actually a misnomer, since these locally supervised employees were not themselves charged with the task of converting people into numbers. Rather, enumerators were to search the darkest corners of the nation's territory, collecting paper "schedules" filled with proper names and verifying the individuating marks of the particular people they found there. The resulting forms, collated and re-copied before being submitted to a central office in Westminster, instance an *ad hoc*, emergent strain of statistical state knowledge.

The schedule shown in Fig. 2.1 shows how the Census' universalizing idiom of forms and grids competes with idiosyncrasies of handwriting and notation particular to this unknown enumerator. Like other documents from this moment of gathering state bureaucracy, Census forms like this one inscribe the simultaneously political and metaphysical tension between singularity and generality, as handwritten proper names fit only uneasily within the standardized grid meant to contain them. In this composite

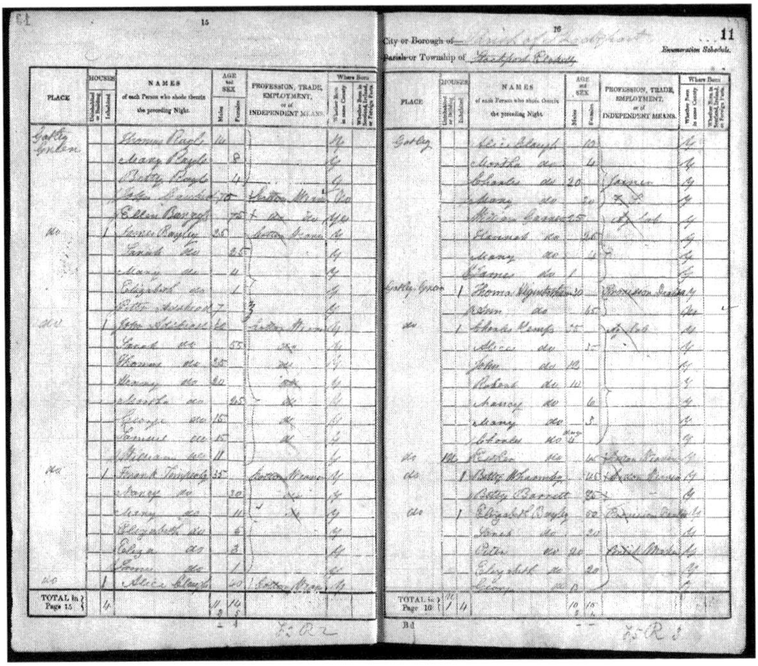

Fig. 2.1. 1841 Enumeration Schedule. Census Enumerator's Book. Stockport Borough; Stockport Parish; Etchells or Stockport-Etchells Township. Schedules filled out by householders were destroyed as part of the enumeration process; this is a copied version, transcribed by enumerators. National Archives HO 107/11/2 (11).

textual performance, categories of singular and general commingle in service of the first centralized collection of biostatistical data in the modern era.[1] From a practical point of view, the collection and verification of such schedules was only the initial step of the 1841 Census' unprecedented project of mass counting and population management. Yet the complications presented by this first interface between the Victorian era's developing bureaucracy and the population it administered were not only logistical. The challenge was conceptual too, as a cartoon of the 1851 census by George Cruikshank suggests (Fig. 2.2).

Like the hybrid Census schedules, which contain the physical traces of unique enumerators within a grid common across England and Wales, Cruikshank's drawing highlights the tension between the particularity of names and the abstract exchangeabilty required for counting. This tension constitutes the central political and aesthetic problem of imperial democracy in the Reform era, when, as historian Patrick Joyce writes, an

Fig. 2.2. George Cruikshank, "Taking the Census" (1851). *The Comick Almanack*, second series, 355.

Fig. 2.3. "&c – / &c – &c – hang me if I can / recollect 'em / all / so it's no use / to try!" "Taking the Census," detail.

unprecedented number of English bodies "became available to be identified as individual and collective objects and subjects of governance" (Joyce 2003: 22).

In Cruikshank's illustration, one household's surplus of bodies threatens to overrun the frame. Names proliferate, and the abundance of (mostly female) individuals overwhelms both the man of the house and the enumerator there to register his burgeoning family; even the cartoonist's handwritten caption must contort itself to accommodate this human profusion. ("[D]on't forget the two babbies!" screams a woman at the rear.) The drawing's visual rhetoric is of humorous alarm. As the frame closes in around him, the householder's effort to list his family in its totality grows more and more desperate. Just as this cataloging effort comes to a crisis, Cruikshank's lineation dissolves into a string of helpless *et ceteras*, as the cramped space of the dialogue bubble, invaded by heads and hair, produces a halting free verse: "&c – / &c – &c – hang me if I can /

recollect 'em / all / so it's no use / to try!" (Fig. 2.3). Here semantic and epistemological projects collapse together, generating a stuttering poetry about the impossibility of comprehending an entire community as named—that is, singular—subjects.

This chapter tracks the tension between abstract category and individual instance as it ramifies across the fields of formal logic, political theory, and aesthetic practice in the middle decades of the nineteenth century. Each of these domains of literary and conceptual activity, I suggest, draws on its particular representational capacities to address the double-sided and finally political problem of membership: on the one hand, particularity must be stripped in any inductive transformation of a singularity into a unit able to be counted in a set; on the other, particularities that avoid the flattening processes of inductive abstraction become for this very reason outside of the category of membership, cast out of belonging and unavailable for what Cruikshank's patriarch calls "recollect[ion]." In material terms, they become the nameless and abandoned bodies populating what historian Gareth Stedman Jones calls "outcast London" (1971). My claim is that the instances of literary thinking discussed in this chapter do not symptomatically replay but actively mediate the dialectic of abstraction and abandonment structuring England's modernizing project in the reform decade.

In fact it would be only at the next step of processing, after the enumerator had turned in his schedules to the Registrar General's Office in London, that the Census' rawest findings could be cleaned, sorted, and rationalized. It was there, at the Central Office, that the Malthusian surplus Cruikshank satirizes would be converted into the fungible, manipulable genre of knowledge we call data, raw material for the technology of governmental administration being consolidated in this mid-century moment. In a letter, the nation's first Registrar General, Thomas Henry Lister, laid out the procedures for producing the state's new human databank. In so doing he pinpoints the moment of conversion from name to number that is crucial both to biopolitical democracy and, I will suggest, to the aesthetic forms that emerged to mediate its most fraught and contested period of expansion, the 1860s.

Lister here describes how locally gathered lists of proper names, scrawled in skewed columns, would be sent to a central clearing house in Westminster. There, state employees would turn this nearly endless jumble of particularized instances into what Lister called "Abstracts." "I will here mention," wrote the Registrar General:

that I would have no Abstracts made but at the Central Office. The duties of the Local Authorities should be confined to the preparation and transmission of correct records of simple facts. The abstraction, condensation, classification and arrangement of those facts should be done upon one uniform system, and upon the responsibility of one person or Board.

(Quoted in Glass 1973: 115–16.)

Lister explains how an uncollected mass of individual names ("simple facts") might be converted into a functional dataset of counted citizens, each potentially commensurable with the next. Because it was the first of such efforts to be nationalized and executed under a single authority, the 1841 Census of England and Wales was the first centralized, state-run project of human abstraction in British history.

The point is that the moment of "abstraction, condensation, [and] classification" identified by Lister marks not just a logistical challenge but a watershed in the history of political rationality. What he outlines is a process of conversion from quality to quantity by which a mass of singularities would be subjected to a process of political induction resulting in an aggregated mass of particular instances, a "new form of knowledge" in which "the common personhood of all those who were counted was somehow more important than their differences" (Joyce 2003: 25). To produce such a dataset in 1841, "upwards of 100 million separate facts were reduced into tabular statements by clerks who [. . .] worked for months [. . .] for twelve hours a day" (W. A. Armstrong 1978: 30–1). In conceptual terms, what these diligent clerks accomplished was the conversion of named human beings into fungible members of the set "citizen."

As Michel Foucault explains in his lectures on biopolitical democracy delivered in the 1970s (2003, 2007), and as the history of public administration in the Victorian era bears out, the form of sovereign power dependent on this new statistical rationality was unique for being directed not at the individual body but at a mathematically aggregated population. Once this social body had been counted by administrators, it could be subdivided by statisticians; analyzed by actuarials; evaluated by reformist demographers like Edwin Chadwick; and subjected to interventions by new bureaus such as the National Vaccine Institution or the General Register Office responsible for marriages, births, and vital statistics (both founded in 1837).[2] Following interventions by Mary Poovey (1995) and Nancy Armstrong (1999, 2005), criticism has long acknowledged that such bureaucratic innovations consolidated a mode of individualism compatible with liberal government in the period. Yet what emerged was not just what Poovey has called statistical liberalism's new "form of subjectivity" (1995: 114) but the idiom of group belonging in which those subjects, massed together, were now to be governed.

As Emily Steinlight has observed (2010), it was by these adminis-trative means that the Victorian state's population could be managed as a population: encouraged to sustain itself and even, by state policy, made to expand. More and more individuals might eventually be included within the era's widening community of administered bodies, those lucky enough to be subject to the state's new dispensation of care. The goal of this expansive political arithmetic was to convert zeroes into ones, "&c's" into names: to fit more and more subjects for inclusion in the era's new life-protecting social calculus. Then as now, bodies inside the biopolitical community thus enumerated would be (in Foucault's plangent formula) made to live—we might think of the compulsory health programs, epidemiological research, and sanitary reforms long associated with the period—while those outside its boundaries, or those expelled from them, might be, Foucault writes, "let die" (2003: 241).[3]

It will be clear that this new political rationality depends upon two forms of violence. The first is the violence associated with the de-particularizing processes necessary for inclusion into the democratic state's biopolitical model of care. This is the flattening conversion by which names become numbers, what is outside is brought inside, and what were once singularities become examples of a type and in that process made fit for counting. The other violence, abandonment, is the precise inversion of this inclusive social mechanism; this extrojective logic produces precarious human bodies uncounted by any category, and makes those cast-off bodies—members of no set—available to the somatic harms explored in more detail in following chapters. To weigh these dialectically intertwined forms of modern injury—where the only thing worse than counting is not to count at all—this chapter builds on the origin story already supplied by *The Mill on the Floss*, examining not legal modernity's rustic prehistory but the forms of conceptuality and representation most characteristic of its full achievement. Teeming with unnamed street people, thronged with uncountable bodies, it was mid-century London that, like the colonial peripheries to be examined later, most fully realized the double movement of uplift and abandonment that characterized the legal modernity Eliot's novel only flickeringly prefigured.

The chapter begins by showing what conceptual work was required to outfit human beings for inclusion in the era's new biopolitical state. This process of abstraction is most sharply articulated, I suggest, in the idiom of formal logic. Viewed as he intended it, as an essay in liberal method, Mill's *A System of Logic, Ratiocinative and Inductive* (1873) does not just defend an empiricist induction against blind belief in a priori categories; it also establishes on the microcosmic level of reason what he advocated at the macroscopic level of policy: namely, the inductive procedure by which countable subjects (citizens) could be produced for a state increasingly organized along the political-economic logic of general human equivalence—that is, "equality."

After charting the political induction driving the democratic expansions of 1867, the chapter explains how the decade's most characteristic fictional genre, the sensation novel, actively reconfigures the epistemological revolution underwriting the democratic fantasy (or, for Tories, nightmare) of total inclusion. As I show, many of these Reform-era novels hinge on the problem of unabstracted particulars or lost people. They end by re-counting the bodies they have cast out, bringing lost people back into the category of "life" in ways that mirror formally the most optimistic hopes of liberal reformers and slum-visitors, who fantasized that eventually, even the most abject bodies might be reclaimed, re-counted, and re-categorized "within the pale of the civil law of Europe," as Collins' *No Name* has it (1998: 139). In this way does the sensation novel replay in an affirmative mode the inductive work of biopolitical democracy, as it labored to draw more and more human bodies onto the right side of those caesuras in the population separating the nameless and unknown from those who belong.

Armadale (1866) goes further. Collins' novel about slave money, naming, and death generates a counterinductive method in order to defend particularity from the violence it associates with both chattel slavery and the regime of exchange Mill names "liberty." In drawing links between forms of injury whose separation was central to the conceptual architecture of progressive idealism, Collins' novel rewires from within the historicism of its advanced liberal contemporaries; it also frames the key dilemmas of liberal violence examined more closely in subsequent chapters. As *Armadale* demonstrates, Victorian networks of abstraction reached far beyond the checkered geographies of metropolitan London. Yet the Empire's world-scaled project of potential inclusion paradoxically produced remainders, castoffs, leftovers: particulars not inducted into, but ejected from, Victorian modernity's seemingly ever-widening community of membership. It was these un-abstracted bodies who would learn first-hand what violence awaits those who, in a world organized by counting, do not themselves count.

A RULE OF EQUATIONS/MILL'S *LOGIC*

John Stuart Mill was not an employee of the Registrar's Office, but as Lister was fine-tuning the state's first centralized census, the logician, literary theorist, and (after 1865) Liberal MP for Westminster was busy creating the Victorian period's most widely read treatise on how to convert "simple facts" into members of the higher-order categories he associated with knowledge. *A System of Logic Ratiocinative and Inductive; Being a Connected View of the Principles of Evidence and the Methods of Scientific Investigation* sets out to offer nothing short of a complete theory of the human mind's ability to turn observed particulars ("facts") into general principles. It details how the processes of what Lister called "abstraction, condensation, classification, and arrangement" ought most rationally to transpire. Containing work Mill had begun in the 1830s, published in 1843, and revised throughout the 1850s and 1860s (appearing in a final edition in 1873), the book spans the Victorian period.[4] It was a compulsory text at Oxford until the end of the nineteenth century, while at Cambridge Mill's work was read widely, both by those students who were made to study it and by those who were not (Snyder 2006: 100).[5] Providing an empiricist method for multiple generations of Victorian thinkers, Mill's *Logic* staked out philosophical territory that even its critics (like the late Victorian liberal Hegelian T. H. Green) were forced to traverse in their efforts to move beyond it.

But if Mill's *Logic* can be understood as the methodological unconscious of the mid-Victorian age, this was only the fulfillment of the author's hope. Though he later recollected his surprise at the popularity of the volume, Mill noted his desire that his work on logic would form the bedrock for nothing short of a liberal revolution. His hope was to use seamless argumentation and a quietly figurative prose to contest philosophy on its own grounds; his aim, mirroring Maggie's developmental story discussed in Chapter 1, was to effect a shift away from blind belief in "intuition" and empower reasonable individuals to come to knowledge through operations of individual of reason (*CW* I). Mill's method thus looked to provide theoretical foundations for the improvements he would later call for in the political sphere: by demolishing what Mill called "deep seated prejudices" and "the great intellectual support of false doctrines and bad institutions," the *Logic* would replace an old regime of philosophical autocracy with a way of thinking appropriate to "these times" (*CW* I). This was a thinking centered, as Mill would explain, on the rational individual's ability to use the logical processes culminating in induction.

Mill's book became, in Leslie Stephen's later assessment, a "sacred book for students who claimed to be genuine liberals" (1895: 75–6), and its story of an old tyranny turning into a new and more logical individualism also structures the explicitly political interventions of *On Liberty* (1859) and *The Subjection of Women* (1869, drafted 1860–61). In multiple idioms, Mill's work from the Reform decade claimed that the pull of human progress would lead society out of belief and into reason, out of force and into a rule of law characterized by consenting relations among equals. This political-theoretical historicism pits an ancient dogmatism against a modern intellectual freedom, a shorthand that persists unexamined in recent accounts seeking to explain this moment.[6] In reference to the *Logic*, Mill refers to the historical transformation he charts as one by which an old philosophy of "Intuition," based on prejudice, turns into a newer, more empirical philosophy of "Experience and Association" (*CW* I). Mill's work on reason has an important but under-recognized relationship to his political writing from these mid-century years. But if this seems obvious from Mill's own commentary, I shift from his own distinction between an old prejudice and a newer rationality to focus on the meticulously outlined but ultimately mystical—or, as I suggest, poetic—processes by which Mill's self-consciously modern vision of abstraction operated. In so doing I highlight the political valences of inductive method and give specificity to Matthew Arnold's observation, in 1861, that democracy was seeking "to *affirm its own essence*; to live, to enjoy, to possess the world" (Arnold 1993: 5, emphasis original).[7]

Mill's project finds him engaging a set of problems in diverse proto-disciplinary languages, his concepts moving between idioms and gaining inflection in that translation. Thus we might notice how *A System of Logic*'s story of something young and impulsive turning into something older and more serious informs the self-fashioning tale in Mill's own *Autobiography* (1873). Likewise the *Logic*'s philosophical focus on aggregated masses of particulars echoes the equally hefty *Principles of Political Economy* (1848), which was being drafted alongside the *Logic*'s early editions. But the *Logic*'s theories of abstraction and aggregation also find Mill working out the fundamental assumptions of the more directly political works, from *Utilitarianism* (1861) and *Considerations on Representative Government* (1863) to *Liberty* and *Subjection*: this is the assumption of a modern state made up of regular, measurable units—countable citizens governed by law, participating in contracts, and entitled to an equal share, as Mill styles it, in a social system understood as an "aggregate." In *Considerations*, Mill insists that the best modern government "is that in which the sovereignty, or supreme controlling power in the last resort, is vested in the entire aggregate of the community" (*CW* XIX).

Mill's most extended treatment of the philosophy of aggregation, *Utilitarianism*, closes with a line from Bentham's "Essay on Representation": "Everybody to count for one, nobody for more than one" (*CW* X). In the modern state, each personal unit is understood to be typical in the sense that it is equivalent to other examples of itself: self-governing but also, by virtue of that autonomy, counted within the larger calculus of costs and benefits that defines Mill's utilitarian democratic program.[8]

The word "aggregate" recurs in Mill's writing with regularity. As a numbered whole or counted mass, an aggregate is a total entity theoretically reducible to equal, interchangeable parts.[9] Leslie Stephen has critiqued Mill for assuming "that man, like molecule, represents a constant unit" (1895: 283). Massed together, these are the regular elements that, in aggregate, act as both subjects and objects in the horizontal liberal sovereignty Mill imagines—an arrangement whereby (in Etienne Balibar's words) "equality is identical to freedom, is equal to freedom, and vice versa" (2014: 46). All of Mill's explicitly political works, therefore, assume a structural distance between named *individua* and the abstract or exchangeable units that are individuated but no longer singular. On the front end of this conversion are incommensurable singularities, while on the back end are examples of the type "citizen": the proper subjects of a count, or aggregate. How is this gulf to be broached? Mill addressed this question not in his multiple political writings on representation and equality but in his *Logic*, doing so with his description of the inductive method.

Induction is the centerpiece of Mill's analytic theory, "the main question of the science of logic—the question which includes all others" (*CW* VII).[10] Mill explains that inferences created in the process of inductive reasoning are more than closed logical circuits (as syllogisms are), and more than matters of definition (as names are): they are the extrapolation from what has been observed into a new order of claim. An induction occurs at the moment, that is, when the human mind transfers between levels, creating new knowledge by moving from particular cases upwards, as Mill consistently figures it, to general or "abstract" principles. This moment of uplift thus works as a mediating step between low and high, a waypoint between empirically observed items and the abstract categories—sets—that would contain them:

> Induction, then, is that operation of the mind, by which we infer from what we know to be true in a particular case or cases, will be true in all cases which resemble the former in certain assignable respects. In other words, Induction is the process by which we conclude that what is true of certain individuals of a class is true of the whole class, or that what is true at certain times will be true in similar circumstances at all times. (*CW* VII)

Mill defines the machinery of induction as a "process" or an "operation of the mind" where an "inference" is able, somehow, to leap between the level of particular observed cases to the level of larger categories. In keeping with his empiricist priorities, Mill is careful to note that the concepts produced in such upward-tending operations are subject to revision on the discovery of new evidence in the future: thus a miracle, for instance, would revise existing natural laws in exactly the ways charted in Chapter 1, by which a *deus ex machina* rewrites codes of expectation within a fictional system. But after being properly abstracted, what were once idiosyncratic particulars can now be termed members of a set, subject to the rules of probability and expectation proper to that set, which Mill calls the "laws" which "govern" them (*CW* XXI; cf. VII).

Properly executed inductive linkages are the crucial features of Mill's politically inflected rational program but its mechanism of abstraction is most clearly visible when he describes classification. As Mill explains, classification requires an initial operation of reason, a first-order step that works to contain a given set of similar particularities under the label of a set, or class. Classes, he specifies, are the "general conceptions" that are "obtained (in metaphysical phrase) by *abstraction* from individual things" (*CW* VIII, emphasis original). Mill's description of the process by which we arrive at higher-order categories calls forth his most detailed account of the conceptual problem of belonging:

> We know that two things are as much as the mind can easily attend to at a time, and we therefore fix upon one of the objects, either at hazard or because it offers in a peculiarly striking manner some important character, and, taking this as our standard, compare it with one object after another. If we find a second object which presents a remarkable agreement with the first, inducing us to class them together, the question instantly arises, in what particular circumstances do they agree? and to take notice of these circumstances is already a first stage of abstraction, giving rise to a general conception. Having advanced thus far, when we now take in hand a third object we naturally ask ourselves the question, not merely whether this third object agrees with the first, but whether it agrees with it in the same circumstances in which the second did? in other words, whether it agrees with the general conception which has been obtained by abstraction from the first and second? *Thus we see the tendency of general conceptions, as soon as formed, to substitute themselves as types, for whatever individual objects previously answered that purpose in our comparisons.*   (*CW* VIII, emphasis added)

Beginning with an individuating "character," Mill shows how we move from that particularity outward, upward, aggregating other examples "in our hand[s]" and then producing, out of those diverse but now-similar phenomena, a "general conception," one "obtained by abstraction" from the first material objects. In this foundational moment of Mill's method, abstraction is born as the type.

Mill explains that the type is an immaterial proxy, different from but linked to the "first" and "second" particularities from which it is abstracted. It is a heuristic or properly immaterial figure that stands in for a potentially endless set of other cases of that type. Its formation allows those once-loose particulars to be seen, now, as iterable members of a similar class, exchangeable with one another within the overarching sameness of a newly created category. (Every particular bird is an example of the type "bird," just as every particular human—in one of Mill's favorite examples—is an example of the type "man.") As the mediating figure or linking concept that can serve to contain two (or many more) distinct items, the type is the immaterial substitute that puts what were once qualitatively distinct particularities into a relationship of equivalence, arranging them into groupings within which each example is interchangeable with the next.

By providing the mechanism by which a qualitatively distinct object can be compared, collated, and aggregated with others of its class, Mill's type performs the function of what Karl Marx called exchange, a parallel that testifies to the wide circulation of this logical problem during the Reform era.[11] In the early chapters of *Capital* that were drafted contemporaneously with the *Logic* in the 1840s and 1850s (in the British Library) and published in the year of the Second Reform Bill (1867), Marx describes the "mystery" of exchange in ways that directly restate Mill's description of the inductive process (1990: 139). For Marx, the particularities at the beginning of the inductive process are qualitatively different goods like linen and shirts. But by a process of conversion called exchange, these two once-dissimilar particularities are first typologized into commodities (objects with exchange value), and then finally equated. Where Mill spoke of two separate "objects" "in hand," Marx writes of corn and iron:

> Let us now take two commodities, for example corn and iron. Whatever their exchange relation may be, it can always be represented by an equation in which a given quantity of corn is equated to some quantity of iron, for instance 1 quarter of corn = x cwt of iron. What does this equation signify? It signifies that a common element of identical magnitude exists in two different things, in 1 quarter of corn and similarly in x cwt of iron. Both are therefore equal to a third thing, which is itself neither the one or the other. Each of them, so far as it is exchange-value, must therefore be reducible to this third thing.   (Marx 1990: 127)

As in Mill's account, what Marx details here is how, when a comparison is forced between disparate objects under a regime of equivalence, a "third thing" is produced that functions as a medium for achieving equivalence between the first two. This "third thing, which is itself neither the one or the other" is the properly idealist "object"—that is, no object at all—that enables relation between the first two qualitatively distinct things. Now members of the same class (here, "commodities"), the typologized objects are fungible in the sense that they can now be organized into numerically represented relationships of equivalence.

What Mill calls "the type" is in other words what Marx calls money: the "third thing" able to convert qualitative difference into ratios of exchange. Like Mill's type, money, writes Marx, "crystallizes out of the process of exchange" (1990: 181). The contours of Marx's political-economic critique of exchange are well known, but for Marx as for several of his later interpreters (notably Theodor Adorno), the historical development of exchange also exacts an acute metaphysical cost. On the level of logical process, the mode of departicularization Mill charts in the *Logic*, and that Marx critiques in *Capital*, subordinates particularity and makes alterity fungible. In the extreme form Mill advanced in the *Logic*, it ensures, on a theoretical level, that all the qualitatively different objects or subjects in the world (as Mill called those items denoted by names) are potentially exchangeable with one another—that they can be made *not different*.[12] In a book-length reading of Adorno, Fredric Jameson calls attention to "the existential or even metaphysical dimension" of exchange, paraphrasing Adorno to describe "the effects [...] of *equivalence* as a new form imposed on reality and of *abstraction* in the broadest epistemological sense as a historically emergent form of organizing the world" (2007: 148, italics original). For Adorno, equivalence "excises the incommensurable" (quoted by Jameson 2007: 149): monetary logic transforms difference into sameness, flattening qualitative distinctions in order to produce repeatable, exchangeable units—equal parts that work, like money or citizens, as the chits of a political-economic system now operating according to a metaphysics of counting. It is in this sense that we should understand Mill's "deep commitment to equality" (Collini 1991: 138).

Mill's inductive method outlines on the level of logical process the theoretical and institutional mechanism by which, in the political sphere, the liberal state's abstract citizens—formally equal and implicitly male, all cases of the same type—were to be produced out of a sea of proper names. After the introduction of money, Marx writes, in an often-cited formulation, "Men are henceforth related to each other in their social process of production in a purely atomistic way" (1990: 187). Describing this atomic relation, Marx clarifies his terms by echoing Mill and other mid-Victorian legal theorists, calling it the "juridical relation, whose form is the contract"

(p. 178n.). This is the legal relation proper to the new regime of money, a juridical relation that, Marx writes, "correspond[s] to the production of commodities" (pp. 178–9n.). Here, in this juridical, monetary modernity—Mill's liberty—exchangeable subjects of law are units that, like commodities, have been moved into that higher-order position in which they stand in as examples of a type Mill called "citizen." They are the subjects and objects of law and, as such, are available, in aggregate, to be managed under the processes of statistical analysis and optimization that defined mid-Victorian biopolitical democracy.

"COUNT OF HEADS": INDUCTIVE DEMOCRACY

Mill's seemingly merely philosophical theory therefore has political stakes. In politics as in logic, Mill's optimistic notion was that all particulars were or should be available for potential abstraction. While running for Parliament in 1865, Mill told audiences that "no man who was competent to manage his own affairs ought to be without a vote" (*CW* XVIII). A newspaper quoted him on the stump that year calling for the "extension of a share of political right to all" and explaining that "[t]hose left without seemed a sort of pariahs" (*CW* XVIII). Mill here explains that "political right" names status as a counted citizen, while those without it are "pariahs": outlying singularities, as yet un-abstracted into the category of political membership. Mill's radicalism lay in his conviction that right might eventually be extended to all.

Mill's universalism in these manifestly political pronouncements mirrors the *Logic*'s description of a potentially limitless field of counted items: no instance is theoretically inassimilable, no human *individuum* unavailable to be converted into an example of the type "citizen." Two years after his election to Parliament on a platform of universal suffrage, Mill would critique the Reform Bill for not yet living up to this ambition of total induction; he claimed that the resulting Act, with a £10 property requirement and still-vast exclusions in the countryside, was not, as he said, a properly "democratic measure," since it did not conform to "what may be called the numerical theory of representation" (*CW* XVIII)—that is, the theory that each citizen of the nation, no matter his borough, was entitled to a mathematically equal share of political right. (The exclusions from Mill's imagined universality, not mentioned in his stump speech, included the mentally ill and those unable to demonstrate a minimal competency in reading and arithmetic.) In pursuit of this mathematical theory, Mill advocated a system in which not localities or boroughs but individual subjects would be represented in Parliament. This individualizing and aggregating democratic position sought to actualize the principle he'd already outlined in *Utilitarianism*, where (as he quoted Bentham) "everybody [would] count for one, nobody for more than one" (*CW* X).

Aside from vexing Tories whose self-interest committed them to supporting the pockets of disproportionate aristocratic representation known as rotten boroughs, Mill's logic of universal abstraction also made waves at a philosophical level. Thomas Carlyle's "Shooting Niagara, and After" (1867) is among the most forceful accounts of the theoretical shift effected by liberal-democratic Reform. That Mill and Carlyle would disagree on this or anything else is hardly surprising. But Carlyle's critique of the logic of equivalence he perceived to animate the 1867 Reform Bill helps highlight in reverse Mill's effort to conceive a typical unit of a democracy now statistically understood.

As he explained with fulminating energy, Carlyle saw the era of mass democratization not in terms of a salutary progress or through the lens of liberal self-cultivation favored in recent studies of Victorian liberalism; instead he saw the fundamental threat posed by Reform as a shift in the matrix of social relations toward number. Quality was now to be replaced by quantity. Despite its grand-sounding name, universal suffrage was nothing more than a perverse version of the Census itself, Carlyle said, a "count of Heads." His outrage gathers into a blast of staccato racism and a citation of history's great men. Reform, he believed, would mean

> Divine commandment to vote ('Manhood Suffrage,'—Horsehood, Doghood ditto not yet treated of); universal 'glorious liberty' (to Sons of the Devil in overwhelming majority, as would appear); count of Heads the God-appointed way in this Universe, all other ways Devil-appointed; in one brief word, which includes whatever of palpable incredibility and delirious absurdity, universally believed, can be uttered or imagined on these points, 'the equality of men,' any man equal to any other; Quashee Nigger to Socrates or Shakespeare; Judas Iscariot to Jesus Christ;—and Bedlam and Gehenna equal to the New Jerusalem, shall we say? (Carlyle 1897: 592)

Carlyle's invective assumes that racial and intellectual factors are the only particularities that would be forced into false equivalence by Reform's abstracting process: not only could corn now be equated with iron, as Marx had it, but Judas was now equal to Jesus and immiserated blacks interchangeable with the greatest white men in civilization's history. (Carlyle's insistently religious language underlines his fear that the flattening processes of what Balibar (2014: 35–66) calls "equaliberty" would be irrevocably secularizing.) Carlyle vastly misjudged the sweep of the 1867 Reforms, of course, which left a majority of urban males disenfranchised, the provinces largely unchanged, and of course—despite Mill's late proposal—kept women out too (Evans 2001: 441). Yet his diatribe shows how the conversion of individuals into abstract subjects registered as a newly acute problem in the 1860s, when a regime of human exchange proper to the biopolitical logic of the Census now became a matter of practical policy. To its advocates and critics alike, mass democracy promised to institute what Mill in *Utilitarianism* had called "perfect impartiality between persons" (*CW* X)—at least inside the boundaries of the abstracting entity, the state, that would produce this impartiality.

It bears recalling that liberally minded authors had used precisely this vocabulary of exchange, equivalence, and counting to critique the most departicularizing effects not of democracy, but of industrialized capitalism in the decades previous to the Reform Bill. Catherine Gallagher has described how, in the 1840s and 1850s, writers spurred by Carlyle's example contested the Utilitarian presumption that value might "emerg[e] from an aggregation of [. . .] facts" (1985: 189). The critique of actuarial thinking animated entire genres of literary representation in the industrial decades, from Condition of England novels like *Sybil, Mary Barton,* and *Hard Times* to sentimental poetry and documentary forays into the sacrifice zones of a newly consolidating urban capitalism. In Elizabeth Barrett Browning's "The Cry of the Children," for example, the wheel's "cold metallic motion" (1995: l. 93) is cold mostly because it ignores the massed-together "children" and their (never particularized) "tender human youth" (l. 92). In *Hard Times,* Sleary's aesthetic ideology stands as counter to Gradgrind's frigid conception that all human difference be treated as "a mere question of figures, a case of simple arithmetic" (Dickens 2008: 8). Engels' *The Condition of the Working Class in England* (1845), meanwhile, also shows how modern exchange strips down human communities into mere instances, a "world of atoms" populated by what Engels, in a term later to be deployed by Marx in *Capital,* calls "monads" (1987: 69). These and other social problem texts of the industrial decades—not a few of which, including Gaskell's *Mary Barton* and *Hard Times,* were dedicated to Carlyle—assert that the final accomplishment of capitalist modernity is to obliterate difference into a false and, because dehumanizing, violent equivalence. Mayhew's *London Labour and the London Poor* (1851) enacts this drama of desubjectification in its form, shifting between generalizing descriptions of social types ("The Coal Heavers," "The Destroyers of Vermin") with quotations from named but allegedly representative individuals.

Liberal-humanist critiques from the 1840s and 1850s deriding the "lives of machinery" led under industrial capitalism (Dickens 2008: 274) would emerge almost unchanged in the 1860s, now to animate what would seem to be a diametrically opposed political project: the conservative critique of the most advanced of liberal platforms, the expansion of the franchise. The conceptual traffic between these seemingly opposed political positions illustrates the extent to which a common conceptual structure animates both democracy and capitalism. It was Carlyle's vexed accomplishment to see continuities between those two modalities of human equivalence and to critique them both—an insight that no doubt helps explain the unpopularity of this bristling intellect in our neoliberal age.

But Carlyle's conservative read on the problem of enumerated man—his romantic and racist nostalgia—might push us to imagine how other commitments might be generated from the critique of a world in which all human relationships—indeed all the world's objects—have been made subject to a utilitarian rule of equations. In a critique of what he calls "the fungibility of all things," Ian Baucom contests the notion that opposing universal equivalence must lead to romantic invective like Carlyle's (2005: 63); it is possible to refuse both monetary exchangeability and the backward-looking nostalgia for what Marx, critiquing this romantic tendency, called a "lost wholeness" (1993: 162). To explain this, Baucom cites the Freudian distinction between mourning and melancholy I noted in Chapter 1, where mourning (1) effects an allegedly successful exchange of the lost object for a new one under a regime of equivalence and (2) asserts the possibility of perfect and remainderless interchangeability between these objects. By contrast melancholy refuses the (false) consolation of this seamless shift from old object to new one, dwelling instead on the non-fungible singularity of what has been lost. Under the monetary logic of mourning, a substitute can always be found for an injury; recompense is always possible; and any given inequality can conceivably, with additional inputs, be brought into equivalence. Against this transactional dispensation of justice, Baucom calls for what he refers to as a "melancholy historicism": a fidelity to past injury that is also an ethical commitment to lost and damaged singularities. As we will see, a similar refusal of historical-ethical equivalence also structures Collins' project in *Armadale*.

The point here is that the texts by Mill, Marx, Carlyle, and others I have read so far engage actively with the problem of interchangeability as it shaped a transforming dispensation of liberal sovereignty in the Reform years—a sovereignty aimed not at disciplining bodies but at managing populations conceived as data. What remains to show is how the genre most attuned to the social novelties of this decade, the sensation novel, emerged to address in formal terms the paradoxical violences of exchangeability and abandonment attending the new kind of sovereign power. Novels about lost women, nameless individuals, and human detritus by

Collins, Dickens, Mrs Henry Wood, Elizabeth Braddon, and others all hinge centrally on the problem of extrojection and abandonment I have suggested is the dialectical other to modern democracy's logic of inclusion. That many of these 1860s novels seek imaginative solutions to this real problem confirms Jonathan Loesberg's point that sensation novels are "manifestations of the same ideological responses that formed the structure of Victorian discussions of parliamentary reform in the late 1850s and 1860s" (1986: 116). Loesberg treats all sensation novels as part of the set "sensation novels," and views them as symptomatic reactions to, rather than as active engagements with, the new political logic of Reform. For the time being I follow that inductive gesture to track the set of novels that most dynamically mediated modern democracy's problem of remainders.

TORN FROM THE LIST OF THE LIVING: *THE WOMAN IN WHITE*

In ways similar to reformist, slum-exploring novels like *Mary Barton*, the encyclopedic compendia of the urban lost by Mayhew and Engels identify frontiers to the project of universal induction Mill envisioned. These inventories of the dispossessed confirm that the fronts of the liberal state's missionary project were those zones where outlying particulars remained to be counted, uplifted, and subjectified—recovered and inducted, that is, into the era's multi-fronted project of producing a populace.[13] Aside from these works of social reportage, another genre emerged to document this movement across the threshold separating those who count from those who don't, doing so in ways specific to the decade of mass democracy. My suggestion here is that a key feature of sensation fiction—the lost ladies, abandoned subjects and, as Collins puts it in *No Name*, "outcasts of the whole social community" (1998: 139)—allegorize as plot the mechanisms of inclusion and abandonment newly characteristic of Victorian biopolitical modernity.

It cannot be doubted that the problem of what Mill called the social pariah was a newly political one in the leadup to the 1867 Reform Bill. In an 1862 review essay called "Centralisation," Mill paraphrases Maine's status-to-contract narrative—and the motion of his own *Logic*—to explain that modernization would inevitably expand the number of those endowed with what he provocatively calls "legal exist[ence]." In previous epochs, Mill writes,

> Law and government recognized, as legally existing, only the few in authority: the slave-masters, the heads of families, the patriarchal chiefs of tribes or

clans. Improving civilization changes this state of things—relieves man from
the power of man, and brings him under that of law.

$$(CW\,\text{XVII})$$

The comment is offered as a simple description of historical facts: "All this
is admitted," Mill says, "and forms no part of the debatable ground." But
it contains an argument about progressive time fundamental to idealist
historicism: "history" here names a gradual extension of the category of
those counted within the protective custody of "the law." "Civilization" is
thus characterized by its ability to increase the number of those "recognized" as "legally existing." Mill lets us see that by 1862, modernization
comes to identify the law's capacity to pull particular human beings inside
the community of the counted.

What Mill describes in the putatively transparent language of political
theory would become fuel for the most scandalous literary plots written to
that point in the history of English literature. Nicholas Daly (2000) has
treated the sensation novel as an aesthetic response to a nascent modernity
construed as sensory shock, and Lauren Goodlad, focusing on *Armadale*,
has demonstrated how Collins' work registers networks of global inequality at the level of historical experience, or *Erfahrung* (2015b: 110–60). But
criticism has also long appreciated how sensation novels meditate obsessively on law and its frontiers. Concerned not just with the vertigos of
urban life or the sublimated relations of core to periphery, sensation
fiction is also obsessed with personal identities, double identities, faked
identities, dead people resurrected, abandoned individuals who get
reclaimed, and, I want now to suggest, with the way in which these
salacious plotlines register as legal problems; thus does the sensation
novel transcode the dialectical motion of political induction into
narrative form.

The plot device of a dead character's resurrection into a new identity
would provide the frisson of Mary Elizabeth Braddon's *Lady Audley's
Secret*, of 1862, which hinged centrally on a drowned person's returning
to life. The plots of Dickens' *A Tale of Two Cities* (1859) and *Our Mutual
Friend* (1865), like Collins' *The Woman in White* (1860) and *No Name*
(1863), among other works from this decade, all turn on misplaced and
excluded bodies that are ultimately "Recalled to Life" (in *A Tale of Two
Cities*) or reclaimed by law (in *The Woman in White*). These lost characters
are most often made to resurface *as* characters in a fashion most vividly
dramatized, perhaps, in the re-emergence of John Rokesmith ("maker of
mist") as John Harmon(y) to reclaim his legal standing in *Our Mutual
Friend*'s money economy, concluding the novel's sequence of Christian-
ized redemption. And though she begins by being pulled down into the

realm of the lost, *The Woman in White*'s Laura Fairlie too finds herself
uplifted, finally, onto "the list of the living" (Collins 2003: 413). Harmon
was recovered from the swirling Thames in 1865, the same year that Lewis
Carroll's Alice lost her identity and escaped sovereign violence, only to
find herself again as a willing bourgeois subject, rushing off to tea; 1859
saw Charles Darnay salvaged from the abyss of France in *A Tale of Two
Cities*; and Magdalen Vane (in *No Name*) reclaimed her name in 1861,
just three years after the female characters of *The Woman in White*—the
novel that succeeded *A Tale of Two Cities* in *All the Year Round*—were
restored to biopolitical visibility.

Drowned, erased, fallen, and abandoned: the 1860s, in other words,
saw literary authors newly preoccupied with the Gothic logic by which
human particularities might be cast out from the field of legal belonging.
Yet nearly all of these stories of social absenteeism offer what Gallagher, in
reference to industrial novels, calls "tropes of reconciliation" (1985:
127–46): they resolve their plots "happily" by affirming not fragmenta-
tion, rupture, or loss but the re-completion of a social totality; they re-
count their lost particulars, re-name their characters, and bring lost people
back into a community conceived in all these novels as isomorphic with
the category of law.

No doubt the mechanisms of democratic reform would emerge as
explicit content in many novels of the period. Anthony Trollope's political
novels such as *Phineas Redux* (1873), for example, retrospectively dramatize the debates of the second Reform Bill in a thinly veiled replay of actual
events.[14] Rather than trace such correspondences, I focus on how novels
of absence and recovery from this period address the question of the law's
expanding reach—and the version of equality it presupposed—as a matter
of structure, as characters shuttled across the boundary line of political
visibility, flitting first beyond and then back within the caesura separating
the biopolitical community from its desubjectified and unrecognizable
outside. Until this moment of decision or cleavage, such bodies remained
in the misty zone between abandonment and identity, stretched like Alice
beyond the very category of the human or, like Rokesmith, rendered a
"living-dead man" (Dickens 1865: 367).

I've cited a series of the most important novels of the 1860s, and
cannot hope to offer readings of each of these texts here. *A Tale of Two
Cities*, in particular, would repay consideration insofar as it narrates a
tension between opposed regimes of legality—an older (and problematically French) *droit de signeur* and a newer (English) contractual
economy—and routes its investigation through the idiom of names
and doubled identities. That conflict between orders of property, legal
personhood, and naming likewise animates *The Woman in White*. In fact

all of Collins' work from this period displays with particular vividness the literary obsessions that emerged in tandem with the political logic I am calling biopolitical induction. (To be clear, I will use these novels as examples to stand for a larger set, returning at the close of this chapter to reflect on this inductive gambit.) Tracing Collins' special preoccupation with legal identity and the reach of law can shed light not just on the predilections of one author who was throughout his life, as his biographer Catherine Peters writes, "intrigued by questions of identity, substitution, and doubling" (1991: 202). It also begins to connect these preoccupations with the changing dispensation of state sovereignty in the 1860s. All three of Collins' long sensation novels of the Reform decade, *No Name*, *The Woman in White*, and *Armadale*, organize themselves around tropes of identity and its erasure; each novel filters this preoccupation through the device of the legally validated proper name to dramatize the great scandal of liberalism's fantasy of total induction: the lost particular.

The threat of legal unbelonging drives the plot in all Collins' 1860s fiction. Centering on figures who hover at the borderline of political existence, Collins' novels during this period rewrite as plot what happens when a given particularity—for Collins almost always a woman—finds itself cast from the margins of biopolitical modernity. "[L]egally speaking," Collins writes in *No Name* (1863), Magdalen Vane "and her sister had No Name" (1998: 181). The Vane sisters, Collins explains, are "outcasts of the whole social community"; they have been cast "out of the pale of the Civil Law of Europe" (p. 139). Written out of her father's will, beneath the field of the state's and even Europe's visibility, Magdalen suffers what Collins calls "practical abandonment" (p. 219). These plots all chart how life "falls away," in Neferti Tadiar's term for the "diminished and disposable forms of life" generated by an allegedly inclusive globalization (2009: 14). Much in the same way that Tadiar, in her study of the Philippines under neoliberalism, describes late capitalism "from the point of view of its human refuse" (p. 14), Collins renarrates legal modernity under the aspect of its human detritus, taking the part of those castoff and uncounted pariahs who belong to nothing at all and who can therefore with indifference be allowed to die.

The Woman in White (1859–60) is the Reform decade's most incisive emplotment of liberalism's dialectic of induction and abandonment. The novel is obsessed with legal belonging: formally replicating the procedures of a criminal trial, *The Woman in White* itself acts as "a supplement to the law" (Dolin 1999: 1). Even before readers have learned what order of rule will be supplemented in these three decks of page-turning incident, law arrives to announce itself as the novel's organizing concern. It is introduced in its universal, capitalized form:

> If the machinery of the Law could be depended upon to fathom every case of suspicion, and to conduct every process of inquiry, [...], the events which fill these pages might have claimed their share of the public attention in a Court of Justice.   (Collins 2003: 9)

Conspicuously framed in the conditional mood, this early sentence, the novel's second, points us toward the interstitial in which the rest of the novel will dwell. This grand "if" marks the distance between the state and its outside, between the machinery of an abstract Law and the stories and subjects that "might have" been, but are not yet, "fathom[ed]" by it. This structure has led Ann Cvetkovich to call attention to the novel's interest in "promot[ing] an extension of the operation of law" (1989: 25).

Not law but "loss," however, is the codeword for the novel's most important turns of plot, and also its most minor: the term and its variants appear more than a hundred times in the novel, describing not just Laura Fairlie's "lost brooch" (p. 275), Fosco's "lost mouse" (p. 236), or Hartright and his adventurers in Honduras, of whom "civilisation has lost all trace" (p. 198). Laura Fairlie is the victim of the book's primary case of ontological misplacement, and the novel refers repeatedly to her fear of becoming a "lost woman"; but Laura's double, Anne Catherick, dead and buried under a gravestone with another woman's name on it, has been absented as well: a "forlorn, friendless, lost woman" (p. 62). That phrase, "lost woman," spans the novel (e.g. pp. 62, 273, 457, 487, 533), a leitmotif of gendered displacement that connects major and minor plots and is buttressed by the consistent reappearance of related adjectives, like "forlorn" (17 occurrences), "absent" (20), "dead" (108), and "gone" (114), to name just a few.

This primitive data analysis stands only to show the novel's interest, across its plotlines and in multiple registers, with the diverse vocabularies of abandonment. When Marian Halcombe engages a housekeeper in a conversation about Laura's double, Anne, Marian asks the servant whether Anne's mother had recently seen this "lost daughter" (p. 209). The housekeeper reports: "'I give her up,' were the last words she said that I can remember; 'I give her up, m'am, for lost'." As *The Woman in White* is at pains to teach us, being lost is to exist in a kind of middle ontological state, physically present but uncounted by law. Alive and breathing but unrecognized by the state's inductive protocols, such characters are particulars but not citizens—in the terms Giorgio Agamben borrows from Aristotle, they are animal but not political life, *zoe*, but not *bios* (1998: 187). Excluded from political belonging, a body that is lost might be found, and might, as happens to Laura, be restored to belonging through the ministrations of a zealous investigator like Hartright. If the Percival Glyde plot reveals the novel's concern with the interpenetration of temporally coded legal orders at this transitional political-historical moment—feudal and modern, customary and contractual—*The Woman in White* also focuses on the limit-cases of governmental induction. Like other sensation novels of the period—*Lady Audley's Secret, Aurora Floyd, East Lynne*—its plot transpires in the caesura between unprotected particularity and the exchangeability proper to a political philosophy of aggregation. The burden of *The Woman in White* will be to find its lost women, to recover their identities (if not their lives) from the abyss of pure givenness, and to pull them back, as Hannah Arendt puts it, from their place "outside normal legal protection" (1973: 275) and re-place them, named and known, into the field of the counting apparatus this novel calls law.

Walter Hartright's often-cited meditation makes explicit what I am suggesting is the novel's central formal and political problem:

> In the eye of reason and of law, in the estimation of relatives and friends, according to every received formality of civilised society, 'Laura, Lady Glyde,' lay buried with her mother in Limmeridge churchyard. Torn in her own lifetime from the list of the living, the daughter of Philip Fairlie and the wife of Percival Glyde might still exist for her sister, might still exist for me, but to all the world besides she was dead. Dead to her uncle who had renounced her; dead to the servants of the house, who had failed to recognise her; dead to the persons in authority who had transmitted her fortune to her husband and her aunt; dead to my mother and my sister, who believed me to be the dupe of an adventuress and the victim of a fraud; socially, morally, legally—dead.
>
> And yet alive! Alive in poverty and in hiding. Alive, with the poor drawing-master to fight her battle, and to win the way back for her to her place in the world of living beings.   (p. 413)

The amazing passage emphasizes three times the finality of Laura's supposed abandonment: "socially, morally, legally,—dead." Invisible to "persons in authority," ripped from "the list of the living," Laura is uncounted by a state designed precisely to count everyone. But this is a recovery narrative, too, and the abrupt conjunction that begins the new paragraph marks her turn from *zoe* to *bios*, from abandonment into political belonging. Collins' ingenious paragraph break delimits the political outside from the visible, breathing world of the biopolitical state, the "world of living beings" that is coextensive, here, with "the eye of reason and law." "And yet alive!": this turn closes the gap between Laura's being abandoned by the law and being inducted into what Mill in the "Centralisation" essay called its "protection." As Collins confirmed in a newspaper interview, "The first part of the story will deal with the

destruction of the victim's identity. The second with its recovery"
(quoted in Robinson 1952: 139).

Hartright's statement can stand as a microcosm for this novel's obsession with the threshold separating the state from its outside. Seeing a lost
person under this sovereign order, as Marian does with Laura a few pages
after this passage, is, we learn, to "recognize the dead-alive" (p. 421).
Perched on the razor's edge between political life and social death, lost
subjects are the ghosts of a counting apparatus that works according to
an empiricist epistemology of visibility. Rendered as non-being, made
visible *as* invisible, such bodies present themselves as the paradigmatic
problem for a liberal sovereignty aimed at, but not yet achieving, a
total count.

Mill told his political supporters that marked subjects of the law were
citizens, while those outside it were "pariahs." If *The Woman in White* is
so obsessed with finding its lost ladies, so consistently interested in
bringing its subjects and characters back into the category of membership, what becomes of the pariahs? Only Count Fosco, the plot's
brilliant and murderous writer-villain, stands definitively beyond the
novel's inductive legal apparatus. He confirms his non-belonging repeatedly, and his self-description as a cosmopolitan "citizen of the world"
(p. 234) is just one way this anti-hero advertises his deracination from
any properly political sphere of membership. Given how perfectly his
plot will bear out Arendt's contention that "cosmopolitanism" is merely
another name for the vulnerability of statelessness, Fosco's pride in this
status proves misplaced.

In ways that accord with Arendt's sense that all bodies of political
membership are constituted by their exclusions, Fosco's final expulsion
from social belonging perversely generates the very community that has
cast him out. The scene finds the political body allegorized by a throng of
citizens both excited and appalled by the spectacle of cast-off life. In the
famous passage, Hartright, in Paris, approaches the line separating his
social community from the abandoned man beyond it:

> Slowly, inch by inch, I pressed in with the crowd, moving nearer and nearer
> to the great glass screen that parts the dead from the living at the Morgue—
> nearer and nearer, till I was close behind the front row of spectators, and
> could look in.
>   There he lay, unowned, unknown; exposed to the flippant curiosity of a
> French mob!   (p. 623)

"Unowned, unknown; exposed": like Laura Fairlie in Hartright's long
meditation above, Fosco is three times cast from the order of social
belonging. What the right-hearted Hartright presses up to is the glass

separating those who have right from those who do not, the legally existing from the "unowned." Against the idealist universalism of thinkers like Mill, Collins anatomizes the mechanism by which a potentially lethal exclusion defines political membership as such.

It is significant, of course, that like Dickens in *A Tale of Two Cities*, Collins locates the scene of this violence in France. The choice politicizes the scene and writes Fosco's death into an allegory of antagonism between opposed sociopolitical systems. The novel is careful to tell us that what Fosco's sacrificial death has excised from its order is an antiquated form of political life, a previous version of law: "His life," reads the death notice Hartright quotes for us, "was one long assertion of the rights of the aristocracy, and the sacred principles of Order—and he died a Martyr to his cause" (p. 625). In expunging "aristocracy" and a capitalized "Order" from the novel, what Fosco's public death consolidates is a liberal community consenting implicitly to a contractual democractic modern-ity, not "Order" but "law," not "aristocracy" but the *demos* gathered here in a "crowd" and "mob": witnesses to an old order dying away, in which group Hartright, the novel's hero, now counts himself ("I pressed in with the crowd."). If this would seem to confirm Goodlad's assessment of Collins as "an apolitical novelist," concerned to naturalize a regime of "complaisant and dehistoricizing providentialism" that anticipates con-temporary neoliberalism (2015: 129), it pronounces these consoling resolutions only halfheartedly or, perhaps, under erasure. As we will see with *Armadale*, for Collins such judgments in favor of liberal idealism come shadowed by darker speculations. If the death scene appears to favor Hartright's right-hearted "mob" over a dead aristocracy, in other words, this bourgeois victory only transpires superficially, since (as readers have long noted) Collins' "strangest," most peripheral, and therefore most revolutionary figures are so often most charged with the novel's sympathetic attention. Fosco may die, but he remains, ambiguously, the novel's hero.

Critics who accept the central analytic categories of liberal orders conventionally chide them for their structural incompletion: they are always unfinished projects. Yet the supposition is that whatever gaps remain in the state's project of uplift and extension should and will be closed eventually: a generalized liberty, disseminated to all, will arrive, in Mill's words, "in the course of ages" (*CW* XXI). But as even its most ardent supporters admitted, idealist liberalism's efforts to complete the circuit of abstraction at universal scale—to bring everyone within the fold—can only ever fail. Logical sets are sets because they include some things and cast others away: likewise are communities of membership defined by the glass that separates them from their outsides. Any order of belonging is thus premised on, and unthinkable without, exclusion; this basic fact of politics and logic both is rendered problematic only from the point of view of universalisms that by definition brook no outside. As Collins painstakingly reveals, exclusion from legal protection was not the exception to liberal universalism's inclusive logic so much as its necessary precondition.

In a well-known speech of 1867, the Radical MP John Bright confirms Collins' analysis. He explains to Parliament that, contrary to Mill's theory of potentially universal induction, which stipulated that everything that can be named can eventually be counted, membership in the set "citizen" could never be extended to all. Some particularities must and should always be excluded. Structurally necessary rather than exceptional, this gap in membership could never be closed: there would always be the cast-off bodies that Bright called democracy's "residuum." He explained:

> At this moment, in all, or nearly all boroughs, [...] there is a small class which it would be much better for themselves if they were not enfranchised, because they have no independence whatsoever, and *it would be much better for the constituency also that they should be excluded*, and there is no class so much interested in having that small class excluded as the intelligent and honest working men. *I call this class the residuum*[.]
> (Quoted in Hall et al. 2000: 98, emphasis added.)

Helplessly dependent and thus permanently unavailable for uplift, this residuum constituted, for Bright, the necessary remainder of a system formulated by Mill and others according to a vision of universal belonging. Bright's analysis concurs with Mill's less celebrated concession, which was that the mentally ill and handicapped—two sectors of society that particularly interested Collins—could never qualify for inclusion. Bright describes the poor, the unspeakably inhuman, those with "no independence whatever," and in so doing puts his finger on what Steinlight, in a reading of Dickens, calls democracy's "problem of remainders" (2010: 229). For Collins it was not a problem to solve but a contradiction to analyze and even to radicalize—a counterliberal tactic he accomplished most effectively through the marginalized, queer, obese, foreign, and disabled characters whom his novels nevertheless perversely imagine as actual subjects. As John Ruskin complained of *Poor Miss Finch*, "the heroine is blind, the hero epileptic, and the obnoxious brother is found dead with his hands dropped off" (1890: 164).

Written seven years after *The Woman in White*, Collins' most extensive reflection on the political status of discounted particulars would dwell on just this problem of who counts, and why. *Armadale* (1866) helps frame the rest of this book's engagement with those superfluous bodies that inhabit liberal universalism's constitutive outside—that zone of indifference inhabited by those without what Arendt calls "the right to have rights" (2004: 296). As the case of *Armadale* will show, not even the set "sensation novel" can be consolidated without remainder: this novel works, not ideologically to smooth over, but critically to contest the forms of human erasure it suggests are generated by modern liberty. Rather than rehearse the affirmative plotlines typical of its form, this singular novel unsettles them from within. Where other novels of the reform decade fetishize progress and propose to exchange a broken past for a peaceful present, *Armadale* asks how the traces of brutal exclusion might live on, unassuaged, archived in the skin and bodies of particular human beings now.

ARMADALE AND THE CHARACTER OF REFORM

Armadale construes abstraction, violence, and political belonging as connected problems generated by democratic reform. This complex analytical project is announced in a throwaway moment from the middle pages of this long, 1866 book about slave money, time, and violence. Here the unsavory son of a man named Bashwood obscures his own character by inhabiting another one. Describing this man in disguise, the narrator tells us:

> No ordinary observation, applying the ordinary rules of analysis, would have detected the character of Bashwood the younger in his face. [. . .] No eye for reading character, but such an eye as belongs to one person, perhaps, in ten thousand, could have penetrated the smoothly-deceptive surface of this man, and have seen him for what he really was [. . .].   (2004: 516)

Repeating the term "character" twice in this short paragraph—along with "ordinary"—the passage draws attention to how a single thing ("one person") can be differentiated from a massive collection of items like it ("ten thousand"). Its emphasis falls on what makes individuals individual, and on how, through a quasi-scientific process of "analysis," one can or cannot tell. Not even an exceptionally astute observer, Collins writes, can "penetrate" the "surface" to see the real Bashwood in his idiosyncratic singularity. A good reader *might* be able to discern the features that differentiate the person marked by the name of "Bashwood the younger" from the one he is impersonating (the "character" legible "in his face"). But here the process of reading fails, and in Collins' knowingly staged scene, Bashwood's ability to exchange his singularity with someone else's allows for a jibe at a modern political order—and a literary community—obsessively fixed (as Collins puts it here) on "reading character."

Taking unconscious cues, perhaps, from scenes like this one, reviews of *Armadale* fixated on precisely this concept—character—judging, for instance, that "Character alone should be the central object of interest for a novelist. And Mr. Wilkie Collins cannot draw character" (Page, ed. 1974: 159). The *Westminster* goes on to associate novels of character with the morally instructive realism of its former editor, George Eliot; in this it speaks for a long line of critics who have praised that author's free indirect discourse and penetrating style—alternately inward and capacious—for their ability to expose the depth of individual minds in a way that seems to distinguish the round Victorian novel from its flatter forebears.[15] But critics who continue to focus on *Armadale*'s apparent preference for plot over character fail to notice that its plot is *about* character—how it can be falsified, how names do or don't match it, how one individual (in disguise) might inhabit several of them in sequence.

Criticism during Victorian Studies' "liberal turn" by Amanda Anderson (2001), Goodlad (2003), and David Wayne Thomas (2003), among others, underscored the importance of character to modern political systems; these critics expanded on Victorian self-assessments to highlight the ethical self-fashioning denoted by this term.[16] But in the decade of the Second Reform Bill, "character" also crystallized precisely the conceptual dilemma this chapter has been tracing, one raised in Bashwood's disguise sequence and treated at length in *Armadale*'s spectacularly complicated plot: the tension between interchangeability and singularity. Citing mid-nineteenth century usages, the *OED* informs us that in fact the term "character" condenses into philosophical dilemma the tension we have seen operating in the Census and in the logic of Reform: it denotes both a general or commonly held morality and also what would seem like its opposite: particularity itself. Character, we learn, meant both "[a] person regarded in the abstract" and "[t]he aggregate of the distinctive features of any thing; essential peculiarity" (*OED*). Marking both singularity and an abstract exchangeability, "character" in other words names the tension between those poles. As Deidre Lynch has observed of *literary* characters, "[t]he character is located—optimally—at the interface of what is particular and what is general" (1998: 46).[17] Or as Matthew Arnold might have put it, character was what kept you from destroying Hyde Park, but *your character* was also what distinguished you from everyone else in the mob.

Armadale exploits this tension to respond to what we can now call the logic of democratic Reform, a strategy that allows this idiosyncratic novel to be classified, provisionally, not just with other sensation novels but with other conceptual texts of the period, including Mill's and Marx's. (The novel will also provide resources for questioning this classificatory operation.) In *Armadale*'s preface, Collins addresses his novel to two sets of readers, "Readers in general" and "Readers in particular" (p. 6), a gesture that announces what will become a central theoretical drama of the novel. While it inherits Mill's assumption of a modern historical stage of equal relations among subjects, Collins' novel ironizes liberal society's tendency to create the economically equivalent, typical units that would participate in those relationships.

It thus offers a principled if self-contradictory critique of mid-century liberalism's domestic project of abstraction. But this globe-spanning novel also expands liberal theory's domestic focus, acknowledging that the Victorian state's mechanisms of equivalence operated abroad as well, in that ever-widening system of actual exchange known as the British Empire. Referring to the novel's "Atlantic uncanny," Goodlad has shown how *Armadale* invests itself in the "disruptive presence" of past injuries like slavery (2015b: 124). My point is that by tracing connections between an older circumatlantic slavery and a newer, equally violent cosmopolitanism (personified in Lydia Gwilt), *Armadale* bears witness to this other, more modern regime of abstraction too. It pursues the British Empire's global money economy through time, from its historical origins in slave-based accumulation into the more contemporary free market in labor that ushers in guilt (as Gwilt) itself.

Collins' 1866 novel is best seen not as ideology but as theory, then, since it performs its own kind of critical link-making: it charts connections among abstraction, exchange, and violence in ways that comment on a moment, the 1860s, when "the free market had become the hallmark of modernity" (Howe 2007: 29). In so doing it provides criticism with new ways of thinking about Reform and Empire together. Read in terms provided by Mill's *Logic*, *Armadale* can be seen to disclose a relationship between the protocols of domestic Reform and those of imperial globalization. By parsing the shared logic of these systems of counting and abandonment, *Armadale* underscores that in the 1860s, it was not just unsavory opinions on race, nor problematic ideologies of development, but a modern and free financial system that both furthered British hegemony and masked its expansion under the sign of peace.

CLICHÉ AS FORM: "THE CIVILIZED
UNIVERSE KNOWS IT ALREADY"

Like Mill's *Logic*, *Armadale* is a wide-ranging document with multiple
subplots. And like Mill's treatise, Collins' sensation novel begins with a
preamble on the philosophical function of names. In the first pages of his
own long work, Mill explains that the business of logic is to analyze
propositions. Because every proposition comprises at least two named
subjects put into a relationship with one another, "the signification of
names, and the relationship generally between names and the things
signified by them, must occupy the preliminary stage of the inquiry we
are engaged in" (*CW* 7.22). *Armadale* introduces this question before we
even open the book. To whom or what does the title *Armadale* refer?
Following the pattern of mid-Victorian triple-deckers like *Pendennis*
(1848–50), *David Copperfield* (1850), or *Phineas Finn* (1867), we might
assume that this novel's title refers to its most conventional hero, the
"light" Allan Armadale. "[T]horoughly English" (p. 55), this Armadale is
represented as typical in a self-conscious sense: he loves sailing, hates
thinking, and sports a lovely complexion and a cheery disposition. But
his opposite number is an Allan Armadale too, though this one bears the
blood of former slaves and introduces himself by the "extraordinary" and
"strangely uncouth name" of Ozias Midwinter (pp. 62, 60). One dark, one
light, one introverted, one plucky, these second-generation Allan Armadales
do not yet exhaust the roll call of potential referents for this novel's name,
for they are the progeny of two other Allan Armadales, the novel's first pair
of doubled potential protagonists.

In total there are five men who lay claim to the proper name of Allan
Armadale. The novel's original Allan Armadale is the England-based
owner of an eighteenth-century slave plantation, in Barbados. This man
is "godfather by proxy" to one Allan Wrentmore (p. 28), whose first name
is Allan in honor of Allan Armadale, but who later inherits his proxy
godfather's sugar fortune—and with it, the wealthy slave-owner's last
name. Because the original Armadale's actual son, also named Allan
Armadale, was disowned, Allan Wrentmore/Armadale becomes "the richest man in Barbadoes," someone who passed his youth "in idleness and
self-indulgence, among people—slaves and half-castes, mostly—to whom
my will was law" (pp. 28, 27–8). Alluding to slavery and sexual excess, this
tale of archaic social form reaches its climax in a lethal conflict between
Allan Wrentmore/Armadale and the disowned son of the original Allan
Armadale, a dispute centering on sexual jealousy and the fate (and fortune)
of a rich English woman suggestively named Blanchard. Armadale the son

impersonates Wrentmore, stealing his intended bride and the English fortune associated with her. But Wrentmore catches up with him at sea, locking his enemy into the hold of a sinking timber ship called, spectacularly, *La Grace de Dieu*. Before he drowned, however, this roguish Armadale had impregnated his "blanching" bride, producing a son in the form of the light Allan Armadale of the novel's main, second-generation action. Wrentmore, now a murderer, goes on to marry a woman of "mixed blood" and "African eyes" (pp. 21, 24) in Trinidad, later fathering a mixed-race son by her. This is the other Allan Armadale, also known as Ozias Midwinter—the one who, as the novel unfolds, is able to overcome his own dark inheritance, ultimately befriending the son of the man his father murdered.

Sensational it may be, but *Armadale*'s double-generational plot also recapitulates in fictional register the more obviously political temporal schemes set out by Collins' advanced liberal contemporaries. Mill's work describes a progressive historical sequence that moves from an era of force characterized by slavery into an epoch of modern peace based on contract. For the *Logic*, this was the transition by which the philosophy of "intuition" developed into that of "experience." In *On Liberty*, Mill refers to it as the distinction between "custom" and "liberty," while Maine's *Ancient Law* figured it as the transition between "status" and "contract." However it is characterized, in this new era of bourgeois freedom, agreements are understood to be based not on coercion or kinship relations but on contracts negotiated freely between autonomous or abstract subjects. Set in the West Indies in the years between 1832 (the year of the first Reform Bill) and 1837 (just after slavery was abolished in the British Empire), *Armadale*'s backstory occurs at the late cusp of what liberal theory understood as a pre-modern, pre-individual political temporality. Characterized by slavery, patrilineal inheritance, and conflicts over women and the fortunes traveling with them, this political temporality is, in the terms laid out by Maine and Mill and ratified by Collins' narration, "pre-contractual."

Armadale's elaborately scandalous backstory establishes the novel's central theme of impersonation, or human interchangeability. But bracketed in the past, in a series of expository letter-writing and dictation scenes, this backstory also provides a temporal-political counterpoint for the novel's main action, which centers on the two modern Allan Armadales who are heirs to these rivals. Starting, as the novel specifies, in 1851—the year of the Great Exhibition—*Armadale*'s diegetic events trace a self-consciously modern plot. But here Collins strays from his fellow theorists of modernity. For where Mill believed that the historical stage of liberty would supersede slavery and thus put an end to bloodshed, for Collins the end of slavery only begins the violence. *Armadale*'s second-generation action revolves around a bewitching series of what Lyn Pykett has called, in reference to Collins' novels, "crimes of advanced capitalism": "crimes which arise from the traffic in paper currency, from the manipulation of documents in a bureaucratic culture, and the control, misrepresentation, or misuse of information" (2005: 149). A writer, a forger, and an expert inhabitant of multiple identities, the female free agent Lydia Gwilt is the most sharply drawn symptom of this monetary modernity. Where the docile Blanchard was passed back and forth between men as an inert object, Gwilt is an autonomous subject, able to alter her own character at will. Bootstrapping herself into any role she imagines, Lydia resembles the Mill of the *Autobiography* far more than any resident of "custom" or "status": Collins exploits this apparent paradox to show that his villain is both a criminal and a perfectly rendered subject of law, what Neil Larsen calls a "monetary subject," whether she has money or is after it (2001: 56–7).

After this professional self-fashioner is defeated in her aggressive effort to defraud the light Armadale of his fortune (and murder him), what emerges in this historical novel is a more conventionally happy ending, one that follows Mill in viewing the emergence of free or abstract subjects as an appropriately uplifting denouement to history's upward arc. This is Goodlad's understanding of the plot, and from one angle it seems true that *Armadale* teaches the (liberal) lesson that the sins of the fathers are not visited upon the sons: it repeatedly suggests, that is, that every subject has the power to abstract himself from his family history by the magic agency of virtuous behavior. "The promise of the Future," we are told, "shin[es] over the ashes of the Past!" (p. 108).

While the Armadales *pères* found themselves bound up by the obligations of status—locked in a pre-modern blood feud—their sons are able to overcome what seems like fate (recall the ship's name, *La Grace de Dieu*) to ratify a peaceful, horizontal relationship between equals. The novel culminates as Ozias and Allan establish a contractual brotherhood: an agreement, sealed by handshake, between the sons of sworn family enemies. This connection finalizes what Elaine Hadley refers to as the Reform era's "shift from an old [...] vertical system of status relations to a new [...] horizontal system in which transactions were commercial, private, and contractual" (1995: 46). Their new union is, in other words, based not on kinship bonds but on voluntary consent: it is a transactional relationship sealed by handshake, a merger. Ozias asks, "while we live, brother, your love and mine will never be divided again?" After which, "They shook hands in silence" (p. 677). This consensual agreement between sovereign male actors rings a change on the indivisible union achieved between

Maggie and her fatally archaic brother, Tom, which was available only in death. Here contract defeats status, and liberty, equality, and a powerfully figurative fraternity (it is not based on blood) close the book on Collins' historical plot.

The novel's juxtaposition of an outdated slavery and a modern union between economically equivalent subjects appears to place its analysis in the territory of Mill and Maine. Following Mill, the novel acknowledges that modern marriage is a contract too, a fact Collins plays for laughs as Allan and Neelie Milroy read naïvely through Blackstone's *Commentaries*: "'Is there nothing about Love?' asked Neelie. 'Look a little lower down.' 'Not a word,' [Allan said]. 'He sticks to his confounded "Contract," all the way through'" (p. 456). The action of *Armadale*'s historical plot seems to naturalize the abstract subjects of such contracts as modern, concluding its historical sequence with a handshake ratifying the equivalence between qualitatively *different* Allan Armadales. This conclusion leads Goodlad to cite the novel's "closing retreat from history and toward post-racial erasure," and tally this as a lamentable misstep in Collins' otherwise radical career (2015b: 132).

But Collins' approval of modern equivalence at the level of novelistic event (its content) is couched within a far-reaching formal and stylistic critique that would seem to contradict it. In fact, and as readers since Ruskin have observed, Collins was fascinated with defending difference, valorizing the idiosyncratic or marginal over the "typical" in ways that self-consciously reverse what Alex Woloch has identified as the bourgeois novel's "distribution of attention" away from minor characters (2003: 12–42).[18] The formal conceit of *Armadale*'s main action highlights this very antagonism between major and minor, figure and ground, as two heroes, one dark and one light, share the same name and compete in structural terms for status as the referent for the novel's title. But Collins' preference for the marginal, idiosyncratic, and counternormative becomes clear in *Armadale*'s treatment of these two potential heroes. The light-haired Allan and the fetching Neelie act their proper parts as hero and heroine of a typical English novel. They exchange banal lovers' talk (though about what their names would be if they were different people (pp. 246–7)), and coo with one another in saccharine tones (albeit as they wade through "the bottomless abyss of the English law" (p. 456)).

In contrast to these secondhand souls, Ozias is what Mill's *Logic* would call an unabstracted particular—a qualitatively *different* thing—and it is to Allan's apparent credit that he notices this:

Allan had seen in him—what he didn't see in people in general. He wasn't like the other fellows in the neighbourhood. All the other fellows were cut out on the same pattern. Every man of them was equally healthy, muscular, loud, hard-headed, clean-skinned, and rough; every man of them drank the same draughts of beer, smoked the same short pipes all day long, rode the best horse, shot over the best dog, and put the best bottle of wine in England on his table at night; every man of them sponged himself every morning in the same sort of tub of cold water, and bragged about it in frosty weather in the same sort of way; every man of them thought getting into debt a capital joke, and betting on horse-races one of the most meritorious actions that a human being can perform. They were no doubt excellent fellows in their way; but the worst of them was, they were all exactly alike. It was a perfect godsend to meet with a man like Midwinter—a man who was not cut out on the regular local pattern, and whose way in the world had the one great merit (in those parts) of being a way of his own.   (pp. 66–7)

The markers that identify these "equally" banal clubmen are social and economic indicators of the English leisure set. But they are also class markers in another way, for they signal the interchangeability of these subjects within an overarching logical category, their "general[ity]." This is classification in the most double-coded sense: going through the motions of inherited activities ("smok[ing] the same short pipes"), these interchangeable Englishmen, all "cut on the same pattern" and "exactly alike," are represented as the very opposite of this text's dark-skinned descendant of a slave. At this point the novel's polemic seems clear, and two orders of characterization, one problematically abstract and one particular, seem in place. Yet even this apparently fully voiced valorization of difference is put into the mouth of the typical hero Collins satirizes—Allan—and we notice, on closer inspection, that this blond man's paean to the powers of individuality refers not to Ozias Midwinter but to "a man like" him. Even here, in the novel's most fully voiced "celebration of diversity," the singular is folded back into the type.

   Internally contradictory as it may be, the novel's interest in valorizing the marginal gives a geopolitical edge to the fact that its most sympathetic character, the one who comes closest to exhibiting absolute singularity, is not English. Dark with the "Creole blood" imparted to him in Trinidad (p. 397), Ozias is represented as the more fascinating of the two modern Allan Armadales, just as the bewitchingly international Gwilt emerges as more colorful than the classically English Blanchard. (In *The Woman in White*, the mouse-toting Fosco remains the most memorable character by far.) Collins' sympathy for characters who are both physically and figurally peripheral cuts against readings of this novel as affirmative, in Marcuse's term (1968) for cultural objects that reinforce rather than stand against the common sense of their moment. Rather than reiterating the ideologies of uplift and progress that define liberal idealism, Collins rewires them from the inside.

His project of valorizing the literally and intellectually peripheral extends to his treatment of setting. Flitting among the West Indies and Thorpe-Ambrose, the Canary Islands and Italy, the novel's dense network of action links multiple points in a mid-Victorian world Eric Hobsbawm describes as "an increasingly dense web of economic transactions" (1989: 62) reaching across the globe. *Armadale* repeatedly emphasizes the fringes of this economic network as the location of a positively charged idiosyncrasy, while its scenes depicting classical tableaux of English domestic novels—the countryside, the family estate—are represented as lifelessly typical, deadening in not only the metaphorical sense.

The novel's famous shipwreck scene occurs on a rocky, gothic crag in the waters off the coast of the Isle of Man. In weird moonlight and with a surplus of particularizing details (including the proper names of specific rocks, "Spanish Head" and "Calf," p. 120), Collins individuates this location, identifying it as distinct from every other place in the world. The town on the Isle of Man is equally particularized, and Castletown, writes Collins, is like no other location on earth:

> It is doubtful if there is a place on the habitable globe which, regarded as a sight-seeing investment offering itself to the spare attention of strangers, yields so small a per-centage of interest in return, as Castletown. (p. 114)

A pun on "interest" allows Collins to satirize the assumptions of transactional logic ("investment," "yields," "per-centage") in order to declare, ironically, that this spot won't repay attention from economically minded travelers.

But Collins himself "invest[s]" no fewer than three full pages describing the features of this allegedly unrewarding town, spinning artful sentences that describe its architecture, its geographical setting, its inhabitants, its "prevalent colour" ("faint grey"), even detailing "various interesting discoveries in connection with the laws and constitution" made by Ozias and Allan (pp. 114–115). When the novel's action shifts to what is described as the "singular place" (p. 239) in the northern moors called "The Broads," we learn that "the shore in these wild regions was not like the shore elsewhere" (p. 255). Similarly individuating language describes other non-English locales, including Germany, Italy, and even the derelict, lawless suburbs of the metropolis itself, site of Doctor Downward's gothically rendered mental institution. (No diegetic action takes place on Barbados or Trinidad.) What these scenes show is that *Armadale* endows the peripheries of England's global network, not its core, with a positively

charged particularity, while the stock scenes of domestic fiction are represented as just that: stock scenes.

The chapter describing the Isle of Man is entitled "Day and Night," a
phrase that aptly describes the difference between Collins' vividly particularizing account of that "happy little nation [that] rejoiced in laws of
its own" (p. 115) and the classically English locale of Thorpe-Ambrose.
Not only does Collins neglect to describe this clichéd countryside
manor, but he makes a joke of not doing so. Miss Milroy says something, and

> Before Allan could reply, they turned the corner of the plantation, and came
> in sight of the cottage. Description of it is needless; the civilized universe
> knows it already. It is the typical cottage of the drawing-master's early lessons
> in neat shading and the broad pencil touch—with the trim thatch, the
> luxuriant creepers, the modest lattice-windows, the rustic porch, and the
> wicker birdcage, all complete.
> "Isn't it lovely?" said Miss Milroy. "Do come in!"   (p. 179)

Thus the English, the domestic, the moneyed—all of this is characterized by both visual cliché and the adjective "typical." (Miss Milroy,
vapid to the end, can do nothing but call it "lovely.") In fact Collins
describes not the cottage itself but an aesthetic rendering of it, in a
drawing-master's practice sketches: doubly mediated, abstracted twice
into images based on other images, to "civilized" eyes the scene is
typical, not itself.

Just as in the depiction of English clubmen who can be exchanged with
one another endlessly, this scene finds Collins satirizing the fiduciary logic
of belonging on another level. Conspicuously *not* particularized, the
cottage is located at the very epicenter of England's "civilized universe";
it thus falls under the abstracting power of metropolitan typicality, where
one cottage can be exchanged with another member of its category
("English cottage") with apparently no loss of descriptive effect. Mocking
the repertoire of clichés proper to modernity's abstracted inside, Collins
directs his descriptive energies instead to its underdeveloped fringes. We
see, for example, that at the "outskirts of the little town of Thorpe-
Ambrose,"

> Nature was uninviting; man was poor; and social progress, as exhibited
> under the form of building, halted miserably. [...] All the wastepaper of
> the town seemed to float congenially to this neglected spot; and all the fretful
> children came and cried here, in charge of all the slatternly nurses who
> disgraced the place. [...] No growth flourished in these desert regions, but
> the arid growth of rubbish; and no human creatures rejoiced but the

creatures of the night—the vermin here and there in the beds, and the cats everywhere on the tiles.   (p. 376)

The picture is far more than a drawing-master's sketch, something different from lovely. In a particularizing mode, *Armadale* traces a relationship between the clichéd realm of "social progress" and the "neglected" regions at its margins; in so doing it registers the economic distance between the two, and their connectedness as part of a single system, at the level of aesthetic practice.

Collins' novel repeatedly draws analogies between the logic of exchange and what it styles as this abstraction's cognate forms, social convention and aesthetic cliché. The multiple levels of *Armadale*'s critique of fungibility become clear in the scenes satirizing Major Milroy's clock, that ill-conceived creative effort in which the "perfect discipline" of the machine's actually wooden characters comically breaks down (p. 224). (The scene finds Collins self-reflexively commenting on what reviewers never failed to call the "machinery" of his own novels.) But *Armadale* extends its critique of mechanical aesthetics even further than this, proceeding to associate modern or "civilized" creative practices like Milroy's with actual violence. Lydia Gwilt's hackneyed lie to Midwinter sets the plot on course toward its final scene—poison gas, an attempted murder, a suicide. The creative villain has made up a story about her past life in order to convince Midwinter she is someone else. But it is a bad story:

> There was nothing new in what I told him: it was the commonplace rubbish of the circulating libraries. A dead father; a lost fortune; vagabond brothers, whom I dread ever seeing again; a bedridden mother dependent on my exertions—No! I can't write it down!   (p. 491)

Gwilt's admission of her guilt frames this novel's distinction between interchangeable literary clichés and vividly particular fiction, wittily reactivating the etymological origins of the word "cliché" in the jargon of cheap printing (*OED*).[19]

Via this oddly sympathetic anti-hero, Collins' autoreferential gesture suggests that, unlike Milroy's clockwork plot or Gwilt's twice-told tale, a specific narrative will have an identity—distinguishing marks that make it singular—while the "commonplace" or commodified fiction "of the circulating libraries" can be reduced, as here, to a list of stock plot devices. That Collins' own novel earned him an unprecedented sum, appeared serially in the respectable *Cornhill*, and circulated in those same libraries are among this passage's distinct ironies. *Armadale*'s self-contradictory critique posits a particularizing literary practice as the realm of the non-exchangeable or incommensurable, an aesthetic ideology whose ironies are further complicated by its treatment of its anti-hero, Gwilt. On the one hand, Gwilt (like Ozias or Fosco) is a sympathetic defeater of clichés; on the other hand, a murderess. And although Gwilt finally dies, this poetic justice was of a feeble sort, according to contemporary reviewers, who complained that this unexampled villain had not been punished enough.

The novel's ambivalence toward its intermittently appealing writer-villain—like Fosco, she is ejected after having focalized what seems like the novel's affective approval—can be taken as evidence of its self-contradictory stance toward the modernity this post-1851 plot documents. Even as *Armadale* naturalizes the freely acting, monetary subject of the contract form as modern (as we saw in the happy ending of Ozias' handshake), it also attacks the deadening effects of that very abstraction: since Gwilt is a murderer, they are literally deadening. As the representative of an epoch of free agents, Gwilt literalizes what Adorno calls abstraction's "rage" to subsume the world (2002: 23), or what Matthew Arnold referred to in 1861 as democracy's effort "to *affirm its own essence, to live, to enjoy, to possess the world*" (1993:5, emphasis original). And when Gwilt wonders "Why am I not always [...] like a wicked character in a novel? Why? why? why?" (p. 559), *Armadale*'s self-reflexive (and internally unstable) critique of exchange logic turns full circle, linking the lethal violence of its plot and the flattening force of aesthetic abstraction. Divided as it may be, this critique of typological procedure registers as a specifically political one in a moment, 1866, when the universal equivalence imagined in Mill's *Logic* was being put into (limited) institutional form by the Second Reform Bill and being enacted, materially, as the British financial empire was extending its networks of exchange across the globe.

Those networks are where *Armadale* takes place. Ranging in time across the entire "Age of Reform," from the 1830s to the 1860s, *Armadale* superimposes over this timeline a spatial configuration that spans the globe: its setting is the imperial network itself (see Goodlad 2015b: 115). At a moment when the expansion of international capital markets meant that England acted "as banker, moneylender, insurer, shipper, and wholesaler to the world at large" (Cain and Hopkins 2001: 163), this plot shuttles over trade and communication lanes connecting London to Barbados to Italy and to the not-incidentally chosen "Isle of Man," among many other locations.

Tracking the movement of money, people, and communications across the mid-century world system, *Armadale*'s double-generational plot also spans time, linking the historical epochs it appears to separate. Like its slave-based backstory, the novel's modern plot can be said to take place *through* Liverpool, that legendary entrepôt of the slave trade and hub, in the 1860s, of a newly global commerce. "I spare you," Ozias writes to Mr. Brock, as the plot begins in earnest, "the account of our stormy voyage, of our detention at Liverpool, and of the trains we missed on our journey across the country" (p. 156). What it means, in a novel explicitly about slavery, for Allan and Ozias to be "detained" in Liverpool is left for the reader to imagine. What is clear is how this plot traces the history of its global setting from its origins in the eighteenth-century slave trade to its current or "modern" phase. Attending to the dark history of the global modernity it documents, *Armadale* reaches as far back as the era of British accumulation in the West Indies; it moves as far forward as the moment when the money issuing from those sugar plantations has been properly forgotten, laundered, "Blanched"—arriving through Liverpool but transformed into cleaner, more respectable English money in the countryside manor of (for instance) Thorpe-Ambrose.

It is true that *Armadale* is partially concerned to expunge the dark past it outlines, sealing it in the past in order to welcome in a more modern (contractual) present. "[O]ut of Evil may come Good," exclaims Midwinter in the novel's final scene, just before his handshake (p. 677). This looks like a completed sequence of historical mourning and an ethical exchange of the past for a peaceful present; yet the grammatical uncertainty of "may" rings against it, and in the novel's ambivalent historicism, good *might* come out of evil, but a series of past crimes, committed under an earlier regime of slavery, reappear as a troubling and unexpungeable specter in the present—the ghost of past damage that will not go away. More lethal than Lydia Gwilt's free agency, more scandalous than Miss Oldershaw's ability to reinvent herself in multiple roles, the primal violence of slavery has power to efface the characters of those who profit from it.

Raised among the "half-castes" to whom he dictated law, Midwinter's white father is destoyed by his association with this economic system, having sustained a "paralytic affection" [*sic*] in the West Indies (p. 15). This desubjectifying disease strips his personhood down to a blank essence, degrading him from *bios* to *zoe*. His eyes roll in his head, and

> the rest of his face [was] as void of all expression of the character within him, and the thought within him, as if he had been dead. There was no looking at him now, and guessing what he might once have been. The leaden blank of his face met every question as to his age, his rank, his temper, and his looks which that face might once have answered, in impenetrable silence. Nothing spoke for him now but the shock that had struck him with the death-in-life of Paralysis. The doctor's eye questioned his lower limbs, and Death-in-Life answered, *I am here.*
>
> (p. 13, emphasis original)

The disease is syphilis, but, unnamed, it is also the crippling, singularity-effacing effect of the most literal form of human exchange. In *Armadale*'s telling, the institution of capital accumulation by human bondage has the power to convert the particularity of its practitioners into anonymized bare life: "*I am here.*" The social death that Orlando Patterson associates with chattel slavery, and that Arendt associates with the bodies excluded from political belonging during World War II, is thus cunningly turned around, since here it is not the slave or stateless person but the master who has "bec[o]me a social nonperson" (Patterson 1982: 5). Inheritor of a slave fortune, despot in a colonial zone, Allan Wrentmore/Armadale is "Death-in-Life," departicularized—the most haunting kind of Victorian object.

Like Mill, who as part of a polemic on the American Civil War argued for the corrosive power of slavery on the civilized societies who practice it, Collins appears here to indulge in the suggestion that the main evil of this social form is its power to degrade its beneficiaries. Mill's review of J. E. Cairnes' *The Slave Power* (1862) argued with a strange assurance that this most basic genre of human exploitation was a thing of the past, an archaic or doomed form that had stubbornly stretched into the current epoch. Mill's historicism had faith that an era of modern liberty would eventually close the door on this violence; he argued, furthermore and in a slightly different context, that "the great extent and rapid increase of international trade" would prove "the principal guarantee of the peace of the world" and "the great permanent security for the uninterrupted progress of the ideas, institutions, and *character* of the human race" (quoted in Howe 2007: 27, emphasis added). *Armadale* redirects Mill's optimistic interest in character, tracing an uncanny linkage between past and present forms of human reification. The very design of this double-generational plot insists not just on the separation between past and present but on their continuity, on the intimate relationship one bears to the other and "the disruptive presence of the past" (Goodlad 2015b: 124).

Perhaps the most obvious way *Armadale* traces the links between old and new forms of human exchange is by echoing Carlyle and Marx to make an analogy between slavery and the modern market in labor. This is the supposedly ennobling institution that is the point of entry, via a newspaper ad, for the novel's murderous governess. When Mrs. Milroy argues for the advertisement that will ultimately secure Gwilt's services, she reasons, "My niece's governess was originally obtained by an advertisement, and you may imagine her value to us when I tell you that she lived in our family for more than ten years" (p. 178). Here Collins makes this respectable woman unwittingly tell us that even in the modern market, a person has "value" and can be "obtained"—even if this servitude is bought on a free market and not a Barbados auction block. Before he becomes Allan's right-hand man, Ozias too has suffered the pains of a free market system, having learned about the civilized world from the bottom up. "It has been my good fortune to see something of Society," he says. "I have helped to fill its stomach and black its boots" (p. 93). What Ozias confirms is that the triangular trade in slavery that made the nearly-dead Armadale "the richest man in Barbados" had, by the moment of the Great Exhibition (when *Armadale*'s action is set) and by the year of Reform (in which it was published), improved into a global system of exchange, uplift, and abandonment characterized by the metaphorical violence of abstraction no less than its more literal forms, allegorized here in sequences of attempted murder, poison gas, and forced detention in Dr. Downward's psychological ward.

In contrast to Mill's paean to the powers of trade, then, Collins' novel charts the persistence of violence from an apparently outdated era of slave accumulation into a newer one, in its novelistic present; in doing so it attends to the historical development of a "contractual" modernity in which violence changes forms but does not go away. *Armadale*'s engagement with progressive idealist thought is direct, therefore, but disobedient. By exploiting the stylistic resources of fiction it reworks the schemes of its contemporary political theories even as it attends to the ghosts that theory believed would soon be past. The novel's bravura closing sentences finalize this double relation. As Midwinter approaches a window, he sees that "the darkness had passed. The first light of the new day met him as he looked out, and rested tenderly on his face" (p. 677). In this stunning conclusion, *Armadale* might seem to perform the retreat from history identified by recent criticism, since it tells us with apparent confidence that an overpowering metaphorical darkness has "passed." But it also says that the "light" arriving to replace that darkness falls directly "on his face": on the very face that, flush with Trinidadian blood, registers the persistence of that banished history into the present, and the future. The novel thus traces how historical injury lives, still, in the bodies of those who survive in its wake.

Attention to *Armadale*'s melancholic historicism opens new questions not just about the aesthetic or political predilections of one author who was throughout his life, as Peters writes, "intrigued by questions of identity, substitution, and doubling" (1991: 202). It also begins to connect these formal and thematic concerns with the material complications of liberal imperialism in the Reform era, when a newly centralizing, increasingly democratic British state, operating under the signs of peace and trade, addressed its power of abstraction to a progressively expanding field of particular bodies within its boundaries. Claiming the power to manage the lives of citizens falling within its count, this state also reserved its ability to exert lethal force on bodies beyond its edges—in those underdeveloped zones, internal and external, where, as Collins wrote, "social progress" was "halted miserably." *Armadale* tracks the broken and expelled bodies whose traces linger miserably within social progress, disrupting from the inside the mechanisms that allowed Victorian theory to conceptualize its modernity.

BECOMING SINGULAR: DICKENS' EJECTA

This chapter's claim has been that Mill, Marx, and Collins responded to the theoretical novelty of the Reform decade by describing the mechanisms of induction and abandonment fundamental to democratic sovereignty. Noting this dialectical relation between inclusion and remainder allows us to more tightly historicize existing accounts of the conversion process of quality into quantity that Adorno and Jameson associate with a generalized modernity.

But it will not have escaped attention that this chapter has performed a series of typologizing moves: it has read Mill's works as a class; claimed examples to stand for larger categories; elaborated a homology between Mill and Marx; and arrayed a particular series of 1860s novels (but not all of them) into a set of texts called "sensation fiction"; it has then argued how one of them, *Armadale*, exceeds its own category. If these analytic gestures have taken the shape of a performative contradiction, as they perform the set-making work of abstraction while critiquing the departicularization such moves necessarily effect, I want to conclude by noting why and how.[20]

Any effort at such reflexivity must start by focusing on the mediating step or translational moment—the moment of conversion between singular and general—discussed above with respect to Mill and Marx. Marx insists that this moment of conversion is mysterious, mystical, or properly unspecifiable in propositional terms: it is, as he puts it, a moment of "magic" or "necromancy" (1990: 169). Mill's inductive program has at its core precisely such an otherworldly mediating leap. In the *Logic*'s many efforts to define induction, Mill describes this "operation of the mind" as an *operation* or a *procedure* or a *process*, an unspecified something that moves us from particular to general. "In other words," Mill writes in one of these efforts, it is "the process by which we conclude that what is true of certain individuals of a class is true of the whole class" (*CW* VII). Though he tries twice just here ("In other words"), Mill has not defined induction but explained its result, restating his original terms ("operation," "process") rather than detailing the procedure they are meant to name. The very unrepresentability of the abstracting moment has led one commentator to observe that "Inductive Reasoning, which has long been the Glory of science," has not "ceased to be the scandal of Philosophy" (quoted in Randall 1965: 60). Mill's proliferating efforts to characterize this scandal of philosophy, his efforts to capture in language the cognitive process that would link the level of facts to that of knowledge, dissolve again and again into a repetition of key terms framed in what we have to recognize as an artful vagueness—what Marx calls a "mystery."[21]

The point is not to critique Mill for a somehow incomplete theory of induction, but to draw attention to this logical method's structuring blindspot, the thing it cannot name—an aporia, we should note, couched at the heart of a program dictating that *all* objects or processes are potentially available for naming. Yet propositional language quails in the face of describing the step that would fit singularities for equivalence. In contrast to Marx, who notes with famous irony that the equational thinking enabled by commodities "abound[s] in metaphysical subtleties and theological niceties" (1990: 163), Mill is driven by a commitment to non-dialectical reason and so must persist doggedly in his efforts to vanquish these subtleties. He refers us to the dangers of making false inductions, cites the perils that follow from improperly using past observations to make bad predictions of future outcomes. Given the provisional nature of all inductions, he asks, how can we be sure that any given induction is valid, that any process of generalization is, as he wrote, "justif[iable]"?

In the end, Mill explains that the guarantee for determining good inductions rests not on the profusion of sensory input, nor any external, measurable, or empirically verifiable function, but on the skill and subtlety of the reasoner himself. Only individuals endowed with the ineffable capacity to produce valid inductions, it turns out, can embody or perform—if not describe—the mediating function between particular and general:

> Why is a single instance, in some cases, sufficient for a complete induction, while in others, myriads of concurring instances, without a single exception known or presumed, go such a very little way towards establishing an universal proposition? Whoever can answer this question knows more of the philosophy of logic than the wisest of the ancients, and has solved the problem of induction. (*CW* VII)

This is how Mill ends his chapter on induction. In this way he, like Marx, leaves an irreducible mystery at the heart of what is still, even after these many pages, "the problem of induction." In the terms provided in this book's Introduction, we might suggest, with several of Mill's commentators, that the creation of valid inductions is a properly creative or poetic event, an "operation of the mind" (in Mill's terms), that mediates in an inevitably creative way between two poles of a cognitive process. As one of Mill's interpreters explains: "Induction is really an 'art'" (Kubitz 1932: 183–4).

For Marx, money was the magic force that could put qualitatively distinct objects into relationships of equivalence; for Mill, the magic that provides that unnameable linkage is "genius." In an 1867 address at Edinburgh, Mill describes Newton as history's most successful practitioner of induction. But this only recast his insight from the 1832 essay "On Genius," written during the early draft stages of the *Logic*. Mill's "Genius" essay invokes Newton as the synecdochal embodiment of the successful movement between observation and knowledge. Here as in the later address, in other words, example stands in for process, and it is instructive to watch Mill circle again the question of what exactly enables men to (as he puts it) "extract[t] the knowledge of general truth" from particular observations. The answer, in the end, is a version of "I don't know":

> Whoever knows anything of his own knowledge, not immediately obvious to the senses, manifests more or less of the same faculty which made a Newton or a Locke. Whosoever does this same thing systematically—whosoever, to the extent of his opportunity, gets at his convictions by his own faculties [. . .]—that man, in proportion as his conclusions have truth in them, is an *original thinker*, and is, as much as anybody ever was, a *man* of *genius*[.]
> (*CW* I, emphasis original)

Mill argues circuitously that whoever is able to proceed by proper induction is a genius, and that geniuses are those men able to perform proper induction successfully. The circularity of this only testifies to the extent to which the "operation of the mind" Mill seeks to specify resists the vocabularies of logical positivism. The "problem" of induction at the heart of Mill's own system, I mean, cannot but remain a problem, since it is unspecifiable from within the stringently non-dialectical critical language he has worked so hard to advance.[22]

In the end it is another fuzzy category, that of "art," that proves crucial to Mill's attempt to use non-dialectical instruments to think the operation by which particularities can be converted to abstractions. Indeed here the aesthetic itself, along with "genius," is pressed into service to structure

Mill's most direct attempts to explain how disparate phenomena might be aggregated into that immaterial or properly abstract object he calls the "type." The chapter in the *Autobiography* that describes Mill's "discovery" of induction is called "A Crisis in my Mental Life," and gives an account of Mill's celebrated mental breakdown that outlines yet again the difficulties attending induction. "At the point which I have now reached [in my work on the *Logic*]," Mill says, "I made a halt, which lasted five years. I had come to the end of my tether; I could make nothing satisfactory of Induction, at this time" (*CW* I).

The chapter on Mill's psychic breakdown has become famous for other reasons: it details how Mill came to see his own legendary educational training as overly rational, too dry and tending toward a diminution of feeling. This dichotomy between a Gradgrindian rationalism and a kindler, gentler capacity called "feeling" is familiar from *Hard Times* and structures genres ranging from Victorian moral theory to present-day defenses of the humanities. In Mill's version, "analytic habits" able to determine what he calls "permanent sequences in nature; the real connexions between Things [. . .]; [and] natural laws" (*CW* I)—these lead to the weakening or atrophying of "the passions and the virtues" (*CW* I). What produced his celebrated crisis, in other words, was induction itself. But if the work of ascertaining the "laws" and "connexions between Things" by abstract reasoning seems to have led Mill *into* this crisis, his chapter also shows how he got out.

This, he says, hinged centrally on the restorative powers of literary art (*CW* I). The Wordsworth poem that for George Eliot modeled how art could suture seemingly antagonistic historical moments for Mill formed "a medicine for my state of mind" as he grappled with the complexities of induction. It is perhaps the Western tradition's most famous articulation of the humanities as palliative: the *Excursion* saved him. Finding himself "at the end of [his] tether," Mill again refers to induction one of the *Logic*'s "really hard knots" (*CW* I). Untying this mysterious knot, naming induction's unthinkable moment of conversion, spurred this famed writer of non-figural prose to produce some of his most mystical writing—and also his most extended claim for the power of literature.

The point is not to critique, under the sign of an allegedly improved rationalism, the poetic function Mill drew upon to explain the transfer between registers of thought unnamable using the idiom of non-dialectical logic. Rather it is to foreground this function of slantwise connection and reclaim it as method: to recover the poetic as a category of knowledge-making. In the "Epistemo-Critical Prologue" to his doctoral dissertation, translated as *The Origin of German Tragic Drama*

(1924–5), Walter Benjamin seeks quasi-mystically to explain that the singular instance or item of historical information—the fragment, the letter, the episode—can stand as an emblem or allegorical representation of a larger whole, without becoming the "example" of its "type." The goal of such an allegorical historicism, Benjamin writes elsewhere, is "to discover in the analysis of the small individual moment the crystal of the total event" (1999: 461). Arranging jumbled singularities into what he calls "constellations," Benjamin's method offers one way by which singular objects might be understood to bear witness to a story that would otherwise seem beyond their own ability to signify, without sacrificing their singularity under the category of that larger narrative. Properly arranged, idiosyncratic objects might poetically express or otherwise evoke "abstract" historical narratives—and true ones— without becoming subsumed under those larger categories.

In the Introduction I evoked the trope of prosopopoeia to suggest that we might embrace rather than deny the function the poet-allegorist plays in the creation of such historical tropes: a critic might speak through her objects. For Benjamin it is only such poetic agents who can, like Mill's Wordsworth and Newton or Mill himself, arrange constellations in which the materials remain only themselves even as they suggest larger categorical claims. The lyric power of those ensembles—their success as tropes—depends on the extent to which the items arrayed for view link to, without becoming identical with, the general claims they mean to evoke. A curating intellect is indispensable to this process, since any instance or object is mute without an intelligence there to draw out of it—that is, write into it—its significance. Any object, Benjamin explains, is "quite incapable of emanating any meaning or significance on its own; such significance it has, it acquires from the allegorist. He places it within it, and stands behind it; not in a psychological sense but in an ontological sense" (1977: 184).

The curatorial approach I have modeled seeks to preserve the singularity of separate objects while linking them with open artificiality to abstract claims I nevertheless hold to be true. This approach is melancholic insofar as it derives from a fidelity to objects beyond the logic of exchange or recompense—*Armadale* is not *The Woman in White*, and vice versa—and curatorial in the sense that it strategically imagines these objects as odd kinds of subjects: subject-objects (in Bruno Latour's phrase) that contain a meaning and significance all their own, albeit one brought to light or, in Benjamin's auratic metaphor, made to "emanate," by the action of a collector focusing attention on them under a dispensation of care.

To be haunted by names, to be obsessed with the lost or marginal singularities denoted by them: this is the challenge Benjamin explains and that *Armadale* invites us to consider. "Let me think," Lydia Gwilt confides to her diary. "What *haunts* me, to begin with? The Names haunt me!" (p. 424, emphasis original). She is talking about the profusion of Allan Armadales, but her comment has methodological resonance here. Mill, Marx, Collins: this chapter has reconstellated its own particulars in order to tell a story about how logical procedure and political practice informed one another at a moment when vast injury was paradoxically produced by the innovations most characteristic of liberty. My suggestion has been that *Armadale* coordinates the logical dilemmas of modern reform with those of financial exchange, shuttling its action across ocean-going networks first carved by transactions in human bodies and linking, in the 1860s, the Empire's increasingly democratic core and its underdeveloped "outskirts." Collins' novel thus addresses itself to a moment when the first liberal empire in history imposed itself across a vast global network—one unrivaled until the even more fully realized moment of empire that is ours.

In *The Life of Dickens* (1872–4), the novelist's friend John Forster included an item he had pulled from the archive, a transcription of diary pages Dickens wrote and then cast off, and which Forster discovered only after the novelist's death. It is a fragment abandoned, a discounted thing. In the final two entries Dickens made to this archival object, a heading was marked with the capitalized title, "AVAILABLE NAMES" (p. 344). Forster reports that this "wonderful list" includes names arrayed into classes and categories, some of which were eventually included in the author's famous novels. But there is also another category, Forster says, a category of names that had fallen out of any category at all. "The rest," he writes, "not lifted into that higher notice by such favour of their creator, must remain like any other undistinguished crowd." Forster enumerates several classes of such figures. "And then," he says, describing Dickens' now-lost page, "come the mass of his 'available names,' which stand thus, without other introduction or comment" (p. 346).

As this book pivots toward the violent outside of Victorian modernity—in the colonies, under martial law—it manifests more directly its commitment to the unabstracted or ungeneralized instance, in both the historical and methodological senses. The point is to model a fidelity to human bodies exiled from the category of legal personhood, but also to those fragments of historical experience unassimilated into any narrative that might grant them meaning. Could the names haunt us? In place of an answer I let the throng Forster found in his dead friend's notebook end this chapter on belonging and abandonment.

TOWNDLING.
HOOD.
GUFF.
TREBLE.
CHILBY.
SPESSIFER.
SITTERN.
DOSTONE.
CAY-LON.
SNOWELL.
LOTTRUM.
LAMMLE.
FROSER.
SLYANT.
QUEEDY.
BESSELTHUR.
MUSTY.
GROUT.
TERTIUS JOBBER.
AMON MEADSTON.
STRAYSHOTT.
MIGDEN.
MORFIT.
GOLDSTRAW.
BARREL.
INGE.
JUMP.
JIGGINS.
BONES.
COY.
DAWN.
TATKIN.
DROWVEY.
PUDSEY.
WARBLER.
PEEX—SPEEX.
GANNAWAY.
MRS. FLINKS.
PEDSEY.
DUNCALF.
TRICKLEBANK.
SAPSEA.
READYHUFF.
DUFTY.
FOGGY.
TWINN.
BROWNSWORD.
PEARTREE.

WODDER.
WHELPFORD.
FENNERCK.
GANNERSON.
CHINKERBLE.
BINTREY.
WOZENHAM.
STILTWALK.
STILTINGSTALK.
STILTSTALKING.
RAVENDER.
HOLBLACK.
MULLEY.
REDWORTH.
REDFOOT.
TARBOX (B).
TINKLING.
DUDDLE.
JEBUS.
POWDERHILL.
GRIMMER.
SKUSE.
TITCOOMBE.
CRABBLE.
SWANNOCEK.
TUZZEN.
TWEMLOW.
SQUAB.
JACKMAN.
SUGG.
BREMMILGE.
SILAS BLODGET.
MELVIN BEAL.
BUTTRICK.
EDSON.
SANLORN.
LIGHTWORD.
TITBULL.
BANGHAM.
KYLE—NYLE.
PEMBLE.
MAXEY.
ROKESMITH.
CHIVERY.
FLINKS.
JEE.
HARDEN.
MERDLE.

FLEDSON.
HIRLL.
BRAYLE.
MULLENDER.
TRESLINGHAM.
BRANEKLE.
MAG.
CHELLYSON.
BLENHAM—CL.
BARDOCK.
SNIGSWORTH.
SWENTON.
CASBY—BEACH.
LOWLEIGH—LOWELY.
PIGRIN.
YERBURY.
PLORNISH.
MAROON.
BANDY-HANDY.
STONEBURY.
MAGWITCH.
MEAGLES.
PANCKS.
HAGGAGE.
PROVIS.
STILTINGTON.
PODSNAP.
CLARRIKER.
COMPERY.
STRIVER—STRYVER.
PUMBLECHOOK.
WANGLER.
BOFFIN.
BANTINCK.
DIBTON.
WILFER.
GLIBBERY.
MULVEY.
HORLICK.
DOOLGE.
GANNERY.
GARGERY.
WILLSHARD.
RIDERHOOD.
PRATTERSTONE.
CHINKIBLE.
WOPSELL.
WOPSLE.

SUDDS.
SILVERMAN.
KIMBER.
LAUGHLEY.
LESSOCK.
TIPPINS.
MINNITT.
RADLOWE.
PRATCHETT.
MAWDETT.

MURDEN.
TOPWASH.
PORDAGE.
DORRET—DORRIT.
CARTON.
MINIFIE.
SLINGO.
JOAD.
KINCH.

WHELPINGTON.
GAYVERY.
WEGG.
HUBBLE.
URRY.
KIBBLE.
SKIFFINS.
ETSER.
AKERSHEM.

PART II
AND ELSEWHERE

3

Form and Excess, Morant Bay and Swinburne

[A]ll this talk of snakes and fire, of blood and wine and brine, of perfumes and poisons and ashes, grows sickly and oppressive on the senses. Every picture is hot and garish with this excess of flaming violent colour.

—John Morley, "Mr. Swinburne's New Poems"
(*Saturday Review*, 4 August 1866)

I am almost ashamed to speak of such acts with the calmness and in the moderate language which the circumstances require.

—John Stuart Mill, "The Disturbances in Jamaica"
(Parliamentary Speech, 31 July 1866)

THE LANGUAGE CIRCUMSTANCES REQUIRE: TWO INSTANCES

The epigraphs above suggest that the summer of 1866 was a challenging one for liberally minded observers of English culture. In those months the Victorian reading public thrilled to accounts of two sets of transgressions, each so lavishly violent that it seemed the precise inversion of English modernity's much-vaunted balance. First, Swinburne. The release of Algernon Charles Swinburne's *Poems and Ballads* by Edward Moxon in mid-July triggered a scandal that has become legendary: the volume "shook an entire generation" (Lafourcade 1928: 447), we are told, and incited critics from across the ideological spectrum to denounce the collection's "unspeakable foulnesses" and "hundred lurid horrors" (Hyder, ed 1970: 24, 26).[1] In the gleeful, hyperbolic torments of Swinburne's verse, even reviewers so sober as John Morley—protégé of John Stuart Mill and advocate of reason in all things—recoiled as though by reflex from their sickening accumulation of necrophilia and same-sex desire. In the epigram above, Morley finds his prose charged by affect, as he breathlessly (and without commas) denounces the collection as "hot and garish with [an] excess of flaming violent colour."

Second, Morant Bay. That same summer, like-minded commentators—in some cases, as in Morley's, the very same individuals—registered outrage at another, and I will say related, dossier of eroticized crimes. This other litany of atrocities took public shape as newspaper reports, cited government documents, transcripts of Parliamentary debates, and quasi-official statements circulated in public media. These bureaucratic and journalistic accounts, shaped into their own kind of art, detailed not classically inflected sadomasochism but a spree of actual violence in Jamaica, an orgy of state-sponsored death in which 439 peasants and one dissident politician were killed, and many more tortured, under regime of martial law. Readers of the dispatches from Jamaica reported being sickened by them. Not even the most rational observer, Mill, could contain his physical revulsion at these reports; and while the task of denouncing this violence demanded what he called "calmness and moderation," even recounting the details of the crimes left him, he reported, "almost ashamed."

This chapter explores the interplay of excess and restraint, violence and law, reason and affect, as those seemingly opposed conceptual categories intermingled in the waning months of 1866. With a self-consciousness about method which I will explain, it reads the episode of sovereign violence in Morant Bay metonymically, *alongside* the generation-shaking effect of Swinburne's collection. This juxtaposition of separate instances emphasizes the non-coincidence of those terms while helping disclose a theoretical and political problem I argue they share. Against the best hopes of a pacifically minded progressive idealism, I mean, what the particular cases of "Morant Bay" and "Swinburne" together expose is that the excess of violence and the restraint of law were not opposite terms, as liberal theory was at pains to uphold, but two names for the same thing. The capacity to kill was the very essence of order, since, as one historian of martial law explains, "in the exercise of violence over life and death more than in any other legal act, law reaffirms itself" (Rossiter 1948: 286). The Governor Eyre controversy conjured outrage but ended with Eyre's successive acquittals and the repayment of his court costs by the British state: the killing Mill denounced as "blood unlawfully shed" (*CW* XXVIII) was shown to have been perfectly legal. Read together, the cases of "Morant Bay" and "Swinburne" help disclose this excess lodged within the law: they shed light, uneasily, on the perverse core of peace itself—a relationship Swinburne's verse stages as the involvement of sublime force within beautiful form.

Seeing how Swinburne's poetry enacts the interplay of two terms progressive idealism held apart demands that we resist the tendency to treat his early work as aestheticist indulgence or formalistic navel-gazing and see it, instead, as political thought enacted in form. This procedure requires, too, that we read non-fictional accounts of "the Jamaica Affair" not as ideological false consciousness or Foucauldian discourse flattened into sameness; still less are these accounts documentary evidence disclosing a historical reality in any unmediated way: they, too, are formally mediated political thinking. Read as instances of thought, the cases metonymically linked by the "and" of this chapter's title expose something about liberal sovereignty that political theory of the period lacked the resources to understand: the apparent paradox by which an excessive, unregulatable force might be lodged within legality itself. Experienced as peace within the legal order's territorial boundaries, this potential for infinite harm would become actual, on bodies paradoxically rendered disposable by Victorian modernity's project of universal inclusion. This chapter advances on the previous one by focusing on the material and legal mechanisms that separated human bodies into categories of protection and abandonment. In so doing it reframes the numerous culturalist treatments of what Mill called "the disturbances in Jamaica" to show how the legal crisis occasioned by Morant Bay identified an unthinkable paradox at the heart of Victorian law, *c.*1866.

The chapter concludes by folding back on its own practice of comparative analysis, reflecting on the metonymic juxtaposition of Morant Bay *and* Swinburne pursued to this point. By what justification this comparison? By what logic the link? The sections that follow shift between those two title instances abruptly, often without transition. This dialectical mode of organization aims to highlight, rather than obscure, the time-honored strategy of literary critical argumentation by which the critic posits a literary instance, adjoins it to an "extraliterary" one, and allows their proximity in time (here, an overlap of a few months late in 1866) to authorize their placement onto a shared conceptual field, "contextualizing" it. As the final pages of the chapter will show, Swinburne's poetry will provide resources for troubling the academic "and" by which scholars almost reflexively conceal from view the procedures of inductive knowledge-making. The case of *Poems and Ballads* in this sense dramatizes how the technology of the lyric poem might become not an object of analysis but a subject of thought: a model or, better, a performance of method. Seen this way, Swinburne's scaled-down exercises in thought productively enact a fundamental fact of political sovereignty that was unimaginable from within the conceptual assumptions of liberal progressivism: that brute violence is ineradicable from even the most peaceful and modern rule of law.

BALLADS OF LIFE AND DEATH

The opening presentation in *Poems and Ballads* is a meditation on violence and art called "A Ballad of Life."[2] In tandem with the collection's second poem, "A Ballad of Death," it announces the collection's political stakes by articulating the key terms of mid-century sovereignty discussed in Chapter 2. In reference to Dickens and Collins, we saw how a newly consolidating British state sought to maintain the biological existences of those within its boundaries, while leaving those beyond its edges uncounted, drowned, or nameless—abandoned to die. As it evokes this dynamic of biopolitical sovereignty, "A Ballad of Life" also sets terms for what have come to be denounced and romanticized as the tortured inversions of Swinburne's art: an aesthetic in which love and pain (like "life" and "death") intertwine, and both are subordinated to the precognitive affective force Swinburne names "desire."

"A Ballad of Life" centers on a beautiful, lute-playing woman, "fervent as a fiery moon" (l. 5), a figure for the spark of poetic inspiration. Unlike the speakers in the dramatic monologues to follow, the "I" of this first poem is unnamed, thus inviting association with the poet himself—since he, like Swinburne, "found in dreams a place of wind and flowers" (l. 1). This speaker gazes at the beautiful woman, is transfixed by her, and then hears the song she plays, notes that shatter its listeners with "extreme sad delight" (l. 56). Like the rest of the collection, this opening poem's thematic emphasis is on "extreme": not a pillar of virtue or embodiment of moderating calmness, Swinburne's figure for poetry is a despot, a kinetic force demanding violent allegiance: "blood burn[s] and swoon[s] / Like a flame rained upon" (ll. 6–7) in her presence. She is an all-powerful muse who exacts worship from "maidens" and earns it from the speaker himself:

> My soul said in me; This is marvelous,
>   Seeing the air's face is not so delicate
> Nor the sun's grace so great,
> If sin and she [i.e. poetry] be kin or amorous.
> And seeing where maidens served her on their knees,
>   I bade one crave of these
>   To know the cause thereof.   (ll. 41–7)

"This is marvelous": in the epiphanic moment that opens *Poems and Ballads*, Swinburne's speaker awakens to the possibility of an aesthetics born of "sin" rather than "grace," "great[ness]," or "delica[cy]." Retooling the juxtapositions he had already framed in his essay on Baudelaire's *Les Fleurs du Mal* (1862)—the first essay in English written on the poet—Swinburne uses a tight matrix of internal rhyme and networked alliteration, along with a formal scheme borrowed from Dante, to fashion "A Ballad of Life" as an essay in poetic order.[3] But lodged within this exhibit in the laws of form is a precise negation of then-ascendant associations of formal beauty with goodness and truth. Swinburne's personification of Poetry finds her image in crime and subjection, not the softening calmness that leads to right reason.

Mid-Victorian links between beauty and moderation—what "A Ballad of Life" calls "grace" and "goodness"—developed through a genealogy that linked Immanuel Kant with John Keats and Matthew Arnold. In his theoretical essays of 1867, for example, Arnold would famously see the finest of literary arts as the epitome of "sweetness and light," the elevating machinery in a program of liberal-aesthetic uplift whereby brute desire would be tempered by the moderating influence of culture.[4] Composed in the aftermath of the Hyde Park riots—another mass political disturbance in the late summer of 1866—Arnold's treatise positioned art as what would cultivate the rational moderation necessary to a liberal state. A mechanism for instructing unruly masses in the virtues of calm, culture was the best vehicle, Arnold thought, for hastening "the growth and predominance of our humanity proper, as distinguished from our animality" (1993: 61–2). But where Arnold followed Kant in separating a cultured humanity from the animalistic drives characterizing desire, Swinburne instead folds these categories together, going further to subordinate rational disinterest to its affective and interested opposite. In Swinburne's poems the vital force of physical transgression (the "animality" of "sin") trumps the virtues of sweetness and light, and therefore "humanity" itself.

In "A Ballad of Life," the allegorical figure for beauty, "kin or amorous" with "sin," is attended by three allegorical male figures. The first stanza's closing lines feature a series of colons, which function as semantic equal signs, converting three successive cognitive processes into the physical energies that turn out to be their motor:

> Then Fear said: I am Pity that was dead.
> And Shame said: I am Sorrow comforted.
> And Lust said: I am Love.   (ll. 47–50)

Swinburne's semantic conversion turns "Pity" into "Fear," "Sorrow" into "Shame," and the most cherished feature of Dickensian sentimentality, "love," into nothing more exalted than its physical instantiation, "Lust." The abstract virtues of Arnoldian humanity are disclosed to be mere façades for embodied impulses, the "emotional, unreflective response[s]" that "preced[e] reflection" (*OED*, "affect," 5a).[5] Adam Smith's *Theory of Moral Sentiments* (1759) had long before argued that fear, shame, and lust are all primal, pre-cognitive physical reactions—"passions," in Smith's terms, "affects" in Kant's, or functions of what Arnold calls "animality."[6] Swinburne's exercise in poetic form rewrites the abstract idealism of Victorian sentimentalism ("sweetness," "light," "love") into vectors of physical matter and equally material physiological response.

Like the rest of *Poems and Ballads*, "A Ballad of Life" was recalled by its publisher for fear of legal action after chastening reviews attended its initial July 1866 publication. Withdrawn instantly from the market by Tennyson's respectable publisher, Edward Moxon, the collection was shortly thereafter republished by a printer of pornographic material, John Camden Hotten. Hotten's version reproduced the original's pagination, green board binding, and mildly decorative gold-leaf flourish on the spine—a similarity of format that did not mask this book's status as potentially demoralizing reading and, as such, a frontal attack on the humane values that literature at least since Wordsworth was expected to instill.[7] Yet the priority of "passion's" bare force over idealist visions of law had already emerged in a more directly political context a year earlier, in November 1865. That month a packet ship arrived from Kingston carrying bundled newspapers and dispatches that described in eroticized terms the force required to put down rebellion among black peasants in Jamaica.

"LICKING AT THE POLICE": THE JAMAICA REBELLION

Eastern Jamaica, early October 1865. In a whitewashed courthouse at the far end of England's largest West Indian colony, a young boy was being tried for simple assault, a minor incident whose fallout would spark what has been called "the most protracted and significant public discussion of the idea of the rule of law during the Victorian era" (Kostal 2005: 16).[8] The reports of the insurrection on the windward side of the island that reached Governor Edward Eyre in Kingston described a shocking anarchy, the very inversion of culture: murdered officials, disemboweled civilians, and a rampage against private property, all sparked by native outrage at the boy's conviction. Eyre later summarized what he'd been told about the threat to his colony's constituted order, providing a report to Lieutenant Edward Cardwell, Colonial Secretary in London, that related the "frightful atrocities" (*Jamaica Papers* No. 1, 86) that, for Eyre, justified the sternest possible reprisals. As Eyre wrote to his superior:

> The Island curate [. . .] is said to have had his tongue cut out whilst still alive, and an attempt is said to have been made to skin him. One person

[…] was ripped open, and his entrails taken out. One gentleman […] is said to have been pushed into an outbuilding, which was then set on fire, and kept there until he was literally roasted alive. Many are said to have had their eyes scooped out; heads were cleft open and brains taken out. The Baron's fingers were cut off and carried away as trophies by the murderers. Some bodies were half-burnt, others horribly battered. Indeed the whole outrage can only be paralleled by the atrocities of the Indian mutiny.   (*Jamaica Papers* No. 1, 86)

Eyre's chaotic vision takes shape in a cloud of hearsay ("it is said"), and uses "the atrocities of the Indian mutiny" (*sic*) to refer to the crimes Indians committed on the English, and not the reverse. But what we should note in Eyre's account is not just how crassly it serves his own interests in defending, after the fact, his decision to invoke martial law. (In fact, as the Jamaica Committee would later point out, the tone of Eyre's report is boastful rather than defensive.[9]) Eyre's dispatch to his superior transforms a peasant insurrection against political and economic apartheid into a fantastic vision of inhumanity itself, where hyperbolic torments—ripping, roasting, scooping, and cleaving—conjure the precise opposite of the regulated order defining modern law.

As we will see, a parallel fantasy of law's absence would provide the rhetorical key for liberal *critics* of Eyre, as they charted the excesses that would come to seem equally fantastic as "the Jamaica Atrocities" became the nation's leading news item. In fact no evidence was ever found to support Eyre's hair-raising allegations—in total, twenty whites were discovered to have been killed.[10] This did not prevent the specter of outrages against law from supplying justification for a massive show of force on the part of the government. "It is very probable," an official reported in a letter to Eyre in Kingston, "that without some military aid, the force at the disposal of the authorities will, in the event of the people carrying out their threats, be insufficient to uphold the law, and, in that case, the worst consequences must be anticipated" (quoted in Semmel 1963: 47). This threat to order justified what would become the most controversial deployment of law-preserving force in the nineteenth century.

The contours of that show of force have been well documented and extensively condemned, by both the liberal Jamaica Committee and the many later accounts that have shared its core assumptions.[11] For his part, Governor Eyre declared martial law in the eastern portions of the island, suspending the normal processes of the courts and instituting a regime of temporary dictatorship that Eyre later said, in a letter to Thomas Carlyle, was "in itself right, necessary, just, and merciful under the circumstances" (quoted in Workman 1974: 96). He sent troops by land and sea to Morant Bay with orders to kill, and charged police and mercenary bands of Maroons with the same task. He arrested a known dissident, George

William Gordon, and transported him from an area where civil law remained in place to Morant Bay, where it had been suspended, and then executed him.[12] He oversaw a spree of violence in which the British command killed 439 black residents by ropes, guns, blades, or whips; flogged some 600 men and women (some of whom, it was later reported, were pregnant); and burned one thousand homes to the ground (Hall 2002: 23). The government suffered no casualties. "This is the picture of martial law," wrote a Captain Ford in his dispatch, "The soldiers enjoy it—the inhabitants have to dread it. If they run on their approach they are shot for running away" (*Jamaica Papers* No. 1, 21).

Swinburne will return us to the topic of enjoyment Captain Ford raises here. Now we can note that while the Jamaica rebellion raised questions of national belonging and racial inequity described in recent accounts, it also, as W. L. Kostal has detailed (2005), posed potentially earth-shaking conceptual problems for a legal order founded on principles of procedural justice and the equal administration of civic rights—that is, on "law." Under what circumstances could modern law be suspended in order to preserve it? Who could and could not be put to death by the British state's temporary imperial dictatorship, and who decided this? Only eight years after the Indian Mutiny, the mandate seemed clear that when the rule of colonial law was under threat, when rebellion was afoot, extraordinary measures could, and should, be taken.[13] (The leader of the campaign to put down the Indian Rebellion, Lord Canning, had earned the name "Clemency Canning" because of his reluctance to do just that.)

Even Mill, the leader of the campaign to prosecute Eyre for the civil murder of Gordon, had acknowledged the right of the state to suspend law at certain "necessary" times: with this granted by all parties, the legal question developed into a dispute about whether this necessity existed, and how far Eyre had gone in excess of that mandate. Still, as Mill wrote in July 1866 on behalf of the Jamaica Committee, the most haunting vision the episode raised was of the possibility of tyranny on British-controlled soil:

> Our lives and liberties have not been, nor can they be safely allowed to be, under the guardianship of the Executive Government alone; they have been, and it is essential that they should remain, under the guardianship of the law.
> (*CW* XXI)

Mill's argument operates under the assumption that executive power and the law are opposing terms, with the former synonymous with tyranny and the latter standing for the multiple processes of checks and balances comprising the British parliamentary system itself. "Our lives," the Committee explains, are and should be under the power of this plural and distributed "law," not subject to the whims of a despotic, or ontologically singular political authority.

By invoking once again the structuring dichotomy of progressive idealism traced in previous chapters, Mill's formula turns away from the question of how "law" might itself rest on the potentially oppressive, singular power he imagines as lodged in "the Executive Government alone." (In this he contravenes Max Weber's canonical definition of the state as the entity with a monopoly on legitimate violence.) But another crucial distinction skipped over in the Committee's account is the content of the pronoun "our." "*Our lives* [. . .] *have not, nor can they safely be allowed to be, under the guardianship of the Executive government alone* [. . .]." It is worth recalling that even the Jamaica Committee's legal strategy did not fully pursue Mill's vision of total lawfulness: the group lodged its persistent legal complaint not against the killing of 439 black peasants but for the murder of Gordon, a single political figure.[14] In fact the distinction between "killing" and "murder" identifies the problem at issue: "murder" names an illegal killing under law, but killing is not a legal category at all, referring to the taking of life *outside* of law—under, for example, conditions of rebellion, insurrection, or open war.

What the Morant Bay affair more than any other episode in mid-Victorian politics thus exposed was how dreams of universal inclusion did more to obscure the problem of state violence than to illuminate it. What emerged was that the legal condition of disposability shadows the very expansive protective mechanisms designed to eradicate it. In Chapter 2 I argued that in a metropolitan context the watchword for mid-Victorian equality was recovery. For urban novels by Dickens and Collins, the injunction was to find the state's lost subjects, "recalling them to life," as Dickens has it in *A Tale of Two Cities*, and to place them, named and known, onto the field of the state's visibility, or what Collins in *The Woman in White* (1859) calls "the list of the living." But even as Mill worked to imagine an endless horizon of equality's reach, an ever-widening list of the living, the outcome of the legal debates about the "atrocities" committed under Eyre would suggest that while a law of life may have been the rule in the metropole, its status in the colonies was far from clear. Outside the bounds of legal belonging, "beyond the pale of [. . .] civil law" (in Collins' phrase), the native Jamaicans deemed to have participated in insurrection found themselves without legal protection at all, a fact that marked their bodies for death in ways that the outcome of the Jamaica case would show were entirely acceptable—that is, "legal"—in conditions of imperial rebellion.[15]

What became known as the Governor Eyre controversy made this central contradiction in liberal theory uncomfortably explicit. Under conditions of duress, the governor of Jamaica had suspended the ordinary procedures of the courts in order to put down what he and his advisors viewed as a grave threat to the stability of the island's proper government. No one argued that martial law was inapplicable in colonial contexts. Rather, as the opposed camps resolved into an antagonism that corresponded roughly to the distinction between liberal internationalists and Tory nationalists, Mill's Jamaica Committee, which included Herbert Spencer, Charles Darwin, Charles Lyell, Thomas Huxley, John Bright, John Morley, and Frederic Harrison, argued that martial law had been misused. As Mill's 1866 speeches to Parliament stirringly explained, Eyre had been right to respond vigorously, but martial law had been inappropriately extended—the floggings and tortures, the Committee thought, had been excessive, "barbarous" (quoted in Hall 2002: 24). Furthermore, the Committee asserted, in killing Gordon, a political opponent of Eyre's and someone not directly involved in the insurrection, Eyre had committed murder. Carlyle's Governor Eyre Defense Committee, which counted among its supporters John Ruskin, Charles Kingsley, Alfred, Lord Tennyson, and, infamously, Charles Dickens, believed that colonial order must be upheld in any case, and that to assume that something so abstract as law applied equally in Jamaica as in Manchester or London was a kind of scandalous joke. It was a blinkered version of the telescopic philanthropy Dickens had already satirized in *Bleak House* (1853), and which Carlyle had derided *en avance* in his "Occasional Discourse on the Negro Question" (1849)—another pitched battle with Mill.[16]

The Eyre affair has come to appear to us a dispute about race, one that tested the limits of a supposed imperial universalism: did blacks have the same status as whites, were both groups "English"? And yet the problem for the black bodies under martial law in Jamaica was not phenomenological, cultural, or ideological, but legal. Did these non-voting subjects of the Crown have rights of legal protection, or not? And if in "ordinary" times they did so, what about "extraordinary" ones, like "emergencies"? The dilemma was genuine, since as late as 1947, legal scholars could lament the "extraordinary fact" of "the complete absence up to now in our legal literature of any adequate treatment of British nationality law" (Mervyn Jones 1947: 1); Victorian legal theorist W. F. Finlason noted in his attempted defense of Eyre that Common Law "only applies to British-born *subjects* and their *descendants*, and not to alien *races*" (quoted in Kostal 2005: 481–2, emphasis added)—a formula that mixes legal status (subjects) and the racial kind (descendants, races) to add more confusion than it resolves.

The legal condition of disposability in which the black Jamaicans of 1865 found themselves, therefore, takes shape as a kind of mystery or muddle.

Understanding it requires nuancing the relationship between race and legal belonging typically presumed in accounts of this event. Culturalist post-colonial criticism has taken as axiomatic that the material violence of Morant Bay follows directly from, or is even identical with, the discursive racism so prolifically evidenced in the period. Accounts of biopolitical sovereignty prise apart this oversimplied isomorphism between cultural violence and the somatic kind. Following Foucault's 1976 lectures on race and the state, later published as *Society Must be Defended!*, Ann Laura Stoler (1995) has argued that the well-documented racism of the Victorian period operated as one mechanism, with others, by which the emergent liberal state articulated its ability to make war. As Giorgio Agamben glosses this same argument, "racism is precisely what allows biopower to mark caesuras in the biological continuum of the species, thus reintroducing a principle of war into the system of 'making live'" (2002: 84). By this reading, race functions not as the site of domination as such (racism *as* violence) but as one tactic in the arsenal available to a biopolitical state as it determines whom to protect and whom to kill, in what Foucault describes as nineteenth-century liber-alism's "coded war" (2003: 52).[17]

The legal structure of the Victorian Empire confirmed this analysis. On the one hand, white settler colonies such as Australia, Canada, and New Zealand participated legally in "the traditions and institutions of representa-tive and responsible self government" and followed the British metropolitan model of power-sharing and democratic procedure (Porter 1986: 4). On the other hand (in the mild words of modern historian Andrew Porter), in those places where populations "seemed unsuited to elective Assemblies"—that is, in annexed, conquered, and ceded territories like Jamaica—"more authori-tarian regimes were established" (1986: 185). In this Crown Colony model, Governors vested with executive authority were advised by Councils or (later) worked in consultation with nominated Executive and Legislative Councils (Burroughs 1999: 185). In practice this meant that black residents of Crown Colonies such Jamaica were subject to imperial law but not fully entitled to the benefits of its protection; they were subjects, not citizens.[18] As Porter further explains, this division in legal status among imperial subjects "paralleled the racial and cultural stereotyping central to imperial life after 1850" (Porter 1986: 4); but the operative distinction was a legal one, since it cleaved democratic participants in imperial sovereignty (in settler colonies) from those who were mere subjects to it.

Mill himself declared that racial or more vaguely philanthropic consid-erations were secondary to the questions the Jamaica case raised about the status of British law. Writing to David Urquhart in 1866, Mill said: "you see that I am not on this occasion standing up for the negroes, or for liberty, deeply as both are interested in the subject—but for the first necessity of human society, law" (*CW* XVI). Of course, in his central programmatic statements *On Liberty* (1859) and *Considerations on Representative Government* (1862), Mill had already stated that not all areas were temporally ready for law, this "first necessity of human society": he notoriously argued in those works that certain swaths of the globe were not yet prepared, developmentally, to participate in the legal forms of equality and participation.[19] Eyre's three successive acquittals for his actions under the martial law he declared would confirm Mill's assessment.

Those legal decisions confirmed—albeit reluctantly, and with considerable contestation—that in imperial locations, politics was in a permanent state of war: the bare right of executive power could show itself at any "extreme" moment, breaking through procedural law with force. As one historian of emergency law confirms,

> In the nineteenth century martial law as a legal concept or practice can hardly be said to have existed in England itself. It is true, however, that it was still an actuality and something of a burning issue for the colonies and Ireland, and in this way martial law was kept alive as a product and a part, although an extraordinary part, of English law.   (Rossiter 1948: 141–2)

By attending to this extraordinary part of British law, this "burning issue," we refine criticism that has tended to inscribe the problem of political belonging into the idiom of universal ethics. Such accounts unwittingly continue Mill's own efforts to transcode the unsettling relationship between law and force into the language of atrocity—outrages against humanity itself. As we will see, Swinburne no less than Morant Bay put impossible questions to this universalist vocabulary.

"SUPERFLUX OF PAIN": *POEMS AND BALLADS* I

Swinburne's *Poems and Ballads* appeared the same month Mill stood before Parliament as the new leader of the Jamaica Committee to announce his intention to prosecute Eyre for what Mill called "blood unlawfully shed" (*CW* XXVIII); as a result they were perhaps poorly timed to elicit popular approval. They did not elicit it. It has been customary for critics to associate this poor reception, "an attack seldom, if ever, equaled for its fierceness in the annals of English literary history" (Hyder, ed. 1933: 37), to the bourgeois naïveté of a Victorian audience. Readings conventionally slot *Poems and Ballads* into a narrative figuring Swinburne as a transgressive hero facing down naïve moralists and "middle-class pressmen" (Pease 2000: 65); in so doing they remain confined to the dynamic of dominance and resistance familiar to readers of cultural studies and the New Historicism. Yet the most articulate critic of Swinburne's collection was no naïf, but one of the most respected and prolific political thinkers of the era, Mill's protégé, member of the Jamaica Committee, and future Liberal MP John Morley. This overlap between poetic criticism and political theory suggests not just that fields of humanistic "discipline" before they were so demarcated were fluid and mutually imbricated—a fact well demonstrated in the pages of trans- or protodisciplinary journals like the *Westminster*, the *Saturday*, the *Fortnightly*, or the *Pall Mall Gazette*, the latter two of which Morley himself edited. It also suggests that, for Morley at least, the response to Swinbune's poems was motivated not by middle-class philistinism but by substantive conceptual and political disagreement.

If one critical tradition has looked to lionize Swinburne for flouting an allegedly imbecilic moralism, another strain has connected his supposed virtues with the republicanism expressed in his later and overtly political *Songs Before Sunrise* (1871).[20] Both tendencies presume the modern critic's superiority to her period of study while leaving unexamined the political investments—typically an implicit secular liberalism—animating this critical melodrama in the first place. Rather than valorize Swinburne's skill at scandalizing the middlebrow, and instead of nodding to the progressivism expressed in his openly republican poems—such as his "Ode to Mazzini"—I propose to unpack the political dynamics of Swinburne's seemingly apolitical verse by putting it in dialogue with the liberal theory it so calculatingly negated. Swinburne's work in *Poems and Ballads* is inassimilable to the secular progressivism modern criticism inherits from its Victorian forebears: these poems romanticize lawless excess and blind power at a moment when events in Morant Bay demanded that liberal England square up as it had never done before to law's relationship with force.

Most of *Poems and Ballads'* experiments in cannibalism, same-sex desire, sadomasochism, and necrophilia were composed in the seven years between 1858, when Swinburne was at Balliol College, and the date of its publication in 1866 (Rooksby 1977: 132), a timeline that places them squarely within the period Walter Bagehot called England's "Age of Discussion." Yet Swinburne's collection meditates not on rational exchange but on torment and violence: a manifesto of excess, it is all pain and sweetness, bitter froth and crushed flowers. Its constituent elements are borrowed from the classical sources whose meters the poems imitate, as well as from Baudelaire, the poet of beautiful evil in whom Swinburne found the limit point where a positively charged pleasure (Arnold's "sweetness and light") coincided with the violence and death that would seem to oppose it. "Not the luxuries of pleasure in their simple first form," wrote Swinburne of *Les Fleurs du Mal*, "but the sharp and cruel enjoyments of pain, the acrid relish of suffering felt or inflicted, the sides on which nature looks unnatural, go to make up the stuff and substance of this poetry" (Hyder, ed. 1970: 30).

Swinburne critiques the "simple first form" of pleasure, that first-order or non-dialectical enjoyment derived from objects that satisfy the Kantian or Arnoldian requirements—disinterested, calming—of "the beautiful." In doing so he announces his acute sense, as one of Swinburne's editors writes, of "the tension of delicately poised opposites," his investment in "the moment when one thing shades off into its opposite, or when contraries fuse" (Rosenberg 1968: xxxi). A dialectical mind but also a theorist of the excessive, Swinburne was also influenced by the Marquis de Sade, although Swinburne's connection to the notorious orgiast goes deeper than the later writer's often cited, but rarely analyzed, sadomasochism.[21] Swinburne read Sade as early as 1862, attesting in an 1865 letter to his belief that Sade "saw to the bottom of gods and men" (1959: 125). This offhand nod to the causal priority of desire will reappear in "Anactoria" shortly.

The role of poetry in giving shape to this antinomian sensibility is evident in the notebooks Swinburne kept at Oxford in the 1850s, when he was composing first drafts of many experiments that would appear in *Poems and Ballads*. Fig. 3.1 shows the first page of Book 11 in a never-published poem called "The Birch." In the poem, Swinburne lovingly describes the pleasures of being beaten with a wooden rod. He lingers on the opened flesh, the dripping fluids, the sublime pleasures of all this. Like other of Swinburne's numerous flogging poems, expertly catalogued by Yopie Prins (2013), "The Birch" is a poem in praise of being beaten.

In the couplet shown in Fig. 3.2, Swinburne's speaker mocks right-minded people who would deny the necessity of what the poem with jarring fondness calls "chastise[ment]." "Never again, they cry, shall schoolboy's blood / Blush on the little twigs of the well-worn rod." Like many of the *Poems and Ballads* also composed in this Oxford period, "The Birch" is written in strict, end-stopped couplets—a grid of masculine rhymes and (mostly) iambs of Popean rigidity that is slashed over, here, with flaying strokes from Swinburne's fountain pen: these marks lacerate the tight form of the poetry they overwrite but do not cancel.

Swinburne's cancellations later in this codex notebook use straight lines to negate a false start in the poem. In the cancellations of Fig. 3.3, for example, the conventional simile "We are like clouds driven by the

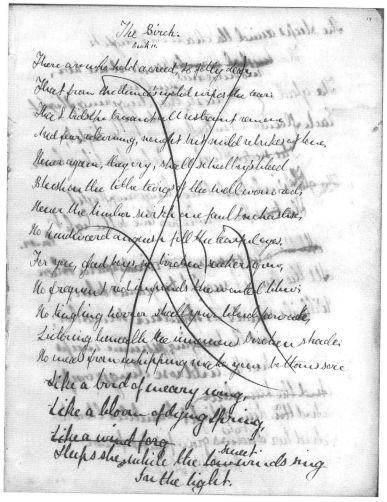

Fig. 3.1. A. C. Swinburne, "The Birch," manuscript poem. John S. Mayfield Papers: Box 5 / Folder 1, Georgetown University Library Special Collections Research Center, Washington, D.C.

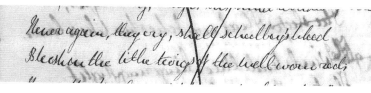

Fig. 3.2. A. C. Swinburne, "The Birch," detail. John S. Mayfield Papers: Box 5 / Folder 1, Georgetown University Library Special Collections Research Center, Washington, D.C.

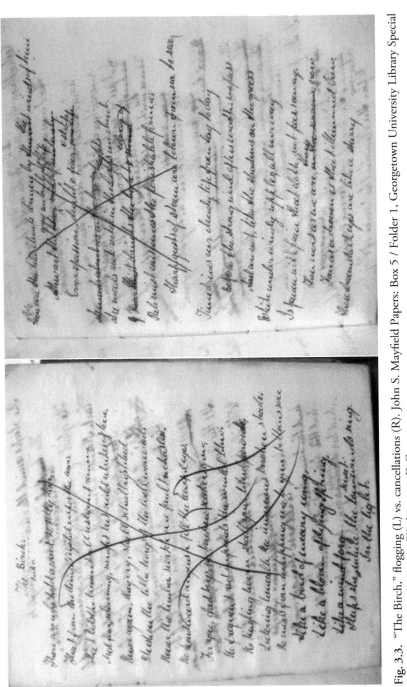

Fig. 3.3. "The Birch," flogging (L) vs. cancellations (R). John S. Mayfield Papers: Box 5 / Folder 1, Georgetown University Library Special Collections Research Center, Washington, D.C.

winds of time" is cut in favor of the more direct and active "Time drives our cloudy life from day to day," which begins immediately following Swinburne's "X." At the opening of Book 11, by contrast, the original text stands in its final version; it has merely been overwritten by the thick, curving strokes of fountain pen with which Swinburne adorns these poetic lines about laceration. Densely inked and sinuous, these markings bear traces of the physical torsions that would have produced them; they evoke for us the embodied processes—the flowing hand, the moving arm—necessary to generate these five- to seven-inch flourishes. In violent, jet-black ink, Swinburne inscribes onto the manuscript of "The Birch" a tension between extravagant lashes and tight, orderly form—a tension between outburst and regulation that this manuscript presentation does not, and need not, resolve. The physical capacities of the manuscript enable this suspension.

In *The Other Victorians*, Steven Marcus dismisses flogging poetry as aesthetically infantile and politically inconsequential. But at least since the 1947 publication of Pierre Klossowski's *Sade My Neighbor*, philosophical and political critics on the left have found room for analysis in the hyperbolic violence of erotico-political prose works like *Justine* and *Philosophy in the Bedroom*.[22] The point is that the Sadean violence of Swinburne's poetry likewise opens itself to political analysis, since it articulates an extrarational drive as the total abrogation of restraint, and figures this force, troped as desire, as "a root form from which all human interaction is generated" (Barrett 1993: 111): the degree zero of political life. Crucially, however, this excess is also, as we will see, uncannily bound up with the regulatory apparatus it seems to contravene.

"Anactoria" is Swinburne's boldest attempt to use the capacities of poetry to chart the unbridled violence animating order. In this monological poem the speaker is Sappho and the object is one of Sappho's lovers: it is thus a love poem, albeit one of a very particular type. To Swinburne's speaker, the pain of love cannot be purged or completed; it is structurally unfinishable, unappeasable. It will not be pacified:

> My life is bitter with thy love; thine eyes
> Blind me, thy tresses burn me, thy sharp sighs
> Divide my flesh and spirit with soft sound,
> And my blood strengthens, and my veins abound.   (ll. 1–4)

The assaulting relation Sappho names "love" lacerates and empowers. The poem's first verb is "is," but what follows are words of motion and force— "blind," "burn," "divide," "strengthen," and "abound"—a sequence that moves out of torment and into power. The violence is what produces that power: "blind," "burn," and "divide" become "strengthen" and "abound," a transition signaled with the conjunction "And" in the fourth line, which suggests that the last two terms are a result of the first three. The driving verse of "Anactoria," iambs thickened with spondees and anapests, underscores the upsurging energy that is the apparently unregulated motor of this poem.

Verbs push forward while the poem construes an intimacy between violence and love. For Swinburne here, both are beyond or outside the purview of anything approaching restraint. Not even death offers a limit to the unappeasable affect Swinburne names "desire":

> Let life burn down, and dream it is not death.
> I would the sea had hidden us, the fire
> (Wilt thou fear that, and fear not my desire?)
> Severed the bones that bleach, the flesh that cleaves,
> And let our sifted ashes drop like leaves.   (ll. 6–10)

Not quite beautiful, "Sappho is identified here," as Prins writes, "only as the effect of a self-displacing, self-disrupting sublime violence" (1999: 133). In a fine reading of "Anactoria," Prins has catalogued Swinburne's formal devices, using a sharp eye for meter and an ear for classical influences to see Swinburne as an aestheticist of the first order. For Prins, the drama of "Anactoria" is that its "verbal violence" "turns pain into poetry" (1999: 126), since it transforms Anactoria's body into an "allegory of sublime rhythm" (1999: 120). Prins' concerns are themselves aestheticist, in the non-pejorative but depoliticizing sense that they are local to poetry itself.

But we can build on Prins' correct identification of the sublime here. In his *Critique of the Power of Judgment* (1790, 1793), Kant had called the beautiful that which the mind views in an attitude of "**calm** contemplation" (2000: 141, emphasis original). A peaceful, contemplating disinterest, one unmarred by what Kant terms "affect," is in this way the condition of possibility for the appreciation of beauty. On viewing sublime sights, by contrast, Kant specifies that the mind is displaced, animated, affected: it experiences a "powerful outpouring" of "vital powers." "[T]he mind," Kant says, "feels itself **moved**" (2000: 129, 141, emphasis original).[23] To appreciate beauty, he further explains, the spectator must be still, void of any engagements, even as beauty itself works to reinforce the disinterested stance whereby the dangerous "movement" of physiological response— "vital force"—is defused enough that sweetness and light might pour in. In Chapter 1 we saw a similar formulation in Eliot's description of Maggie's preternaturally modern intellect, "poised above pleasure or pain."

As if to anticipate Eliot's depiction of Maggie's most mature mental processes, Kant explains that the cognitive remove necessary to appreciate beauty cannot be inflected with any merely physical interest. "**Emotion**," he writes, "a sensation in which agreeableness is produced only by means of a momentary inhibition followed by a stronger outpouring of the vital force, does not belong to beauty at all" (2000: 111, emphasis original). Motion and stasis, force and inhibition: the pairings multiply, and as it makes a distinction between calmness and excitement, culture and anarchy—all of it always folding back toward reason—Kant's distinction between beautiful and sublime responds to and helped shape a long history of thinking on the topics, the genealogy itself confirming that these conceptual categories developed as a political configuration no less than an aesthetic one. Arnold had read Kant as early as 1845 (Allott 1959: 254–66), and while he did not share the German philosopher's rigor, Arnold would translate a version of Kant's idealist philosophy into applied social criticism, calling for an art that would likewise defuse outpourings of vital force ("anarchy"), using a subtler machinery, culture, "to draw ever nearer to a sense of what is indeed beautiful, graceful, and becoming" (1993: 64).[24]

In Kant's political-aesthetic terms as in Arnold's, where a beautiful or calming reason works toward the preservation of order, and the peace of disinterest is the definition of political modernity, "Anactoria" unfolds a mesmerizing counternarrative. The poem is supercharged with the vital energy Kant calls the "dynamical sublime," the forces of nature that "make our capacity to resist into an insignificant trifle in comparison with their power" (2000: 144):

> I would my love could kill thee; I am satiated
> With seeing thee live, and fain would have thee dead.
> I would earth had thy body as fruit to eat,
> And no mouth but some serpent's found thee sweet.   (ll. 23–6)

In this love poem, the violence goes further:

> I would find grievous ways to have thee slain,
> Intense device, and superflux of pain;
> Vex thee with amorous agonies, and shake
> Life at thy lips, and leave it there to ache;
> Strain out thy soul with pangs too soft to kill,
> Intolerable interludes, and infinite ill;
> Relapse and reluctation of the breath,
> Dumb tunes and shuddering semitones of death.   (ll. 27–34)

"Superflux" is from *King Lear*, but Swinburne twists Lear's term for the unfathomable sky to mean somatic injury that would exceed any limit: a superflux of pain. Sappho's imagined crimes are knit together by alliteration and assonance, which link opposites ("amorous agonies") and intensify already vivid nouns ("shuddering semitones"). Internal slant rhymes ("strain" and "pangs") further unify these vectors of human damage. Pain and love fold into a drive toward unity that's evident in this passage's movement from a series of active verbs ("find," "vex," "shake," and "strain") to a strange stasis. The long sentence culminates in a clause that is not a clause at all; a noun phrase sits in place of a verbal one: "Relapse and reluctation of the breath / Dumb tunes and shuddering semitones of death." Frenzied activity results in stasis, and the false dynamism here—action that is really a standstill—replays the odd inertia evident in the poem's first line ("My life *is* bitter with thy love"). This is, Jerome McGann writes, "poetry which fascinates and absorbs, but which in the end goes nowhere" (1972: 41).

How to understand a poetry that is excessive and immobile too? In "Anactoria" the speaker is sovereign and everything folds into her power. "I Sappho," she says, "shall be one with all these things" (l. 276). Here love is absolutism, and as with Swinburne's later hyperviolent heroine, Hertha, Sappho here (in the words of E. M. W. Tillyard), "contains all being and all processes within herself" (1948: 89). This ontological unity means that the monologue must proceed not by development but by accretion: the speaker's being can be modified and intensified, but since it is monolithic and potentially all-encompassing it cannot be made substantively dynamic. At a poetic level this monism means that figural patterns multiply while metaphors mix and stack; the result is a riot of intersignification, a frenzy of cross-cutting reference, as difference folds into unity so relentlessly as to justify Tennyson's famous dismissal of Swinburne as "a reed through which all things blow into music" (quoted in Noyes 1968: 299). In *Poems and Ballads* we confront a world

> Where air might wash and long leaves cover me,
> Where tides of grass break into foam of flowers,
> Or where the wind's feet shine along the sea.   ("Laus Veneris," ll. 53–6)

Excessive in their very metaphoric surplus, these love poems concern themselves with a world structured by killing, breaking, and cleaving, all of it filtered through a figural arsenal aimed at transforming diversity into unity, the many into the one: here air turns into water, which transforms into leaves and flowers and grass before transforming once again into what it was before—the wind, troped as the "feet" of poetic meter itself, flitting along the surface of the ocean.

Excessive, yes, but immobile too. Built around "natural" desire, omnivorous sameness, and surplus force, "Anactoria" also tells a story of consumption. Its drive toward ontological totality finds one body (Sappho's) consuming and being consumed by every other body in her field. McGann again cites Swinburne's propensity "toward forms which do not so much move forward as they spin off from a center, accumulating all the while what can be a bewildering variety of figures and images which are constantly interacting with one another" (1972: 41). These poems operate according to a logic of accumulation, with modifiers added to static nouns that in the end "shade into their opposites" anyway, creating a larger and more powerful whole. The grand and philosophically static monism of "Anactoria" explains its profusion of modifiers, the ceaseless rain of intensifiers and the cumulative logic of Swinburne's notorious adjectivalism: "Ah sweet, and sweet again, and seven times sweet" (l. 117).

The accretion of violence and sweetness in "Anactoria"—its antidevelopmental, additive force—builds intensity while it moves toward the total sameness of metaphor, in Roman Jakobson's sense of metaphor as a rhetorical form that converts difference into uniformity (1956).[25] This monist or rhizomatic ontology—as a single entity extends outwards, horizonally, without differentiation—structured the poem's composition too. In manuscript, Swinburne composed "Anactoria" in freestanding couplets and chunks of them, sometimes just a single couplet at a time. These discrete pieces he scrawled all over the page in an apparently random order, only later recombining them into the full-length poem (Fig. 3.4). The result is a kind of assemblage of semi-autonomous and quasi-interchangeable components. Yet the irreducible unit of the poem's assemblage logic—its indivisible conceptual building block—is the couplet, that rhymed pairing of different lines by which binary difference is forged into union. The way these constituent units accrete in the final version may be why McGann, without having seen the manuscript, compares Swinburne's poetry to coral: it does not so much develop as grow layers, build in mass, make more of itself. The blooming mass of couplets extends over the page, a sprawling aggregation on blue foolscap that can be divided into its constitutive units only with great difficulty.[26]

The poem's rhizomatic composition helps underscore its monistic logic, a compounding unity that in turn helps explain how the poem handles the problem of distance. Another of the poem's distended sentences begins by suggesting a proximity between its two lovers. Such a link of contiguity ensures individuation of the compared objects according to a logic of metonymy. Blood begins by being "against" blood, but pain soon folds these terms into a single sensing body:

> I feel thy blood against my blood: my pain
> Pains thee, and lips bruise lips, and vein stings vein.
> Let fruit be crushed on fruit, let flower on flower,
> Breast kindle breast, and either burn one hour.   (ll. 11–14)

In this play of sameness and difference, difference folds into identity in a semantic and conceptual struggle that results, finally, in ontological totality ("flower on flower"). As in the logic of metaphor, one term is consumed by the other, carried over and appropriated by it to create a new whole. The poem tells us that if a more conventional, moderate, or

Forms of Empire

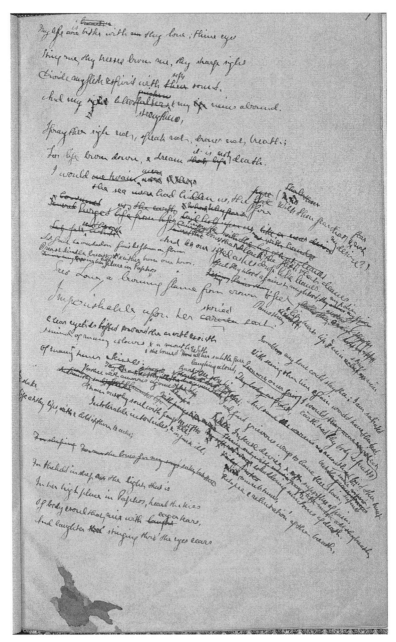

Fig. 3.4. A. C. Swinburne, "Anactoria" manuscript page. Courtesy of Harry Ransom Center, The University of Texas at Austin.

properly sympathetic love poetry might police the distance between its instances, this metaphoric logic finds one thing repeated, redoubled, aggrandized into totality, "one with all these things" (l. 276).

Pushing toward this scandalous unity, the poem generates a model that is the precise reversal of what Mill understood in his political theory as modern. The energy of "Anactoria" aims not toward the diffusion, plurality, or individuation that modern critics and their Victorian forebears presume to constitute modernity, but toward what Mill's *Considerations on Representative Government* (1862) refers to as a problematically unified political ontology. The burden of Mill's treatise is to de-ontologize sovereign power, to sever it from belief, making this practical guide to parliamentary liberalism the precise negation of "Anactoria"—and vice versa. "[T]he ideally best form of government," Mill explains, "is that in which the sovereignty, or supreme controlling power in the last resort, is vested in the entire aggregate of the community" (*CW* XIX). A "supreme controlling power" is, "in the last resort," "vested" in an "aggregate": for Mill sovereign power has no proper location, and should not have it: power's crystallization into singular form is a thing most seriously to be avoided. ("Our lives and liberties have not been," as he said in reference to Jamaica, "nor can they be safely allowed to be, under the guardianship of the Executive Government alone"). In *Considerations*, Mill explains how in the system of representation he outlines, the government's three branches share authority equally, each having the power of "thwarting and obstructing the others" in order to prevent the government's "powers from being exerted aggressively" (*CW* XIX).[27]

In "Anactoria" the speaker is sovereign and her power is aggression personified. Sappho describes a fevered lust for another body that builds and builds, gaining power only to fold back into her own physical nausea:

> Yea, all sweet words of thine and all thy ways,
> And all the fruit of nights and flower of days,
> And stinging lips wherein the hot sweet brine
> That Love was born of burns and foams like wine,
> And eyes insatiable of amorous hours,
> Fervent as fire and delicate as flowers,
> Coloured like night at heart, but cloven through
> Like night with flame, dyed round like night with blue,
> Clothed with deep eyelids under and above—
> Yea, all thy beauty sickens me with love[.] (ll. 47–56)

Like the rest of this poem, Sappho's lacerated trance is here cast in the "stopped form" of heroic couplets (Saintsbury 1961: 341), a form that might work, in Mill's language, to "thwart" and "obstruct." Yet Sappho's stopped-form aria, bookended by a word for political assent that is also an archaic invocation ("Yea"), blows through its endstops, enjambing crucial phrases to enact an unstoppable forward energy (ll. 49–50, 53–4). Three successive "alls"s combine with three "and"s to further advertise the superflux breaking through the thwarting and obstructing seemingly accomplished by the poem's end-rhymes. Through this litany of vexations the verb is deferred; we pass through the compound subjects of "fruit," "lips," and "eyes"—all draped in elaborate qualifiers, four lines in the case of "eyes"—until we reach, finally, the climax of this coital scene, which is not a climax at all but offers an inversion where the release should be: a dash, a line break, and then we come to rest, exhausted, with the physical response of this dramatic monologue's speaker: "Yea, all thy beauty sickens me with love."

Staging restraint, Swinburne answers with excess—but why? From what does this commitment derive? In the middle of the poem, Sappho imagines what she would do if she had limitless power—and answers with a question: "God knows I might be crueller than God. / For who shall change with prayers or thanksgivings / The mystery of the cruelty of things?" Amid the swirling vortex of her totalizing violence, Sappho concedes to the inexplicability of her own desire, its final unavailability to rational explanation. The "cruelty of things" is a "mystery" that is, she suggests, unalterable by the "prayers or thanksgivings" of those, however well meaning, who would intervene against it. These are lines 152–4 of the 304-line poem. Astonishingly, this means that Sappho's dark political theology, her desire for a violence that would exceed any supervening power—"God knows I might be crueller than God"—sits at the precise mathematical center of these layers of coral accumulation. Like a pearl adding opalescent layers one by one around a grain of sand, the poem's accreted surplus can now be seen to have built up around a central, irreducible mystery that is, at bottom, a political one. The center of this pearl is an aporia also known to the black Jamaicans who found themselves, by whip and sword and hanging rope, on the wrong end of "exigency." "The mystery of the cruelty of things": the unjustified, unjustifiable violence that is the obscene center of sovereignty itself (Fig. 3.5).

This fact may help explain why Tillyard, in his post World War II assessment of Swinburne, asserts flatly of another poem that it "contain[s] the doctrine of fascism" (1948: 4). Pursuing a reading of "Hertha" not unrelated to the one of "Anactoria" I've just attempted, Tillyard files Swinburne's verse into a category he borrows from George Santayana, "the Poetry of Barbarism" (1948: 92). With fascinated disbelief—Tillyard seems to love the poem, but is flummoxed by its anti-liberal worldview—he explains that Swinburne rejects the progressive notion that history moves toward increasing comfort and peace, and instead construes "progress" to name the

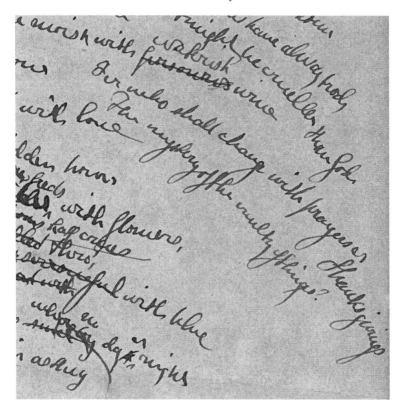

Fig. 3.5. "But who shall change with prayers or thanksgivings / The mystery of the cruelty of things?" A. C. Swinburne, "Anactoria" manuscript, detail of what would become lines 153–4. Courtesy of Harry Ransom Center, The University of Texas at Austin.

successive removal of restraints, the gradual realization of pure essence. ("To many of his age's activities," Tillyard says, Swinburne "would have thought himself hostile" (1948: 103).) Tillyard cites Swinburne's "fanaticism" (p. 111), his anti-individualism, and evinces some internal conflict when he notes that "Swinburne would never himself have been a Fascist, but he was the unsuspecting mouthpiece of the ideas out of which Fascist doctrine was made" (p. 97). "The intoxicating quality of Swinburne's verse," he concludes, tempts otherwise right thinking individuals to "surrender the individual will" to forces beyond themselves (p. 101). If Tillyard's own postwar historical position forces him to associate collective life with Fascism, he concedes that Swinburne could not have been precisely Fascist—but only because the "immense apparent stability" of Victorian England authorized him

to experiment with "irresponsible" ideas (1948: 97). What Tillyard's asssess-
ment symptomatically reveals is how successfully a poem like "Anactoria"
scrambles, and by scrambling detonates, the conceptual presumptions of
progressive idealism.

In "Anactoria" the scene of unspeakable violence is hermetically sealed
and mediated by myth, locked in a vacuum of pre-classical Greek history
and poetic autoreferentiality. It seems, as Prins notes, to be centrally
concerned with poetry itself. The poem's extravagant aestheticism seems
willfully to refuse any concrete historical reference, a deracination that
suggests why efforts to politicize Swinburne's verse in contextual ways—
by reading for content—can only fail.

But another of the monologues in *Poems and Ballads*, "Laus Veneris,"
specifies and concretizes its field of reference while radicalizing further the
sadomasochistic reconfiguration of sovereignty theory in "Anactoria." This
poem in praise of Venus repeats the dialectical energy of "Anactoria" but
places its political-erotic drive toward death in the context of colonial war.
In the poem the knight Tannhäuser, fresh from a Christian crusade,
considers the sources and extent of love. This poem finds its speaker (now
male) complaining that more moderate lovers "pluck sweet fruit of life and
eat" (l. 98). His derisive suggestion is that normal lovers comport themselves
toward their loved objects according to a logic of first-order pleasure that
presumes a relationship of autonomous separation and polices distance
between lover and loved. This form of love is made moderate, here, by
the cloyingly smooth internal rhyme of "sweet" and "eat." For these lovers,
Swinburne tells us through Tannhäuser, the plucking and tasting of a loved
object might seem to be an act of "sweet[ness]," of light, an act (we can
now say) that operates according to the calming logic of neo-Kantian or
Arnoldian beauty that provided a "higher" pleasure to Maggie Tulliver.
Swinburne's obsessive knight rejects this and construes love, instead, as an
all-devouring process. Some lovers regard their object from a polite distance,

> But me the hot and hungry days devour,
> And in my mouth no fruit of theirs is sweet.
>
> No fruit of theirs, but fruit of my desire,
> For her love's sake whose lips through mine respire;
>   Her eyelids on her eyes like flower on flower,
> Mine eyelids on mine eyes like fire on fire.   (ll. 99–104)

If there is light to go with this sweetness it comes from "fire." Like Sappho,
Tannhäuser here folds together with his object of lust, cancelling distance
and becoming one with her. As Swinburne's verse specifies, they share the
same lungs.

The knight's obsessive consumption of and consumption by his love's object, his oneness with what he desires, "does not," as Kathy Psomiades writes, "allow for the distant dispassionate musing that usually characterizes beauty's onlookers" (1997: 82). Psomiades alerts us to the closeness here, as a repetition of key terms combines with a reiterative structure, the doubled sequence joined by a simile: "her eyelids on her eyes like flower on flower." Is this sameness, or difference, or, rather, a totalization that obliterates that distinction? As Psomiades writes of another section in "Laus Veneris": "*Too close* to be distanced and described [...] or contemplated in its loveliness, Venus' face is part of Tannhäuser's flesh" (1997: 89, emphasis added). This folding-together collapses the metaphysical distinction between autonomous instances on which pluralism depends; Swinburne's metaphoric procedure accomplishes instead the conversion of difference into totality that Deleuze in *A Thousand Plateaus* enacts with a performative formula: "PLURALISM = MONISM" (1987: 20).

"I Sappho shall be one with all these things": Prins cites this line of "Anactoria" but explains that Sappho is paradoxically *not* driving toward a stable or completed self: her violence may never be completed. Recall the conditional tense: "I *would* my love could kill thee." The observation allows for an analysis of how pleasure is figured in this and other of *Poems and Ballads*' sadistic experiments. Writing of Baudelaire, Leo Bersani describes the libidinal pleasure associated with this type of antinomian tendency toward the sublime. Bersani is discussing how Baudelaire prefigures Freud's understanding of sadism (in Freud's "Instincts and Their Vicissitudes" [1915]) to describe how "agonies" could produce a "second-order" pleasure whose proper libidinal result derived from the fact that it exceeds all boundaries of experience—a superflux of pain. Bersani writes:

> The usual notion of pleasure and pain would therefore have to be revised and subordinated to a more inclusive view of sexual pleasure as a component of all sensations which go beyond a certain threshold of intensity. [...] Pleasure and pain continue to be different sensations, but, to a certain extent, they are both experienced as sexual pleasure when they are strong enough to shatter a certain stability or equilibrium of the self. [...] The crucial point to hold onto is the association of sexuality with the organism's experience of something excessive. [...] [T]he pleasurable excitement of sexuality occurs when the body's normal range of sensation is exceeded and when the organization of the self is momentarily disturbed (deranged) by sensations somehow 'beyond' those compatible with psychic organization. (1977: 76–7)

Describing Baudelaire, Bersani also assesses the structure of thanophilic excess in *Poems and Ballads*. Here outpourings of Arnoldian animality repeatedly, even flagrantly "go beyond," in Bersani's words, "a certain threshold of intensity," until, as a character in Swinburne's only novel, *Lesbia Brandon* (written 1859–68), puts it, "one can't tell where the pain or the pleasure begins or ends" (quoted in Barrett 1993: 114).[28] I have offered a short, programmatic reading of "Anactoria" and nodded to "Laus Veneris" to make a claim about the place violence and excess occupy in this collection. A more sustained engagement (with readings of, for example, "Faustine," "The Leper," and "Dolores" especially) would show that, with local modifications and with certain ironic complexities, Swinburne's first major collection undertakes a program of exploring what Bersani calls in reference to Baudelaire "a dizzying transgression of limits which has no other end but its own explosive and fatal force" (Bersani 1977: 89).

Poems and Ballads' vision of power as excessive and singular and aimed toward death did not help its author's position with Victorian critics, nor yet with their neo-Victorian epigones like Tillyard. The collection's reception upon its original publication has become legendary. In one of the most often cited of all Victorian reviews, Robert Buchanan would later (in 1871) denounce Swinburne alongside D. G. Rossetti for what he saw as their perverse voluptuousness, in an article he called "The Fleshly School of Poetry." But the critic also wrote a review of *Poems and Ballads* in the summer of 1866, one of three hostile notices of the work to appear on 4 August. In that earlier note Buchanan observed that where Shelley and Keats showed the virtue of "passionate sweetness" and Wordsworth modeled "cold severity," Swinburne "stain[s] the current of our literature with impure thought" (Hyder, ed. 1970: 30). Insincere even in his perversity, Swinburne is, Buchanan concludes, an unworthy successor to the "transcendent purity" of England's poetic tradition (Hyder, ed. 1970: 30). Recurring to a standard lexicon of moralized denunciation, though one that is also, in its degraded way, neo-Kantian—"insincerity," "purity"—this review did not disturb Swinburne.[29] Its terms, as he recognized, recycled reactionary tropes in ways that the poet's friends, who had predicted the shock his volume would produce, had warned him about.

Another notice, by John Morley, was not so easily written off. Morley avoided reference to Swinburne's blasphemy and paganism in order to object in the more piercing terms that, his biographers note, affected Swinburne more than any other of *Poems and Ballads*' many negative reviews. In his article on 4 August 1866, just five days after Mill appeared before Parliament to denounce "the Disturbances in Jamaica," Morley identified another set of disturbances for readers of *The Saturday Review*:

> [Swinburne] is so firmly and avowedly fixed in an attitude of revolt against the current notions of decency and dignity and social duty that to beg of him

to become a little more decent, to fly a little less persistently and gleefully to the animal side of human nature, is simply to beg him to be something different from Mr. Swinburne. (Hyder, ed. 1970: 22–3)

Morley's critique deploys the language of moralized idealism we have traced so far: here "decency," "dignity," and "social duty" oppose "the animal side of human nature." Morley sees in Swinburne a program of affective deregulation that arrays him in opposition to the political spirit of the age, a spirit that Morley, like his predecessors in this idealist tradition, conceives in terms of limitation. (As one account of Morley's political career attests: "Progress, ordered movement, inevitable improvement—these are the themes in which Morley wanted to believe" (Hamer 1968: 19).[30]) In his literary review, Morley recognizes in Swinburne the antithesis of this orderly upward motion, citing "the nameless shameless abominations which inspire him with such frenzied delight" (Hyder, ed. 1970: 23).

But if the critic's own poetic zeal in this assessment, as he rhymes "nameless" and "shameless," makes Swinburne's point that restraint and violence share an equally zealous core, Morley gains focus as the essay goes on. His account continues by identifying in Swinburne "a mind all aflame with the feverish carnality of a schoolboy" (Hyder, ed. 1970: 23). He is obsessed with crime, vexation, stinging, biting—and "much else that is nameless and abominable" (p. 24). "Mr. Swinburne," Morley writes, "riots in the profusion of colour of the most garish and heated kind" (p. 26). (He again, in the passage I cite as an epigraph, calls attention to "the excess of flaming violent colour" and the "biting and burning" (p. 25) throughout these pages.) Too vivid by half, the sensual supercharging "inspir[ing]" Swinburne's verse threatens the equilibrium that a cooler rationality would secure, and opens up the dizzy possibilities of what can happen when reserve is abandoned: "There are not twenty stanzas in the whole book which have the faintest tincture of soberness. We are in the midst of fire and serpents, wine and ashes, blood and foam, and a hundred lurid horrors" (p. 26).

The point is that the protégé of Mill and future MP here casts his objection to Swinburne's poetics in directly political terms. In doing this he puts his finger on what I am suggesting is *Poems and Ballads* political theory of affective surplus. During the summer of 1866 Morley also reviewed Eliot's *Felix Holt* (in the *Saturday Review* of 16 June). In that anti-political novel, the follower of Mill found much to appreciate. The novel that featured its title character defusing social revolution through the persuasive power of sober speech stirred from Morley the highest compliments: Eliot, Morley thought, "looks out upon the world with the most entire enjoyment of all the good that there is in it to enjoy, and with an enlarged compassion for all the ill that there is in it to pity" (Morley 1866: 723). Citing Eliot's expansive broadness of mind—her "enlarged compassion"—Morley well identifies the cosmopolitan wandering I described in Chapter 1 as Eliot's content for the term "modernity." In doing so the critic makes plain his own political-aesthetic affection for "the benign, elevated, and calm spirit which breathes through the authoress' style" (Morley 1866: 723). Rather than read these as conventional phrases of bourgeois praise, I am suggesting that they are also coded political messages, where calmness, elevatedness, and dispassion—what Amanda Anderson calls "the powers of distance"—have themselves been elevated into what I am suggesting is the political aesthetic of mid-century progressive idealism.

Morley sums up his August 1866 denunciation of *Poems and Ballads* with praise, but soon unfurls the now explicitly politicized terms of his objections. "Not all the fervour of his imagination," Morley writes, not

> the beauty of his melody, the splendour of his many phrases and pictures can blind us to the absence of judgment and reason, the reckless contempt for anything like a balance [. . .]. The lurid clouds of lust or of fiery despair and defiance never lift to let us see the pure and peaceful and bounteous kindly aspects of the great landscape of human life.   (Hyder, ed. 1970: 29)

Swinburne's poems articulate an alternative vision that Morley deals with in starkly political terms: devoid of "judgment and reason," evincing "reckless contempt for anything like a balance," *Poems and Ballads* represents for Morley's account, as for my own, the diametric inversion of what the liberal imagination envisioned as law.[31] It is customary for criticism to invoke Swinburne's reviews as evidence of a hopelessly backward bourgeoisie, the "middle-class pressmen" Allison Pease dismisses in her reading of Swinburne in *Modernism, Mass Culture, and the Aesthetics of Obscenity* (2000: 65). But I have quoted Morley's review at length because I take his judgment to reveal the operative categories of advanced liberal thought at this post-Mutiny, Reform-era moment. Identifying correctly the antinomian surplus Swinburne took pains to encode in his verse, Morley's reading articulates as an aesthetic problem the very conceptual antagonism between restraint and surplus that would become evident shortly, as a more widely touted crisis took shape over what role violence might play in the benign and elevated mission of the British Empire.

"OUT THERE, YOU SEE REAL GOVERNMENT": MILL *AVEC* STEPHEN

In an 1868 letter Mill noted with due horror what he called the "wanton torture & death of many hundred men & women" (*CW* XVI) during Eyre's temporary dictatorship in Jamaica. But Mill moves on from this to explain that it is *not* these horrors that motivate his interest. The Jamaican crimes were no doubt terrible, Mill writes.

> Yet if all human sympathies could be cast aside together, the importance of instituting a judicial enquiry into the proceedings in Jamaica would still be paramount in the eyes of all thinking persons who look upon law & justice as the foundation of order & civilization.   (*CW* XVI)

Parallel ampersands betray the reflexive equation Mill's thought presumes between "law & justice" and "order & civilization," where each side of the equation is "foundation[al]" to the other. The Jamaica case threatened both. Before breaking with Mill's Jamaica Committee in June of 1866 over a dispute about precisely the question of law's relation to force, James Fitzjames Stephen served as its lead counsel, producing in that spring an opinion that supported the Committee's charge that in killing Gordon, Eyre had gone in excess of his charge. (After Eyre's first acquittal and when the Committee, now under Mill's direction, decided to pursue Eyre for civil murder, Stephen withdrew from the Committee, arguing over what Stephen viewed as Mill's excessively sentimental connection to the case (Stephen 1895: 230).)

Before this split Stephen had argued that martial law existed *within* the common law, as part of that order's self-defensive architecture.[32] Martial law, Stephen wrote in his 1866 opinion, was nothing more than "*the common law right* of the Crown and its representatives to repel force by force in the case of invasion or insurrection, and to act against rebels as it might against invaders" (*Jamaica Papers* No. 1, 70, emphasis original). Stephen's definition explains that the status of insurgents was equivalent to that of invading national armies, though without foreign national status. What is of note is that for Stephen, the apparent excesses of martial law were immanent to the common law, one mechanism, with others, by which the state could lawfully defend itself against threats to its stability. His sense of martial law's fundamental lawfulness aligns Stephen's early opinion with the Millite presumption that even in the most extreme moments, even under the gravest challenge to its constituted order, the rule of law had no outside.

Later in his career Stephen would cease to count himself among Mill's "thinking persons" who see "law & order" as one with "order & civilization." After his noisy break from Mill during the height of the Jamaica prosecution, and after a two-year stint as a magistrate in India, Stephen's views on the relationship of violence to law had drastically altered.[33] This iconoclastic thinker, the man who "of all the Victorian critics of democracy [was] at once the most radical and the least encumbered with substitute religion" (White 1967: 17), would explain how "order & civilization" is authorized only by force; Stephen's major theoretical work would go further to argue that "wanton torture" and "death" were built into the very apparatus of order Mill and his Committee were interested in defending. Force, for Stephen, was the very name of peace.

After his time as the Jamaica Committee counsel, Stephen served as a member of the Legislative Counsel in Calcutta for two years. On the journey home from that tenure, the jurist produced what may be the Victorian era's most trenchant critique of the principles of Millite liberalism, *Liberty, Equality, Fraternity* (1873). In India Stephen developed an abiding respect for what he, like the progressive idealist thinkers he would come to oppose, called "the rule of law." But while Mill in repeated arguments signaled that the term signified the culmination of a historical motion into horizontal relations of contract, for Stephen the rule of law best understood as another term for authority. "He always said," Stephen's modern editor writes, "that his experience in India was a second university education, and that *Liberty, Equality, Fraternity* was 'little more than the turning of an Indian lantern on European problems'" (White 1967: 1).

Though composed in the 1870s, then, Stephen's argument in *Liberty* engages directly with Mill's positions in *On Liberty* and other idealist handbooks from the Age of Equipoise, but refracts those ideas through the experiences of Jamaica and India.[34] Stephen's critique would hold Mill to account for his historical optimism; for his empty use of abstract terms like "liberty"; and, most importantly here, for what Stephen considered Mill's jejune belief that violence could somehow be eradicated from politics. "Disguise it how you will," Stephen judged, "it is force in one shape or another which determines the relations between human beings" (1967: 209).

Stephen patiently unravels the presumption that history tends toward peaceful equality, and that (as he argues in the context of *The Subjection of Women*) inequality among the sexes "stands out as an isolated fact in modern social institutions"—"in radical opposition," as Mill had written, to "the progressive movement, which is the boast of the modern world" (*CW* XXI). Stephen invokes Sir Henry Maine to refute the progressive supposition, axiomatic for Mill as for so many of his contemporaries, that through the course of history, "force" gives way inevitably to a peace based on contract. "I say," Stephen writes,

> that all that is proved by the fact that status, to use Sir H. Maine's expression, tends to be replaced by contract, is that force changes its form. Society rests ultimately upon force in these days, just as much as it did in the wildest and most stormy periods of history. (1967: 226)

To further explain this refutation of what he styles the optimistic historicism of Mill and Maine, Stephen goes on to grant that the appearance of peacefulness may certainly have developed in modernity; but what has happened is not an eradication of force but its metamorphosis into subtler form.

Given that Eliot drew on the same source to elaborate her own model of progress into cosmopolitan modernity in *The Mill on the Floss*, it is ironic perhaps that to make his argument Stephen has recourse to the historical novels of Walter Scott. He refers readers to Scott's *The Fair Maid of Perth*, and grants that on first appearance, fourteenth-century Scotland would seem to have been ruled by violence. He grants, too, that the "quiet industry, farming, commerce, and amusement" of present-day Scotland (1967: 228) would appear to prove that force had been replaced by peace. "Look a little deeper," however, and we see that the reason modern force feels less powerful is that

> no one doubts either its existence, or its direction, or its crushing superiority to any individual resistance. [. . .] [D]eliberate individual resistance to the law of the land for mere private advantage is in these days an impossibility which no one ever thinks of attempting. Force not only reigns, but in most matters it reigns without dispute, but it does not follow that it has ceased to exist. (Stephen 1967: 203)

Stephen's argument would be recapitulated in Foucault's conception of politics as permanent war no less than in Max Weber's observation, in *Politics as Vocation* (1919), that the state is that entity which claims a monopoly on the legitimate use of physical violence. This claim sharply counterpoints the story of inevitable pacification and moral improvement Eliot derived from her own reading of Scott. (Morley's reading of *Felix Holt*, meanwhile, celebrates exactly this forward-driving historical tendency.) "Force is an absolutely essential element of all law whatever," Stephen writes later in his book, channeling the maxim of positivist sovereignty theory since Austin. "Indeed law is nothing but regulated force subjected to particular conditions and directed towards particular objects. The abolition of the law of force cannot therefore mean the withdrawal of the element of force from law, for that would be the destruction of law altogether" (1967: 223). The fact that this articulation of a basic tenet of sovereignty theory could be offered as a polemic measures how completely the question of violence had been sidestepped by mainstream Victorian theory.

For Stephen, societies could never improve *beyond* relations of force because force defines sociality as such. Stephen would go further, to associate the ineradicable presence of force within modern law with war itself: war, he would explain, is the condition of possibility for everyday life. In an observation Foucault would transform into aphorism in his lectures of 1975–6, Stephen argued that the state of open somatic harm that we call war is merely the force relations of daily life rendered manifest. (Peace, Foucault says, is a "silent war" (2003: 16).) From this point of view, what Mill described in his speeches on Jamaica as the "sanguinary licenses" of "temporary dictatorship"—the excesses of tyranny—did not indicate the rule of law's absence but its very truth made explicit.[35]

Within weeks of John Morley's 4 August review of *Poems and Ballads*, and in the same magazine, Stephen published a series of essays on sovereignty for the *Saturday Review* that began to develop the realist political philosophy that would soon animate *Liberty, Equality, Fraternity*. In essays that appeared while the Jamaica controversy was taking shape, Stephen called on Hobbes as the prototype for his own ideas that force is the condition of possibility for political order. "[T]o imagine a society in which there is no sovereign," Stephen wrote in one of these essays, "is to imagine a society that is not a society, but an anarchy" (1866: 58). Every one of these essays on Hobbes appeared just before or during the Jamaica case, with the earliest one, "Hobbes on Government," appearing on 26 August 1865, three months before the first news of insurrection reached London.

Stephen returned to Hobbes as the controversy heated up: "Hobbes' Leviathan" appeared on 29 September, while "Sovereignty"—reprinted later as "Hobbes' Minor Works"—appeared in the *Saturday* on 10 November 1866, just days after Stephen resigned from the Jamaica Committee. It is difficult not to see these essays working out in the idiom of theory the more practical dilemmas Stephen faced in the Jamaica case. "[Hobbes] saw clearly," Stephen wrote in the first of these essays, "what very few people see even now, that [. . .] what is usually claimed under that name is not liberty, but dominion. That part of our life as to which the law issues no commands is the province of liberty. The possession of control over others is not liberty at all, but power" (1865: 12). But it is in the 10 November essay entitled "Sovereignty" that Stephen expresses his sympathy with Hobbes' sense that order flows not from any historical process superseding violence, but from an onto-logically singular, power-wielding force, a sovereign (in Stephen's words) whose "commands [. . .] may be equitable or inequitable [. . .] but they cannot be unlawful, for they are themselves the laws" (1866: 55). This idea may seem scandalous to contemporary tastes, Stephen admits—as I noted in the Introduction, Maine would nuance it in his own writing on sovereignty, from 1874—but Stephen's sense was that Hobbes' doctrine "is intimately connected with many of the most practical controversies of the day" (1866: 54). Stephen does not cite Jamaica by name in this short piece, but his argument is indeed "intimately connected" to the crisis of legality in which a governor deemed that certain (black) bodies would feel without mediation the state's power to preserve itself—and was then acquitted in three successive trials. The word "deem" itself expresses a moment of non-procedural sovereign decision.

Responses to Stephen's *Saturday Review* essays on Hobbes do not survive, but he was fiercely attacked for his views in *Liberty, Equality, Fraternity* by his former associates on the Jamaica Committee, Frederic Harrison and (once more) John Morley. Harrison adopted positivist objections to Stephen's polemics, but Morley, now writing for the *Fortnightly* (in August 1873), attacked from what Stephen's biographer and brother, Leslie Stephen, in reference to this episode, calls "Mill's point of view" (Stephen 1895: 339). Stephen had explained that the peace of Victorian modernity was actually a state of permanent war, one where force relations might resolve into equilibrium and pass all but unnoticed, but could emerge at any exceptional, crushing moment to make their presence known. During Stephen's sojourn to post-1857 India he realized, as he recalled, that seeing law work in the empire was "the best corrective in existence to the fundamental fallacies of liberalism. Out there, you see real government" (quoted in White 1967: 11). By turning India's lantern toward domestic politics, Stephen argued again and again his fundamental point that sprees of brutality apparently exceptional to the rule of law in fact defined that rule. This sense of how "many dissimilar things" "run into each other" (1967: 43) helped him appreciate how absolutism and democracy, despotism and liberty—all jargon terms he contests—shade into one another. Stephen predicted correctly that English political commonsense would be unsettled by this scandalous defiance of the law of non-contradiction.

Colonial records vindicate Stephen. Martial law's seemingly exceptional status had been long regularized as a tool for administering colonial zones by the time Morley and Harrison voiced objections to Stephen's theory. The burned and hanged bodies framed by Felice Beato in the Introduction may stand as synecdoche for these instances. "In the colonies during the nineteenth century," we learn, "martial law" was invoked on a number of occasions when the white man's burden became unwieldy. The list includes servile revolts in Barbados (1816), Demerara (1823), and Jamaica (1831). To this may be added the native revolts against taxation in Ceylon (1848) and the uprisings of Negro labourers in St. Vincent (1862) and Jamaica (1865). The attacks of border tribes called forth proclamations of 'martial law' in the Cape of Good Hope in 1835, 1846, and during the period 1850–53. An attempt to collect a poll tax from the Zulus of Natal in 1906 led to a race war which in turn called forth a prolonged period of martial rule over the natives. Martial law was twice proclaimed in Lower Canada during the "Patriote" Rebellion of 1837–38. Still other cases might be mentioned.   (Fairman 1930: 53)

Liberal England's endless war was a reality that from Stephen's perspective made perfect sense. From within the terms of Mill's theory—or Morley's derivation of it—it could only be explained by recourse to the categories of time and development, atrocity and humanity. Where a Millite commitment to the principles of non-contradiction and identity meant that law (as peace) and war (as violence) could only ever sit at opposite ends of a moralized continuum, Stephen saw in theory what the practice of martial law made concrete: that the brute force on the world system's periphery was no "accidental disturbanc[e] of right theory" (Stephen 1895: 231), but the necessary precondition of the mid-Victorian global order.

"INDIFFERENCE WAS IMPOSSIBLE TO HIM": SWINBURNE'S BLAKE

In essays on Byron (1866) and Blake (published 1868, drafted 1866), Swinburne framed his own distinction between the material forces "which really stir mankind" and "right theory," claiming, like Stephen, that the former determined relationships among men. Swinburne's introduction to Byron is concerned to justify a reconsideration of the romantic poet's artistic virtues. While readers of the contemporary period, Swinburne writes, "have become used to better verse and carefuller workmen" (1875: 239), Byron's "excellence of sincerity and strength" recommends him to readers today: his verse is the source of an "imperishable excellence" (1875: 239). These rather conventional words of praise take a telling swerve later on, when Swinburne offers a description of Byron's procedure that sheds light on his own poetic strategy, opening up, in the process, links this chapter has developed between the poet's antinomian sensibility and the material intertwinement of law and violence exposed in Jamaica.

It is here that Swinburne develops his own political theology, elaborating his sense of the political effectivity of a singular drive based on a nonnegotiable demand. The source for this demand, he specifies, is in a commitment whose only metaphors can be taken from the natural world. "Turn now to Byron or to Shelley," Swinburne writes:

> Their passion is perfect, a fierce and blind desire which exalts and impels their verse into the high places of emotion and expression. They feed upon nature with a holy hunger, follow her with a divine lust as of gods chasing the daughters of men. Wind and fire, the cadences of thunder and the clamours of the sea, gave to them no less of sensual pleasure than of spiritual sustenance.   (1875: 245)

The role of "fierce and blind desire" in Swinburne's own poetics has already been explained, and the other terms Swinburne uses to praise these poets—"wind and fire," "the clamours of the sea"—are the key images structuring *Poems and Ballads*.

For Shelley as for Byron, Swinburne writes here, "divine lust" and "holy hunger" are the driving forces for an affective poetics of belief, one charged with an archaic spirit proper to the era of gods that is "sensual" but also "spiritual." (In 1877 Swinburne praised *Wuthering Heights* along similar lines, setting the stage for the modern recuperation of what he styles as the bracingly "savage" novel (2004: 404–6).) In the essays from the *Poems and Ballads* period, Swinburne goes on to explain that while Shelley's work may please us, it is Byron who most courageously revels in the force relations animating a world charged with the blind commitments of desire. To Byron, says Swinburne,

> Tempest and rebellion and the magnificence of anguish were as the natural food and fire to kindle and sustain his indomitable and sleepless spirit. The godless martyrdom of rebels; the passion that cannot redeem; the Thebaid whose first hermit was Cain, the Calvary whose first martyr was Satan, these, time after time, allured and inspired him. Here for once this inner and fiery passion of thought found outer clothing and expression in the ruin of a world.   (xiii–xiv)

Swinburne reads Byron as a poet of of passion, rebellion, Satanism.[36] All are for Swinburne positive terms: while the world may be frozen over in a veneer of tranquil equanimity, the forces underneath that placid surface seethe and groan. The poets who acknowledge this see, like Sade, the passions that sit at "the bottom of gods and men." Swinburne's neo-romantic allegiances find him praising these outdated (because open) antagonisms, the archaic commitments of "rebels," "martyrs," "rebellion." All of these stances of inspired resistance find proper form, Swinburne says, not in sentimental meliorism but in facing without consolation the generalized damage that finds "outer clothing," he says, in "the ruin of a world."

Byron's attractively outdated interest in the abrogation of law impressed Swinburne more than Shelley's, whose signature political tract was called "A Philosophical View of *Reform*"—not revolution. But even more than Byron, the poet who exemplified for Swinburne the dialectical possibilities of unblunted conviction was William Blake. "[M]ade up of mist and fire" (Swinburne 1968b: 358), Blake was for Swinburne the very paradigm of a positively charged frenzy. Here again, Swinburne names this privileged vision "belief." In the essay on Blake that has long been seen as the key articulation of his own aesthetic program,[37] Swinburne explains his appreciation for Blake's effort to create his own category of the good, to transform the world into his own image in a lifelong mission akin to a religious crusade.

In a political modernity governed by the immanent workings of de-ontologized sovereignty, evacuated of belief, Swinburne finds in Blake an inspired counterpoint. "[T]he main part of him was, and is yet, simply inexplicable," Swinburne writes:

> In a time of critical reason and definite division, he was possessed by a fervour and fury of belief; among sane men who had disproved most things and proved the rest, here was an evident madman who believed a thing, one may say, only insomuch as it was incapable of proof. He lived and worked out of all rule, and yet by law. (1968b: 359)

Creating his own law, toiling in pursuit of an absolute of his own devising, Blake's "faith was absolute and hard, like a pure fanatic's; there was no speculation in him" (1968b: 359). Swinburne goes on in his praise by invoking each key term of Victorian liberalism I have discussed so far— Bagehot's "Age of Discussion," Kantian disinterest, and the procedural law of Mill's deontological liberalism—only to refuse them each in turn:

> His outcries on various matters of art or morals were in effect the mere expression, not of reasonable dissent, but of violent belief. [...] Indifference was impossible to him. Thus every shred of his work has some life, or some blood, infused or woven into it. In such a vast tumbling chaos of relics as he left behind to get in time disentangled and cast into shape, there are naturally inequalities enough; rough sides and loose sides, weak points and helpless knots, before which all mere human patience or comprehension recoils and reels back. But in all, at all times, there is the one invaluable quality of actual life. (1968b: 360)

Invoking "actual life" and "violent belief" as the positive counterpoint to "reasonable dissent," Swinburne voices a preference for belief's "invaluable quality"—a quality that supersedes all value. Against secular modernity's belief in the disinterested fungibility of all things, Swinburne arrays the singular and inexchangeable, the precarious: a "vast tumbling chaos of relics," full of "weak" and "helpless" jagged edges.

The vision Swinburne extrapolates from Blake stems from belief and takes shape as a melancholic fidelity to a ruined world, a catastrophic commitment rooted in the intertwined drives toward damage and desire he would soon call love. Accounting for "the special and distinctive character of passion," in *Wuthering Heights*, Swinburne triangulates ruin and its seeming opposite, love, in just these terms:

> The love which devours life itself, which devastates the present and desolates the future with unquenchable and raging fire, has nothing less pure in it than flame or sunlight. And this passionate and ardent chastity is utterly and unmistakably spontaneous and unconscious.   (2004: 405)

Swinburne's celebration of ardent chastity rewires the circuitry between catastrophe and redemption, and would seem, in so doing, to romanticize destruction itself and confirm Tillyard's intuition of Swinburne's proto-fascist millennialism. But Swinburne's melancholic investments cut against this reading, insisting on attention to the unexpungable damage of history and the equal ruin of the present moment: this commitment to parsing disaster led him to praise those same qualities of Blake and Brontë, and perhaps to find them there. In poems about injury in *Poems and Ballads* like "Dolores" and "Itylus," Swinburne maintains what he represents as the fundamentalist conviction that past violence cannot and will not go away— that "sorrow," "travail," and "melancholy" are, as in "Anactoria," "blind inexpiable things" (ll. 166–70): damage that cannot and will not be redeemed.[38] His rewriting of the Procne myth in "Itylus," for example, reworks the traditional theme, common to Keats, Arnold, and T. S. Eliot, by which the story of Philomela's rape and subsequent transformation into a nightingale becomes an allegory of pain turning into poetry. In this poetic tradition, the transformation of trauma into beauty mirrors the procedure of cognitive exchange psychoanalysis understands as mourning: expiation is possible, reparation achieved.

Swinburne's retelling refuses the consolations of such exchanges. His Procne myth forestalls the closure that, for example, Arnold gives the tale in "Philomela," insisting instead on the melancholic persistence of past damage, its inability to be purged from the historical record. Instead of narrating the conversion of pain into poetry—exchanging injury for something else under a logic of equivalence—Swinburne models an ardent chastity that enjoins speaker and reader to witness a violence that cannot be exchanged or otherwise erased. This is the poem's final stanza:

> O sister, sister, thy first-begotten!
> The hands that cling and the feet that follow,
> The voice of the child's blood crying yet
> *Who hath remembered me? who hath forgotten?*
> Thou hast forgotten, O summer swallow,
> But the world shall end when I forget.
> ("Itylus," ll. 55–60, emphasis original)

The stanza's final line forms what would seem to be the closure of its C–C rhyme, as "forget" concludes the rhyme initiated by the "child's blood crying yet." But what works poetically as closure is thematically positioned as its precise opposite, open-endedness: no forgetting happens here, no closure is achieved. The speaker realizes the strangeness of her commitment to remembering, marking it as the opposite of what "thou" would do. If Swinburne finds in Blake some image of this fanatical dedication to the past—with the past understood not as a sequence of progressive stages but as a fragmentary jumble of damage, what Benjamin called "the Passion of the world" (1977: 166)—then his own poetry would hold out as a good the focused, extrarational allegiances that make such commitment possible.

Like Stephen's essays on Hobbes, Swinburne's depiction of Blake's "perpetual freshness and fulness of belief" (1968b: 364) was finalized during the height of the Jamaica crisis. In their different ways, Swinburne and Stephen both responded to this historical conjuncture by proposing a re-ontologization of power, a return to conviction and reanimation of the category of ends. In so doing, both men diagnose the sovereign violence that sits at the heart of any order that imagines itself to have left violence behind; Swinburne went further to model a fidelity to the damage accrued in this savage modernity, conceiving it as a loss whose human cost cannot be repaid.

Swinburne finds the figure for this frantic commitment in the term "love." "Laus Veneris" recounts the knight Tannhäuser explaining that his love is an all-consuming obsession, what in reference to *Wuthering Heights* Swinburne called "[t]he love which devours life itself." The crusade poem underlines the countersecular thrust of this position by giving it theological content. Tannhäuser is not just any warrior but a Christian one: a religious warrior just back from an actual holy war. Speaking of God, the Christian knight admits to fanaticism:

> Though [God] search all my veins through, searching them
> He shall find nothing whole therein but love.   ("Laus Veneris," ll. 383–4)

Given over entirely to commitment, Tannhäuser is consumed by an affective drive coterminous with total violence, one encoded as part of his very physical makeup, in "all my veins through." This physicalized "love" harries the knight, he says, sticking to him and scorching him: he is unable to shake it. It is "clinging as a fire that clings / To the body and to the raiment, burning them; / As after death I know that such-like flame / Shall cleave to me for ever" (ll. 404–7).

In this heretical reversal of Christian eternity, "Laus Veneris" rewrites the endlessness of the afterlife as the unceasing pain of an obsessive conviction. In doing so this religious knight tells us what the term "ecstasy" already implies, which is that religious fervor and sexual desire go hand in hand; he does more, insisting that as extreme positions or absolutes, love and war, *eros* and *thanatos*, intertwine to the point of indistinction. Tannhäuser imagines himself in the crusades, and describes his killing of enemies in terms that echo his own cleaving passion for his loved Venus. In a flashback he confronts "Some certain of my foe's men," then tells us:

> The first red-bearded, with square cheeks—alack,
> I made my knave's blood turn his beard to black;
>   The slaying of him was a joy to see.   (ll. 243, 245–7)

Compared to the metaphoric violence of love, this actual violence (a killing, a cleaving) is rendered with strange indirectness, a reticence that serves paradoxically to highlight the killing, and the sexualized "joy" it effects.

I have so far provided terms for suggesting Swinburne's ideological complicity with Tannhäuser: I have left room for assuming that Swinburne imagines this crusading knight—slaughterer of infidels, prey to a consuming passion—as a "good" figure. In allowing for this I have emphasized how Swinburne seems to make his fanatical knight, like Sappho, a somehow sympathetic character, the hero of the story. But in moving to conclusion I want to recall Swinburne's work, in "Itylus," to witness rather than celebrate the violence that constitutes historical and political life. Note that the form of Swinburne's dramatic monologues in *Poems and Ballads* allows for a precisely ironic reading of their hyperbolically violent Sapphos and Tannhäusers. McGann has made the case that Tannhäuser is ironized—"not really a tragic figure [...] but a pathetic one." Swinburne, he continues, "uses him as the moral example of an attitude which ruins the possibility of a fully human life" (1972: 256). I close this section on Swinburne's materialist theology of violence—"God knows I might be crueller than God"—by suggesting that the ambiguity of Tannhäuser's position is one of the many ways that Swinburne does not so much fetishize violence as stage it for our view. Uncontent with abstractions, seeing to the bottom of gods and men, Swinburne catalogs the forces that seethe and groan under the calm surface of idealist rationalism. His efforts allow this chapter to swerve a final time to the political world, so as to measure the fanaticism structuring the very rule of law that believed it might cancel fanaticism forever.

"CASES OF EXTREME EXIGENCY": MILL'S EXCEPTIONS

In his July 1866 speeches for the Jamaica Committee, Mill framed the debate over Eyre's guilt as a contest between restraint and excess, a peaceful law versus the unchecked executive power Mill understood as law's neg-ation. Which side was England on? Referring to martial law as "arbitrary power—the rule of force, subject to no legal limits" (*CW* XXVIII), Mill stood before a full session of Parliament to denounce the arbitrary aspect of this unlimited force. He used an uncharacteristic rhetorical energy and a formulation whose terms justify extended quotation:

> [I]f men are let loose from all law, from all precedents, from all forms—are left to try people for their lives in any way they please, take evidence as they please, refuse evidence as they please, give facilities to the defence or withhold those facilities as they think fit, and after that pass any sentences they please, and irrevocably execute those sentences, with no bounds to their discretion but their own judgment of what is necessary for the suppression of a rebellion [. . .]; when there is absolutely no guarantee against any extremity of tyrannical violence, but the responsibility which can be afterwards exacted from the tyrant—then, sir, it is indeed indispensable that he who takes the lives of others under this discretion should know that he risks his own.
>
> (*CW* XXVIII)

Mill's account draws on a vocabulary common to neo-Kantian aesthetics, referring to the "forms" of "law" and "extremit[ies]" of "violence" to cast the problem of Eyre's lawless despotism as one of unregulated motion, vital force overflowing its proper container.[39] If colonial governors can do "as they please," Mill says, the regulative functions of law have been abrogated entirely.

This speech to Parliament predates Matthew Arnold's well-known chapter of *Culture and Anarchy* on "Doing as One Likes" by three years, but Mill's story replicates Arnold's terms with an accuracy that highlights the analytic resources of liberal theory in the period. In the chapter Arnold outlines the threat mass democracy poses to the harmony of the state, arguing that the times are tending toward individual whim. Freedom, Arnold surmises in the context of the 1866 Hyde Park riots, had leaned too far. "More and more," he says, "this and that man, and this and that body of men, all over the country, are beginning to assert and put in practice an Englishman's right to do what he likes; his right to march where he likes, meet where he likes, enter where he likes, hoot as he likes, threaten as he likes, smash as he likes. All this, I say, tends to anarchy" (1993: 84–5). As Chapter 2 showed, Arnold's fears were catalyzed in contests over who might count or not count in the lead-up to the 1867 Reform Bill.

The problem became more acute when the horizon of potential inclusion was expanded beyond England's internal "residuum" to the world's external one. In Arnold's domestic context as in Mill's imperial one, what remains inassimilable from within this conceptual opposition is how "anarchy" itself—the violence that knows no law, that is prior to and beyond the law that it is invoked to enforce—had long been established as a tool for securing liberty and culture in the first place. Arnold himself had worried over the seeming distinction between legal justification ("right") and brute force two years before. In "The Function of Criticism at the Present Time" (1864), he cites approvingly the French Epicurian Joseph Joubert, who

> has said beautifully: "C'est la force et le droit qui règlent toutes choses dans le monde; la force en attendant le droit." (Force and right are the governors of this world; force till right is ready.) Force till right is ready; and till right is ready, force, the existing order of things, is justified, is the legitimate ruler.
>
> (1993: 33)

The mechanism that would blur to the point of indistinction the seeming opposition between "right" and "force" was martial law. This had enjoyed a long and controversial history in England before Morant Bay: its roots lay in the Riot Act and Acts of War, and as the term indicates, "martial law" referred originally to the military law that would apply to invading armies or other enemies of the state. Known in the French tradition as the state of siege, martial law in England thus named the rules of war governing troops in the field: it was administered by the military, to the military. But in English common law, insurgents rising against the state's lawful power arrayed themselves in a state of war. Like invaders under an enemy flag but without the benefit of national status, those participating in insurrection entered a state of enmity with respect to the government, becoming in that act unprotected by civil law and falling instead under the jurisdiction of the laws of war. Henry VII and Henry VIII, among other monarchs, had invoked this function to put down rebels from within England's own population, and by the nineteenth century the term began

to take on new meaning, now also referring to temporary executive power
in a state of emergency.

In his 1930 survey of martial law's long history, Charles Fairman lists at
least five competing definitions of the term operative by the time of his
writing. By October of 1865, as W. R. Kostal writes, "the law of martial
law was dauntingly complex, perhaps utterly incoherent" (2005: 10). Still,
out of the chaos of theory at least two traditions began to be consolidated
around the time of the Jamaica Rebellion—martial law as military law and
martial law as a temporary executive dictatorship. Both were qualitatively
separate from the normal operations of constitutional procedure.[40]

Since the insurrection at Morant Bay was "triggered by 'necessity'" but did
not involve foreign military agents, it fell, most heavily, under the auspices of a
temporary dictatorship. As we will see, even Mill's *Considerations on Representative Government* acknowledged that in an emergency situation, the state
preserved the right to secure itself by any means necessary—since "necessity,"
as Oliver Cromwell had long before noted, "hath no law."[41] "It is a matter of
common knowledge," Fairman confirms,

> that governors [...] of British colonies and dominions do in various
> emergencies issue what purport to be proclamations of martial law. These
> usher in an extraordinary regime wherein the military authority issues
> regulations for the conduct of the civil population; individuals deemed
> troublesome will be seized and held without judicial process, and in some
> instances may be tried and sentenced to death by a military tribunal. Soldiers
> may be ordered to take life to prevent the commission of a felony, or to
> punish, or perhaps to produce a moral effect.   (Fairman 1930: 23)

What is outlined here is not just the process by which "an extraordinary
regime" could take power over a colonial population, or how that regime
could come to occupy the position of supreme sovereign, "deem[ing]"
certain sections of the population to be threats in a pre-procedural act that
itself confirms a singular site of decision. By invoking "common knowledge," the passage also begins to unveil one of the central paradoxes at the
heart of emergency law, which is how this "law" coincides uneasily with
the "fact" of its own execution. As the confused record indicates, "martial
law" is lawful less because it is legal than because it happens, because of
"necessity." Stephen's Hobbesian argument from August 1866 already
showed how the state's right to invoke this suspension is based on its self-
preserving or constituting power; it precedes the prescriptions of legal
forms in the sense that it derives from the very power that authorizes those
procedures in the first place. ("The commands of [the] sovereign may be
equitable or inequitable," Stephen wrote, "but they cannot be unlawful,
for they are themselves the laws [...].") (1892: 55).

But Mill did not see it this way, and could not: from within the tenets of his logical-political system the question resolved into one concerning boundaries. Was martial law "inside" or "outside" of law? In the moment that Mill, in *Considerations*, had called "the last resort," where did sovereignty reside? The Jamaica Committee's statement of 27 July 1866 outlined its intention to argue that though martial law had been executed as if it were *outside* of the law, it should be brought back *within* the law's reach. Mill sought "to have it determined by authority whether the law which these courts [of martial law] assume to administer is really law at all, or sanguinary license which the law will repress and punish" (*CW* XXI). The binary formula that separates "sanguinary license" from "the law" positions embodied affect against regulatory reason in ways that once again recapitulate the language surrounding the Swinburne poems condemned by Morley just five days after this speech. Mill and his collaborators seek to make the obscene excesses of martial law something "which the law will repress and punish."

Referring to the "authority" that will "determine" whether martial law is or is not law, Mill and his colleagues beg the question the case is most concerned with solving. Precisely what is at stake is who has the authority to determine what constitutes a legal exception, what justifies this decision, and what measures may be undertaken under the auspices of such an emergency. Here Mill is assuming that it is the English state, based in London, that bears this sovereign authority, while Carlyle's Governor Eyre Defence Committee held that it was the governor who held it.[42] In either case, the spatial metaphors of insides and outsides suggest a fundamental confusion about the mechanisms by which a state can preserve its own power.

In staging the debate about law and sovereignty in spatial terms, Mill anticipates the moves of more recent thinkers who, spurred by newer crises, have looked to analyze the relationship of law and violence in the contemporary era. In his 2005 book on the law of exception, Giorgio Agamben cites two historians to describe martial law as "'a point of imbalance between public law and political fact' situated in an 'ambiguous, uncertain, borderline fringe, at the intersection of the legal and the political'" (2005: 1). As the historian Charles Fairman concludes in his 1930 analysis, "'Martial law'" "runs close to politics" (foreword, n.p.). Concerned with boundaries, edges, and relations of proximity and reversal, Fairman and Agamben both reach for spatial tropes to describe the "position" martial law occupies with respect to the constitutional or normal legal regime: for Fairman it is "close" to politics, and for the historians Agamben cites, it is "a point [. . .] between" that "is situated" "at the intersection" of political necessity (fact) and legal form (law). Both critics thus raise another seeming paradox of "the law of martial law" (Kostal), namely its ambiguous *location* with respect to the state's normal proceedings.

Mill's *Considerations on Representative Government* faces a similar representational challenge. As noted above, that work takes pains to illustrate the virtues of a political system moderated by checks and balances, where the sovereignty resides in "the aggregate of the people" "in the last resort." But earlier, Mill makes a striking admission of the *position* excess occupies in the context of this moderating law. "I am far from condemning," writes the author of *On Liberty*,

> in cases of extreme exigency, the assumption of absolute power in the form of a temporary dictatorship. Free nations have, in times of old, conferred such power by their own choice, as a necessary medicine for diseases of the body politic which could not be got rid of by less violent means.   (*CW* XIX)

Mill moves on from the biopolitical metaphor of excision to note that a temporary dictatorship is only justified if this cancellation of liberty is itself aimed at expanding liberty.

Suspending the law, Mill writes, "even for a time strictly limited, can only be excused, if, like Solon or Pittacus, the dictator employs the whole power he assumes in removing the obstacles which debar the nation from the enjoyment of freedom" (*CW* XIX). How this will be guaranteed is not mentioned. Apparently resting on discussion, communicative rationality, and the dynamically pacifying influence of parliamentary procedure ("law"), Mill's model of government in this moment reveals its dependence on a more naked sovereign power that might show itself in "cases of extreme exigency." In doing so it alludes momentarily to the supervening power that exists behind the operations of the system outlined in the rest of the treatise's many pages. Who decides when a case is of "extreme exigency"?

The violence in Jamaica would apply strong pressure to the crucial internal tension in Mill's earlier text. Despite efforts on both sides of the Eyre affair to determine whether martial law was internal to law or external to law, what emerged, after three straight acquittals, was that martial law "occupied" both "positions": it defined the set of "law" without itself belonging to that set. This fact in turn exposed the inadequacy of spatial metaphors for describing this relation of simultaneity. The threat of total violence was the very guarantee of imperial peace. As Agamben admits, "[i]n truth, the state of exception is neither external nor internal to the juridical order, and the problem of defining it concerns precisely a threshold, or a zone of indifference, where inside and outside do not exclude each other but rather blur with each other" (2005: 23). This book's final chapter will engage critically the metaphors that continue to emerge as if by reflex to structure attempts to describe legal violence. (Agamben still refers to a "zone.") Here I note that the relationship Agamben describes in the context of the American situation in 2005 underscores what the outcome of the Jamaica case likewise made clear. In a most material sense, it was the exception that defined the rule. That which was "external" to law (martial law) could nonetheless exist "within" it, and this "threshold" concept is what, in its very exceptional status, defined the very order it appears most violently to abrogate.

The paradoxes of this scenario have already come to life for us in those sections of *Liberty, Equality, Fraternity* where Stephen explains how the liberal buzzword "liberty" in fact refers to its apparent opposite, coercion. The foundational force that Benjamin called "lawmaking violence" is not itself part of the legal order it defines and upholds: it is the law's abrogation, its excess, but at the same time it is precisely this excess that expresses the identity of its set, upholding and defining the category it seems to transgress.[43] "I am the law," is what martial law announces, but that announcement—the temporary and total violence of martial law—is not itself legal. This seemingly fussy deconstructive point provides terms for understanding how a law-establishing violence of the kind troped in *The Mill on the Floss'* world-ruining apocalypse might return later, elsewhere, and on bodies deemed available for killing, but now to uphold rather than abolish a regime of legal order.

No doubt it is this simultaneously law-cancelling and law-establishing aspect of martial law that led Mill, in his parliamentary speeches, to compare Governor Eyre to Robespierre—an association between martial law and revolutionary violence that became a cliché in the liberal and radical presses in these years. A profusion of cheaply printed pamphlets on the Jamaica events remediated the Committee's own reports with sometimes moralizing, sometimes salacious additions. With various calibrations of pornographic delight and recoil, these described the excessive violence on the island. Always they drew on imagery borrowed from the counterrevolutionary lexicons of observers like Carlyle, Eliot, Dickens, and Edmund Burke. Henry Bleby's *The Reign of Terror: A Narrative of Facts Concerning Ex-Governor Eyre, George William Gordon, and the Jamaica Atrocities* is exemplary in this respect, since it heightens still further the already garish terms of the governor's report about the "ripping," "roasting," and "cleaving" of the rebels' (supposed) revolutionary assault, though to opposite political effect. Breathlessly, Bleby's pro-Jamaica Committee account describes a scene that could have been a reversed outtake from *A Tale of Two Cities* or its source text, Carlyle's *The French Revolution* (1837). The state's counterrevolutionary forces ravage black bodies without restraint: "[T]he savage hordes which [Eyre] let loose upon the people without any check to their ferocity," Bleby reports, "and with no instructions but to ravage and destroy, gorged themselves with blood" (1868: 50). In a formula that anticipates Mill's own affective response to the counterinsurgency—his blush of shame— Bleby quotes approvingly a Rev. Henry Clarke, island curate in the parish of Westmoreland: "every honest Englishman [should] blush with shame for the savage barbarities his countrymen are capable of when left to the exercise of their natural propensities, unrestrained by any fear of public opinion or of the law" (1868: 11). Bleby's denunciation of these Swinburnian crimes—this "hell-like saturnalia of martial law," as the book's epigraph has it—takes shape as a critique of martial law's irredeemable anomie, its "unrestrained" cancellation of "the law."

Eyre's successive acquittals ran counter to this vision of law. In 1866 and after, political and legal debates surrounding the outpouring of vital forces at Morant Bay grasped with uneven success for a vocabulary that might explain the force that defines the peace. The non-dialectical idiom held in common by the practitioners of these debates took as axiomatic the principles of classical logic whereby, among other things, nothing could be both itself and its opposite simultaneously. This identitarian thinking, common to liberal idealism as to so much of our own criticism about it, ensured that the violence structuring modern legality could be legible only as paradox, as confusion, as embarrassment, over and over again.

THE LAWS OF METER: LYRIC AS THOUGHT

If the excesses of martial law sat unspeakably at the core of what Mill called the "forms" of juridical protection, I want now to show how Swinburne's *Poems and Ballads* also worked to lodge surplus within an overarching formalism, one that several critics of British poetry have seen as the very image of artistic order. Against the helpless progressive idealism of the jurists and politicians just surveyed, Swinburne exploits the affordances of the poetic medium to stage the seemingly self-contradictory involvement of legality and atrocity as a generative friction between content and form. The technology of the lyric, I suggest, enables Swinburne to ring changes on the logical presuppositions of his era, and to marshal the full resources of poetic presentation to set opposites into tension while fusing those same contradictory elements into an unbreakable conceptual totality. The resulting dialectical images—the poems—do not represent or describe so much as enact the paradoxical scenario of martial law, and are best thought of, for that reason, not as discourse or art but as political thought crystallized in form. In linguistic terms, Isobel Armstrong writes,

> Swinburne's poetry effectively [...] creat[es] a language which may be determined but which is nevertheless out of control in the sense that it is outside the law, or outside humanly made laws.   (1993: 406)

So much we have seen. And yet all studies of Swinburne that either romanticize or critique his status as a rebel are forced to confront the fact that his odes to vitality, death, fanaticism, and damage are precisely "lawful" in their forms: these are some of the most accomplished exercises in poetic formalism of the Victorian age.

A 1908 article entitled "The Metrical Forms Used by Certain Victorian Poets," we are told, "furnishes some statistics [...] estimating that Swinburne used 420 metrical and stanzaic forms, almost twice as many as Tennyson (240) and Browning (200)" (Faverty 1968: 244). Swinburne's work represents a surplus of ordered forms. But rather than seeing Swinburne's numerically impressive formal variety as another way of demonstrating his excess, we might instead follow McGann and others in construing this formalism as one half of Swinburne's dialectic strategy: the frisson of a poem like "Anactoria," for example, which dramatizes Sadism but does so in heroic couplets, comes precisely from the drama it stages between the excess of its content and the restraint of its meter, between driving violence and what Victorian metrical theorist George Saintsbury called "stopped form" (1910: 341). The questions this dialectic poses are those we have already seen in reference to martial law: is the violence of Swinburne's excess "inside" or "outside" the forms in which it is couched? Is the violence "contained" by those forms, or rather, as I want to suggest here, do the poems stage that very tension as their central drama?

McGann cites Swinburne's love of static, eternal forms, a tendency toward order which for McGann is most evident in Swinburne's use of the roundel, that repetitive, eleven-line form in which the opening of the first line is repeated as a refrain in the fourth and eleventh lines. (Swinburne adapted his own exceptionally difficult roundel form from the French rondeau, fourteen-line poems with only two rhymes, where the first and second, seventh and eighth, and thirteenth and fourteenth lines repeat.) "If you don't have to depend on your own improvisations for the fundamental sound structure," McGann writes of Swinburne's roundel, "but can look to a form which possesses *an anterior and objective existence*, all the practical music of the verse will take its character from the given, 'unsought' rhyming pattern" (1972: 44–5, emphasis added). In a later poem simply called "The Roundel," Swinburne gives poetic shape to the point here, emphasizing the ringlike coherence of this strict form:

> A roundel is wrought as a ring or a starbright sphere,
>> With craft of delight and with cunning of sound unsought,
> That the heart of the hearer may smile if to pleasure his ear
>> A roundel is wrought.   (ll. 1–4)

Tightly meshed, circular in its internal self-reference, giving the pleasure of unity like any other example of Kantian beauty or New Critical coherence, the poem enacts formally what it describes. "Given," "unsought," "anterior," and "objective," as McGann says, the laws of form—here, the roundel—work for Swinburne as the orderly template within which the "sadistic" or lawless programs of poems like "Anactoria" can unfold.[44]

In his 1857 "Essay on English Metrical Law," Coventry Patmore anticipated the New Criticism by describing successful poetry as a management of tension: the best poetry, he wrote at the height of the Age of Equipoise, achieved "the coordination of life and law" (1961: 7).[45] For Patmore "life" is the name for vital substance of poetry, its content, while "law" derives from the poetry's meter. In a now-familiar gesture Patmore suggests that meter is thus a regulating force, or what, in reference to Swinburne, Prins calls a "disciplinary measure" (Prins 1999: 122): it is what tempers and restrains the spirit of poetry's content. Calming embodied spirit, meter thus operates according to what we can say is the regulative Kantian logic of the beautiful. Citing Patmore as her key example, Prins, in an important essay on "Victorian Meters," goes further to explain how meter worked to rationalize unruly energy:

> The Victorians increasingly conceptualized meter as a formal grid or pattern of spacing, created by the alternation of quantifiable units. Their interest in quantification has the effect of detaching poetic voice from spoken utterance, and marks—literally, in the making of metrical marks—a graphic distinction between meter and rhythm.   (2000: 90; see also Martin 2012)

Describing rationalized grids and quantifiable units of meter, Prins outlines a political economy of form, one where rhythmic units of "voice"—what Swinburne called his poems' "shining feet"—have been converted into regularized, and thus fungible, metrical units. The rough edges of "spoken utterance" and its "rhythm[s]" are smoothed out, equalized under law.

As Meredith Martin has observed, these general comments on Victorian meter take a more specific turn in Saintsbury's *A History of English Prosody* (1910). Saintsbury's massive, three-volume project looks to chart what it styles as the historical progression of English meter, a *Bildungsroman* of poetic form that redeploys Mill's earlier historicism to trace a trajectory running out of chaos and into law. Literary history, he says, progresses upward from the stormy twelfth century (before the "regimenting" accomplished by Chaucer (Saintsbury 1910: 170)) to the regularized, rationalized forms of the present day. For Saintsbury's Whig history of poetic development, modernity arrives in the guise of a new formalism that the critic calls, in important language, "the practical abolition of the strict syllabic theory, and the admission of Substitution and Equivalence" (1910: 171). With a long history of older, more "tyrran[ical]" forms superseded—that is Saintsbury's language (p. 170)—a new, modern order of "Substitution and Equivalence" has, after "abolition," emerged into freedom. "Now," Saintsbury says, "things are different" (p. 170). As Martin and Prins have variously shown, Saintsbury's account of poetic advancement thus sketches in aesthetic terms the Millite story of status turning into contract, a story by which a new regime of equivalence emerges from the stormy periods of unregulated force. We finally arrive, Saintsbury says, at "the exercise, deliberate and unrestrained, of the franchise of English prosody" (p. 296, quoted in Prins 2000: 93). In this stunning political-aesthetic performance, Saintsbury tells a story by which "English prosody becomes a national heritage, with a political as well as a poetical purpose in resisting 'tyranny' and establishing a 'new ordered liberty' for the English nation. It has its own law and order" (Prins 2000: 93).

The story of archaic violence turning into the substitution and equivalence of modern legality has its own interest in relation to the liberal historicism discussed in this and earlier chapters. What matters here is that the poet Saintsbury calls upon to represent the apogee of history's motion toward lawful order is not Matthew Arnold, whose preference for culture over anarchy we have already charted, but Algernon Charles Swinburne. Representing, with Tennyson, "this new ordered liberty" (Saintsbury 1910: 296), Swinburne is modern poetry's latest exponent, Saintsbury says, one whose "unsurpassed versatility and virtuosity" in formal metrics is the fruit of "the growth and development of seven centuries of English language and English literature" (p. 351, quoted in Prins 2000: 93). Morley's unbalanced, atavistic follower of Sade is also the very image of lawful modernity.

Both readings are correct. Aside from superficial compliments to Swinburne's poetic talents, Morley's denunciation did not address poetic form, concentrating instead on the excessive content of *Poems and Ballads* to structure its politicized objections. What Saintsbury's account allows us to see is what Swinburne's undergraduate manuscript also disclosed: that this excessive and lawless poetics is also a lawful and orderly one, a contradiction the poem freezes within its own presentation in ways that defeat logics of non-contradiction and identity and press instead toward irresolvable dialectical intertwinement. In reference to Brontë, Swinburne referred to an "ardent chastity": what his poems disclose is the capacity of lyric form to signify, enact, or perform this simultaneity between ardency and chastity, embodied drive and severe restriction. Swinburne's lyrics in this way mobilize conceptual resources that liberal theory of the period lacked, and as a result are best considered as a modality of thinking: lyric as thought.

In the political-aesthetic terms this chapter has traced through Arnold (via Kant) and through Mill (via Morley) and, now, into Swinburne, the poet's dialectical program could be represented as in Fig. 3.6. Swinburne explains this complex situation in clearer terms in his essay on Blake, whom he represents as an inspired mystic and forger of his own laws. But Swinburne explains, as well, that the apparently untamable force of Blake's commitment is bound by limits. Blake seems to destroy all order, "[o]nly there are laws, strange as it must sound, by which the work is done and against which it never sins" (1968b: 372). Swinburne goes on to explain the process, in Blake's poems, by which those laws emerge out of what seems like chaos. The "savage abstractions" of Blake's titanic imagination speak with "vast lax lips," Swinburne says; the earlier poet's jumbled riot of disordered sound seems a frenzy of utterances, "barren of all but noise." However,

> Slowly they grow into something of shape, assume some foggy feature and indefinite colour: word by word the fluctuating noise condenses into music, the floating music divides into audible notes and scales. The sound which at first was the mere collision of cloud with cloud is now the recognisable voice of god or daemon. Chaos is cloven into separate elements [...]. Upon each of these the prophet, as it were, lays hand, compelling the thing into shape and speech, constraining the abstract to do service as a man might.   (1968b: 374)

Charting how a foggy "noise" and floating "music" divides, condenses, and is constrained into shape, Swinburne describes a process by which law emerges out of chaos, order out of the pure force of belief.

Poems and Ballads has long been read as a key monument in the aestheticist tradition, an exhibit in the movement toward the aesthetic ideology of modernism and an example of an "*art pour l'art*" return to form. This chapter has treated Swinburne's formalism as one that acknowledges, even flaunts its own impurity, even as it retains a melancholic attachment to the damage it understands to result from the very violence it so extravagantly appears to romanticize. By locating these biting, burning poems in a circuit of global violence centered in London and dispensing its

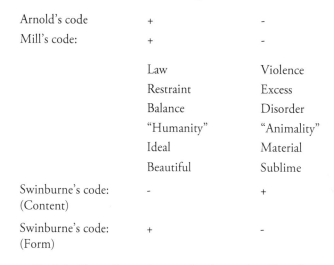

Arnold's code	+	-
Mill's code:	+	-
	Law	Violence
	Restraint	Excess
	Balance	Disorder
	"Humanity"	"Animality"
	Ideal	Material
	Beautiful	Sublime
Swinburne's code: (Content)	-	+
Swinburne's code: (Form)	+	-

Fig. 3.6. Chart of commitments: Swinburne, Arnold, Mill.

force all over the world, I have argued that Swinburne's apparently apolitical poetry mediates actively the single most important legal issue for Britain's imperial democracy as it pivoted from its so-called Age of Equipoise toward the open militarism of the Empire's post-1870 downward phase: the question of which bodies would be protected and which allowed to die. Bringing the full resources of poetic presentation to bear on the political problem of legal violence, Swinburne can be said not to have offered its solution but to have staged it, and by staging revealed its operations to view.[46]

Years after the crises of both *Poems and Ballads* and the Jamaica Affair, in December of 1876, Swinburne reflected belatedly upon the spree of violence at Morant Bay in a letter to his friend Theodor Watts-Dunton, his only comments I know of on the topic. The unpublished note sits in the British Library. Written in black ink on stationery framed with a tight black band, it reflects on the fantasia of death now almost exactly ten years in the past. Watts-Dunton has counseled Swinburne that he runs the risk of libel action for comments critical of Eyre. Swinburne responds by referring to the "vaunted atrocities of Eyre & his gang"; he cites the "shame & physical nausea" that resulted when he reread the blue books containing what he calls "the loathsome detail about 'the whops made of piano-wire' being 'fresh [?] tried on the backs of women' & showing 'that their skins were easier to cut'" (Swinburne 1876: n.p., *sic*). And he concludes by noting that the possibility of libel is absurd on its face, since

the letters & despatches from Jamaica for a month or more read like a series
of connected extracts from the very worst chapters of <u>Justine</u>. If you remember anything of the hideous & beastly details (nor, mind you, charges
brought by enemies, but gloatingly and boastfully avowed by the perpetra-
tors) you cannot but admit that these facts did actually rival in open daylight
(as to cruelty & brutality & unmanliness) the delirious dreams of the
Marquis de Sade in solitary confinement. [...] No word of mine on the
mater [*sic*] is a quarter, a tenth part, as strong, as what was most justly said at
the time (in the House of Commons & elsewhere) by Mill & many others.

(Swinburne 1876: n.p.)

The letter states in no uncertain terms Swinburne's position on the matter
of Eyre's cruel and brutal—he says "unmanl[y]"—episode of extrajudicial
killing; it is something ripped, he says astonishingly, from the pages of
Justine, a surprising critique for this early adopter of Sadean aesthetics. In
this the note would seem to confirm criticism's comfortable sense of the
later Swinburne as a glorious Republican and archetype of conveniently
self-confirming liberal-democratic sympathies. I resist that conclusion here.
Rather than reading this late admission as confirmation that Swinburne was
all along (as he suggests here) of Mill's party, I emphasize how relentlesssly
his own early poetry detonates such comforting moral certainty, dismantling
too our own self-satisfied moral identifications with it. My reading has
sought to show, then, how an inert and self-confirming analysis of "the
political Swinburne" is exceeded by the conceptual capacities of the poetry
itself. The dramatic monologues of *Poems and Ballads* surveyed here,
I mean, improve on the poet's admirable but smugly moralizing rhetoric
to Watts-Dunton insofar as they frame for our consideration an unappeasable sovereign violence and implicate us, the reader, in the judgment of it.
What do we see?

HISTORICAL TROPES

The juxtaposition I have risked here has staged an oscillation between a
book of poems on the one hand and an outbreak of imperial violence on
the other. This shuttling between culture and materialism has placed two
separate things next to one another, in this way operating by a poetic logic
of metonymy—one thing *and* another—where both instances are arrayed
on separate planes with proximity, rather than conceptual identity, to
suggest their connection. Morant Bay and Swinburne, a "historical" case
and a "literary" exemplar: the form of argument is a familiar one in
historicist criticism, even a cliché. But what is this academic "and"?

In *Culture and Imperialism* (1994), Edward Said describes his method—and his book's title—by calling attention to exactly this metonymic relationship between its subject areas, explaining that he has "deliberately abstained" from "advancing a completely worked out theory of the connection between literature and culture on the one hand, and imperialism on the other." He goes on:

> Instead, I hope the connections will emerge from their explicit places in the various texts, with the enveloping setting—empire—there to make connections with, to develop, elaborate, expand, or criticize.   (Said 1994: 14)

Said's grammatically complicated description of method says that "connections [. . .] will emerge" with a "setting" "there to make connections with." In this foundational, metonymically titled work at the origin of postcolonial criticism—Culture *and* Imperialism—the two levels of Said's title can only be proximally linked together, set into contact. The dynamic of their mediation is absent. If this contrapuntal procedure circumvents the standards of validity proper to inductive logic, it also takes pains to delay the question of how cultural productions relate to the material processes of extraction, expropriation, and killing; its focus is on the figurative violence of representation rather than the warmaking and acquisition that structured British rule in the nineteenth century.

Swinburne proposes a different method. Minutely attuned to violence and physical harm, the accretion of *Poems and Ballads*—the collection's incessant, additive force—builds intensity while it moves toward the overarching oneness of metaphor. Rather than proposing a metonymic relation between separate individuals or discrete instances that would police the distinction between compared objects—one thing *and* another—the play of sameness and difference in a poem like "Anactoria" finds difference folding into identity, as the speaker condenses into her lover in a semantic and conceptual struggle that results in ontological singularity, a union. If, in logical terms, this acquisitive metaphoric procedure represents the triumph of a specific type of inductive method—the violent subsumption of the multiple under the category of the one—then Swinburne's poetics can frame questions about this chapter's method, as it has looked to stage its own encounter between the seemingly disconnected fields of culture and imperialism.

In contrast to the metonymic procedure of Saidian cultural studies and the New Historicism, where connections wait to emerge, Swinburne's speaker reaches for totalizing monism: "I Sappho shall be one with all these things" ("Anactoria," l. 276). Capturing particularities and transforming them in her own image, subsuming them under her category, Anactoria performs the singularity-effacing inductive work we traced in

Chapter 2, whereby phenomena are stripped of their idiosyncracy and transformed into instances of a type. But this is Sappho, not Swinburne, and in this grand drama of metaphoric logic, couched within quieting forms, the poem puts on display *both* the promises of totalizing method and its inherent violence. Parting from Said's refusal to provide synthesis and Sappho's overmastering insistence on it, I have worked to allow my chapter's two instances—"Morant Bay" and "Swinburne" and the archival evidence arrayed under those headings—to remain separate, proximate, broken into sections. But I also insist that this split-screen story is a way of narrating a real configuration of law and violence at a specific moment in the British Empire's long plot of dispossession and injury.

In a discussion of Adorno in *Marxism and Form*, Jameson (1974: 3–60) explains that criticism is always allegorical and thus figural in nature: any act of reading substitutes one narrative (the interpretation) for another (the text). The charge of a properly dialectical criticism is to renarrativize or, as Jameson says, recode a given narrative level into another one, switching tactically between registers in an effort to disclose the ultimate involvement within the same totality of these apparently separate narratives. The injunction is to create a critical constellation that would temporarily freeze into the same frame of analysis what were, before that act of reading, disconnected "worlds." As I noted in the Introduction, Jameson explains that a historical trope is the "setting into contact with each other [. . .] two incommensurable realities" (1974: 189); when effective, such ruptured allegories permit us to apprehend the involvement of apparently separate sociocultural in-stances or levels in a single story we would do best to call "history," even while exposing its artifice in performing that suturing move. This chapter's arrangement of instances has attempted to defend the separ-ation of its singular cases, asserting their noncoincidence as materially discrete ensembles. Yet it has also insisted on their ability to allegorize a larger and real conceptual and political story in which, I argue, they both participate.

Swinburne's poetry challenges us to move past the metonymic procedure still regnant in contemporary criticism. As Jameson noted as early as 1992, in the still-operative paradigms of Foucauldian cultural studies and the New Historicism, "[e]legance [. . .] consists in constructing bridge passages between the various concrete analyses, transitions or modulations inventive enough to preclude the posing of theoretical or interpretive questions" (1992: 188 *et passim*). Swinburne's metaphoric procedure spurs us to forgo the "bridge passages" that would "successfully" complete the circuit of methodological induction; in this it provides a language for challenging the nominalist tendency to aggregate facts or catalog instances, leaving the relations to emerge. Instead I am following Swinburne to propose a version of totality—call it "history"—under which we might constellate via the logic of metaphor any number of particular instances, even while remaining aware of the metaphysical cost of this act. So: Morant Bay *and* Swinburne: my sense is that by highlighting rather than obscuring this metonymic "and," we might radicalize rather than avoid the operations of mediation that so much of historical literary criticism still leaves nameless.

As the argument of this book shifts from the legal emergency that seemed to rupture forever the equipoise of mid-century England and open what Hobsbawm calls "the Age of Empire"—it had always been an age of Empire—it also shuttles forward in time. Jumping from 1866 to 1885 helps chart how a material downturn in England's geopolitical posture after 1875 produced new challenges for literary form. In the decades of unwinding that saw British hegemony dissolve into an increasingly militaristic dominance while the pole of global leadership shifted as if by gravity across the Atlantic, *action* would become an aesthetic no less than a political problem. Set against the Jamesian realism they negate, H. Rider Haggard's African romances turn out to engage this problem actively, as they disclose at the level of form the splintering cognitive efforts required to renarrate England's global project of expropriation as heroism.

4

The Philosophy of Romance Form

More claymores, less psychology.

—Andrew Lang

SYSTEM, EXEMPLUM, IMPERIUM

Across three chapters this book has explored the foundational but unfigurable role of violence in Victorian theories of legal modernity. Doing so has entailed taking measure of the seemingly paradoxical situation by which "law" could stand as both a peaceful modernity's most perfect realization and force in its purest and most atavistic form. Seen under the aspect of progressive idealism and its logical principles of non-contradiction and identity, this duality could only appear as paradox or hypocrisy. Yet as Eliot, Collins, Swinburne, and others have variously apprehended over the course of these pages, legal order and violence were not opposite terms so much as two complementary aspects of sovereign power. This disorienting fact—that liberal rule just like the illiberal kind required violence to guarantee it—generated a stunning diversity of forms, literary technologies that exploit their own capacities of mediation to stage, enact, or otherwise perform some version of modernity's curious intimacy with harm.

This chapter turns to the darkening years of the war-torn *Pax Victoriana*, the 1880s, to track how the form most characteristic of this transitional geopolitical moment, the adventure romance, developed its particular features so as to examine critically the role of violence in a global Empire whose self-description unfolded not in the language of brute conquest but principled emancipation. As economic and world-systems historians have noted, the 1880s were a transitional moment in the long period of Victorian global rule. A domestic economy newly dependent on national debt and novel instruments of credit; a global military supremacy challenged by rising powers; a periphery under constant threat: the 1880s were not so much the "climax of Empire" Hannah Arendt and later critics have identified in this violent and jingoistic decade, but the moment when the once-stable hegemony of the British system began to fray, the seeming equipoise of mid-century now spinning into a baldly militaristic anomie.[1] An example plays out in miniature the consequences of this geopolitical shift for literary form.

In the first year of the British Empire's autumnal decade—late spring 1881—a letter posted from the imperial frontier arrived in London, containing a son's update to his mother. In a style that avoids introspection, it cites "disaster," "death," "anihilat[ion]" (*sic*), and "slaughter," but does not dwell on those things:

> Hilldrop
> Newcastle,
> NATAL

My dearest Mother,

I have to thank you for your long letter written from London at the time of the bad weather. At any rate with all our troubles we are spared frost and east winds. Long before this gets to you you will have heard of our third disaster and of the death of poor Sir George. We heard the guns going the day before yesterday and then came the news that 500 men had been anihilated [*sic*] on the top of the square mountain we see from our verandah. Thank God it is not quite so bad as that, but still it is a crushing defeat and so far as we can judge a most unnecessary one. [. . .] It is very sickening to be continually talking to men one day and the next to hear that they are dead, yet that is what happens to us every day now. We do not know what the next move is to be any more than the troops themselves, in fact everything seems to be in more or less of a mess. [. . .] [T]he slaughter amongst the officers is tremendous. War is a fearful thing when you are face to face with it. We had a nice little alarm here the other night. Louie had just gone to bed and I was sitting in the drawing room when I heard a mysterious noise and saw a cocked revolver coming round the corner of the door of the verandah which was open. I looked out and perceived an officer of the mounted police followed by a line of armed troopers advancing with the greatest caution along the verandah. It appeared that they believed the place to be in the possession of the Boers and had come to see the truth of it. They stated that there was a patrol of them 500 strong on the farm so we did not have a very comfortable night, however nothing happened to us. Altogether these are not very comfortable times but Louie shows wonderful pluck about it, the fact is one gets used to anything.

H. Rider Haggard

(Haggard 1881: 2nd 18:A Box 1, c.1)

The 25-year-old Haggard, still four years from becoming one of the best-selling authors in English history, ends this unpublished letter not with a pitched battle but with a non-event. The near-death experience he describes results not in resolution but in more waiting, as pressing danger dissolves into temporary relief. "Nothing," Haggard concludes, "happened to us." The intimate account by Victorian literature's clumsiest stylist bears witness to wars waged along the edges of a world system now shuffling toward downturn. It addresses this macrohistorical context in a minor key: the violence of a splintering imperium is here an everyday fact, catastrophe itself hardly rising to the level of narratable event. Haggard cites "our third disaster" and similarly de-emphasizes the loss of his friend George Colley just a month before ("You will have heard [...] of the death of poor Sir George"). Yet incident punctuates this everyday violence eventually: the British camp is almost, but not, overtaken by Boers, causing Haggard a "nice little alarm."

This sample text could be seen as teaching us something about the metaphysics of anticipation, where silence-shattering events alternate with the empty time of expectation. Or it could be read as a study in the trauma of wartime, as emergency is routinized and sensitivity dulled through prolonged exposure to human damage.[2] Haggard's letter pursues neither of these angles: in fact it pursues no angle at all. That is the point I want to make about it. What the letter stands here to represent is how diligently its prose works to avoid addressing conceptual or theoretical issues of any kind. Part of this is down to genre: the son's plucky letter to his mother was likely scribbled in an instant—we do not know, since the only copy exists in typescript, "from a copy of a letter found amongst Aunt Ellie's papers" (1881) (Fig. 4.1)—and would anyway always be reluctant to dilate on emotional matters. But Haggard's admittance of relief is extravagantly superficial, not just un- but anti-reflective. The letter ends by feinting toward a disclosure of some mental process: Haggard describes a not "very comfortable night" and parallels this with the "not very comfortable times." But this doubled negation of "comfortable" indicates a bodily state, not a mental one, and even this letter's most reflective moments ("War is a fearful thing") describe only physical bodies in material relationships: anticonceptuality is its most theoretical intervention.

In bringing us (in the letter's phrase) "face to face with it," Haggard's dispatch from the edges of the British system labors to collapse cognition into action, *dianoia* (thought) into *praxis* (deed). Any inward emotion, conscious deliberation, or characterological attitude has been, as Erich Auerbach might have put it, "scrupulously externalized" (1946: 3). In the first chapter or *Mimesis*, Auerbach describes the Homeric

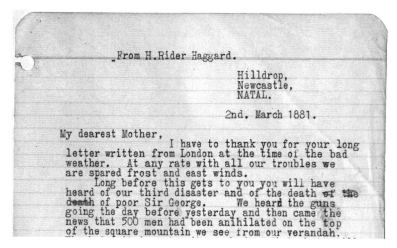

From H.Rider Haggard.

Hilldrop,
Newcastle,
NATAL.

2nd. March 1881.

My dearest Mother,
          I have to thank you for your long
letter written from London at the time of the bad
weather. At any rate with all our troubles we
are spared frost and east winds.
          Long before this gets to you you will have
heard of our third disaster and of the death of the
death of poor Sir George. We heard the guns
going the day before yesterday and then came the
news that 500 men had been anihilated on the top
of the square mountain we see from our verandah.

Fig. 4.1. Letter from Haggard to his mother, 2 March 1881 (detail). H. Rider Haggard Papers, David M. Rubenstein Rare Book & Manuscript Library, Duke University.

style in terms that also describe the pseudo-archaic technique of what will become Haggard's romance style, the highly artificial effect of immediacy I will investigate in what follows. "Clearly outlined, brightly and uniformly illuminated," Auerbach writes of Homeric epic, "men and things stand out in a realm where everything is visible" (p. 3). Georg Lukács, too, would index literary mode to social form, explaining in *The Theory of the Novel* (first published in 1920) that the epic is the only genre proper to pre-bourgeois experience; this is because "the autonomous life of interiority" on which novel form is predicated was not possible when human societies had yet to be disaggregated into individuals (1971: 66).[3] It bears noting that the aesthetic and political progressivisms of Lukács and Auerbach are but later reconfigurations of the Marxian and liberal narratives from the 1850s I charted in Chapter 1. As I will show, the status-to-contract storyline these thinkers all share, now transformed into a theory of fictional style, is legible in the pages of Haggard's romances no less than in the diverse conceptual writings of Haggard's sponsor, Andrew Lang—a connection between nineteenth-century "ideology" and twentieth-century "theory" that productively disrupts habitual critical divisions between those categories.

    Three years after writing the letter cited above, the young Haggard, fresh from his African experiences and seeking to make his way in the

London literary world, would find himself championed by Lang, whose work as a folklorist, literary impresario, and Homer scholar had already placed him at the center of the dynamic mass media environment of the 1880s and 1890s. Among many other accomplishments, Lang would prove instrumental in spurring Haggard to shift modes, guiding him from the failed domestic melodrama of *Dawn* (1884) and *The Witch's Head* (1885) toward the brutal and immediate romance plots Lang later judged to be "as good as Homer!" ("Norwich" 1920: 5).[4] In his letter, Haggard anticipates what would become the neo-Homeric practice of romances like *King Solomon's Mines* (1885), as he turns even so tumultuous an experience as being nearly murdered in bed into something palpable, visible, on the surface. Here as in his later work, in other words, Haggard's prose operates as a machine for converting thought into deed, internal deliberation into physical action. In so doing, it reverses the modernizing movement that George Eliot described as the progress from naïve to sentimental style (see Chapter 1) and dwells instead in the "absolute immanence of life" that Lukács, inheriting the categories Eliot herself derived from Schiller (who derived them from Kant), explains is proper to the epic mode (Lukács 1971: 35).

The progressive historical model these thinkers hold in common is one that has been traced across multiple registers in preceding chapters. Here as before it is a political story with aesthetic stakes: the developmental ideology shared by so diverse a group as Eliot, Mill, Auerbach, and Lukács presumes that a brutal and immediate violence gives way, over time, to a pacified and deliberative modernity: action gives way to thought, embodied affect to disembodied rationality. In modernity, Lukács explains, "interiority and adventure are forever divorced from each other" (1971: 66). Yet this aesthetic and political ideology of modernization, so often ascribed to the liberal proponents of time's forward motion like Mill Spencer, also structured the thought of late-century partisans of romance like Lang and Haggard, who (again anticipating Lukács) wanted to turn back the clock.

This chapter reconstructs an 1880s debate over the proper shape of literary fiction to show how the seemingly merely aesthetic controversy between "realism" and "romance" habitually cited in accounts of these years in fact mediated an important political problem in this pivotal decade: the newly obvious but still unspeakable role of violence in a declining liberal Empire. Written into causeries and magazine columns, attack-pieces and essays of method, the so-called "realism wars" of this decade pitted a deliberative and introspective American realism, conceptualized by William Dean Howells and exemplified in the work of Henry

James, against a self-consciously atavistic and stalwartly non-cognitive romance, a faux-epic style concretized in the novels of Haggard and devised as a theoretical mode by Lang, his literary handler. One consequence of reconstructing this antagonism over leadership of the transatlantic literary field in the 1880s has to do with the category of value. The brute immediacy of Haggard's romances is still treated as bad by a post-New Critical, post-Jamesian critical tradition: it is, to nearly all its critics, clunky, ham-fisted, and amateurish, more ideology than theory. But this fact says more about us than our objects, since it confirms that our own categories of analysis emerged from a struggle over literary value that Haggard's camp did not win.

My point is that this victory was political no less than aesthetic, since the dispute over the proper role of incident in literature transpired across transatlantic circuits of print production, connecting two imperial centers and two rival author–editor combinations: Lang and Haggard wrote from what was once the center of global print culture (London), with Howells and James blasting back from the rising literary and cultural marketplaces of Boston and New York. As the participants themselves note, this inter-imperial rivalry over the proper depth of fiction was among other things a displacement into literary practice of the tectonic geopolitical transition of this moment, when an ascendant bourgeois empire, an American one, began to assert its place as the globe's rising sovereign power in the years after 1875.[5] This chapter shows how the dispute between "realism" and "romance" transforms the seeming paradox of liberal violence into an aesthetic problem, doing so at a moment when dreams of perpetual peace unraveled into the endless wars of annexation and pacification in the waning years of British global power. Violence had always been the rule of Empire. But if the wars necessary to sustain equipoise took place largely outside the consciousness of metropolitan writers like Eliot, the late century found the brute work of sustaining Empire under conditions of decline all but impossible to ignore. As Hannah Arendt notes, "rule by sheer violence comes into play where power is being lost" (1970: 53).

This claim about late imperial violence and the mediating conceptual work of romance unfolds in three parts. First, the chapter reconstructs the transatlantic debates that gave rise to Haggard's idiosyncratic style—the veering and immediate prose to which post-Jamesian criticism still condescends. Second, it explains how this stylistic dispute shapes Haggard's treatment of so-called just war at the edges of Britain's newly contested global empire, as sovereign brutality and humanitarian impulses mutually inform *King Solomon's Mines*. The chapter concludes by showing how the seeming antagonism between liberal and illiberal fictional modes, what Lukács referred to as "adventure and interiority," belies a deeper kinship between them. Another member of the Lang coterie, Robert Louis Stevenson, investigates this uncanny affinity in *The Strange Case of Dr. Jekyll and Mr. Hyde* (1886), which reconfigures as dialectic the genre-inflected political dispute those other thinkers treat as simple opposition. As it allegorizes the struggle between realist deliberation and romance action, between liberal restraint and anti-liberal brute force, it casts this struggle not as opposition but as an irresolvable antinomy of liberal modernity. Seen this way, romance does not so much provide imaginary solutions to real problems—as symptomatic readings, following Althusser's famous definition of ideology, have long presumed—as strategically mediate liberalism's relationship to violence during this transitional period, when dreams of equipoise splintered and brute violence lurched into the light.

REALISM WARS: JAMES/HOWELLS, LANG/HAGGARD

When the elephant-blasting hero of *King Solomon's Mines* is asked, in the book's first pages, whether he will join an aristocrat and a navy man named Good on a quest into the heart of Africa, readers are presented with what is announced as a moment of inward mental deliberation—Quatermain is supposed to be thinking. It is a big decision, and between question and answer intervene "four or five days," an interlude the text fills with concrete descriptions of sunsets, flora, fauna, and other details of para-anthropological local color. At last the decision arrives:

> I rose and knocked out my pipe before I answered. I had not made up my mind, and wanted the additional moment to complete it. Before the burning tobacco had fallen into the sea it was completed; just that little extra second did the trick. It is often the way when you have been bothering a long time over a thing.
> "Yes, gentlemen," I said, sitting down again, "I will go[.]"   (2007: 32)

In the decisive moment, pages of externalized waiting collapse into a single instant of decision. It is passively narrated ("it was completed") and almost atemporal: "just that little second did the trick." And yet, what Quatermain uses here is not quite the embodied or arational processing that goes by the name "affect." For Allan has been "bothering for a long time" over his decision; but the novel has refused to disclose the mechanisms of that bother. Instead, this moment of deliberative cognition—one of the novel's very few—is translated into an entirely physical episode: "I rose and knocked out my pipe." And the relentlessly physicalizing aesthetic of romance plays out in miniature.

Under Lang's direction, the campaign against an upstart American realism by the advocates of romance during the mid-1880s was "one of the most important literary debates in Britain during the late 19th century" (Michalski 1995: 13), though it is chiefly remembered not *as* a debate but with isolated references to its most widely anthologized interventions: Lang's "Realism and Romance" and James' "The Art of Fiction." In that 1884 article, James used his title's then-polemical genitive to solidify the medium he had chosen—fiction—as worthy of the label "art." This pointed foray into the era's shifting literary field required a new vocabulary, James intuited, one able to separate penetrating works of high culture from their shallow others. "[T]he deepest quality of a work of art," James continued, "will always be the quality of mind of the producer"; no good writing "will ever proceed from a superficial mind" (1884: n.p.). That James' metaphors of superficiality and depth register now as platitudes measures the astonishing success of James and his early sponsor Howells in deciding the future of novel form; it also indexes the efficiency of these actors in casting an evaluative criticism in spatial terms. James' reference to "deepest qualities" and "superficial minds" is noteworthy, I mean, not just because this surface/depth dichotomy predates the Freudian moment so often taken as originary in genealogies of literary hermeneutics. It is important also because these categories, now deracinated from their historical origins, continue to structure debates about method. Given the backstory I trace here, Haggard's anti-deliberative aesthetic is best seen as reversing extravagantly the value judgments still clinging to the surprisingly resilient metaphors of surface and depth in literary criticism: for Haggard, cognitive states are accessible only by way of the bodily actions that express them, and the post-Jamesian distinction between bad surface and good depth (or, as in recent so-called postcritical methods, the reverse) dissolves into incoherence.

Still it is true that a seeming unsophistication of technique has authorized readers from the 1880s forward to view Haggard's novels as conceptually unsophisticated too. At least partially for this supposed naïveté, *King Solomon's Mines* continues to be understood as the first instance (Brantlinger 1988), the most offensive specimen (Chrisman 2000), and a "nearly pure example" (Patteson 1978: 113) of an entire genre of mass-cultural ideology we might have done better without. Shepherded into publication by Lang and then puffed by him in almost innumerable outlets (a rumor was that he had written twenty-four separate positive reviews), Haggard's allegedly simple-minded tale was for Lang akin to the best of Walter Scott and

Homer. The comparison to these artifacts of high culture was partially motivated by Lang's assiduous efforts to "logroll" his friend's book, and was always meant to scandalize. Given that the novel had been written on a dare to imitate Stevenson's *Treasure Island* and is dedicated "to all the big and little boys who read it," claims for the novel's timeless value would always register as hyperbole. The novel's famous publication event, a watershed moment in the marketing of literary commodities, came directly in the wake of Britain's greatest late-century imperial embarrassment, the abortive 1885 campaign to rescue General Gordon at Khartoum, and at the height of the openly militaristic "New Imperialism" of the mid-1880s. It was thus well packaged (as children's literature) and perfectly timed (at a time of national-imperial crisis) to perform the "consolatory form of magical thinking" that criticism has long seen as the signal cultural work of Haggard's literary practice (Hultgren 2014: 23).[6]

But in contrast to the later critics who treat Haggard's work as mechanistically expressive of a jingoistic mass culture, Haggard's most perceptive contemporaries recognized that his stumbling productions represented an active intervention into novel theory. "Does not Mr. Rider Haggard make even his African carnage pleasant?" (quoted in Edel 1962: 178). The question comes from James himself, and it is meant ironically; but the Master's aside was written during the period when, as Leon Edel notes, he was building from the ground up his own sense of how an artist-author should best navigate between the poles of inwardness and action, "character" and "plot" (Edel 1962: 322–4). James' answer is that it should be different from Haggard. Writing to Stevenson in August of 1887, James continued his defense of the fanatical introspection that would characterize his own late style, finding in the "beastly bloodiness" of Haggard's prose (quoted in Edel 1962: 178) the negative image of his own more involuted practice:

> Such perpetual killing and such perpetual ugliness! It is worth while to write a tale of fantastic adventure, with a funny man, etc. and pitched all in the slangiest key, to kill 20,000 men, as in *Solomon*, in order to help your heroes on! [. . .] They seem to me works in which our race and our age make a very vile figure—and they have unexpectedly depressed me.
>
> (quoted in Edel 1962: 178)

James had read all of *King Solomon's Mines* and half of *She* (1887) when he registered this depression. It was enough to spur a visceral response to "the unspeakable Haggard" (James 1980: 128), an affective or reflexive revulsion that is ironic given James' status today as the least embodied and most reflective of modern novelists—literary history's chief defender, with Eliot, of fiction's effort to plumb the depths of spatially imagined human psyches in order to expand and cultivate the sympathetic capacities of readers.[7] Fiction should elevate what James called the "moral sense" (quoted in Miller 595–6) and not, as he suggested of Haggard, "depress" it. We do not often think of Jamesian style as bearing a necessary, because mutually defining, link to children's literature. But as Edel explains, these letters were composed in the twilight hour between James' famed "early" and "late" phases, and his dismissal of Haggard reveals him in the process of developing the method that he would devise to counter the surplus of shocking event he identified in Haggard no less than in his own early work. This was the involuted style that elevated a "nervousness about overt action" into an aesthetic desideratum (Markovits 2006: 145).

In the prototypically early novel, *The American*, of 1877, published serially in Howells' *Atlantic*, James had somewhat hamfistedly announced a new man, Christopher Newman, as the protagonist in what would become his novels' ongoing international drama. But that novel featured a duel with pistols—albeit one that happens off the page—and by 1907, in the preface to the novel's New York edition, James would find cause to apologize for the lack of "tact" he displayed in veering so indelicately into the "disconnected and uncontrolled experience [...] which romance [...] palms off on us" (1907: n.p.). In the preface the late James chides the early one for slumming in the realm of novelistic incident. Before he had gained that kind of remove, in "The Art of Fiction" (1884), James had already ventured that cognitive operations might be actions too: "it *is* an incident," he declares, "for a woman to stand up with her hand resting on a table and look at you a certain way; or if it not be an incident, I think it will be hard to say what it is" (p. 512). The extravagantly attenuated concept of incident being tested here—the hesitation is legible in James' prose—already finds him finding value not in material event or realized action but in the deliberative process occasioning it. This reworking of "incident" to describe interiorized cognition, study, and reflection—the Kantian faculty of disembodied judgment traced in Chapters 1 and 3—explicitly rejects the melodrama of James' own early work in, for example, *Watch and Ward* (serial 1871, book 1878). It also reiterates the conventional understanding, in force since Aristotle, that unwitting, unconsidered, or reflexive actions do not properly count as actions at all, since (in the words of one summary) "*what* is done" is less important than "*why* it is done" (Ackrill 1980: 94). The sentiment is Aristotle's, but could be James', for even *Watch and Ward*, which James later disavowed for its ostentations emphasis on action, features a hero for whom "it was quite out of his nature to do a thing without distinctly knowing why" (1878: 8–9).

The later James could have an entire novel build up to the question, as he put it in the New York edition Preface to *The Portrait of a Lady*, "well, what will she *do?*" (emphasis original): 600 pages build toward a single event, which James nevertheless says is hardly an event at all, since the climax, he explains in the Preface, is "a representation simply of [Isabel Archer] motionlessly *seeing*, and an attempt withal to make the mere still lucidity of her act as 'interesting' as the surprise of a caravan or the identification of a pirate" (1907, n.p., emphasis original). Haggard's novels are packed full of the Arabian Nights-like devices that James derides here ("caravan[s]," "pirate[s]"); they refuse James' inward turn; they work hard to avoid what Quatermain calls the "detestable habit of thinking" (2007: 146); and they propose a theory of action that is the precise opposite of James' neo-Aristotelian and liberal-idealist deliberative rationality, where an action can only occur when it is undertaken knowingly and after consideration, by a sovereign individual, with an "equilibrium" of the soul Aristotle calls "ethos," or character (1902, n.p.).

It is a critical truism that James' mode, particularly in his later fictions, is deliberative consciousness realized in form: ever-longer sentences, thick with dependent clauses, tensely vibrate between observing minds that are themselves engaged in acts of *"seeing."* Such techniques as free indirect discourse mediate that densely cognitive deliberativeness as literary device. The vibrating, oscillating, or internally dividing character of this consciousness enacts, in this way, the etymology of *dianoia* (διάνοια, "thought"). As opposed to *noesis* (νόησις), which designates immediate or reflexive apprehension of the material world, *dianoia* denotes thinking in motion: through or over (διά), the "movement from one side (of an issue) to the other to reach balanced conclusions; full-orbed reasoning (= critical thinking)" ("Dianoia" 2001). Contrasting with such poised deliberation or thinking-around—always aimed at the equilibrium that James, anticipating the New Critics, idealizes as "form"—Haggard's abrupt tonal shifts and rigorously non-cognitive approach attack the very idea of balance, and (from this perspective) can only ever appear as formless.

James' most sustained investigation into the aesthetic and, I am suggesting, political problem of action, *The Princess Casamassima*, of 1886, inflects with class valences the dilemma of cognition versus event that is its main problematic. Here the tension between an upmarket humanistic contemplativeness and a low-rent emphasis on deeds becomes the backstory of the novel's hero, Hyacinth Robinson. Robinson is the son of a murdering prostitute and a sublimely passive aristocrat. His dilemma is the one also allegorized in George Gissing's *New Grub Street* (1891), where Reardon's anti-commercial art-aesthetics lose out to the opportunistic Jaspar Milvain and his ability to write anything, anywhere, instantly. It is also, as we will see, the problem framed in Stevenson's *Dr. Jekyll and Mr. Hyde*, where a civilized thinking man and an animalistic man of action struggle for control over a single body.

The chapter in Edel's biography that discusses *The Princess Casamassima* is called "The Divided Self" (1962: 324), and while Edel is talking about James, the label applies also to his hero: Robinson is half action and half thought, half low and half high. Which inheritance will he claim? While he dabbles in the possibility of joining "the party of immediate action"—a cell of leftist revolutionaries—his "mixed, divided nature, his conflicting sympathies, his eternal habit of swinging from one view to another" (1987: 478) makes worldly action difficult. In framing Hyacinth's choice, the novel asks itself whether its protagonist will be more like Haggard or more like the late James. Will Robinson do it? Where the less reflective Princess was "apt to kindle [...] at the idea of any great freedom of action" (p. 487), Robinson balks; he deliberates; he thinks for pages of dialogue-free paragraphs; and finally he decides to not decide: "[T]hen the old man said, 'Well, [Hyancinth], promise me that you will never, under any circumstances whatever, do anything'"(p. 564). Robinson agrees to this stunningly broad prohibition, and doesn't assassinate the man he's been directed to. But rather than refuse to perform this act—that would be an action too—Robinson demurs, killing himself offscreen in the novel's final (unrepresented) event. As Stefanie Markovits observes, "Like Isabel Archer's, Hyacinth's yearning for action belies a deep-seated passivity" (2006: 161). This tendency toward deferral and deliberative delay is what the hero shares with the novel form that is his mind's most appropriate medium.

Against such nobly elevating smoothness—form raised to a principle of liberal-humanistic cultivation—Lang positioned Haggard as a gleefully savage other.[8] As I've noted, Lang was Haggard's early champion and editor; he read *King Solomon's Mines* in manuscript and helped arrange for its publication, going on to collaborate with Haggard throughout the waning years of the nineteenth century and even authoring a badly reviewed novel with him, published by the house for which Lang was an asset, Longman's—*The World's Desire* of 1890. "[P]erhaps the most influential critic of the last two decades of the nineteenth century" (Weintraub 5) and an almost comically tireless worker,[9] Lang carved out multiple avenues for reaching the public he loved to amuse: magazine columns, folklore criticism, Homer scholarship, and literary criticism, among many other areas of production. During his lifetime Lang authored more than 300 books—the precise figure is still unknown—and throughout the 1880s and 1890s used his mastery of multiple media platforms to establish "a dominant influence beyond any individual critic before or since" (Elwin 1939: 183). He cultivated a coterie of adventure writers and intellectual fellow-travelers. With these collaborators he militated for a rejuvenating, savage, or neo-epic mode centered on explicit event—on action, as he tirelessly insisted, not thinking.

Filtering this literary partisanship through his interests in the cultural anthropology then being pioneered by E. B. Tylor, Lang conceived his action-oriented mode as reanimating a tradition reaching back, he thought, not only to Walter Scott, a fellow Scot Lang had always admired, but also to the cultural forms Lang (with Tylor) associated with premodernity itself: savage folklore and Homeric epic. To the critics who demanded from their fiction probability of events, domestic settings, and deep psychology, Lang responded by making connections among Haggard, Homer, and the marvels of supernatural myth. His citation of the *Odyssey* as "the typical example of [. . .] romance," for example, pointedly demolishes the then conventional association of the Greek poems with elevated nobility. Rather than the ennobling or rationalistic virtue Arnold had indirectly suggested might emerge from the poet in his lectures *On Translating Homer* (1860), Lang finds in Homer something to charge "the barbaric element [. . .] of our blood [. . .], a childish love of marvels, miracles, man eating giants." In "Realism and Romance" (1887), Lang's rhetoric reaches a crescendo with a dig at Howells:

> "Public opinion," in Boston, may condemn us, but we will get all the fun we can out of the ancestral barbarism of our natures. I only wish we had more of it. The Coming Man may [well] be bald, toothless, highly "cultured," and addicted to tales of introspective analysis.   (Lang 1887: 689)

Lang's polemic against a refined and bloodless "Coming Man" rests on the claim that archaic romances stir a "barbaric element" that has not yet died in us, even at this late phase of civilization. Lang's polemic against an enfeebled civilization jibes at the scientific theories of Spencer to mock—but not refute—the idea that the process of modernization will inevitably dim what Lang calls "the ancestral barbarism of our natures." But the Boston dig aims directly at Howells, with whom Lang was by this time engaged in a battle that pitted the coming man of American realism against the atavistic throwbacks of English romance. As Howells later wrote, using Lang's own terms against him, the childlike instinct in "[m]odern English criticism likes to be melted, and horrified, and blood-curdled, and goose-fleshed," while an appropriately modern, adult, and American criticism, Howells maintained, will always prefer the more involuted and thus sympathy-extending pleasures of an allegedly mature psychological fiction (quoted in Demoor 1987a: 417).

Against the self-consciously atavistic English practices Lang advocated—figured throughout these debates as childish, an accusation Haggard and Lang were happy to embrace—Howells used a series of articles from the mid-1880s to assert realist form as the idiom in which a maturing American modernity might articulate itself. The art of Dickens and Thackeray was now "of the past," Howells explained, and "the new school [...] which is so largely of the future as well as the present, finds its chief exemplar in Mr. Henry James" (1882: 28). The dispute between deliberation and event was in other words nothing less than a tension between an English past and an American future:

> To spin a yarn for the yarn's sake, that is an ideal worthy of a nineteenth century Englishman [...]; but wholly impossible to an American of Mr. Henry James's modernity. [...] To such a mind as his the story could never have value except as a means; it could not exist for him as an end; it could be used only illustratively; it could be the frame, not possibly the picture.
>
> (Hayes, ed. 1996: 234)

With the past obsession with yarns set against an interest in human complexity more appropriate to the future, Howells' polemics call for a bourgeois modernity characterized by "artistic impartiality" and painstaking "analysis of motive" (1882: 318, 320). Howells is careful to pitch his intervention as a timely one, necessary "now," in 1886:

> realism seeks now, to widen the bounds of sympathy, to level every barrier against aesthetic freedom, to escape from the paralysis of tradition. [Romance] exhausted itself in this impulse, and it remained for realism to assert that fidelity to experience and probability of motive are essential conditions for great imaginative literature.   (1992, vol. 2: 21)

These tactical interventions into the transatlantic literary field find Howells rewriting in international terms the status-to-contract story we have traced in earlier chapters. Here, an exhausted British romance is announced as an archaic phase of status (spinning yarns, curdling blood), while a new realism, waiting in history's wings, readies to ascend new heights of liberal-idealist cognition, "level[ing] barrier[s]" and spreading not just moral sense and "sympathy" but what Howells does not shy from terming "freedom." This storyline could only be told provided Howells ignored the fact that just a few decades earlier this very bourgeois aesthetic found its proper home in England, and its proper expression in Eliot. By the 1880s, however, the liberal freedom of American realism (in Amy Kaplan's words) "emerges in literary history in bellicose terms—as a *war, a struggle, a campaign*—and William Dean Howells appears as the leader of this charge" (1988: 15, emphasis added). It is an ironic characterization given that this mode's main characteristic was a studied avoidance of each of the forms of violence listed here.

The realism wars would alter forever the shape of the novel. As readers will recall, Haggard's narrative structures are first-person and extremely limited: his novels unfold as found texts mediated by editors, disclosing nested sets of adventures, one inside of another, that are narrated always from a single simple man's point of view.[10] (In *Homer and the Epic*, Lang had described a similar digressive, nested structure in the *Odyssey*.) By contrast, in James as in Eliot, the narrative voice dips first into one perspective, then into another, and ascends, finally, to cast ironic judgment on all of them in a process that expands webs of intersubjective sympathy while it "deepens" the capacity of readers insofar as it pushes them to experience separate aspects of their own experiences, as "perspectives." Free indirect discourse, with its emphasis on the minute apprehension of other minds and the specific linguistic processes by which they operate (see Fludernik 1995), was the formal device proper to the bourgeois consciousness Howells sought to institutionalize in its internally divided or liberal-sentimental form. In an early version of a still-common argument, Howells claimed that reading stories that model this intersubjective process would in turn expand the sympathies of readers, rendering them more "human."

This backstory helps us see that one accomplishment of F. R. Leavis' *The Great Tradition* was to collapse into a single, allegedly timeless liberal-humanist tradition what was in fact a complicated historical and international rivalry between English and American bourgeois forms. Out of inter-imperial rivalry Leavis generated a "human" identity alleged to transcend nationality. In his encomium to the soulmaking ambition of James' own procedure, its salutary capacity to humanize you, Leavis explains correctly that Eliot and James share a success in translating the cognitive dispensation of individualized, interiorized modernity into fictional form; they concretize, in Michael McKeon's words, "at the micro-level of style and the sentence, [. . .] that (variously figured) condition of detachment or distance" (2000: 485) that liberal theory then as now associates with modernity as such. Put another way, the densely deliberative practice of Jamesian realism works as the aesthetic mediation of, and argument for, human rationality in its post-Kantian, self-divided, and self-regulating guise. (It is this dispensation of consciousness that Lukács critiques when he explains that "happy ages have no philosophy" (1971: 29)). James himself suggests this when he explains that the process of creating true art (not romance, not melodrama) induces "an immense increase—a kind of revelation—of freedom" (1884: 515). My point is that, in the 1880s, this new claim to freedom represents a claim for a specifically American version of it, and constitutes an effort to relocate the place of bourgeois "depth" from an older side of the Atlantic to the newer one. It may be true, as D. H. Lawrence said, that of all the novelists "it was [George Eliot] who started putting all the action inside" (quoted in Markovits 2006: 89). But after 1880 the figure of modern detachment was an American.[11]

Lang for his part conceded the dichotomy Howells and James framed between surface and depth, character and incident, but maintained that the retrograde pleasures of story, however asynchronous with their present, could for that very reason provide a bracing tonic for men lapsed too far into a timid civility. While "[t]hey all talk about their emotions forever," Lang sneers, "the natural man within me, the survival of some blue-painted Briton or of some gipsy [is] equally pleased with a *true* Zulu love story" (1887: 689, emphasis original). If one surprise of this theory is that it places Haggard's clunky novels on the level of myth, another is that all such primitive forms have the power to stir within modern man an older way of living that is no longer ours: a Zulu or "gipsy" mode of life Lang inflects not with a negative but a positive valence. Lang's program thus accepts the modernizing timeline on which liberal developmental schemes are based, but inverts the dichotomy of value Arnold had already made, in *Culture and Anarchy* (1867), between our "best" and "worst" selves. Lang pulls not for the calm moderation of a hypercognitive disinterest, but for the passionate physicality of animal man. In reading Homer, Lang contends, "our own sense of vitality is [...] in a measure increased, and, as it were, there is a kind of transfusion into our veins of the heroic blood, of the vigour in the limbs of the sons of Gods" (1893: 11).

Lang had begun his career as a decorated scholar of Homeric poetry while studying at Oxford, and was influenced there by Tylor and other participants in the new developmental historicism of culture then reshaping ethnological method.[12] For Lang, the key aspect of Tylor's theory was the doctrine of survivals, or holdovers from previous cultural stages. What Lang took from this innovation were two key points. The first was the idea that myths were the crystallization of a kind a common language or *pensée sauvage*, a deep structure shared by all human cultures at a given stage of development, no matter the the myth's temporal or geographical origin. Thus Welsh folktales, Icelandic sagas, African myth, and Homer could equally be adduced in Lang's (many) published collections of folktales, fairy stories, and *Märchen*, as representing a primitive prehistory that was our common heritage. The second point was that "older" forms—idioms further down this universal scale of thought—nevertheless have the power to reach beyond their proper time and place, productively contaminating the present moment with dead forms: magical thinking from the childhood of culture could re-emerge later, in adult epochs that had become problematically disenchanted.

"KILL! KILL! KILL!": *KING SOLOMON'S MINES* I

In the late Victorian period, little thinking was more magical than Haggard's, and since the 1980s, the protocols of Marxian hermeneutics and Foucauldian cultural studies have authorized literary criticism to read these alleged fantasy constructions symptomatically. Such approaches figure Haggard's novels as either (in the first case) the unwitting displacement of sociocultural dilemmas or (in the second) instantiations of an undifferentiated imperial discourse whose "anxieties" remain for the critic to decode. This work has produced insights insofar as it has sketched the putatively unknowing relationship of *King Solomon's Mines* to the racism, sexism, and cultural jingoism of its moment. There is an irony, of course, in accusing Haggard's novel of imperialism given that its author was an avowed supporter of Empire—in fact a soldier in the cause who, it is routinely cited, personally raised the British flag during the annexation of the Transvaal.[13] More pressing than such critical circularities is the fact that symptomatic approaches replay the theoretical presuppositions of the objects they mean to analyze, such that, for example, the method of historical reading Lang developed via Tylor is used to understand Lang and his acolyte and imitator, Haggard. As Kathy Psomiades has noted (2013), this pair's sense of the present as a jumbled archive of enciphered remnants, legible only through the hermeneutic energy of later witnesses, would be fleshed out in a more theoretical language by Lévi-Strauss. From that source it would come to structure Fredric Jameson's method for reading what he calls "sedimented" generic signals, passing from Jameson to inform (for example) cultural criticism's presumption that Victorian literary forms, construed as ideology or discourse, encrypt unbeknownst to themselves a given culture's subconscious desires or "anxieties."[14] Rather than engage in exhumatory or stratigraphic readerly practices like these, we might instead track these practices in their processes of emergence and institutionalization. One result would be that literary objects like *King Solomon's Mines* stand not as instances of unwitting magical thinking or reflexive enclosure but as political conceptuality: not passive ideology but enacted thought.

What Haggard's breakthrough novel chronicles is a fight for law itself. The plot's main episode shows how British military expertise helps reinstate a rational, just ruler, "a magnificent-looking man" (2007: 40) as the sovereign of a formerly despotic African state. After this operation, our three representative British characters depart, leaving Kukuanaland safe in the hands of a new, more enlightened regime, one that promises to replace the random executions of the former state with the equivalence and peace of modern law. "[B]loodshed shall cease in the land," promises the reinstated prince, Ignosi. "No longer shall ye cry for justice to find slaughter [. . .] No man shall die save he who offendeth against the laws" (p. 142).

Narrated in the neo-archaic style that was directly shaped, as we will see, by Lang's pioneering translations of Homer, this story of international intervention in defense of universal norms—call it "nation-building" or "modernization"—coexists with another tale more directly in line with the muscular imperialism Haggard avowed in public statements; here, resource extraction and the expansion of British territorial sovereignty emerge as the ultimate results of the intervention staged by Quatermain and his band. It is not the presence of one or the other of these imperial strategies—emancipatory or jingoistic, "informal" or "formal," Liberal or Tory—but their coexistence that marks this text as canny translation, into form, of the late empire's political strategies.[15]

Alternating between moralistic denunciations of violence and gleeful accounts of it in a sensationalizing mode, Haggard's romance shows how a strategy of direct political annexation worked hand in glove with the kind of softer influence, still imperial, that was advocated by mid- and late-Victorian opponents of "imperialism." Fused together in Haggard's prose, these two apparently conflicting political positions map roughly onto the paired strategies available to British power in the late century. As Bradley Deane (2014) among others has explained, the "soft" or humanitarian motivations generally adduced by Gladstonian liberalism traded blows with the more muscular approach favored by Tory lawmakers in the run-up to the 1886 elections. Corresponding broadly to the distinction between formal and informal or indirect imperialisms—open violence or the secret kind—this broadly sketched division itself recapitulates what David Harvey has called the "contradictory fusion" of late modern imperialism's twin strategies (2003: 26), where the first formally incorporates resources and territory, and the second works to link previously excluded economic points into a world-systemic network under the signs of modernization and improvement (see also Arrighi 2007: 211 *et passim*). One produces an empire of conquest, the other an empire of liberty.

It is the distinction of *King Solomon's Mines* to dramatize both strategies simultaneously: "formal" and "informal" imperial strategies overlap and inform one another in Haggard's plot, with the first avowedly acquisitive narrative taking shape at the level of plot, even as a civilizing or modernizing narrative (call it progressive, or "liberal") emerges in the explicit pronouncements of Haggard's imperial characters. This snarled aesthetic and ideological program generates Haggard's most characteristic effects of prose, and attention to this effect of mediation shows how, in a liberal empire facing the prospect of its dissolution, ultraviolent capitalist expansion and humanistic universalism could come wrapped in a single package.

The plot of Haggard's fantasia unfolds episodically, and begins as Allan Quatermain is approached in Durban, South Africa, by Sir Henry Curtis and the straightforwardly named Captain Good, a naval officer. The details of their quest are familiar to millions of readers: the team of characters allegorically denoting the three estates of an idealized British nationalism—an aristocrat, a military man, and a freelancing capitalist entrepreneur—join with their native guide, Umbopa, to follow a vividly drawn map into the heart of Africa. They cross a desert, climb a mountain ("Sheba's left breast" (p. 25)), enter a cave, find a dead explorer, then pass into the lush valley of Kukuanaland, a lost civilization distantly related, we are told, to the Zulus. In Kukuanaland the white men prove their superiority by using an icon of Western technical rationality (an almanac) to predict an eclipse.[16] The novel's main episode transpires as the trio helps organize a rebellion against a murderous king, Twala. Having used their newly proven supernatural powers (and their ability to organize a coup), the heroes restore their former porter to his rightful place as king, then enter the mines of the book's title, where they are locked into the treasure chamber by a shriveled witch-goddess, Gagool. They escape, and on the return journey through the desert they find Sir Henry's brother seemingly at random. After returning to Durban, all adventurers re-enter civilization, now more or less rich thanks to the few diamonds they were able to fit in their pockets.

All of this unfolds in the episodic or segmented "empty time" Bakhtin and others treat as a distinguishing feature of counter-realist narration since ancient times (Bakhtin 1981: 91). In this antidevelopmental chronotope, characters are static and positional rather than dynamically characterological. Plot is generated not from personal development or "inner" change but from a series of confrontations between stable actors and variable external stimuli. Unlike bourgeois forms such as the *Bildungsroman* or the probabilistic realism of James or Eliot, romance has a logic that is (in Bakhtin's words) "one of random contingency" rather than sequential development: "'suddenlys' and 'at just that moments' make up the entire contents of the novel" (1981: 92). Thick with "suddenly" (44 appearances) and "and then" (42 appearances), Quatermain's world is one designed with perfect indifference to the gradualist sequential patterns and probabilistic regimes of modern-bourgeois narration, those upwardly tending arcs built not on chance encounters with other actors but on the internalized "process of *becoming-man*" (Lukács 1971: 62, emphasis original).

My own quick sketch of a plot that was itself quickly sketched—Haggard boasted that he composed the novel in a six-week burst, never having thought about the structure deeply (Cohen 1960: 85)—will have already suggested why the text has been seen since the 1990s as an unthinking tool of late imperial mythmaking. Yet if it seems to work as a mechanistic ideological vehicle, reiterating gentle-manly gender ideology (Deane 2014), late-century racism (Brantlinger 1988), or imperialist fantasy (Chrisman 2000), attention to its formal procedure shows how it also works actively or positively, to mediate into new language the legal precarity and thus disposability of human beings inhabiting "semi-autonomous" areas of a British world system under threat.

It is often overlooked that the novel's central episode is not dia-mond extraction or sexualized exploration but a crisis of international sovereignty, one whose form of appearance is a dispute over dynastic succession. Haggard's Kukuanan characters set the stage for British intervention by recounting their nation's convoluted political history in a tale that forms the third backstory within the novel's major quest narrative.[17] The details of the crisis are these. Long ago the civilization's king, Kafa, fathered twin sons, Imotu, the first born, and Twala, the present king (pp. 92–3). Because the custom in Kukuanaland is to kill the weaker twin, the mother hid Twala away, with Gagool providing protection to the child for several years. Meanwhile Imotu became king, eventually bearing a son, Ignosi. When Ignosi was three years old, a famine swept the land. Gagool blamed Imotu, and when the witch doctress unveiled Twala, who had secretly been kept alive, Twala was greeted as king by a starving populace. Imotu's wife, now widowed, fled the country to the south, raising the former king's son (Ignosi) under the name Umbopa. "Then if this child Ignosi had lived," Quatermain helpfully inquires, "he would be the true king of the Kukuana people?" (p. 103) The answer is yes, and the baroque scenario is clarified by a family tree, adapted from Richard Patteson's (1978) structural analysis of the novel (Fig. 4.2).

The revelation that Umbopa the servant is really Ignosi the king forms the *anagnorisis*, or moment of recognition, considered by commentators from Frye to Bakhtin as a distinguishing feature of romance. Umbopa has not *developed* from servant to a king, as the plot of *Bildung* would dictate; he has discovered he always was one. Haggard's melodrama of discovery thus draws on the resources of romance form to trace a story of regime

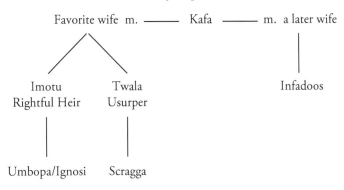

Fig. 4.2. Sovereignty in Kukuanaland. Adapted from Richard Patteson, "*King Solomon's Mines*: Imperialism and Narrative Structure," *Journal of Narrative Technique* 8(2) (1978), p. 118.

change on the margins of the British system. Successfully resolving it will require acrobatic balancing from Haggard's text, for it must partially disavow ulterior motives on the part of the British liberators (they are only helping), even as it acknowledges the benefits that accrue to them because of their intervention. If they get diamonds from and power over the regime they set up, these advantages accrue only by accident: the real motive was a humanitarian one.

With curious good cheer, the adventurers consent to assist in the new civil war, with Sir Henry and Captain Good agreeing to help for different but equally "humorous" reasons—Henry because "I have always liked Umbopa," Good because "a row is surely good, and warms the cockles of the heart" (p. 116). The rationales are cartoon versions of the strategies available to British administrators at a moment when Gladstone's liberal imperialism was succeeded by the New Imperialism of Disraeli and his successors. In Haggard's prismatic reworking of liberal imperialism's constitutive conceptual impasse, intervention can be justified either via a Disraeli-esque lust for brute force ("a row [. . .] warms the cockles of the heart"), or because of the seemingly more advanced, Gladstonian obligations of loyalty that friendship incurs upon a stronger power ("I have always liked Umbopa").

Quatermain's response is more telling, since it combines these alternatives, freezing into a single ambiguous utterance the peculiar combination of reluctance and action—a kind of accidental warmaking—this text is at pains to ascribe to its laconic hero. Umbopa has offered to pay the British men as mercenaries. With a smirk, Quatermain reveals that what motivates him is loyalty—and acquisition:

"Umbopa, or Ignosi," I said, "I don't like revolutions. I am a man of peace, and a bit of a coward" (here Umbopa smiled) "but, on the other hand, I stick to my friends, Ignosi. You have stuck to us and played the part of a man, and I will stick to you. But mind you I am a trader, and have to make my living, so I accept your offer about those diamonds, in case we should ever be in a position to avail ourselves of it." (p. 116)

Umbopa's well-timed smile allows us to see that Quatermain is less a "coward" than a warrior in search of mineral wealth, albeit one who mouths phrases of non-violence and loyalty. The tension Haggard's prose crystallizes is that between Quatermain's feigned liberal idealism ("I am a man of peace") and an actual diamond-grabbing realpolitik, a doubleness of motive that rewrites the antagonisms of Britain's concrete presence on the African veldt into a grinning performative contradiction Haggard's prose stages but—and this is its most powerful intervention— feels no need to resolve. Quatermain's strangely acquisitive critique of violence means that instead of policing the distance between ideological poles, *King Solomon's Mines* discloses their fundamental interconnection: liberation and expropriation, friendship and subjection are here cemented together.[18] The result is a hybrid packaging of a fading empire's contra- dictory logics. On the one hand, a nightmarishly violent episode of capital extraction, resource theft, and puppet sovereignty; on the other, a reluc- tant intervention on behalf of values construed as "human."

Just as earlier we have learned that "for a timid man, I have been mixed up in a deal of slaughter" (p. 11), Quatermain's speech about being a man of peace could stand for Britain's national position in this, its late imperial or downward phase. On the one hand, it glances at the virtues of peaceful free trade appropriate to a civilizing or incorporating imperial mission, one aimed at bringing in and then uplifting sites and peoples formerly outside its auspices. This allegedly peaceful process of universalist integration is what Eliot no less than Mill and Collins held as the content for the term "modernity." Yet Quatermain's conflicted announcement also underscores the resource extraction and expansion of British power that were the material results of the campaign waged with this uplifting incorporation ostensibly in mind ("mind you I am a trader"). Rather than seeing liberal incorporation and Tory acquisition/extermination as antagonistic strategies, Haggard's text sets both into motion at once.[19]

It is a familiar fact that *King Solomon's Mines* and other of Haggard's African tales translate into fiction his real-life experiences as attaché to Theophilius Shepstone, special commissioner for the Transvaal, a pos- ition Haggard held from 1875 until he returned to England (and began writing books) in 1881. As noted already, critiques of the novel's seeming jingoism habitually note that Haggard himself seems to have raised the Union Jack in the 1877 annexation ceremony of the Transvaal: "I think that [. . .] I did the actual hoisting, but of these details I am not quite sure" (1912: 1, 106–7). (The territory was ceded back to the Boers in 1881.) Given the fraught back-and-forth of Transvaal sovereignty in this period, it is little surprise that the chapters of *The Days of My Life* dealing with the annexation find Haggard mulling over the special problems these territories posed for British legal paramountcy. Haggard reports that after Shepstone's 1876 appointment, the commissioner enjoyed a kind of personal despotism over the area, a total individual sovereignty structurally akin to the tribal despots he was dedicated to fighting. On reflection, Haggard admits, it was "a great authority to leave to the discretion of a single man," since Shepstone held personally and without supervision the "powers, if he thought fit, to annex the country, 'in order to secure the peace and safety of our said colonies and our subjects elsewhere'" (1912, vol. 1: 73). Such annexation is in fact what came to pass.

Yet this stated motive of protection—"to secure [. . .] peace and safety"—in fact concealed an aggressive policy of expansion aimed at propping up an Empire now being threatened by rising powers. As part of the so-called Cape to Cairo policy, Shepstone's supervisor, the British colonial secretary Lord Carnarvon, had as early as 1876 expressed his determination to extend British political suzerainty over large swaths of African territory; his goal was to position England against potential European competitors now rising on the world stage. As Haggard himself suggests, Carnarvon's realpolitik effort to shore up England's geopolitical posture came cloaked in a rhetoric of disinterested protection of values now branded as universal. It is a fact that numerous British wars on the continent, including the Zulu War of 1875, were waged with the stated purpose of overthrowing unjust, violent, uncivilized, or otherwise hostile regimes. Yet such wars (in the words of one contemporary observer) "often terminate[d] in annexation" (Callwell 1906: 28). The 1877 Zulu war, for example, was started because the Zulu prince Cetywayo was "a standing danger to Natal," but "ended in the incorporation of the kingdom in the British Empire" (p. 28). Thus did wars of liberal principle reveal themselves to be wars of realpolitik acquisition, the two finally proving impossible to distinguish.

Haggard's self-published first book, the nonfictional *Cetywayo and His White Neighbors* (1882), takes the historical case of the Transvaal/ Zululand as its topic and documents a real-life version of the pseudo-accidental annexation later to be fictionalized in *King Solomon's Mines*. Haggard's eyewitness account of the Zulu cycle of acquisition and abandonment—annexed in 1877, "retrocessed" to the Boers in 1881—argued, against "amateurs and sentimentalists" (1882: x), that England should annex Cetywayo's territory and install a new king appointed by the colonial governor. The rationale Haggard adduces for this extension of British sovereignty is a humanitarian one: Cetywayo must be removed because he stood opposed, Haggard explained, not just to British strategic interests but to values common across humanity.

Cetywayo offers what Haggard frames as an expert's testimony of the native chief's fantastic and irredeemable cruelty. Where English philanthropists and "lady advocates" (1882: 11) might turn a blind eye on the affronts to nature perpetrated by this criminal regime, Haggard advocates a reluctant interventionism. Stepping in is necessary, he explains in an appendix called "A Zulu War Dance," because of England's special relationship to universal justice:

> When the strong aggressive hand of England has grasped some fresh portion of the earth's surface, there is yet a spirit of justice in her heart and head which prompts the question, among the first of such demands, as to how best and most fairly to deal by the natives of the newly-acquired land.
>
> (1882: 278)

The point is that the ethicopolitical rationale Haggard marshals in this hectoring non-fiction account—a strong but fair England guarantees universal values like "justice"—would generate the frisson of the most overlooked (yet central) matter of plot in *King Solomon's Mines*. In keeping with Haggard's commentary in *Cetywayo*, and with Quatermain's official position on nonviolence, the novel frames the British effort to depose Twala as a hesitant interventionism, a just war to unseat a regime whose policies extravagantly contravene norms conceived as universal.

In a chapter of *King Solomon's Mines* whose title, "The Witch Hunt," advertises a ceremony that is the very paradigm of arbitrary state violence, the Twala regime is painted as a bloodthirsty and random tyranny that is the precise negation of British legal rationality. (Witch hunts then and now stand as emblems of illiberal political barbarism.[20]) The "glorious show" of Haggard's fictionalized hunt (p. 119), in which random citizens are selected to be murdered, finds Twala's armies assembled for a rally of ceremonial murder. The grisly but disconcertingly hilarious scene recodes Victorian field accounts of warlike Zulu tribes (and Haggard's own experiences with them) into an African *Triumph of the Will*:

> The king lifted his spear, and suddenly twenty thousand feet were raised, as though they belonged to one man, and brought down with a stamp upon the earth. This was repeated three times, causing the solid ground to shake and

tremble. Then from a far point of the circle a solitary voice began wailing a
song, of which the refrain ran something as follows:—

"What is the lot of man born of woman?"

Back came the answer rolling out from every throat in that vast company—

"Death!" (p. 120)

Chapter 2 showed how the British legal order operated domestically in
an uplifting mode, working to produce life and to care for it. Legal
modernity was defined by the administrative regime of management
that stood opposed to what Foucault calls "the old power of death"
(Foucault 1978: 139–40). In bold strokes, Haggard's scene paints
Twala's sovereign power as old in precisely this sense: its thanophilic
operations invert the life-giving or abstracting aspirations of modern
political rationality.[21]

Over the course of these chapters we have seen at least three ways in
which liberal universalism produces its outside: (1) with metaphors of
childhood or nonage; (2) with metaphors of imbecility or irrationality; and
(3) with the related figures of temporal distance or premodernity. Such
tropes as "savagery" cement together several techniques of exclusion (here,
irrationality and archaicism). The common ideology of Victorian progressive science by which ontogeny was alleged to repeat phylogeny—that the
development of man as an individual played out, in microcosm, the
developmental sequence man as a species—was another combinatory
strategy. For if ancient races lived in a state of social childhood then
they were, as Mill infamously asserted, not yet ready for the liberty
appropriate to adults. The point is that because any human community,
to be a community, must have an outside, these figural tactics are best seen
as tools in the arsenal of liberal universalism's exclusionary logic. They are
ways to generate the "biological caesura within a population" (Foucault
2003: 255) necessary to partition the elect from the abandoned and to
consolidate a social body as such. In his depiction of Twala's death cult,
Haggard introduces us to a fourth way to produce this boundary between
inside and outside. His novel imagines a sovereign government whose
principle of rule inverts the life-giving or abstracting administration of the
modern state. In their archaic refusal to protect and preserve the category
of "life"—indeed in their thanophilic hatred of this category—Twala and
his functionaries reveal themselves to be enemies of modernity in just
this sense.

The novel's case against Twala's regime paints it as the negation of
(British) administrative rationality in its guise as "law." The text pursues
relentlessly this opposition between law and its other, but nowhere is it
more visible than when Twala's rogue regime exercises its archaic form of

power on the physical bodies of its citizen. When the first random warrior is summarily executed with spear and club, the three heads of state blurt out their nation's anti-ethic. The law of *this* land, we are made to understand, is no law at all:

> "*Kill!*" said the king.
> "*Kill!*" squeaked Gagool.
> "*Kill!*" re-echoed Scragga, with a hollow chuckle.
> Almost before the words were uttered the horrible deed was done. One man had driven his spear into the victim's heart, and to make assurance double sure, the other had dashed out his brains with a great club.   (p. 122)

It is worth noting how Haggard's prose ascribes a non-cognitive involuntarism to these colonial executioners—the killing is accomplished "[a]lmost before the words were uttered"—even as it confirms their perverse effectiveness as overlords. No deliberation, in that word's legal or cognitive senses, has preceded this executive action. It is *praxis* without *dianoia*. The ceremony's "exhaust[ing]" work of counterliberal death is continued until "some hundreds of bodies were stretched out in rows behind us" (p. 123).

These excessive scenes are critical to the novel's seemingly differential political scheme. (I say "seemingly" because as we have seen, such involuntary or non-deliberative violence has already been advertised as the key feature of the novel's favored form of British masculinity, in Quatermain, a figural inversion that Stevenson will radicalize for us shortly.) Here, Haggard's narration of Twala's African death cult shows the enemy regime to uphold Foucault's "old power of death" in ways that mark it as the negative image of the liberal state's rationalized or life-protecting functions. The cancellation of modernity accomplished in the native government's anti-ethic (*"Kill! Kill! Kill!"*) comes full circle when Twala calls his extravagant process of random execution by exactly the name it is not: "'Let the law take its course, white men [Twala says]. These dogs are magicians and evildoers; it is well that they should die'" (p. 123). Focused on law and its reversal, Haggard's novel conjures a figurative beyond to the modern legal order, and Twala's death cult is the hyperbolic state of nature whose antagonism to life limns the threshold separating the inside of modern legality from its outside.

After he returned from Africa but before beginning his career as a romancer under Lang's direction, Haggard was a middling barrister in London, and his novel's obsession with framing the distinction between civilization and barbarism in legal terms no doubt stems from that experience. In *King Solomon's Mines*, the Hobbesian state of nature in Kukuanaland becomes the constitutive lack that, as observers from Frantz Fanon to Achille Mbembe have noted, Africa so often represents in

Western self-representations: it is the negative term that defines the positive one.[22] Quatermain is the figure who exposes this relation, having already explained that he at least adheres to the principle of restraint that governs rational nations the world over. "I have killed many men in my time," he says, "but I have never slain wantonly or stained my hand in innocent blood, only in self-defence" (p. 11). Quatermain's exculpatory formulation gives voice to what, in *Cetywayo*, Haggard called England's "strong aggressive hand" that was nevertheless tempered by "a spirit of justice" (1893: 278).[23]

Offered in clunky but legalistic prose, Quatermain's lesson about the morality of colonial violence—don't be wanton, don't kill innocents—repeats English common sense and a bowdlerized Christian ethic. It also invokes legal categories ("innocent," "self-defence") that establish his slaying of "many men" as just. In ways that predict Quatermain's involuted explanation—and that may have provided a source for it—Victorian legal writer W. L. Finlason argued in the context of the Jamaica Rebellion that during colonial emergencies, soldiers could kill, maim, torture, and terrorize as many people as necessary, in whatever ways they deemed fit, with perfect legal protection—provided they also observed "those rules of common justice and humanity, which are universally obligatory" (quoted in Kostal 2005: 482). This was a defense of Eyre. How the opposed injunctions to defend humanity and fight "a war of *extermination*" (quoted in Kostal 2005: 481, emphasis original) were to be observed simultaneously is left for the reader to guess. Quatermain's no less strained effort to legalize his own killing of "many men" invokes theories of just war propounded by theorists following in the wake of Spanish jurist Francisco de Vitoria, an itinerary reaching from the medieval crusades and witch hunts of the Thirty Years' War to the Kantian theory springing from that context; it pressed forward from there to Haggard's own moment of nascent international law, surviving as justification for American intervention against Islamic fundamentalism in the present (see e.g. Elshtain 2003).

In the 1880s, anyway, the so-called "standard of civilization" in international law—it is still in force—ensured that infinite harm could be visited on enemies of universal principles. This legal standard drew a line between the protectors of humanity and its sworn enemies, a geographical and political caesura that would have large consequences for the human residents of Southern Africa, for example, who found themselves poised on the threshold separating protected inhabitants of the international community from those who, by virtue of their antagonism to that community, became perfectly disposable.

JUST WAR, UNJUST ENEMIES:
TRANSVAAL *c.*1885

None of Haggard's slanders on native regimes is surprising given his reputation as the ultimate mythmaker of Empire. But the cultural distinction between civilization and savagery so often preoccupying recent critics of Haggard's novels enabled and sustained distinctions in international law that had life-and-death consequences for those on the far end of British equipoise: bodies available to imperial power but uncounted by its bureaucratic calculus. Where post-Saidian cultural criticism takes as axiomatic that the racism and the cultural othering accomplished by "imperial discourse" constitutes the central content of imperialism's damage, Haggard's text discloses that these cultural and racial distinctions are best seen not as causes but techniques, weapons for carving lines in a now-globalized social body that was always, if sometimes only imperceptibly, at war.

According to what is still called "the standard of civilization in international law," status as a civilized state, and the recognition by international law that comes with it, presupposes a state's internal capacity to regulate itself and operate according to the institutionalized codes of reason understood as the rule of law. In the system of international law reaching from Kant to the present day and codified during the last decades of the nineteenth century, the requirements for recognition as "civilized" include all the elements of modern political form discussed in previous chapters: working institutions of public bureaucracy, a regular army, "a published legal code and adherence to the rule of law," the willingness to follow international laws of war, and the capacity to honor contracts (Bowden 1997: 6). For a state to be recognized as a sovereign and autonomous actor by international law it must conform to these universal (i.e. European) norms, standards that mirror on a national scale the deliberative and self-regulating behavior that thinkers like Kant and Rawls—and, as I have suggested, Howells and James—identify as the constitutive attributes of properly modern ("human") individual subjects.[24]

Describing the Victorian roots of the distinction between self-governing, and thus recognizable, political entities and those cut off from membership in the international community, historian Mark Mazower explains how the standard of civilization worked in the Victorian imperium to demarcate the edges of political belonging. This standard drew hard frontiers between areas legally "[i]nside Europe" and those zones "[o]utside this sphere," where "the potential costs—in terms of legalized violence—of failing to attain the standard of civilization were most evident" (2006: 557).

Requirements for inclusion in "the sphere of civilized life," Mazower continues, are those familiar from the modernizing narratives we have already traced: private property, "the rule of law"; disaggregated or non-despotic state sovereignty; regular armies (as opposed to guerrilla forces); and (particularly relevant to this discussion of Howells and James) "freedom of conscience" (2006: 557). The structuring distinction in Victorian international law thus relied on the cultural dichotomy Haggard's novel is at pains to rework. A civilized inside, which Haggard's text leaves implicit, as "our" common sense, sits in tacit opposition to the uncivilized or premodern outside depicted in Twala's death cult. Thus is the novel's world divided in legal terms between those who would act within the bounds of universally valid reason and those who are either unrecognized by or enemies to that law—"outside" its "sphere."[25]

"It is scarcely necessary to point out," confirms the Victorian legal theorist E. W. Hall in his influential *Treatise on International Law* (1880), written five years before *King Solomon's Mines*, that "international law is a product of the special civilization of modern Europe." To enter this special community, "states outside European civilization must formally *enter into the circle* of law-governed countries. They must do something with the acquiescence of the latter [...] which amounts to an acceptance of the law in its entirety" (1880: 42–3, emphasis added).[26] Hall's account gives voice to the positivist legal consensus that within "the special civilization of modern Europe," something called law holds sway, while "outside European civilization" exist states which cannot be properly considered sovereign states at all, and are thus not entitled to the legal status and consequent protections membership in the international community ("recognition") confers. To gain such status they must "formally enter" the circle by "acquiesc[ing]" to the values just described.[27]

The spatial metaphors of this inside–outside movement will become important later, when they collapse into incoherence in the body of Henry Jekyll. Here the point is how Hall's effort to demarcate the edges of "the sphere of law" (1880: 43) gives legal form to the efforts of *King Solomon's Mines* to set into binary opposition universal justice and its bloodstained opposite, as it plots Twala and his autocratic advisory board as the very image of what civilized modernity is not.

Such unjust or anomic enemies have a long history, and recent work has shown how Roman law, canon law, and early modern sovereignty theory all produced figures—the pirate, the savage, the infidel—on whom maximum harm could be visited so as to secure the integrity of values deemed universal. But it is the bourgeois philosophical system in Immanuel Kant's *The Metaphysics of Morals* that describes the unjust enemy in terms that most explicitly articulate the policies that would be codified in late Victorian international law. That law would go to great lengths to identify communities whose criminality, political "childishness," or collective "imbecility" render them ineligible for standing in the international sphere. (The terms are James Lorimer's, from *The Institutes of the Law of Nations* of 1883, and come as he identifies human communities without international legal standing (pp. 156–7).) For Kant, the unjust enemy is an actor whose "publicly expressed will [. . .] displays a maxim that would make peace among nations impossible and would lead to a perpetual state of nature if made into a general rule" (1996: 170). Kant's "someone" is ambiguous, referring at once to individual actors and rogue collectivities. But as his text specifies, such outliers to the human community threaten the structure of civilization itself.[28]

Carl Schmitt cites this passage in Kant to describe how in the period after the Treaty of Westphalia (1648), which brought to a close the appalling and unlimited violence of the Thirty Years' War, conflict among civilized or European states was bracketed—that is, limited—by the recognition of both parties' status as sovereign international actors. Disputes between parties within these brackets were horizontal or what Schmitt calls properly political, insofar as they were oganized confrontations between equals in which each party was a *justus hostis*, or just enemy. Lorimer's 1883 treatise refers to "belligerent recognition" (p. 156) as what is required to confer protections in such areas as the treatment of prisoners. Hall's 1880 account explains that in situations of unequal civilization, absent the recognition that equality guarantees, a "parent state" (p. 33) may deem it useful to treat a belligerent community as an equal. But such a decision could be based only on charitable feeling, or "moral duty" (p. 34). That is because an unrecognized "belligerent community is not a legal person," and as such it "can have no rights under [. . .] law" (pp. 34–5).

Haggard suggested in the nonfictional *Cetywayo* that the actually existing Zulu sect he describes was just such a legal nonentity, and for that reason was available to be exterminated if exigency demanded. According to British officials and Haggard's account, Cetywayo and the community he led expressed a maxim of despotic tyranny antithetical to the healthy existence of a world organized according to the principles of exchange and self-governance arrayed under the heading "law." Haggard quotes a Mr. Osborne, who reports how Cetywayo "is putting people to death in a shameful manner, especially girls. The dead bodies are placed by his order in the principal paths, especially where the paths intersect each other [. . .] It is really terrible that such horrible savagery should take place on our own borders" (Haggard 1893: 17). Shameful, terrible, horrible savagery: the terms serve to identify this group not as a recognizable belligerent—an equal—but as an instance of piratical criminality on whom endless violence might justifiably be visited. From the perspective of international legal theory, I mean, because enemies like Cetywayo existed not only outside the international sphere, but also as antagonists to that sphere, they could and did become objects of wars unlimited in scope.

Being uncounted by any sovereign or rights-guaranteeing body, the human beings outside the pale of international recognition thus found themselves excluded from what Arendt calls "the right to have rights": stripped of standing, they became available to be dealt with in whatever way the greater power or (in Hall's language) "parent state" deemed fit. In Chapter 3 we saw how, in Swinburne's "Laus Veneris," the unbracketed wars of the Crusades enabled the Christian knight Tannhäuser to pursue a "goodly fight" against the "blinkard [*sic*] heathen[s] stumbling for scant light" (ll. 212, 210) while remaining confident that "Though [God] search all my veins through, searching them / He shall find nothing whole therein but love" (ll. 383–4). Swinburne emphasizes a seeming paradox of secular universalism, whereby justice and ruination aim toward the same goal: the killing happens precisely in service of love.[29] That a doctrine for just war derived for religious crusades could re-emerge, in secular form, as the governing logic of liberal universalism shows the traffic between these two allegedly opposed worldviews.

As Swinburne intuited and Haggard elaborates here, it is on the fringes of the recognized world that secular universalism's unbracketed violence registers its full force. For parent states dealing with enemies for whom, in Lorimer's words, "the claim even to belligerent recognition falls to the ground" (1883: 156), two options emerge: they can either be forcibly brought within the sphere of recognition, uplifted into law and incorporated; or eliminated entirely. The former course of action might sometimes be wise, but at other moments elimination made tactical sense. As Anthony Trollope infamously noted in a different context, one way or another, "the Australian black man [...] has to go" (2003: 73).

In a field manual first published in 1896, *Small Wars: Their Principle and Their Practice*, British colonel C. E. Callwell confirms that the techniques available to the civilized nation in combating such disposable enemies was unchecked by all restriction save prudence and the prosecutors' imaginations. He explains that it is advisable to follow the laws of war wherever doing so is practical. But should necessity demand it, the parent state should not shy away from "the destruction of villages," "raids on livestock," and "the destruction of the crops and stores of grain" (1906: 40, 41). This how-to guide goes on:

The most satisfactory way of bringing such foes to reason is by the rifle and sword, for they understand this mode of warfare and respect it. Sometimes, however, the circumstances do not admit of it, and then their villages must be demolished and their crops and granaries destroyed; still it is unfortunate when this is the case.   (Callwell 1906: 41)

Concerned, like Kant or Victorian international law, with "bringing [. . .] foes to reason," the manual goes on to note that the European rules of war only recently (in 1864) codified in Geneva do not apply in cases when the enemy is unrecognized by—because he does not himself recognize—European norms of war.[30] As in the case of the martial law declared in Jamaica, an unreasoning, unregulated violence would police the integrity of a civilization whose very definition turned on the principles of reason and self-regulation ("law") here explicitly contravened. *Jus ad bellum*—the justification for going to war—and *jus in bello*—the conduct within war—sit in diametric opposition.

Edward Adams (2011) has charted how the paradoxical injunction of liberal imperialism—to kill so as to put a stop to killing—produced torsions at the level of literary and historical representation. In ways similar to those Adams details, Haggard's novel sharpens the apparent paradoxes of liberal just war by condensing them into a story not of regular armies but of representative adventurers. When Haggard's three-man band helps organize the coup against Twala, the British characters act as military advisors for native soldiers. But the operation proceeds in a manner appropriate not to a skirmish among irregular corps but to autonomous European powers. Sir Henry Good commands a regiment called "The Greys," while Quatermain and Ignosi lead "the second attacking regiment," "The Buffaloes" (2007: 158–9). Obsessive attention to how these groups are organized—"in a triple-line formation" and "a similar three-fold formation" (p. 161)—bolsters the novel's infantile militarism even as it differentiates these regularized forces from the scattered guerrillas they meet in battle.

Despite the orderliness of this quasi-British proxy army and in keeping with Callwell's prescription for conflict on the colonial fringes, the war for Kukuanaland's liberation is no bracketed confrontation between equals but a baroque extravaganza of slaughter: thousands are killed, blood is everywhere. Amidst this chaos of human attrition, Haggard takes pains to show us that in contrast to the enemy, Ignosi and his armies follow the laws of civilized combat even if they are not bound to. Ignosi orders his troops not to kill Twala's wounded, "and so far as [Quatermain] could see this order was scrupulously carried out" (p. 163). What this "mythic potpourri" of fact and fancy (Monsman 2000: 289) labors to portray is a war whose grisly means are justified by their civilization-spreading ends.

"ALMOST UNBOUNDED RIGHTS OF
SOVEREIGNTY": *KING SOLOMON'S MINES* II

The slaughter finally concludes; Ignosi is restored; a new law is established. The sequence would seem to conclude a sequence of Kantian just war, since the reinstated monarch wastes little time in renouncing the arbitrary and violent ways of the previous regime. Quatermain has already instructed the future king by emphasizing the importance of universal values in their guise as legal proceduralism. He tells Ignosi: "We [English] shed no blood of man except in just punishment" (p. 108). Even before the military coup is waged, the English party has stressed that the installation of modern legal institutions (not diamonds, not influence) is their only interest. They exact a promise that Ignosi's successor will reign in accord with the principles of procedural rationality the British characters only intermittently embody but in any case seek seek to spread. The novel represents this as a promise between friends:

> "Ignosi," said Sir Henry, "promise me one thing."
> "I will promise, Incubu, my friend, even before I hear it. [. . .] What is it?"
> "This: that if you ever become king of this people, you will do away with the smelling out of witches such as we have seen last night and that the killing of men without trial shall not take place in the land."   (p. 130)

What the Englishmen demand is the installation of a deliberative proceduralism in which state killing will transpire under the sign of administrative rationality rather than despotic whim. Accepting this proviso would ensure that Ignosi's new state will accord with maxims of universal civilization and thus complete its cycle of uplift into the folds of modernity: it would complete what Callwell (1906) called "bring[ing] foes to reason."

Haggard's non-fictional description of the sovereignty transfer in *Cetywayo* hints at the shadow autonomy *King Solomon's Mines* grants to its new state. The earlier text recounts an 1873 episode, in Natal, in which Shepstone declared Cetywayo king. Shepstone specified that the new regime would operate according to principles he dictated in four simple points. Haggard writes that Shepstone,

> standing in the place of Cetywayo's father, and so representing the [Zulu] nation, enunciated the four following articles, with a view to putting an end to the continual slaughter that darkens the history of Zululand:
>
> 1. That the indiscriminate shedding of blood shall cease in the land.

2. That no Zulu shall be condemned without open trial, and the public examination of witnesses for and against, and that he shall have a right to appeal to the king.

3. That no Zulu's life shall be taken without the previous knowledge and consent of the king, after such trial has taken place, and the right of appeal has been allowed to be exercised.

4. That for minor crimes the loss of property, all or a portion, shall be substituted for the punishment of death.   (Haggard 1892: 11–12)

The four-step prescription repeats the minimal requirements of sovereign states in Victorian international law; its language emerges in Haggard's novelistic account nearly unchanged. (The real General Shepstone, like the novel's Sir Henry, demands a halt to "the indiscriminate shedding of blood in this land.") In the novel, Ignosi cannot accede to such demands entirely: he explains that "[t]he ways of black people are not the ways of white men [. . .] nor do we hold life so high as ye" (p. 130). Still he avers at least that he will enforce a certain local version of the rule of law. "Yet will I promise it," Ignosi says. "If it be in my power to hold them back, the witch-finders shall hunt no more, nor shall any man die the death without judgment" (p. 130). Sir Henry takes Ignosi's promise as the necessary condition of their help in the fight: "'That's a bargain, then,'" he says (p. 130).

For Kant, the victor in a war against an unjust enemy is both empowered and obligated to impose on the defeated people "a new constitution that by its nature will be unfavorable to the inclination of war" (quoted in Schmitt 2003: 170). In keeping with this nation-building injunction and with British policy in the Transvaal, the war in Kukuanaland, fought with a British advisory team and enacted on territory full of moveable capital in its purest form, leads to what Kant called "a new constitution," one amenable to the universal principles of legality to which Quatermain has already given voice. Ignosi provides a helpful summary of what has transpired, describing how "the white lords from the stars, looking down on the land, had perceived its trouble, and determined, at great personal inconvenience, to alleviate its lot" (p. 141). The establishment of Ignosi as "rightful king" (p. 141) and his adoption of new constitution forges what seems to be relationship of friendship and mutual honor between the liberators and the newly installed government. The Englishmen—"at great personal inconvenience"—will "stand by" them.

In this way does Haggard's Kukuanan plot conclude the liberal-universalist sequence by which a formerly extralegal body is brought into the fold of the comity of nations, made to "accept the law in its entirety" (Hall 1880), or "brought to reason" (Callwell 1906) in a process that ends with recognition as a sovereign actor. From this angle the plot to replace Twala with Ignosi reads as an effort to carve a civil society from a lawless state of nature, a mission that is incorporative in the sense that it mirrors on an international level the individuating and abstracting political induction charted in Chapter 2.

Such a story would presume the sovereignty or achieved individuality of the resulting nation-state, its ability to enter international civil society as an actor endowed with the self-regulating power Kant and the later positivist tradition require of national subjects. (It must be able, for example, to conclude contracts, or what Ignosi calls "promise[s]."[31]) In keeping with this requirement, the Quatermain cadre's intervention appears to be capped when the trio explains that Ignosi "could exercise almost unbounded rights of sovereignty" (p. 156). The "almost" will become important, but it appears now that when the adventurers depart Kukuanaland with the full state honor of a tickertape parade, the narrative of national incorporation is in place. The British have waged a war for justice; they have set up institutions toward this end; they have maintained no military or administrative presence in the liberated zone. And if they have taken diamonds they have done so reluctantly, leaving most of the wealth where they found it.

But again our attention is drawn directly to the question of who is in charge, as Haggard's neo-Homeric idiom registers Kukuanaland's compromised autonomy in the aftermath of its externally engineered military coup "to overthrow this tyrant and murderer" (p. 115). Certainly the signs of the restored ruler's "almost unbounded rights of sovereignty" are apparent. The departure of his white benefactors stirs from Ignosi a speech full of nationalist vigor, the sure sign of the autonomy necessary for recognition in the international sphere:

> "But listen, and let all the white men know my words. No other white man shall cross the mountains [. . .]. If a white man comes to my gates I will send him back; if a hundred come, I will push them back; if an army comes, I will make war on them with all my strength, and they shall not prevail against me." (p. 223)

It is a noble sentiment, but just after Ignosi's inaugural speech as sovereign, readers learn that there is an exception: the three white men can return whenever they please. And the novel suggests that when they do, they will continue to exert influence over the native people as they did before they left. What is that influence?

Fifty pages before Ignosi's declaration of total autonomy from white men, we are informed that our three British heroes have retained a certain power, one that extends indefinitely into the future. Ignosi gives an order that we three were to be greeted with the royal salute, to be treated with the same ceremony and respect that was by custom accorded to the king, and the power of life and death was publicly conferred upon us. (pp. 182–3)

That political sovereignty is coextensive with what Quatermain here calls "the power of life and death" is a commonplace of sovereignty theory from Bodin and Hobbes forward: it is what defines sovereignty as such.[32] By conferring this ultimate authority on Quatermain's band, the novel discloses that Ignosi's new sovereignty is in fact no sovereignty at all. With the Englishmen bearing the power "by custom accorded to the king," Ignosi's government is but a native front for British interests, albeit in their guise as a universal legal modernity.[33] Haggard's prose in other words registers the dense complications of sovereignty theory at the margins of the civilized world, and forces us to ask what model of autonomy might be imagined in which a new ruler might "promise" something to his white benefactors "even before [he] hear[s]" the proposal (p. 130).

As if to answer the question, the same page of *Mines* that tells of Ignosi's "almost unbounded rights of sovereignty" also contains an exchange in which Quatermain is himself revealed to be the power pulling the strings. What plays out is a power drama writ small, in which an apparently sovereign state defers decision to its parent—whom Ignosi here in fact calls his "father":

"The last word is in Ignosi, the king, for it is a king's right to speak of war; but let us hear thy voice, O [Quatermain]," [said Infadoos].

"What sayest thou, Ignosi?" [Quatermain] asked.

"Nay, my father," answered our quondam servant, who now, clad as he was in the full panoply of savage war, looked every inch a warrior king, "do thou speak, and let me, who am but a child in wisdom beside thee, hearken to thy words." (pp. 155–6)

Here Infadoos and Quatermain make overtures toward Ignosi's status as sovereign, his "king's right" to offer "the last word," and Ignosi himself appears in his most powerful guise, "looking every inch a [...] king." Yet this "quondam [former] servant" is a dependent and "friend" who may look like a sovereign but isn't: the passage reworks the language Mill and Kant used to describe the "nonage" of premodern subject races to explain that for this child, the power of decision rests with the father. When Quatermain later tells Ignosi that he, Ignosi, "camest a servant, and now *we leave thee* a mighty king" (p. 222, emphasis added), Quatermain's language is crucially ambiguous. "[W]e leave thee" can refer to the British team's departure—they are leaving him as king—or to the fact that they are allowing him to be king, giving him leave.

Elaborately unresolved here, the ambiguity captures a political distinction between autonomy and dependence that is revealed, at the micro-
stylistic level of prose, to be no distinction at all. Yet whether the new
state is a sovereign nation or an indirectly ruled puppet regime, this
proxy war has yielded a legal order remade in England's image—one
ready, at last, to be brought under the auspices of civilization and a rule
of law now internationally scaled.

Haggard's prose sharpens the question of justification yet further,
though, and while maintaining its anti-deliberative superficiality discloses
a secret compact between the moral discourse of liberal nation-building
("justice," "law," "freedom") and a visceral exultation in death seemingly
more at home in the blood-and-soil language of Tory realpolitik. Is this
violence scandalous or delightful? Which side is the novel—and are we—
on? During the course of the British-led civil war, the killing is called
"awful," but then described as "music[al]," an interplay of negative and
positive valences Haggard's prose does not seek to resolve:

> The slaughter was something awful, hundreds falling every minute; and from
> among the shouts of the warriors and the groans of the dying, set to the
> clashing music of meeting spears, came a continuous hissing undertone of
> "*S'gee, s'gee*," the note of triumph of each victor as he passed his spear
> through and through the body of his fallen foe.   (p. 163)

The words "shocking" and "awful" recur multiple times throughout the
fourteen-page battle scene. But is this language condemning "the slaughter" or reveling in its "clashing music"?

The answer is both, and as it narrates the hyperviolent just war that
unseats Twala, the oscillating tone of Haggard's prose mediates the
paradoxical valences of just war doctrine, such that the codes of civilized
ethics (those that would *produce* the judgment of the violence's "awful[ness]")
are the very reason why this violence is undertaken in the first place. As
in the entire tradition of what Adams calls "liberal epic," the contradictory
commitments of Haggard's narration here generate what seems to be
a tension between, on the one hand, the ethicopolitical language
appropriate to "civilization" and, on the other, the pseudo-Homeric
total war appropriate to this atavistic African periphery. "It was a mighty
struggle," Quatermain says of the battle, "*and* an awful thing to see"
(p. 173). In Haggard's sentence, an "and" sits where a "but" should
be, and this surreal, self-contradictory prose imagines mutually exclusive
codes for understanding violence simultaneously. From within the presumptions of progressive idealism, killing in service of peace could only
appear as unthinkable contradiction. Yet Haggard's text, with joyous
perversity, evinces no contradiction at all.

"AS GOOD AS HOMER!": ANDREW
LANG'S EPIC FORM

The influence of Lang is crucial in understanding the simultaneously stylistic and political effect I have charted so far. For George Eliot at the high moment of British hegemony, 1860, the cosmopolitan modern mind could be understood to travel to "the banks of the Zambezi" in wide-angled flights of imagination, as the physical geography of the Empire became a cognitive space available to the enlightened citizens of the metropolitan center. For Haggard in the 1880s, these banks of the Zambezi can be narrated only as a zone of compromised sovereignty and hyperbolic bloodshed in pursuit of order, a space not of cognitive dilation but of incessant physical conflict, endless in scope and unbracketed in the scale of its material damage. Scrubbed of interiority, reveling in unconsidered physicality, the mode Haggard devised in tandem with Lang emerged as the technology whose effects proved best able to capture the paradoxes of this excessively violent geopolitical decline.

Lang's nostalgia for the world's outdated forms, his embrace of "the natural man within me," put him in conflict with his academic colleagues more in step with modernity, including Friedrich Max Müller. A longtime fixture at Oxford and its first Professor of Comparative Philology, Müller elaborated from that institutional position a racialized system of myth that understood forms like the Indian Vedas (his prime example) to be so-called diseases of language, antecedent versions of a mythological system later to be perfected by subsequent civilizations. Lang's countervailing theory held that these stories represented a shared savage past that was (for him) lamentably all but expunged in the modern age, even though its broken traces persisted, unevenly, into the present moment as survivals. For Müller, in other words, the study of archaic forms revealed progress into a more regulated and rational time, "the perfect manhood of the Aryan mind" that he would find in Kant (1881, trans. Müller: lxi)—a modernizing story that told in the language of myth the story of progressive rationalization George Saintsbury described for poetry in Chapter 3. For Lang, by contrast, the present moment was not so much the culmination of a modernizing arc but a ciphered, jumbled archive of past thought-forms, savage conceptual idioms whose intimacy with the brute facts of existence was preferable, Lang thought, to the inward dilations of the Coming Man.

Lang's dictum "More claymores, less psychology" captures this preference for outdated action. But a sketch he sent to Stevenson in a letter, depicting an episode of *Kidnapped*, expresses yet more sharply the apparently tangled logic of the heroic violence Lang sought to recapture (Fig. 4.3). Despite

Fig. 4.3. "*Un bon coup d'épée.*" Andrew Lang to Stevenson, 29 August 1886. Beinecke Rare Book & Manuscript Library, Yale University.

the loving attention paid in this drawing to coat button and shoe buckle, Lang's loose, scribbly line encapsulates the reputation he'd cultivated for unpretentious accomplishment, "an easy grace of style" (Elwin 1939: 183) that is most visible here, perhaps, in the "m"-shaped suggestions of birds and their jokey label, "Eagles." (His notation of "Jura" on the twin mountains identifies the "Paps of Jura," the Hebridean formation along Breck's route in *Kidnapped*—and suggests, too, where Haggard may have got the idea for his own breastlike mountains, in the infamous woman-map in *King Solomon's Mines*.[34]) The point here concerns style: Lang's drawing appears naïve and immediate, dashed off in an instant and betraying total confidence and scarce evidence of conscious formal design. On second glance, however, we see that this naïveté is far from natural, as Lukács would presume of genuine epic style. Note the effect of compositional balance in the shaping form of the sail, swooping over Breck's head; the crosshatch that rhymes deck and mountain; or the vertical axis of the mast, structurally dividing friend and foe.

At the core of this characteristically easy virtuosity—what James derided as Lang's "beautiful thin facility" (quoted in Elwin 1939: 191)—matters of life and death intercede, and ferociously: a sword-tip emerges through the back of its victim, as Mr. Shuan's flailing body is literally lifted off its feet by the force of the blow. Set against this brutality, Lang's wobbly, humorous approach registers nostalgia for the lost age of heroism and force he depicts. That the handwritten caption is in French—"*Alan Breck donne un bon coup d'épée à M. Shuan, trois pousses de fer bravais dans le ventre*," "Alan Breck gives a good sword thrust to M. Shuan, three hits [or doses] of fer bravais into the guts"—only heightens the oddity of effect, since the language of both civilized culture and quasi-medieval chivalry conveys, in anatomically precise detail, the anarchic brutality of the Scots periphery. It also lets Lang pun on a pseudo-scientific health tonic popular in the 1880s, fer bravais, to jokily equate violent death with bodily cure.[35]

Lang's scholarship on Homer developed in tandem with his work on folklore, which itself unfolded in connection to his ongoing polemics on literary romance. His numerous interventions in the contested field of Homeric criticism (he argued that one person wrote all the poems), included *Homer and the Epic* (1893) and *The World of Homer* (1910), both of which collected work Lang had done during the 1880s and 1890s. While Müller was finalizing his groundbreaking English translation of Kant's *Critique of Pure Reason* (1881), a text Müller judged to represent the manhood of the Aryan mind" in its self-reflexive, "non-dogmatical" modern form (p. lxi), Lang was translating Homer, "puzzl[ing] over the brutal and irrational features of Greek myths" (Dorson 1968: 206). Lang's obsession with outdated thought developed in productive interchange with his literary work as editor, critic, and translator. In addition to 1884's *Custom and Myth* and 1885's *King Solomon's Mines* (which as we have seen he helped usher into print), the period just before and during the "realism wars" saw Lang producing two of the Victorian period's most popular translations of Homer, collaborating with S. H. Butcher on a prose version of the *Odyssey* (1879) and with Walter Leaf and Ernest Myers on an iconic prose treatment of the *Iliad* (1883), which has been called the most widely read translation of any kind in the Victorian period.[36]

These vastly influential works on epic have yet to be analyzed in Victorianist criticism on the romance. Lang's appreciation for Homer came from his understanding of this poetry not as high art but savage culture, the literary remains of a society organized by social rules and mental structures we no longer share. "The epics are not only poetry," he wrote in *Homer and the Epic*, "but history, history not of real events, indeed, but of real manners, of a real world, to us otherwise unknown" (Lang 1893: 7). Like Auerbach and Lukács, for whom the Greek poems record the "absolute immanence of life" of premodern social form (Lukács 1971: 35), Lang here imagines a mode of being antecedent to bourgeois modernity and extrapolates from this a representational form. Epic's static characterization and counterdevelopmental temporalities reflected a unified way of living, Lang thought, one that would only later be parsed into the divided selves characteristic of the (realist) novel form. As Lukács writes in language Lang will soon ratify, in the epic world

> [t]here is not yet any interiority, for there is not yet any exterior, any 'otherness' for the soul. The soul goes out to seek adventure; it lives through adventures, but it does not know the real torment of seeking and the real danger of finding; such a soul never stakes itself; it does not yet know that it can lose itself, it never thinks of having to look for itself. Such an age is the age of the epic.   (1971: 30)

It was precisely such an undivided age that Lang sought to recapture in the romances he defended from his post at *Longman's Magazine*.

Lang's practice as a translator pursues into the realm of stylistics the philosophical-historical program Lukács outlines here and that Lang defended in his theoretical writing on epic and romance. For Lang as for Lukács, epic was the shape of an irredeemably savage art that disclosed a heroic way of life now all but extinct. Any faithful translation of Homer should thus convey the strangeness and immediacy of a world in which, as Auerbach observes in a related observation, all thought is rigorously externalized into scenes of physical action and quoted speech. In *The World of Homer*, Lang develops this observation about the externality of the epic mode, praising Homer's mastery by describing (repetitively) the unchanging nature of his characters' essences: "[s]o consistent, so delicate, so strong a delineation of character [. . .] every person is drawn with equal firmness, delicacy, and consistency" (1910: 250).

Lang's repetitive emphasis on the "consistency" of Homeric actants accords with Bakhtin's sense that the characters of romance are static entities whose narrative dynamism comes from inhabiting a world of "miraculous chance" (1981: 152); it also mirrors Auerbach's claim, in *Mimesis*, that the injunction of epic style is "to represent phenomena [. . .] completely fixed in their spatial and temporal relations. Nor do psychological processes receive any other treatment: here too nothing must remain hidden and unexpressed" (2003: 6). Arguing alongside these later critics for an isomorphism between social and literary form, Lang understood that the mental undergirding of epic life predated rationality construed in its post-Kantian or Jamesian guise as internal self-division, self-reflection, and sentimental self-alienation. (All these faculties, I have suggested, are translated into literary practice by a technique like free indirect discourse.) By contrast, romance form proceeds from the presumption that premodern cognition works not as cognition at all but as physical sensation or affect; its formal mode must therefore convey this temporally and politically coded absence of *dianoia*, or thought.[37]

Lang's scholarship had convinced him of the cognitive difference between the epic age and "ours"; it had also proven to him that Homer's poems were written in an already archaic dialect of Greek: the language of the epics, he thought, was old-fashioned even to Homer's original audiences. In keeping with this, Lang cast his epics not into verse but prose—the better to convey immediacy and reach common audiences—and reasoned further that his prose translation should recreate the original's archaicizing effect. He thus settled on an "old and plain" style he linked in his preface to the *Odyssey* to the Bible (1928: ix), a connection between Hebrew and Greek idioms Auerbach would also make. The result was the same quasi-King Jamesian prose line, loaded with thee's and thou's, later to be be transposed almost without alteration into the pages of Haggard's pseudo-Homeric combats. For the twentieth-century critic George Steiner, these techniques constitute Lang's "contentious" intervention into the tradition of Homeric translation (1996: 372; see also Dentith 2006: 48–63).

In Book XI of Lang's co-translated 1883 *Iliad* (he was responsible for Books X–XVI), a spree of premodern violence becomes an action scene worthy of Haggard, old and plain and unremittingly brutal:

[Agamemnon] spake and dashed Peisandros from his chariot to the earth, smiting him with the spear upon the breast, and he lay supine on the ground.

> But Hippolochos rushed away, and him too he smote to earth, and cut off
> his arms and his neck with the sword, then tossed him like a ball of stone to
> roll through the throng.   (p. 185)

In Lang's treatment, immediacy of detail combines with an archaizing
linguistic affectation ("smite," "smote") to create an action scene reminiscent of the all-out battle scenes in *King Solomon's Mines*. When Lang
tells us that Agamemnon "cut off his arms and his neck with the sword,"
his simple declarative statement conveys action, as predication, in its
most direct form: subject, verb, object. In Robert Fagles' 1990 treatment, by contrast, the content is just as violent (it is in the original), but
Lang's direct verbs have been lengthened. The original (*Iliad* 11.143–7)
also uses participles, τμήξας ("cutting off") and κόψας ("severing"), a
grammatical form retained by Alexander Pope and Robert Fagles but
pointedly rejected by Lang. The present participles Fagles maintains via
Pope—and from the original Greek—are forms that, in English,
lengthen and diffuse the actions Lang chooses to render with ostenta-
tious directness. So even as they transcode Greek syntax "directly,"
participial renderings also introduce what Adams critiques as the "cor-
rected or civilized violence" of liberal epic (2011: 83): "Hippolochus
leapt away, but him he killed on the ground, / slashing off his arms with
a sword, lopping off his head" (trans. Fagles, 1990: XI, 167–9). Lang's
sharp, hard verbs have been evened out, and the shock of decapitation
(Lang uses "cut") has been softened into the figurative "lopping."[38]
Characterized by plain speech and brute violence, Lang's Homer contains what Haggard called "mighty struggles"—ones that are not so
much "awful" as entertaining to see.
    The point is that the flatly material mode of Lang's Homer would be
transposed directly into *King Solomon's Mines* and the other romances
Lang helped usher into print. This mode can be called superficial only
provided the value judgments of our post-Jamesian critical tradition be
stripped from that term. As Lang wrote in *Homer and the Epic*, "The
epic, in the *Odyssey*, becomes a romance, the best of all romances"
(1893: 7). Shaped in dialogue with Lang's translation of premodern
myth, Haggard's prose shifts between scenes incredible violence (what
James called *King Solomon's Mines* "bloodiness!") and a stagy archaicizing idiom, a tonal oscillation only further radicalized by the novel's
infamous humor. But that's okay, since, as Lang said of Homer's world,
great deeds, feasts, and pitiful violence—"humour too"—sat next to one
another without transition, since all of these facets of existence constituted elements of a unified society in which softer distinctions would have

been unthinkable (1893: 6). "[W]ith his clear vision of the end of all living, he combines the gladdest enjoyment of life," Lang writes of Homer (p. 5). Or as Haggard explains, the savage chronotope of the African countryside has no place for "soft transformation scene[s]" or "breathing-space" between one thing and another: "for in these latitudes," Haggard writes, "twilight does not exist. The change from day to night is as quick and as absolute as the change from life to death" (2007: 102). Given Haggard's avowed refusal of the transitional buffering of modern prose—its emphasis on dilated mental processes, the cognitive pauses before an action—it is hardly surprising that Lang proclaimed Haggard's work "as good as Homer!" ("Norwich" 1920: 5).

What I have argued is that the adventure romance was generated from prior forms, at a period of England's global geopolitical decline, as a technology of mediation that might rekindle an epic life turned residual under the pressures of Victorian modernity in its late or downward phase. Once we appreciate the importance of free indirect discourse and its concomitant figures of depth, deliberation, and delay to the self-consciously modern fiction then rising from Boston and New York, we are in a better position to historicize the alleged deficiencies of romance style. If free indirect discourse captures the subtle, probing machinery of bourgeois thought, then Allan Quatermain's rebuttal stands as fit description of its romantic opposite: "Elephant hunters are a rough set of men," Quatermain says, "and don't trouble themselves with much beyond the facts of life" (p. 19). In Haggard's novels, all is surface and everything, as Howells wrote of Haggard, is "a great, whirling splendor of peril and achievement, a wild scene of heroic adventure, and of emotional ground and lofty tumbling" (Howells 1892: 106). Howells meant this to sound bad. But the excessive and kinetic qualities of Haggard's Lang-Sponsored prose become evident as a stylistic strategy, rather than simple defect, when we historicize rather than reproduce the judgments of the realism wars' winning side.[39]

This process works both ways, however, and can reframe our understanding James' late style to see it less as the culmination of novelistic development and more as the product of a moment in which the content of the term "novel" was being actively contested. While the realism wars escalated to maximum tension, another member of the Lang coterie stretched the novel form yet further to show how, during a period of systemic transition a seemingly archaic violence and modern deliberation might not be opposites so much as two phases of the same being.

RADICALLY BOTH: STEVENSON'S STRANGE CASE

The Strange Case of Dr. Jekyll and Mr. Hyde (1886) has been described as crude pulp fiction and sophisticated psychological drama: at once a shilling shocker, an early detective novel, and a member (with *King Solomon's Mines*) of the category Brantlinger calls the "imperial gothic" (1988: 228). It "is not," observed the flummoxed *Academy* in January 1886,

> an orthodox three-volume novel; it is not even a one-volume novel of the ordinary type; it is simply a paper-covered shilling story, belonging, so far as external appearance goes, to a class of literature familiarity with which has bred in the minds of most readers a certain measure of contempt. [But] [. . .] [a]ppearances [. . .] are deceitful; and in this case they are very deceitful indeed [. . .]   (Maixner, ed. 1998: 203)

Powerless to discern the true self hidden beneath *Jekyll and Hyde*'s "external appearance," the reviewer recapitulates the plot he analyzes. In the final accounting, is this a respectable novel or a "contempt[ible]" one, an ennobling thing or a debasing one, more like Jekyll or more like Hyde? The reader's confusion can signify for us the sophistication with which Stevenson's novel diagnoses the intertwined generic and political antagonisms structuring its moment. In the years leading up to *Jekyll and Hyde*, Stevenson corresponded regularly with both Lang and James, and his 1886 novel emerges directly out of the debates over action and deliberation then gripping the literary field in which he was already, thanks to *Treasure Island*, an established property.[40] *Jekyll and Hyde* stages as psychological agon the generic tension between realism and romance as it was then being debated by Stevenson's own friends and correspondents; in so doing, this self-consciously idiosyncratic novel—this strange case—shows that modern restraint and epic violence are not opposed terms but complementary aspects of liberal modernity's sovereign power as it expresses itself under conditions of geopolitical transition.

In works like *Treasure Island* (1883) and *Kidnapped* (1886), Stevenson had already perfected the mode Lang was then busy branding as romance. Those adventure tales privileged action over introspection and set their stories of piracy and event in a milieu that self-consciously borrowed from the work of Lang, Scott, and even Haggard—though Stevenson refused a request by Lang to collaborate on a novel with Haggard, citing the latter's sloppy prose style. Stevenson's most surreal romances hinge their mode on geographical distance from modernity's center. But his third novel is not about tropical resource acquisition (like *Treasure Island*) or an escape from slavery that takes place beyond the reach of English power

(like *Kidnapped*). Nor is it, like *The Dynamiter* (1885), formally bifur-
cated into, on the one hand, sexualized adventures taking place on the
world system's periphery—a "Hoodoo camp" in Cuba, a Mormon sera-
glio in Utah—and, on the other, a realist plot unfolding in London. All
those texts follow Lang and Howells in enforcing a generic distinction that
is also, for Stevenson here, a geographical and political one: realism and
romance, civilization and barbarism, are differentiated along a continuum
of modernization understood to correspond to the geographic distinction
between core and periphery.[41]

Where a text like *The Dynamiter* formally separates this interlocked set
of modal and political binaries, *Jekyll and Hyde* folds them together. In a
novel that uses physical space to mirror the mental lives of its inhabitants
(and vice versa), Jekyll's once-grand house is an outpost amid creeping
neglect. It's positioned among "a square of ancient, handsome houses,
now for the most part decayed from their high estate and let in flats and
chambers to all sorts and conditions of men; map-engravers, architects,
shady lawyers and the agents of obscure enterprises" (2002: 16). Passages
like this have been adduced as evidence of the text's preoccupation with a
new professionalism. But "anxiety" cannot capture the conceptual and
periodizing work happening here: "now" once grand houses have become
"decayed from their high estate," and a once comfortable bourgeois
economy has degenerated into apartment-living and a penumbral money
economy, as each of the Empire's signal disciplines—mapping, building,
law, and finance—move in while a formerly stable order moves out.

As Dr. Jekyll's final narration will explain, those processes of historical
transformation and material decline conclude when the doctor's "bonds of
obligation" find their "solution" (2002: 57) in a bare physicality, figured as
Hyde, that breaks through the forms of restraint associated with the
villain's law-abiding host. The novel marks this civilized host with a
comic excess of bourgeois uprightness, listing his titles—"Henry Jekyll
MD, DCL, LLD, FRS, &s" (p. 11)—and calling him "one of your fellows
who do what they call good" (p. 9). By contrast to the philanthropic
rationalism of this upstanding citizen, Hyde betrays a Quatermain-esque
anti-deliberation that is inhuman or animalistic, in the repeated language
of existing criticism, only if we follow the assumption that Jamesian
cognition constitutes humanity as such. (The fact that criticism continues
to use these terms to read the novel only testifies to the persistence of
liberal idealism's categories into current method.) Recall that Hyde's
brutal acts of violence take place "with extraordinary quickness" (p. 15),
"all of a sudden" (p. 21), "and next moment" (p. 22).

These and many other markers of temporal synchronicity serve conspicuously to erase deliberative processes. In so doing they depict Hyde as,

in this too, the opposite and yet secret truth of his politely modern host. In all of his symbolic registers, then—savagery, inhumanity, darkness, and unthinking action—Hyde is liberalism's extravagant other. Yet he is not. In a famous passage, the doctor drinks the potion, shudders, and

> [t]hen these agonies began swiftly to subside, and I came to myself as if out of a great sickness. There was something strange in my sensations, something indescribably new and, from its very novelty, incredibly sweet. I felt younger, lighter, happier in body; within I was conscious of a heady recklessness, a current of disordered sensual images running like a millrace in my fancy, a solution of the bonds of obligation, an unknown but not an innocent freedom of the soul. I knew myself, at the first breath of this new life, to be more wicked, tenfold more wicked, sold a slave to my original evil; and the thought, in that moment, braced and delighted me like wine. I stretched out my hands, exulting in the freshness of these sensations; and in the act, I was suddenly aware that I had lost in stature.   (p. 57)

Stevenson here documents how a civilized body might "come to itself" as brute violence. When Jekyll-Hyde realizes he has "lost in stature," for example, we assume with nearly every film adaptation—and the later references to Hyde's baggy clothing—that he's referencing physical height, but the "stretch[ing]" and "exulting" here argue otherwise. The terms help us know that this socially striving doctor has lost something else too: social respectability and moral uprightness, "stature." All are "lost," as Jekyll is simultaneously liberated and enslaved. "Solution" works as a hinge between conceptually exclusive readings too, since the doctor's descent/ ascent into physicality is both the answer (solution) to Jekyll's restrained and philanthropic liberalism—Hyde feels "younger, lighter, happier in body" (p. 57)—and its precise negation, a "[dis-]solution."

Stevenson's style negotiates two sets of conceptual oppositions at once. It joins together, first, physical and social registers (stature/stature) and second, the theory that violence is the perfect abrogation of liberal restraint with the (opposite) claim that it is liberalism's purest essence. A solution. This collapse of opposed readings through the workings of style shows that for Stevenson, the "zone" of romance is less a space of symptomatic fantasy or naïve wish-fulfillment and more like our own home, albeit a home now made akin to the "terror formation" of the colony (Mbembe 2003: 24). Terror, we learn here, is what lives within and secretly animates precisely those figures who do the most of "what they call good."

It is crucial to note that Stevenson's presentation does not offer the emergence of Hyde from Jekyll, brutality from civility, in the context of "the shipwreck of [Jekyll's] reason" (p. 49) as simple paradox. Mere opposition does not capture the complicated inter-involvement of these heavily allegorized positions. In fact Hyde is described as the radicalization or externalization of the impulses already lurking within someone who, we are assured, "inclined by nature to industry, fond of the respect of the wise and good among [his] fellow-men" (p. 55). Violence and brutality are, in other words, already constitutive elements of Jekyll's seeming civility. As Jekyll reports, he is "in no sense a hypocrite": "I was no more myself when I laid aside restraint and plunged in shame, than when I laboured, in the eye of day, at the furtherance of knowledge or the relief of sorrow or suffering" (p. 55). Rather than splitting into opposition the politicized modal functions I have traced—ultraviolent romance and civilized realism, Lukács' "adventure and interiority"—Stevenson shows with bravura intensity that they are two names for the same thing, a dialectical scenario concretized in Jekyll's signature, for example, or in those famous sentences—"He, I say—I cannot say, I"—in which the very grammatical structure of identity collapses under the weight of the "solution" Stevenson has in mind here. "[O]f the two natures that contended in the field of my consciousness," Jekyll-Hyde reports, "even if I could rightly be said to be either, it was only because I was radically both" (p. 56).

In accord with twenty-first-century historians of empire so diverse as Giovanni Arrighi and Niall Ferguson, Stevenson fixes this openly violent and seemingly atavistic turn in England's global fortunes to the mid-1870s, "close on a generation ago" (p. 16). If we understand the novel's present to be 1886, the year of its composition and publication, then when Dr. Lanyon says that "it is more than ten years since Henry Jekyll [. . .] began to go wrong, wrong in mind" (p. 12), the physician dates Jekyll's deterioration—and Hyde's emergence—to 1876. In this and other of its conspicuous but unremarked periodizing gestures, *Jekyll and Hyde* anticipates the macrohistorical arguments of those economic historians who, like Arrighi (2010), Ferguson (2004), and Cain and Hopkins (2001), fix the mid-1870s as the turning-point in the long-term fortunes of England's global power, the pivot in its transition from global hegemony to violent late imperial dominance.

What I am emphasizing is how Stevenson's allegedly symptomatic morality play cannily manipulates the generic antagonism between realism and romance to dramatize the place of political violence at the twilight hour of empire. Where Haggard and James were content to inhabit two sides of this opposition—Haggard happy to be called childish and James desperate to play the sober adult—Stevenson refuses to choose, and shows instead how these interlocked sets of binary terms—romance and realism, brute force and modern civility, "nonage" and adulthood—are but liberal idealism's own inadequate vocabulary for understanding the seeming paradoxes by which incredible violence might not stand against but

secretly structure political modernity in its most peaceful or even philanthropic dispensations. Children's bodies trampled in the street; human
beings clubbed to death at night: what Stevenson discloses is that such
scenes of extravagant brutality are not legal modernity's abrogation so
much as its ultimate expression or limit case—where its perverse core
becomes manifest. It is therefore Utterson, the lawyer, who is perhaps best
positioned to appreciate, as he tours the ruined avenues of his modern city,
what he calls in ambiguous syntax the "terror of the law" (p. 23).

Conclusion

Endless War Then and Now

This book has tracked the sovereignty concept across the battle-scarred career of the *Pax Victoriana*, when dreams of cosmopolitan emancipation unfolded alongside no fewer than 200 separate wars. This story began at the bright noon of a relatively secure geopolitical hegemony, at mid-century, and concluded in the half-light of decline, amid the anomie, dissolution, and overseas challenge of the 1880s. Throughout this arc I have emphasized how the dogged persistence of killing in an age of liberty disrupted the conceptual assumptions of progressive idealism; how the very inseparability of law and violence, never more painfully evident than in episodes of colonial war and legal emergency, collapsed the logical principles of non-contradiction and identity that remain our common sense. The disorientation generated by this implosion of bourgeois thought spurred Victorian writers to grope toward new forms of conceptuality, new genres of thought, and in so doing to generate the literary effects that might perform them.

Conceptual breakdown as engine for literary innovation; form as the enactment of thought. In showing how Eliot, Collins, Swinburne, Haggard, and others navigated this process of conceptual generation I have treated their works not as ideological symptoms or passive transfer points for discourse but as performances of political thinking. These creative acts did not so much enforce or recapitulate the intellectual repertoires of their moments as test and even, sometimes, exceed them. They actively model thought. Yet as I noted in the Introduction, no choice to read *this* way instead of *that* way can ever be guaranteed by anything outside the reading encounter itself. All interpretation presupposes an affective and intellectual relation between subject and object, even perhaps an erotic one, that can change shape, intensify, and reverse itself but that can find no authorization anywhere but in the reading itself. My allegiances have pushed me to ascribe critical agency to apparently inert historical objects by a kind of tactical prosopopoeia—to see them as processes, not things, as agents of thought rather than recipients of it. But this choice can only ever be a willed act, a decision in the sense of a wager, or choice without guarantees. Is the mode of reading I've pursued here "correct"? The question misses the point, since such a decision—here, to read objects of the past as demonstrating creative critical abilities, actively modeling thought—can only ever be a response to the undecideable made in relation to first principles or extrarational commitments: not facts, but values. Not means, but ends.

What commitments drive our reading? The allegiances that have informed this book about political violence rest, perhaps paradoxically, on the normative value of care. They do so in two senses. On the one hand, the readings arrayed here have sought to care intrinsically, within the reading encounter: they have trained repartive attention on individual cultural objects in ways that, I hope, come some way in honoring the concrete specificity of those objects, the textured idiosyncrasy of thought forms not our own. On the other hand, these encounters are driven by care of an extrinsic kind, a care directed outside the hermetic closure of textual analysis. In that sense, this book has labored to maintain affective solidarity with the historical damage and expunged human singularity that all documents of Victorian modernity cannot but transcode into form.

It will have escaped no one's attention that the historical problem the foregoing chapters all in some way engage—the modern state's relationship to killing—persists unresolved into the present. We have yet to live beyond the dynamics of harm and exclusion documented in these pages. This seemingly obvious point generates difficult questions for method. All historical thinking depends on a dialectic of sameness and difference, foreignness and domestication. On the one hand, the past is absolute otherness, and to posit analogies with the present is to efface the specificity of some particular configuration of historical-political time. On the other hand, to construe historical difference as an unbridgeable gulf—to imagine the past as radically singular, a foreign country separated from us by impermeable borders—is to close off the past from the present and deny the historicity of our own moment. *Forms of Empire* has worked to play the irresolvable dilemma of historical thinking two ways at once. The book's extended engagements with individual texts I hope stand as evidence that its primary investments are in the specificity of the works, situations, human actors, and historical moments under examination. To that end I have resisted the temptation to treat singular instances—be they texts, events, or human beings—as types, stand-ins, or fungible instances of something other than themselves. The names should haunt us. This commitment to particularity explains why so little has been said in these pages about the nature of abstract categories like "realism" or "aestheticism" or "popular fiction." As we saw in Chapter 2, the impulse to flatten qualitatively different instances into exchangeable examples of a category is itself a feature of Victorian modernity.

So the past and its forms of thought are radically themselves, untranslatable across time. Yet the stakes for this book's exercises in historical particularization also derive from a sense that the instances arranged here retain some ghostly relevance beyond themselves: that they are, if only in some slanted sense, generalizable. The period during which this project was conceived, researched, and completed was characterized, at first, by the late phase of a broadly optimistic, post-Cold War sense that history's end had lately arrived. This optimism about the emancipatory potential of elements of liberal ontology such as rational disinterest, individual agency, and idealist logical method—along with their material condition of possibility, capitalism—gave way as in a fever dream to a profusion of warmaking in service of emancipation.[1] The project of perpetual peace once more proved to be entangled uncomfortably with its opposite. Then as now, modernity's unceasing wars are not the exception to its promise of liberation but that promise's perverse realization.

From this perspective, nineteenth-century thinking is productively seen not just as radically singular—escaping instrumentalization and refusing the exchange relations of historical analogy—but also, and in direct contrast to this, useful: a resource for addressing conceptual and material crises now. Among other things, this means that if a temptation is to seal the "Victorian world" under antiquarian glass, lacquering the dynamic energy of the past into an inventory of theses or ideologies available for our later moral judgment, we might instead imagine the Victorian age as worth caring about not least because the world's first liberal empire—ours is the second—underwent a phase of geopolitical hegemony and contraction, and produced dynamic aesthetic and conceptual forms to mediate those processes, in ways that bear an oblique relation to our own period of war-ravaged post-Enlightenment.

The hyperviolent twilight of our American century has been bracketed under various periodizing rubrics, including neoliberalism, late capitalism or, with Elizabeth Povinelli (2011) and others, "late liberalism," the "lates" and the "neos" suggesting at once continuity and rupture. The capitalist consensus named by those terms has in turn generated genres of reaction familiar to students of the nineteenth century: resurgent ethnonationalisms, romantic anticapitalisms, and Carlylean fantasias of purer times. All of this feels shockingly familiar, uncannily repetitive. The macrohistorical models of economists like Arrighi (2010), which posit "patterns of recurrence and evolution" (2010: 4) stretching over successive phases of world leadership, would push us to posit such analogies, even isomorphisms, between comparable cycles of imperial rule: Genoese, Dutch, British, and American all in a row. But the ghostly persistence of Victorian liberal paradigms into the present should not be taken to mean that the dynamics of modern violence are quasi-natural facts or historical inevitabilities, as I have provisionally left room for assuming in these pages. *Longues durées*, cycles of empire, phases of capital accumulation, recurrences, autumns, and death: such figures and the determinist frameworks they evoke have their uses, insofar as they help generate previously unseen linkages and authorize connections between otherwise sequestered historical moments.[2] In an important sense, the Victorians are us, and vice versa.

But any allusion to suprahuman historical laws, however provisional, must instantly be countered with the fact that in matters of human history nothing is settled in advance. Far from being the result of inevitable processes or quasi-natural cycles, the obscene and ongoing violence of our contemporary—like any historical configuration—is a result of human will. It emerges from a political rationality that is human-made and for that reason subject to change. Marx's 1852 maxim about individuals' intertwinement with historical forces—"Men make their own history, [...] but under circumstances [...] given and transmitted from the past" (1852: n.p.)—is itself an insight of the Victorian period. As belated readers of that earlier liberal empire, we are charged with the task of using its archive to help remake the present.

Notes

INTRODUCTION

1. Bayly notes that the uprisings later denoted "The Mutiny" were just the largest in a series of acts of revolt against British capital expansion (1990: 170). For short accounts of the events, see Joshi 55–66 and Herbert (2009: 3–5), who note (with others) that the London press was all but unanimous in its calls for vengeance; W. H. Russell's dispatches were conspicuous in their dissent. In any case, the aim of the British counterinsurgency, as one late Victorian historian recalled, was "to punish and to awe" (quoted in Joshi 59), a policy applauded by even such otherwise sentimental onlookers as Dickens (cf. Joshi 50n., 49).
2. See e.g. Favret (2009), Cole (2012), and Saint-Amour (2015).
3. The event is also known as the Bibighar Massacre and became the rallying point for British popular sentiment during the rebellion. Havelock's soldiers retook the courtyard and found themselves "'ankle-deep'" in the blood of executed civilians: "blood covered the floor and the rooms were littered with pieces of clothing, daguerreotype cases, bonnets, shoes, and other 'unspeakable remnants' of violent death"; rumors elaborated these findings, adding severed feet in shoes and babies bayoneted to the walls (quoted in Tickell 2013: 70).
4. Citing historian Richard Drayton, Bell notes that "sidestepping imperial violence has been a recurrent theme in the historiography of the British Empire" (Bell 2015: 989). On the Cold War as foundational moment for Victorian Studies, see Vernon (2005). The characterization of modernity as an "unfinished project" is by Habermas. Like imperial war, the death penalty crystallizes this fundamental tension in the liberal state's self-representation; unsurprisingly, John Stuart Mill vigorously engaged with this issue in the 1860s.
5. Kostal notes that "[f]or the moralizing fragment of the governing class," the unbridled violence against black peasants in Jamaica, ultimately judged legal, produced "confusion and self-contradiction" (2005: 483).
6. For a detailed treatment of the way in which this inside/outside dynamic worked at the level of legal procedure, see Hussain (2003: esp. 1–34), which charts "the potential conflict between state power and legal authority, between what the state perceives as necessary power for survival at certain moments and what the law makes available—a tension between [. . .] the requirements of sovereign emergency and the contraints of a rule of law" (p. 2).
7. As Farwell's case indicates, such empirical studies are most readily found in the genre of military history. Like the related euphemism "low-intensity conflict," "small wars" refers to irregular, sometimes covert military operations like counterinsurgency or so-called peacekeeping, often undertaken under executive authority, which do not typically involve massed armies on

an open battlefield. I use it here to underscore the perversity of the idea that any war is small to those killed by it.

8. Bell has likewise observed that nineteenth-century "[l]iberalism was a protean phenomenon, a shape-shifting amalgam of philosophical arguments and political-economic practices encompassing diverse views on the self, society, economy and government." Thus "[r]eductive generalizations [. . .] are usually more misleading than illuminating" (Bell 2016: 1, 2).

9. Banerjee (2010) shows how discourses of liberal citizenship provided ammunition for anticolonial movements in India; Sartori (2014) has likewise demonstrated how "liberal" assumptions about property ownership enabled new idioms for imagining peasant independence within the imperial structure of British India.

10. My sense of the past as a repertoire of possible futures borrows from Grosz's work on Darwin (2004: esp. 244–61). On presentism in Victorian Studies, see Levine (2015: 1–23) and Goodlad (2015: 268–93).

11. The valuable work of parsing liberalism's vast significations has been done by others including Bell (2014: 683). Citing the definitional flexibility charted by Bell, Gunn and Vernon (2011) note that "liberalism" is most often used to denote: (1) particular dynamics of state politics, or schemes of "political representation and the relationship between the individual and the state" often characterized as liberal; (2) the political economic model—bourgeois capitalism—that arose in tandem with and sometimes tension with those state forms; (3) the micropolitical category of the Liberal Party itself, which did not properly exist until as late as 1868; and finally, (4) the much more generalized notion of liberalism a "diffuse rationality" that is "seemingly everywhere and nowhere" (Gunn and Vernon 2011: 8–9; see also Parry 1993). For Bell (2016: 2, 30), claims of liberalism's static relation to empire too often draw their evidence from "*canonical* interpretations of liberalism" by figures like Locke and Mill. I focus on this "canonical" strain, and expand its cast of characters, to underscore our conceptual debt to this post-Enlightenment tradition.

12. A representative sample of this now-massive body of work would include Mehta (1999); Gunn and Vernon (2011); Hall (2002); Lasourdo (2014); Mantena (2010); Claeys (2012); Mufti (2007); Muthu (2003); and Pitts (2005). For a coherent overview, see Sartori (2014: 3–5); Bell (2016); Goodlad (2015a).

13. The marketing copy for Mehta's book suggests this inversion of common sense as its key selling point: "We take liberalism to be a set of ideas committed to political rights and self-determination, yet it also served to justify an empire built on political domination" (http://press.uchicago.edu/ ucp/books/book/chicago/L/bo3623192.html).

14. For the debate see e.g. Goodlad (2015a); Goodlad and Sartori (2013); Best and Marcus (2009); the recent work of Rita Felski (2015); and the V21

Manifesto (2015) and the many responses to it. I borrow the ideology/theory distinction from Psomiades (2013).

15. For an opening onto the vast topic how cultural liberalism relates to seemingly "anti-liberal" politics, see Brown (2006); for a treatment of this process at the level of aesthetic practice, see Davis (2015: 27–67).

16. The preceding sentences rework similar ones in Hensley (2015). For macroscopic, macrohistorical accounts of the "British world," see Darwin (2011); Arrighi (2010); Cain and Hopkins (2001); Belich (2011). Thomas S. Davis summarizes: "Unlike other theories of conceiving the world that tend to foreground cultural flows, ethical encounters, or multiple versions of something dubbed 'modernity,' world-systems analysis prioritizes the interplay of force and capital accumulation that link different states, geographical areas, and international actors" (2015: 14).

17. My approach charts a middle course between the smaller-scaled, human-focused work in the so-called New Imperial History and the systems-level approaches typified, recently, in the work of Darwin, Cain and Hopkins, and others: I construe power from the point of view of political violence (and thus in the top-down political-economic and statist terms favored by Darwin et al.), but my investments in this follow postcolonial studies, subaltern studies, and the New Imperial Historians by coming from the bottom up.

18. Asked in an interview whether "the military model" seems "the best one for describing power," Foucault explained: "This is the problem I now find myself confronting. [...] Isn't power simply a form of warlike domination? Shouldn't one therefore conceive all problems of power in terms of relations of war? Isn't power a sort of generalized war which assumes at particular moments the forms of peace and the State? Peace would then be a form of war, and the State a means of waging it" (1984: 123).

19. Both tendencies are evident in Mbembe's widely cited "Necropolitics" (2003), which cites these passages of Foucault, but frames their central questions in the eternalized vocabulary of political metaphysics.

20. "Epistemic violence" is Spivak's phrase, but the statements authorizing the slippage between ontological and somatic understandings of "violence," and the work of institutionalizing this slippage in literary studies, came from the figure whose work she helped introduce to the academy. See Derrida (1967), "Violence and Metaphysics," and "The Violence of the Letter" (1987: 101–40). The academic fascination with Carl Schmitt in the past two decades—and the otherwise inexplicable traction of his separation of "the political" into a separate and allegedly higher ontological realm—is perhaps best seen as a symptom of such linguistic models' inadequacy to lived experience after 2001.

21. Arthur Clennam in *Little Dorrit* meets an official who explains, "I can give you plenty of forms to fill up. Lots of 'em here. You can have a dozen if you like. But you'll never go on with it" (quoted in Levine 2015: 98).

On documents as a genre, see Gitelman (2014: esp. 20–52); on form in telegraphic messaging, see Menke (2007: 1–30).

22. Bigelow (2013) shows a similar process in action at the level of literary genre (historical novel and national tale); Stoler (2010) shows how everyday institutional documentation discloses hesitations and caesuras in colonial thought. Like Bigelow, my focus falls on the strongly shaped idioms of literary writing, but with Stoler I aim to show how interfaces between human idiosyncrasy and institutionalized forms of writing (like literature) can generate new forms, and thus new thought.

23. It is this procedure that Levine has in mind when she critiques approaches (like that of Cleanth Brooks) that equate the "boundedness" of a lyric poem, for example, with the "boundedness" of closed political orders, seeing in the aesthetic artifact an analogue of the social one (2015: 25).

24. This distinction is usefully illuminated with reference to the disagreement between Paul de Man and Derrida over deconstruction. Where Derrida's work to "deconstruct" Rousseau in *Of Grammatology* had implicitly figured deconstruction as something *a reader* does, de Man countered that Rousseau's text had itself generated this effect, shifting the work of deconstruction to the object (de Man 1983a: 133). I'm grateful to Forest Pyle (2015), and to Zach Samalin for reminding me of this distinction.

25. Kirshenbaum cites Abigail Sellen and Richard Harper's *Myth of the Paperless Office* (2001) to explain that affordances "are all about possibilities for action, which determine how human beings interact with the physical things in their environment" (2012: 32). I expand this emphasis on the "raw, literal, physical materiality of different kinds of objects and media" (p. 31) to account for the shaping constraints of semi-material forms like (say) heroic couplets or literary realism; these shaping codes are instantiated in physical objects like codex books and lineated manuscripts but are not reducible to their materials of transmission. The point is to account for the traffic between physical equipment and literary performance.

26. Goodlad draws on Jameson's vocabulary but, in emphasizing authors' individual insights and acts of apprehension, leaves ambiguous whether she follows him in viewing texts as operating symptomatically. For an account of literary form's capacity to figure otherwise inapprehensible phenomena, see Davis (2015). Like Davis and at least one strain of Goodlad's argument (2015b), I hew more closely to Gilles Deleuze's sense that works of literature, rather than readers of them, perform critical work: "Authors, if they are great, are more like doctors than patients. [. . .] [T]hey are themselves astonishing diagnosticians or symptomatologists. [. . .] [A]rtists are clinicians [. . .] of civilization" (quoted in Smith 1998: xvii).

27. Lacoste (2010) remains the most and perhaps only authoritative source on Beato's biography. I gratefully draw on it here. I part ways with even Chaudhary's modified symptomatic approach, but my account is indebted to his superb treatment of Beato. I thank Tom Prasch for sharing his research

on Beato, and Colin Macwhirter at the Canadian Centre for Architecture for sharing his knowledge of the archive.

28. Chaudhary recounts an astonishing story in which he discovered a reference to a Beato diary entry allegedly explaining the photographer's intention in making "Secundrah Bagh" (1858). When Chaudhary contacted the author of the 1980 article hoping to find the original document, the author confessed that he had been so desperate to ground his reading in authorial intention that he had forged the entry (2012: 220n.).

29. For Azoulay, any reading must account for "all the participants in photographic acts [. . .] approaching the photograph (and its meaning) as an unintentional effect of the encounter between these" (2008: 23).

30. In information and library sciences, deciding what something is "about" constitutes an interpretive act in its own right; turned into metadata, this primal act of interpretation instantly becomes invisible. See Hutchins (1977).

31. Given that "more was written about the revolt than about any other epoch of Indo-British connection" (Chaudhary 2012: 7), we might ask to what extent its violence could be considered buried. Critical projects like W. H. Russell's seem to have exposed British violence, as, for example, when he recounts the casual execution of a child by pistol-whipping (1860: 347–8). But the fact that these reports "aroused a storm of indignation" (Chaudhari 1979: 12) confirms that violence unredeemed by national myth remained for a tiny minority of voices to document. Beato's image brings this contradiction to view.

32. About another Beato image of disinterred bones, Chaudhary writes that it "render[s] visible the violence that preserves daily social relations" and offers "a glimpse into the other side of [. . .] production" (2012: 99). I add that these metaphors of disclosure and unburial are built into the image's own form.

33. For the idea of "reading-with" as a form of solidarity, I am grateful to Stephen Squibb.

CHAPTER 1

1. For the novel as a modified *Bildungsroman*, see Buckley (1974), Fraiman (2002), Stewart (2009: 127–73), and Esty (2002: esp. 63–4). My account runs parallel to Esty's sense that "[m]odernization in this novel kills off central characters and social practices" (p. 55), and rhymes, too, with Stewart's claim that *The Mill* "may be the most Hegelian thing, let along the most Lukácsian thing, that the philosophic Eliot ever wrote" (2009: 164).

2. "The Mill" of the book's title is actually on the Ripple, not the Floss, as Eliot noted to her publisher, John Blackwood, who had come up with the title. (One of Eliot's initial title ideas was "The House of Tulliver," which highlights the quasi-feudal clan identities at the novel's core. See Haight 1968: 319.)

3. Like *On Liberty* (1859) and *Ancient Law* (1861), Darwin's *Origin* (1859) also emerged in the period surrounding 1860, though like the others it began

germinating decades before. Burrow emphasizes that evolutionary thinking was widespread in the years surrounding 1860, and warns against seeing all such thought after 1859 as caused by Darwin (1966: 153). Eliot read *Origin* while writing book 2 of the *Mill*, but experienced it not as a revolution but as a relatively unimpressive addition to the Spencerian developmental theory she already knew. Rather than emphasizing biographical details such as the fact that Eliot invested all the profits from the 1859 *Adam Bede* in Indian railways or that Lewes' son Thornie died from an illness sustained in the Cape Colony (as Nancy Henry does, in her helpful *George Eliot and the British Empire*, 2006), I am concerned with how the problem of political violence structures Eliot's version of the Victorian modernity plot.

4. Investigating the connection between mid-Victorian "equipoise" and the Anglo-American Cold War project's self diagnosis as an "empire of liberty" is beyond the scope of this chapter. Vernon writes that positive assessment of Victorian equipoise was "at its most influential in the decades following the Second World War, when modernization theory became enchanted by what it saw as the Victorian achievement: the peaceful transition to an industrialized market economy, the formation of a democratic civil society, and the largely voluntary origins of the welfare state—all achievements predicated on a new ethics of individualism" (2005: 273). Woodward's influential *The Age of Reform: 1815–1870* (1938, rev. 1962) captures this tendency in microcosm, drawing explicit parallels between the Victorian and interwar situations, a topic Esty's forthcoming project now investigates.

5. In the post-Cold War moment Amanda Anderson called for a reintroduction of the term "modernity" to the evaluation of Victorian political practices, a move that self-consciously returned to the temporal-political schemes invented by the Victorians, with modifications from Habermas and Rawls. Anderson's project shares with the ideologies it recapitulates a relative incuriosity about the material practices subtending the idealist "distance" or positively charged indifference it endorses.

6. Hewing closely to Eliot's own pronouncements, full monographs treat e.g. *Memory and History in George Eliot* (Li 2000) and *George Eliot and Victorian Historiography* (McCaw 2000). Stewart's superb chapter on *The Mill*, in *Novel Violence*, is called "Of Time as a River" (2009: 127–73).

7. Benedict Anderson (1991) follows Eliot in situating the grave as the privileged figure of political time. For Anderson, the (dead) Unknown Soldier represents the sacrifice that must be encoded into the time of the past for a nation to acknowledge its status as a legitimate power in the present (p. 9). I thank Sarah Lincoln for this insight.

8. Eliot's research program for *The Mill* has been well documented; see Rignall (2000). Eliot's notes, including her observations on floods and geological events, are collected in *A Writer's Notebook* (1981). In the 1851 essay "The Progress of the Intellect," Eliot cites "the great inductions of geology" as support for her sense of history's "undeviating law[,] [. . .] that invariability of sequence which is acknowledged to be the basis of physical science, but

which is still perversely ignored in our social organization, our ethics, and our religion" (1963: 31).

9. Secord emphasizes the local struggles of individual geologists within institutions, critiques "high level theory" (1986: 318), and arguably underplays how developmental stories in the idiom of science recoded those in other seemingly separate spheres, like "politics" or "fiction." My point is that geology was one sphere of cultural production (with others) in which the state of the modern state was being devised and contested.

10. Cuvier's statement of method in his *Discours* parallels Jameson's almost exactly: "it was necessary," he writes, "to restore these monuments of past revolutions, and to detect their meaning: I had to collect and arrange in their original order the component relics; to remodel the creatures to whom the fragments belonged; to reproduce them in their just proportions and with their proper characteristics; and then to compare them with those beings now existing" (Cuvier 1825: 1). Jameson aims to "momentarily retur[n] to life [. . .] the essential mystery of the cultural past" and "allow [it] once more to speak, and to deliver its long-forgotten message in surroundings utterly alien to it" (Jamieson 1981: 19). To do this requires "detecting the traces of that uninterrupted narrative [of history] [. . .] restoring to the surface . . . the repressed and buried reality of this fundamental history" (p. 20). The geological metaphors are crucial to Jameson's account of historical reading. Any text, Jameson says, is the "sedimented or fossilized trace" of historical experience (p. 117).

11. "What I am striving to keep in our minds," Felix tells the "Working Men" in Eliot's 1868 essay, "is the care, the precaution, with which we should go about making things better, so that the public order may not be destroyed, so that no fatal shock may be given to this society of ours, this living body in which our lives are bound up" (Eliot 1963: 422).

12. The essay has proven central to political readings of Eliot's novels. Anderson (2001) and Tucker (2000) use it to read the much later *Daniel Deronda* (1876), ignoring the fiction most contemporary to the essay and implicitly ascribing false continuity to Eliot's ideas regarding organicism over this period. For these changes see Paxton (1991).

13. Horowitz (2006) sees Eliot's "radicalism" as a secret form of "conservatism," but the point is that Eliot seeks to unite progressive and stabilizing functions through the mechanism and metaphors of social organicism.

14. In ways that disclose Habermas' links to Enlightenment idealism, Kant notes: "If it is now asked whether we at present live in an *enlightened age*, the answer is: No, but we live in an age of *enlightenment*" (1991a: 58). Kant also ancipates Eliot's idealist position that mental liberation must precede the material kind (1991a: 55).

15. One is tempted to consider whether pastoral is the signal genre of geological uniformitarianism, where tragedy best gives shape to catastrophist thinking. In any case these are the two generic templates that struggle for pride of place

in—and organize competing critical labels of—Eliot's novel, a doubleness that is symptomatic of the ambiguity I chart here. On *The Mill* as Eliot's signal pastoral novel, see e.g. Levine (2001).

16. Via *Deronda*, Psomiades (n.d.) argues that consent constitutes the key indicator of modernity for 1870s political, anthropological, and novelistic thinkers. Kahn's account of early modern contract (2004) cites *Ancient Law* as the beginning of a modern contract theory tradition, running, for her, into the Cold War and beyond.

17. On the despotism-constitutionalism distinction as a mobilizing force in the Crimean war, see Anderson's analysis (1967), in one of the few Cold War texts to examine this dynamic, *A Liberal State at War*.

18. For these notes, see *George Eliot's Middlemarch Notebooks* (1979: 202–7). For Eliot's list of "Books for Historical Studies," see *George Eliot: A Writer's Notebook, 1854–1879* (1981: 57).

19. Beer's 1986 recounting of Maggie's struggle should be read symptomatically, I suggest, as evidence of the extent to which Eliot's figural system comports with the liberal feminist imagination: "It is this expression of female desire, the desire for knowledge, for sexual love, for free life, which is the unremitting narrative urgency of *The Mill on the Floss*, a desire for new forms of life unrealizable in terms of the old order and the fixed stereotypes by which [Maggie] is surrounded. The desires (for knowledge, sexual love, freedom) are not different from those of men; the difference is in the breaking of the taboo on them, the claiming of them as female desires" (Beer 1986: 98).

20. Spencer's 1857 "Progress" essay also imagines history to aim toward individuation. And Marx, in his 1857–8 notebooks later compiled as the *Grundrisse*, refers to "the naturally arisen clan community, or, if one will, pastoral society" sharing "communality of blood, language, [and] customs" as what is eradicated by an urbanized modernity (1993: 472).

21. Burrow notes that the "early 1860s mark something of a watershed" in the history of progress-thinking, while 1861 was "something of an *annus mirabilis*," since it saw publication of *Ancient Law*, Buckle's second volume of the *History of England*, Mill's *Considerations on Representative Government*, and Max Müller's *Lectures on the Science of Language* (Burrow 1991: 58). We might add *Great Expectations* (serial 1860, book 1861) and, I'm suggesting, *The Mill on the Floss*.

22. In *The Mill*, Eliot makes the idealist argument that an atavistic love for battle is the rationale for warfare abroad, and thus that war will be eradicated in the future. As Tom fantasizes about fighting abroad, the narrator wryly notes: "It is doubtful whether our soldiers would be maintained if there were not pacific people at home who like to fancy themselves soldiers. War, like other dramatic spectacles, might possibly cease for want of a 'public'" (2003: 185).

23. In *Feeling Global*, Robbins argues that the goal of an ethical cosmopolitanism "would be both to defend the social welfare state and, as much as possible, to

extend it outward—for example, toward residents who are noncitizens" (1999: 36); but Robbins would find cause to revise this thesis by 2012, when his collected essays appeared under the title *Perpetual War: Cosmopolitanism from the Viewpoint of Violence*.

24. Maggie's book is *Pug's Tour Through Europe, or, The travell'd monkey: containing his wonderful adventures in the principal capitals of the greatest empires, kingdoms, and states* (1825). It is a poem about a monkey on a Grand Tour, and frames for children a pedagogy of local turning global, and coming back again. Maggie thus repackages an anti-cosmopolitan allegory (stay home, don't go abroad!) into a story about cross-cultural exchange.

25. Even when she fails this cognitive test of modernity—imagining another's experience as your own—Maggie somehow succeeds. When she forgets about Tom's rabbits, she feels Tom's (imagined) reaction as her own— "and so am I sorry" (2003: 34).

26. As Graver (1984) explains, for Tonnies *community* is the name for the largely "rural" or pre-capitalist way of relating, what he calls "the lasting and genuine form of living together" (Tonnies 1957: 35). *Society* is a "mechanical structure" of relations, coextensive with "public" life (33). "*Gemeinschaft* is old," Tonnies summarizes, "*Gesellschaft* is new" (1957: 34).

27. I thank Sarah Lincoln for the Nietzsche reference, and for her many other incisive comments on this chapter.

28. Here Jameson (2002) faithfully represents Marx's own position. In the chapter of *Capital* on "The Process of Exchange," Marx specifies a relationship of determination between base and superstructure: "This juridical relation, whose form is the contract, [...] is itself determined by the economic relation" (1990: 178).

29. But note that the narrative challenge of figuring "transitions" between stages receives sophisticated treatment in Jameson (1981: 96–7); on the problem of narrating periods, see Jameson (1998) and Hensley (2012).

30. Burke may be the most well-known advocate of *durée* over event: for him, a revolution was "an irregular, convulsive movement" that would shock the biotic order of any appropriately historical society. "The course of succession is the healthy habit of the British constitution" (1987: 22).

31. Already in 1956 Larry Rubin could refer with some exhaustion to the "critical controversy long standing" regarding the novel's conclusion (p. 18). Rubin notes that E. A. Baker "sees the flood as a 'melodramatic contrivance'" (quoted on p. 18), then lists a series of other scandalized responses to the ending that James and Leavis had trained New Critics to defame.

32. By calling it "supernumerary," Badiou indicates (2006: 178) that the event is not among the elements of the situation that gives rise to it. See also Hallward (2003: 107–51). Leavis judges that Eliot's "flooded river has no symbolic or metaphorical value," arguing with Badiou that the flood does not *stand for* anything: it is pure presence, beyond the exchange relations of metaphor (1948: 45–6).

33. Writing of politics and revolution, Jean-Luc Nancy concurs with Arendt and Badiou: "The surprise—the event—does not belong to the order of representation" (2000: 173). Arendt's 1963 *On Revolution*, in valorizing what it styles as the exceptional stability of the American Revolution (in distinction from the violent French one), shares an affinity for equipoise with the Cold War liberalism that animated Asa Briggs. The footnotes denouncing black radicalism in *On Violence*, embarrassing to read, make this counterrevolutionary position explicit.

34. Summarizes Hallward (2003: 114–15): "The event reveals 'the inadmissible empty point in which nothing is presented,' and this is why every event indicates, in principle, a pure beginning, the inaugural or uncountable zero of a new time (a new calendar, a new order of history)."

35. For Rubin, certain scenes "poin[t] with the impersonal assurance of a road sign to the actual drowning scene" (Rubin 1956: 21). The road sign metaphor alerts us to the difficulties of interpretation being negotiated here: how obvious *is* this "road sign," and to whom? Maggie's observation that signification and reference break down during the flood event confirms Eliot's awareness—and conscious management—of this hermeneutic dilemma.

36. The evental site is Badiou's name for a set or order in which the elements that make up that set are not yet legible, but are known to exist. It is at this "site" where the momentary (or literally atemporal) actualization of these heretofore unspecifiable potential elements takes place—this is the event. For Badiou, events have to be immanent, i.e. they can't come from outside the situation. As Hallward notes, a foreign invasion, being an incursion from without, cannot properly be termed an event (2003: 116). Thus were the "Long Haired Sea Kings" and "Roman Legions" of St. Ogg's folded into the long history of the village, while the flood, generated from the situation itself, is, like a popular uprising, there, in potential form, waiting to surge.

37. I do not have the space to parse the implications of the flood's status as a sublime event, but such a detour would lead through Kant and Burke, and begin by noting the connection both thinkers draw between sublime natural violence and that of political revolution.

38. Divine violence, which I do not treat here, is problematically the messianic end-time of this cyclical process of revolution, duration, and counterrevolution. Eliot is not eschatological in Benjamin's more severe sense, since as the retrospective form of the novels assures us, a future always awaits.

39. The unjustifiable character of revolutionary violence was well known to Eliot herself. In an 1856 essay she wrote: "A revolutionary must not only dare to be right, he must also dare to be wrong—to shake faith, to wound friendship [. . .]" (*Essays* 265). But if this sounds like a defense of revolutionary fidelity, it is instead the opposite: "Perhaps the best moral we can draw is that [. . .] our protest for the right should be seasoned with moderation and reverence, and that the lofty words—(great words, *'megaloi logoi'*)—are not becoming to mortals" (1963: 265).

40. Derrida's reading of Benjamin in "The Force of Law" is illuminating insofar as its language—of a "homogenous tissue of history [. . .] ripped apart with one decision," in an act of "violence that in itself is neither just nor unjust"— reproduces the language I have been tracing in Eliot's ending and her readers' impressions of it (1992: 13–14).

41. Psomiades analyzes in these terms a similar scene in *Daniel Deronda*, in which Grandcourt is the atavistic, lizardlike aggressor (representative of an older sovereign power), and Gwendolyn finds herself unable to "decide" on an outcome, though she (like Maggie) specifies her inability to consent. This scene also takes place on a boat, the emblem for the undecided zone between custom and law in Eliot's political imagination (see Psomiades n.d.). Though he is a "guest," Stephen's force is not yet fully alien to St. Ogg's; by 1875, Grandcourt's *patria potestas*—along with his double-signifiers of aristocracy, "grand" "court"—would seem doubly anachronistic.

42. After Maggie attests to her inability to consent, Stephen "let go her arm" (2003: 499), giving up the control over female bodies that history itself (so we're told here) has rendered obsolete.

43. Yeazell (2009) attests to the continued lure of associating Eliot's realism with the painterly kind.

44. Eliot read Schiller early and often, mentioning him in the second paragraph of "The Future of German Philosophy," written just before she began work on *The Mill*. He was Eliot's favorite German author in her first years reading the language; she wished she herself had written the works of "our divine Schiller" (quoted in Rignall 2000: 356; Eliot 1958–78: 3.8, 13). See Guth (2003: e.g. 25), which also lists the Schiller works Eliot read, with dates and editions.

45. In words that could have been Lukács', Eliot's narrator explains: "There is no sense of ease like the ease we felt in those scenes where we were born, where objects became dear to us before we had known the labour of choice, and where the outer world seemed only an extension of our own personality: we accepted and loved it as we accepted and loved our own sense of existence and our own limbs" (1860: 160). Chapter 4 traces how this nostalgic modernity story fares under pressure of advanced imperialism.

46. Adorno's ironic comment in *The Dialectic of Enlightenment* captures the force of Maggie's experiments in self-denial: "The history of civilization is the history of the introversion of sacrifice—in other words, the history of renunciation" (Adorno and Horkheimer 2002: 43).

47. In MS (Eliot n.d.), Eliot's Wordsworthian framing device is even more prounouced: "I remember those large dripping willows . . . . . . I remember the stone bridge. . . . .": in MS the ellipses are extended to six periods in the first instance, five in the second, excessively marking the rupture in experience denoted by the frame structure. By contrast a later moment, at the end of Book I, gives Tom's halting speech this way in the print version: "And— and—poor father—" In MS it is: "And . . . . and . . . . Poor Father. . . . .": four, four, and five ellipses respectively, suggesting that Eliot understood four to be

standard and an extra period to conclude the sentence. Later on the same page (MS 344/368) ellipses appear with four periods (twice) and three periods (also twice); all this suggests that the elongated ellipses marking the frame structure denote a reverie even further separated from the main action than the print edition of the novel, with its standardized ellipsis, could convey.

48. Lewes gave Eliot a full set of *Waverly* novels as a New Year's present as she was beginning work on *The Mill*, inscribing it: "To Marian Evans Lewes, The best of Novelists, and Wives, These works of her longest-venerated and best-loved Romancist [*sic*] are given by her grateful Husband 1 January 1860" (quoted in Haight 1968: 319).

49. Maggie's episode with Stephen and her love of injured animals demonstrate her sympathetic bent, but the disabled Philip, a "poor crooked creatur" (2003: 194), is the novel's most visibly injured object and therefore prime target for Maggie's self-expanding charity of mind. Brown (2006) argues that tolerance discourse "substitutes emotional and personal vocabularies for political ones in formulating *solutions* to political problems" (p. 16, emphasis original).

50. The book Maggie reads is a compilation of essays from Addison and Steele: *The Beauties of the Spectator; or The most elegant, agreeable and instructive pieces selected out that renowned work* (London and Paris, 1804).

51. In ways that rhyme with Barthes' analysis of the photograph, Derrida understands the trace as that which reaches forward from the past: the unassimilable remainder of a past (singular) event of inscription. The mark thus testifies to the absence of the cut, wound, or act of writing that produced it (all Derrida's examples) even as it draws us toward that event's impossible recovery (1982: 13).

CHAPTER 2

1. While enumeration of the nation's inhabitants had long been practiced by such local bodies as the Overseers of the Poor (Armstrong 1978: 30), the 1841 Census was the first to be centralized and nationalized. McClure shows that statistics at this moment enabled "effective displacement of responsibility for the production of authoritative social and political knowledge from citizens to the state itself" (2015: 58). On the history of the Census, see Nissel (1987: 1–3) and Glass (1973). On statistics as a genre of knowledge, see Porter (1986) and Poovey (1995).

2. See Poovey (1995). Chadwick's *The Sanitary Condition of the Labouring Population* was published just a year after the 1841 Census and should be seen as a linked project. Reasoning that "general conclusions can only be distinctly made out from the various classes of particular facts" (1842: 2), Chadwick's famed report presents its particulars in tabular and numerical form, thus crystallizing Foucault's insight that statistical knowledge is the epistemology appropriate to modern governmentality.

3. See especially Foucault (1990: 135–43) and (2003: 239–63). Steinlight approaches the problem of biopolitics in sensation fiction by describing

surplus populations of characters within novels. Poovey's emphasis on "disciplinary individualism" (1995: 99) follows from Foucault's early work on that topic, while the emphasis on population management and biopolitics—focused not on individuals but on masses—emerged only later in Foucault's writings.

4. The book went through eight editions during Mill's lifetime, "including an inexpensive edition for working-class readers" (Snyder 2006: 100). Mill made some 5,000 emendations to the text over the course of its publication history (Whitaker 1975: 1035). For an account of these, see *CW* VII, headnote.

5. Mill's *Logic* continues to animate debates in logical method, and is still "the standard view of induction" in philosophy primers today (Snyder 2006: 100). Mill's work on the metaphysics of the proper name continues to animate debate in the discipline of analytical philosophy. I am grateful to David Coombs for discussions of this. For an introduction, see Reimer and Michaelson (2014).

6. In Anderson's *Powers of Distance* Mill stands with Eliot as exemplar of the book's polemic on reason, praised for his ability to "privilege the capacity to achieve distance from one's own perspective and interests, conceiving the movement toward truth as result of a continuously enacted impartiality on the part of the individual" (2001: 17).

7. Mill's essays on reform help periodize the window of time I focus on here. "Thoughts on Parliamentary Reform" appeared in February 1859, followed directly by "Recent Writers on Reform" (April 1859), which appraises "the present Reform movement" (*CW* XIX). *Considerations on Representative Government* was first published in 1861, reprinted again that year and then once more in 1865 (see headnote, *CW* XIX). The Reform Bill itself, of course, passed in 1867. Mill's "Centralisation" essay appeared in April 1862.

8. I read Mill as part of the casuistical tradition Forrester has outlined in his ongoing work on the case form, adding that the problems of particularity and aggregation that the case brings together are the key dilemmas of democratic reform. Forrester hints at this by explaining how the case form captures the paradox by which "the rise of statistical thinking put in question the notion of the individual, through the very process of refining what it might mean to have knowledge of a number of individuals" (p. 3). On cases, see also Chandler (1998) and Baucom (2005).

9. In an 1862 usage, the *OED* gives us "aggregate," in legal terminology, as something "Composed of many individual bodies united into one association"; a second definition, with usages from 1824, 1859, and 1876, simultaneously biologizes and politicizes this definition. An aggregate, here, is a thing "[c]onstituted by the collection of many particles or units into one body, mass, or amount; collected, collective, whole, total." For Foucault, "Utilitarian philosophy was the theoretical instrument that underpinned the government of populations" (2007: 74).

10. In a brief discussion of the *Logic*, Forrester claims that "[f]or Mill [...] reasoning is always from particulars to particulars" (1996: 6). But his focus is solely on Mill's treatment of syllogisms. While Mill did argue against the a priori existence of classes (or "natural kinds"), as Forrester suggests, the *Logic* explains at length how scientific classes or "generalizations," however provisional, could and should be determined: this is by induction, a mode of reasoning Mill describes as central to his method, but which Forrester does not discuss.

11. Marx was explicitly in dialogue with Mill's work, citing him by name in several derisive instances in *Capital*. My point is that this logical problem underwrote a political shift, and informed multiple genres of expression, during the Reform years. Without reference to Marx, Poovey has argued that "[t]he modern system of abstraction [...] was produced in relation to a complex set of problems, which were simultaneously economic, political, and administrative" (1995: 31).

12. As Mill explains, "If [...] we knew what all names signify, we should know everything which, in the existing state of human knowledge, is capable either of being made a subject of affirmation or denial, or of being itself affirmed or denied of a subject" (*CW* VII). The quietly radical position here is that *all* observable or conceivably observable phenomena in the world—objects, concepts, clusters of either—are potentially nameable as "facts"; they are theoretically able to be marked as particular "subjects" available for (later) mental processing.

13. In ways that anticipate the arguments in Chapters 3 and 4, another work of urban reportage, Booth's *In Darkest England and the Way Out* (1890), advances an analogy between metropolitan sacrifice zones like St. Giles and the colonial periphery.

14. In *Phineas Redux*, the advanced liberal character Monk uses just the language traced here: "Equality is an ugly word and shouldn't be used. [...] But the wish of every honest man should be to assist in lifting up those below him, till they be something nearer his own level than he finds them" (1973: 128).

15. The *North British Review* judged similarly of Collins that "to this author plot and incident are all in all, character is nothing" (Page 1974: 141). On the importance of free indirect discourse to what we could call the nineteenth-century "rise of depth," see McKeon (2000: 485–91), and Chapter 4.

16. See Anderson (2001), Thomas (2003), and Goodlad (2003). These works followed each other in close succession and helped define a liberal turn in Victorian studies in the years after 2000, a phenomenon that coincided with, and helped advance, the abandonment of Victorianist postcolonial studies in ways future work might historicize.

17. In this obvservation Lynch follows Lukács' Hegelian argument that the labor of the bourgeois novel has been to articulate the general in the idiom of the particular, squaring the dialectic of part and whole through the mechanism

of character such that (as Lukács writes of Scott) "living human embodi-ment" and "historical-social types" might, by means of artistic genius, be made to coexist in a single fictional entity (1983: 34).

18. As Pykett summarizes, "His fascination with social outsiders is matched by a well-developed interest in crime and criminality" (2005: 138). For a sense of how this fascination with the marginal reverses trends in a broader novelistic tradition, see Woloch (2003: 12–42).

19. "Cliché" comes to English via the French term for wooden stereotype printing blocks (*OED*). Note also the Grub-street origins of "stereotype," as both a secondhand trope and a physical plate taken from the type to print (as opposed to printing from the type itself): a traffic between the aesthetic and material realms of literary production Collins no doubt has in mind here.

20. Berlant notes that scholarship interested in what she calls "the singularity concept" often contradicts its own assertions in practice, mobilizing "a whole variety of descriptive and interpretive processes of determining likeness, generality, or patterning" in service of an argument *against* exactly those methods (2007: 663n.).

21. The central "problem" in the *Logic*, says one commentator, is "how [to] get from facts to science, 'by experience'" (Randall 1965: 66). Poovey also describes "the problem of induction" as "the methodological problem of moving [...] to general principles" (1998: 313–14). I am emphasizing how Mill's non-dialectical logic commits him to seeking (unsuccessfully) to solve this "problem," while dialectical procedures like Benjamin's or Collins' radicalize or refigure it *as* a problem.

22. David Russell has noted the seeming cleavage between Mill's early aesthetic-work and his later pleas for rigorous rationalism (2013: 20–3). The *System of Logic* spans this career, and I am suggesting splints those projects together while revealing their generative misfit.

CHAPTER 3

1. Lafourcade's *La Jeunesse de Swinburne* (1928) was the first and remains among the most authoritative biographies of the poet. For Lafourcade, *Poems and Ballads* "demeurera le livre qui bouleversa toute une génération" (1928: 417).

2. In the Bonchurch edition and several modern reprints, the first of the *Poems and Ballads* is Swinburne's "Dedication" to Edward Burne-Jones, but both of the 1866 editions put it at the end, beginning with "A Ballad of Life," thus placing life and death front and center.

3. On the form of these opening poems see Lafourcade (1928: 441–2), who cites W. M. Rossetti's early reading to offer a genealogy of Swinburne's influences (here, Italian). For a recent overview of Baudelaire along lines I outline here for Swinburne, see Sanyal (2006).

4. J. Hillis Miller frames the distinction between Arnold and Swinburne in terms that have connections to those I draw out here: "Arnold always keeps

himself erect and aloof [. . .]," but for Swinburne, "the more powerful the sensation, the better" (quoted in McGann 1972: 34).

5. The *OED*'s authority here is Kant's *Metaphysics of Morals*, a detail further confirming that Victorian idealist rationalism shares its structuring dichotomy of "affect" and "reflection" with that philosopher.

6. See Smith (1982: esp. 1–66). In the *Critique of the Power of Judgment* Kant explains that "affects" are unruly, extralegal feelings—"tumultuous and unpremeditated"—while "passions" are "sustained and considered" (2000: 154), thus linked to reason's regulative functions.

7. The only observable differences between the editions are (1) that Moxon's cover board is embossed with a design, and begins with advertisements for *Atalanta in Calydon*, which had been published by Moxon the previous year; (2) that the Moxon also includes a section entitled "Opinions of the Press," eight pages of single spaced agate type citing favorable reviews of that earlier work, a feature absent in Hotton's edition; and (3) that Moxon takes three pages for the table of contents, while Hotton cramps it into two.

8. My account of the Morant Bay events draws on Kostal (2005), Semmel (1963), Hall (2002), Heuman (1994), Winter (2016), and Baucom (1999). Nicole Rizzuto has recently examined the Rebellion in terms similar to mine here, tracking in twentieth-century narratives of the event the role of witness and memory in the production of (retrospective) vindications of colonial law (2015: 127–77).

9. In his dispatch, Eyre cites the "utmost promptitude and efficiency" with which his subordinates "carried out" "all my wishes" (*Jamaica Papers* No. 1: 92), making its closest generic equivalent perhaps the award acceptance speech.

10. See *Jamaica Papers* No. 6: 9. The Committee's document presents a quantitative table which juxtaposes the numbers of those "Killed and wounded by negroes on the 11th Oct, 1865, at Morant Bay," with a tabulation of those "Killed and wounded by authorities in resisting rioters on the 11th of October" and "Punishments by authorities afterwards." The assumption of this utilitarian calculus is that black bodies count the same as white ones, an assumption that did not take account of the varied legal statuses of those bodies—in one column citizens, in the other subjects—and that therefore proved optimistic. (The black lives did not matter.)

11. Hall explains that her personal cathexis to the case sprang from "what might be characterized as a humanist universalism, an assumption that all human beings are equal, [that] was integral to the shared vocabulary of the Left [. . .] but the unspoken racial hierarchy which was the underlying assumption of that humanist universalism had not been confronted in my psyche" (2002: 5). That this 1994 account would replicate rather than analyze the conceptual and ethical categories it shares with (some of) its objects of study confirms the persistence of Victorian progressive idealism into even the most committed critical practice. For a critique of Hall's culturalist position see Sartori (2014).

12. The hanging of Gordon was a particular flashpoint for debate, since for critics it was political murder, an exact transgression of a system understood to operate by discussion and procedure. As Bagehot wrote: "In causing Mr. Gordon to be hanged, Eyre's greatest offence is that he put an affront on the majesty of law, and, for a time, cancelled the ripest fruits of our civilization'" (quoted in Kostal 2005: 468).

13. For a comprehensive account of the status of emergency law in colonial contexts see Hussain (2003), on whose treatment I draw in these pages.

14. Gordon was a "coloured" landowner, a descendant of both ex-slaves and colonists whose unsettled racial status no doubt enabled his body to exist in a legal no-man's-land.

15. Or perceived imperial rebellion. One issue the Committee disputed was that any genuine insurgency existed at all. In the event it was proved that the *belief* in a revolt was enough to establish the (extra-)juridical condition of "rebellion." Arendt's canonical analysis of statelessness shows that to be stripped of political or "civil" status—as in a state of rebellion—*should* be to return a body to the shared state of "humanity" that putatively stands as the baseline guaranteeing rights to life and status. Paradoxically, however, "[a]ctually the opposite is the case. It seems that a man who is nothing but a man has lost the very qualities which make it possible for other people to treat him as a fellow-man" (1970: 300).

  For Agamben such depoliticized bodies are transformed from subjects to objects, the stateless remainders of a legal order that remain available to receive the state's full force at any time the state should deem fit. Slavery and its legacies complicate this picture, since slaves never had "legal personality" to begin with and were objects in ways the Zong case, for example, made explicit; freed slaves were in a similarly anomalous position. Lindsay Kaplan (2015) traces the etymology for the term slave (from *servus*) from the practice of salvaging life after battle in the classical period. A body thus plucked from the scene of death could be killed or "salvaged"; in the latter case, it was recovered into the category of dependence and became a literal form of remaindered life.

16. Many of Dickens' later commentators have lamented this lapse from the reformist sentimentalism of his earlier period (though recall his stance on the Indian Mutiny, noted in the Introduction). The entertainer channeled Carlyle's "Occasional Discourse" in an 1865 letter: "The Jamaica insurrection is another hopeful piece of business. That platform-sympathy with the black—or the native, or the devil—afar off, and that platform indifference to our own countrymen at enormous odds in the midst of bloodshed and savagery, makes me stark wild. Only the other day, here was a meeting of jawbones of asses at Manchester, to censure the Jamaica Governor for his manner of putting down the insurrection! So we are badgered about New Zealanders and Hottentots, as if they were identical with men in clean shirts at Camberwell, and were to be bound by pen and ink accordingly" (Dickens 1999: 114–15).

17. As Stoler notes (1995: 55–94), Foucault himself avoids the question of empire, even while his analysis spurs criticism to move beyond construing racism as an end of empire to see it as a technique in empire's maintenance.

18. In 1848, a petition declaring loyalty to Queen Victoria from "your sable subjects of Jamaica, of African descent" avowed "how much we prize and value our privileges as free people." But even while citing their own freedom, the authors refer to their legal claims not as rights but as "privileges," affirming their status as subjects to a law by which they were not represented (quoted in Sheller 2012: 103–4, emphasis added).

19. Says Mill in *Considerations*: "A people of savages should be taught obedience, but not in such a manner as to convert them into a people of slaves. And (to give the observation a higher generality) the form of government which is most effectual for carrying a people through the next stage of progress, will still be very improper for them if it does this in such a manner as to obstruct, or positively unfit for them, the step next beyond. Such cases are frequent, and are among the most melancholy facts of history" (*CW* XIX).

20. In her unmatched *Victorian Poetry* Armstrong (1993) reads Swinburne as an "agonistic republican," while raising a connection between Swinburne and Morant Bay: I flesh out and historicize those insights here.

21. Lafourcade explains that "le sadisme de Swinburne dépasse de beaucoup une simple théorie de l'amour; de purement instinctif et sensuel, il devient bientôt raisonné et intellectuel. Eclairé par les doctrines du Marquis de Sade, et jusqu'à un certain point poussé par une conviction personnelle, Swinburne découvre dans la nature cette même loi de souffrance universelle et de mort qui lui était apparue dans le mécanisme des passions. La ruine et la destruction sont les grands principes qui régissent le monde. La nature ne peut créer sans tuer, ne peut faire vivre sans faire souffrir." (1928: 431).
    ["Swinburne's sadism goes far beyond a simple theory of love; from (being) purely instinctive and sensual, he quickly becomes well-reasoned and intellectual. Enlightened by the Marquis de Sade's doctrines and pushed, up to a certain point, by personal conviction, Swinburne discovers in nature this same law of universal suffering and of death which had appeared to him in the mechanism of passions. Ruin and destruction are the major rules that govern the world. Nature cannot create without killing, cannot cause life without causing suffering." I thank Anne O'Neil-Henry for translation help.]

22. A short list of philosophers who have engaged seriously with Sade would include Simone de Beauvoir, Gilles Deleuze, Jacques Lacan, and Maurice Blanchot. For Blanchot, Sade "was drawn to [revolution] only to the extent that it constituted for a short time the possibility of a regime without law, since it represented a transition period from one set of laws to the other" (1965: 45). In "Kant with Sade" Lacan (2006) observes that Sade's outrages are the secret truth of Kant's tyrannical morality, while the chapter in Adorno and Horkheimer's *Dialectic of Enlightenment* called "Juliette; or Enlightenment and Morality" conceives the two as a dialectical pair (Adorno

wrote the chapter). Relatedly, Barrett shows that Eliot and Swinburne share a sadomasochistic imaginary "neither narrow nor deviant but of the most central and far reaching significance" (1993: 118).

23. In a move with implications that will be traced below, Kant also describes the importance of "form" to the beautiful object—with "form" understood as a restraint that is in the sublime object entirely absent: "The beautiful in nature concerns the form of the object, which consists in limitation; the sublime, by contrast, is to be found in a formless object, insofar as **limitlessness** is represented in it [...]" (2000: 128, boldface original).

24. A full engagement with Kant's political-aesthetic system is beyond the scope of this study. Despite Coleridge's early reading, this had yet to be fully understood in Victorian England by Arnold's day, though Arnold was important in spreading Kant's thought (Muirhead 1930:434). "By the thirties," we are told, "through the influence of Coleridge, De Quincey and Carlyle, Kant's name had become familiar in circles far beyond 'the learned.' Henceforth it occupies a conspicuous place in the histories of philosophy" (Muirhead 1930: 432). For a useful overview of the complex relationship between Kant and political liberalism, see Flikschuh (2000). I am indebted to Bill Knight for sharing his knowledge of Kant.

25. On metonymy versus metaphor, see Jakobson (1956). De Man's concern in "The Rhetoric of Temporality" (1983) is to valorize metonymy over the totalizing Romantic technique of metaphor; my point is that Swinburne's metaphoric procedure provides a counternarrative to the comfortable (postmodern, poststructuralist) assumption that totalization is bad. For the early Swinburne the issue is descriptive: totalization and violence is all there is, and to pretend otherwise is to lapse into what Bataille in a similar vein calls "a revolting utopian sentimentality" (1985: 101)—a trap into which Swinburne's later republican poetry arguably falls. If there is a politics to these tropes, it would appear that metaphor is "anti-liberal," being the chosen figure of, for example, Marxist theories of totality. De Man's metonymic sensibility would thus be considered "pluralist" in its opposition to this unification, as Jameson's critique of American deconstruction in *Postmodernism* (1992) suggests.

26. Describing rhizomatic structures—tubers, swarms, the bulbs of plants— Deleuze and Guattari might be writing of Swinburne's MS for "Anactoria" or the action of poem itself: "The world has lost its pivot; the subject can no longer even dichotomize, but accedes to a higher unity ... [A]ny point of a rhizome can be connected to anything other, and must be" (1987: 6–7).

27. The dead metaphor of the governmental "branch" presupposes the "arborescent" subordination of hierarchical elements that is the precise inversion of the accumulation modeled by Swinburne here. As Deleuze and Guattari write in their call for a similar monist ontology: "We're tired of trees" (1987: 15).

28. For Isobel Armstrong (via Bataille), Swinburne's "poetics of excess place[s] value on the wasteful, exorbitant expenditure of energy in violation and

transgression." The aim is "[t]o break through ethical, psychological, and sexual categories in desire and lust, madness, violence, incest, is to assert a plenitude which recognizes no limit and begins to assuage that furious dependence on the literal by which the poet is bound" (Armstrong 1993: 407).

29. For Kant, "sensations [...] justifiably count as beautiful only insofar as [they] are **pure**, which is a determination that already concerns form" (109, emphasis original). If Buchanan is invoking Kantian categories he certainly has no idea he's doing so.

30. Morley's conviction that the peace of "humanity" would triumph over what he styles as its opposite is perhaps most clearly evident in his critical, even anxious lectures on Machiavelli, of 1897. For Morley, it is unfortunately true that Machiavelli "represents certain living forces in our actual world," but "this is because energy, force, will, violence, still keep alive in the world their resistance to the control of justice and conscience, humanity and right" (1897: 49–50).

31. As Bevington describes in his history of the *Saturday*, the attack on Swinburne's collection issued from a unified sense—John Morley is mentioned as advancing this idea—that the poet, whom the journal had earlier encouraged, had now gone too far (1941: 220).

32. As Leslie Stephen writes in his biography of his brother: "The law, as understood by Fitzjames, comes, I think, substantially to this. The so-called 'martial law' is simply an application of the power given by the common law to put down an actual insurrection by force..... The so-called courts-martial are not properly courts at all, but simply committees for carrying out measures adopted on responsibility of the officials; as the proclamation is merely a public notice that such measures will be employed" (1895: 229).

33. Leslie Stephen's biography describes the effect of the tenure in India on Stephen's legal beliefs in a chapter called "Indian Impressions" (1895: 292–300).

34. Stephen explains in the first pages that he has chosen Mill's work to critique because it "the popular view [...] of the religious doctrine of liberty" (1967: 54).

35. Of his schooling at Eton, Stephen later said that "The process taught me for life, the lesson that to be weak is wretched, that the state of nature is a state of war, and *Vae Victus* [woe to the conquered] the great law of nature" (quoted in White 1967: 4).

36. For Bataille as for Swinburne and Swinburne's Byron, catastrophe "is that by which a nocturnal horizon is set ablaze, that for which lacerated existence goes into a trance – it is the Revolution – it is time released from all bonds; it is pure change; it is a skeleton that emerges from its cadaver as from a cocoon and that sadistically lives the unreal existence of death" (1985: 134). Bataille describes revolutionary violence, but could be describing martial law. In either case he well describes Swinburne's lawless verse; see Armstrong (1993).

37. Hyder suggests that it was with Swinburne's *William Blake*, written 1863–6, that "modern appreciation of Blake began" (1933: 133). Entire passages of Swinburne's reading of Blake could be transposed without edit into a discussion of Swinburne's own work: "[T]he fiery and lyrical tone of mind and speech, the passionate singleness of aim, the heat and flame of faith in himself, the violence of mere words, the lust of paradox, the loud and angry habits of expression which abound in his critical or didactic work, are not here absent" (1968b: 363).

38. Here and above, quotations from Swinburne's *Poems and Ballads* are taken from the Penguin edition, edited by Kenneth Haynes (2000).

39. A central tension of the *Critique of Judgement* stems from Kant's effort to recontain the displacing power of the sublime within the realm of beauty. This dynamic stages the same problem as martial law: is the sublime inside or outside the regulative apparatus of reason? Kant brings his displacing violence inside, pacifying it, but exposes a faultline in his argument in doing so.

40. "Thus we see," writes a team of legal historians, "that the English legal/constitutional system [. . .] is aware of two regimes: the standard one and martial law. The second triggered by 'necessity' is nothing but a temporary suspension of ordinary rights" (Ferejohn and Pasquino 2004: 239).

41. In histories of martial law, Cromwell's quote is typically invoked alongside Cicero's dictum that "when arms speak, the laws fall silent." It is a neat historical coincidence that Cromwell led the original expedition to steal Jamaica from Spain in 1670, perhaps invoking his own maxim, as part of the project of acquisition he and his New Model Army called "The Western Design" (Dunn 2000: 152).

42. As Mill said to Parliament on 31 July 1866: "We want to know [. . .] who are to be our masters: her Majesty's judges and a jury of our countrymen, administering the laws of England, or three naval and military officers, two of them boys, administering, as the Chancellor of the Exchequer tells us, no law at all" (*CW* XXVIII).

43. Derrida outlines how the event that defines a rule or a set of laws is precisely that which exceeds the rule but, by exceeding it, defines it. "It belongs without belonging" (1980: 65).

44. For McGann, "Swinburne's flagellant verse, *precisely because it is so schematic*, clarifies an aesthetic attitude specifically allied to the masochistically inclined personality. The art of Sacher-Masoch, Swinburne, and Genet exhibits similar formal properties" (1972: 281, emphasis added). See also Prins (2013).

45. Similarly would John Crowe Ransom explain in *The New Criticism* (1941) that a poem "is like a democratic state, which realizes the ends of a state without sacrificing the personal character of its citizens" (quoted in Eagleton 1996: 44).

46. Swinburne thus provides a genealogy in the sense Foucault describes when he says that we might, "by following lines of fragility in the present," aspire to "grasp why and how that which is might no longer be that which is" (1994: 126).

CHAPTER 4

1. World-systems historians like Giovanni Arrighi (2010), John Darwin (2011), and P. J. Cain and A. G. Hopkins (2001) have noted that the 1880s were a watershed moment in the history of global capital cycles and the imperial political systems they underwrote. For Arrighi and others, the post-1875 phase of financialization serves as a macroeconomic indicator that the seat of global power was at this moment moving across the Atlantic, and a contracting British hegemony was being replaced, slowly, by a rising American system that would by the turn of the century be able to claim status as the world's new arbiter of universal values. What was at stake in this transitional decade, then, was which bourgeois empire, the old or the new, would lay claim to the mantle of global modernity.

2. Saint-Amour describes the temporality of air war as "the routinization of emergency" (2004: 131), and notes that on the imperial frontier, where the idea that "wartime and peacetime are absolutely distinct" is "negated," time is marked by the anticipation of disaster where emergency is the rule (2015: 1–46).

3. See the catalog of overlaps between imperial ideology and epic form in Tucker (2008) and Dentith (2006).

4. Hultgren gives a deft account of Haggard's relation to melodrama, focusing on *The Witch's Head* in particular (2014: esp. 63–92). Green (1979) shows how fully the counter-domestic adventure novel and its parent form, melodrama, predated the late-century heyday of the genre.

5. Positing provisionally a cyclical or wave-based model of macrohistorical time, whereby a fading bourgeois empire is replaced, after a period of transitional contestation, by a new one, helps place Eliot's characterological realism at the crest of an earlier cycle of what Arrighi (2010) calls global leadership or geopolitical hegemony. I examine these metaphors of waves, cycles, and lifespans in more detail in "Allegories of the Contemporary" (2012).

6. The almost universal tendency to treat Haggard's novels as the displacement of ideological investments unknown to the texts themselves repeats in another register the aesthetic ideology being shaped in this period. Thus do popular writers like Haggard, Henty, and Corelli find themselves cast in the role of the ideological, passive, or symptomatic "bad objects" while the role of the critical, active, or theoretical "good object" (to be read *with*) is reserved for novels ennobled by the post-Jamesian taste for internalization: most often Schreiner, Conrad, and James himself. The point is that our tacit choices between critical and affirmative reading practices repeats the evaluative presumptions being naturalized in this period.

7. Recent dustups around so-called "surface reading" can be taken to index the longevity of the vocabulary James here works to naturalize. See, canonically, Best and Marcus (2009). Sedgwick shows how criticism repeats "a particular psychological model of the self, one with an inside and an outside and with certain material ('the irrational') on the inside that could or should pass outside" (1986: 255).

8. Leavis' canonical judgment makes these class values explicit: "there is nothing bogus, cheap or vulgar about [James'] idealizations: certain human potentialities are nobly celebrated" (1948: 12).

9. Contemporary accounts of Lang marvel at his ability to write at any time no matter the circumstances. One story describes Lang scribbling out a magazine article while animatedly chatting during a train ride, never losing concentration on either "conversation." See Hensley (2013).

10. Lang, collaborating with Haggard in *The World's Desire*, made the disastrous aesthetic decision to tell a novelized version of the Odysseus story in third person omniscient voice, a mode of distanciation fatally mismatched to the content of these neo-Homeric tales (Lang and Haggard 1890).

11. This conflict between American and British claims on the future of the novel was mediated by the changing dynamics of international publishing and the rise of professional authorship during the 1880s: the triple-decker was dying; the circulating libraries were withering; and in their place rose illustrated literary magazines and cheap one-volume novels, the total number of which literally doubled in the years between 1880 and 1891 (Colby 1990: 116). These and other seismic changes in the technological and commercial dynamics of the literary field mean that the causal spring of the Lang–Howells rivalry is diffuse and finally indeterminate. Yet as Howells and Lang themselves acknowledged, one determinant was geopolitical, and I work here to understand how these impresarios used a struggle over the role of action in literature—and the campaign to promote their respective literary brands—to play out a contest not just about what constituted a novel, or *the* novel, as such, but what geopolitical empire might retain the power to decide that question.

12. Lang met Tylor at Balliol, where Lang read classics but was exposed to the "epoch-making" work of John McClennan, in *Primitive Marriage* (1865) (quoted in Dorson 1968: 207). Lang and Tylor disagreed about the coincidences of oral and material culture across race and distance as well as, e.g., spiritualism, "Tylor dismissing it as a 'monstrous farrago,' while Lang thought the element of animism—though not of automatism—to be a survival" (Dorson 1968: 208).

13. "Imperialism," Haggard said while introducing his friend Kipling to a club of writers, is "in the divine right of a great civilising people—that is, in their divine mission" (quoted in Etherington 1984: 93).

14. In this way Lang's own folkloric research, following Tylor's and radicalizing it, can be seen as a kind of ironic source code for Jameson's hermeneutic method—ironic because Lang's position as a founder of romance makes him a symptom or object of study rather than source of "theory" within Jameson's own account. As suggested in Chapter 1, Jameson's methodology can be described as a theory of survivals at the level of genre, a haunting or sedimentation, as he calls it, of older forms within newer.

15. I here rely on Cain and Hopkins' definition of imperialism, where its distinguishing feature "is not that it takes a specific economic, cultural or political form, but that it involves an incursion, or an attempted incursion, into the sovereignty of another state. [...] What matters [...] is that one power has the will, and if it is to succeed, the capacity to shape the affairs of another by imposing on it. The relations established by imperialism are therefore based on inequality and not upon mutual compromises of the kind which characterize states of interdependence" (2001: 54).

16. One of the novel's ironies is that this modernity-ratifying episode was based on errors of scientific fact resulting from Haggard's faulty understanding of eclipses. So while the scene would seem to valorize Western "science" over native superstition, Haggard's own lack of scientific precision meant that he, and perhaps his novel too, are best aligned with the scene's dumbstruck savages rather than its techno-rationalistic explorers; Haggard amended the text in future editions to bring his narration in line with the western reason he purported, sometimes, to value (2007: 257n.).

17. The other two are Sir Henry's story about his lost brother, at the outset of the novel, and Allan's narrative about the history of the mines, a story which itself contains Jose Silvestre's translated first-person account of the diamond mines. This structure of nested picaresques mimics Lang's description of the *Odyssey*'s form, as noted above.

18. During Haggard's tenure in Africa the blunt work of expansion was frequently leavened with the language of justice and friendship. Like the earlier annexation of Natalia (1843), the acquisition of the Transvaal was explained as a humanitarian endeavor: Shepstone framed it as a gesture of protection, but as a Boer Burgher explained: "We bow only to the superior power. We submit because we cannot successfully draw the sword against this superior power, because by doing so we could only plunge the country into deeper miseries and disasters" (quoted in Meredith 2007: 73).

19. After 1875, pressures on Britain's world position drove it to consolidate territories that provided tactical advantage (in an incorporating mode) while pushing it to secure material resources (in an expropriating mode): by 1873, £1.6 million worth of diamonds were streaming out of the Kimberly Mine each year (Meredith 2007: 37), destined to prop up a metropolitan economy whose domestic production had fallen into steep decline. Quatermain references this when he fantasizes that the mines' mineral wealth might "pay off a moderate national debt, or [...] build a fleet of ironclads (p. 209)."

20. If, for us, witch-hunts recall the McCarthy Hearings, they would have conjured for nineteenth-century readers the savagery of the Thirty Years' War (1618–48), when the technique figured prominently. Not unrelatedly, this conflict spurred the development of modern sovereignty theory; see Schmitt (2003).

21. An extended footnote in *Cetywayo* describes the "real" witch-hunts Haggard and his friends witnessed in Zululand. "These instances," Haggard concludes after listing several, "will show how dark and terrible is the Zulu superstition

connected with witchcraft, and what a formidable weapon it becomes in the hands of the king or chief" (1893: 19n.). The point is not to chase alleged correspondences between life and art but to note how *King Solomon's Mines* derives from these moralizing observations a legal vocabulary for establishing Cetywayo/Twala as an enemy of universal values.

22. Fanon explains how "The native is declared insensible to ethics," since "[h]e represents not only the absence of values, but also the negation of values. He is, let us dare to admit, the enemy of values, and in this sense he is the absolute evil" (Fanon 1963: 41). On the persistence of this figuration into current discourse on globalization, see Mbembe (2001).

23. By suggesting that "only [. . .] self-defense" is a valid rationale for violence, Quatermain repeats Vitoria's influential maxim that "*the sole and only just cause for waging war is when harm has been inflicted*" (quoted in Bain 2013: 74, emphasis original). In England this became a benchmark, though one with wide applicability; as Lord Palmerston said as early as 1841, "It is the business of government to open and to secure the roads for the merchant" (quoted in Lynn 2009: 105). "Self-defense" could thus be interpreted to include threats to private enterprise and the global economy itself, a latitude of interpretation persisting today.

24. The chapter on rogue regimes in Lorimer (1883) is titled: "Of communities that are cut off from [international] recognition, on the ground that [they are prevented from] expressing or reciprocating will" (p. 162); the term "will" here confirms the isomorphism between individual and state subjects common to the idealist tradition traced here.

25. See also Bell (2007). On the persistence of this distinction into the present, see Bowden (1997); on its early history, see Anghie (1999).

26. In his UN-era *A Concise History of the Law of Nations* (1947), Nussbaum cites Hall's treatise as an authority and explains that Victorians liked it too: "In England its reception was so favorable that [there were] four posthumous editions, the last one in 1924, increasing the total to eight" (p. 236).

27. A key detail is that "European" is not a merely cartographic term, since it allows geography and cultural standing to commingle in ways familiar from the civilizational discourse of law charted in earlier chapters. "European" states, Hall explains, need not be located in Europe but usually are. The white settler colonies comprising "Greater Britain" are exceptions, and as Banerjee explains, the strategic manipulation of this rhetoric by Indian subjects, for example, testifies to the confusions—and thus malleability—of international law's socio-geographical (il)logic.

28. On Kant and the unjust enemy as the "other" of humanity, see Baucom (2009: esp. 124–5) and Schmitt (2003: 168–71). I draw inspiration from Baucom's account in the following pages.

29. "A preventative war against such an enemy," Schmitt explains, "would be considered even more than a just war. It would be a crusade, because we would be dealing not simply with a criminal, but with an unjust enemy, with the perpetuator of the state of nature" (2003: 169).

30. "[I]n small wars against uncivilized nations," specifies a British general in 1923, reflecting on the Victorian period, "the form of warfare to be adopted must tone [*sic*] with the shade of culture existing in the land, by which I mean that, against people possessing a low civilization, war must be more brutal in type" (quoted in Mazower 2006: 557). Mazower notes: "The 1914 *British Manual of Military Law*, too, emphasized that 'rules of International Law apply only to warfare between civilized nations [. . .] They do not apply in wars with uncivilized states and tribes'" (quoted on p. 557).

31. Lorimer explains that to be recognized internationally, a state must "possess subjective will as well as objective freedom; it must be autonomous or self-ruling, as well as autarchous [*sic*] or self directing" (1883: 155). Ignosi's new state is none of these, though the novel goes to great pains to let him pretend otherwise.

32. Mbembe summarizes that "the ultimate expression of sovereignty resides, to a large degree, in the power and the capacity to dictate who may live and who must die. Hence, to kill or allow to live constitute the limits of sovereignty, its fundamental attributes. To exercise sovereignty is to exercise control over mortality" (2001: 11–12).

33. Haggard's source text, *Cetywayo*, details how Shepstone supposedly ceded but in fact retained sovereignty over the Zulus in 1876 in just this way. Before Cetywayo emerged as a tyrant in his own right in the 1880s, Shepstone was to nominate him as king in another, earlier effort to establish a friendly regime. But Zulu law had no mechanism for understanding how someone who was not a Zulu king could grant sovereignty to a king. The solution, Haggard says, was to "inves[t] Mr. Shepstone with all the attributes of a Zulu king, such as the power to make laws, order executions, &c., and those attributes in the eyes of Zulus he still retains" (1893: 10). The result is one that Haggard finds amusing: Shepstone to this day holds sovereignty over the Zulu nation to which he ceded independence.

34. I am grateful to John Pfordresher for noticing this correspondence, and for his advice on Stevenson.

35. I thank Anne O'Neil-Henry and the anonymous reader for help in this translation; for more on this letter, see Demoor (1990: 102).

36. According to Hugh Kenner, in preparing *Ulysses* Joyce used Samuel Butler's 1897 translation of the *Odyssey*, not the more vulgar and fantastic translation by Lang and Leaf that would have been orthodox. For Kenner, the Butler was preferable because its Homer is "an observer and an ingenious transposer or actualities": a realist rather than a romancer. Lang and Leaf say "fair court" where Butler says "tower" in Book I, a substitution Kenner says inspired Joyce's use of the tower to open *Ulysses*' first episode (Kenner 1971: 46–9).

37. For a literary-historical account of the necessary relation of epic form to "heroic society" that predates Lukács, see Ker (1931: 1–34) (first published 1896). In the terms of Peter Brooks, melodrama captures the sense of superficiality and providence Lang associated with magical thinking and Homer, though this mode of course predates the fin-de-siècle efflorescence

of "romance." Writes Brooks: "There is no 'psychology' in melodrama in this sense; the characters have no interior depth, there is no psychological conflict. It is delusive to seek an interior conflict, the 'psychology of melodrama,' because melodrama exteriorizes conflict and psychic structure" (1976: 35–6). My point is that Lang reanimates this long anti-psychological tradition. Hultgren (2014) adapts Brooks to read Haggard's *Jess* in ways I draw on here.

38. Adams' analysis of the internal conflicts of liberal epic helps us appreciate how the same passage in Pope's translation is yet more mediate, transforming the "immediate and technical original" into "distanced and generalizing heroic couplets" (Adams 2011: 75). Thus: "[...] Pisander from the car he cast, /And pierced his breast: supine he breathed his last. / His brother leap'd to earth; but, as he lay, / The trenchant falchion lopp'd his hands away; / His sever'd head was toss'd among the throng, / And, rolling, drew a bloody train along" (Pope 1899: bk 11, n.p.). I thank Mark McMorris for sharing his knowledge of Greek translation.

39. Ker notes that in epic literature, characters "cannot go on talking unless they have something to do; and so the whole business of life comes bodily into the epic poem" (1931: 9). This physicality generates in part the "weight and solidity" of epic against the "mystery and fantasy" of romance (p. 4); Haggard would meld the two, muddling also the distinction Ker makes between an egalitarian epic mode, in which even "the great man is a good judge of cattle" against the class condescension structuring the later (aristocratic) romance, with its "insuperable difference between gentle and simple" (p. 7).

40. See the oddly parallel works *Henry James and Robert Louis Stevenson: A Record of Friendship and Criticism* (Smith 1948) and *Dear Stevenson: Letters from Andrew Lang to Robert Louis Stevenson* (Demoor 1990), both of which make a case for the shaping power of Lang's friendship for their subject's life and work.

41. I here draw on Steer's superb account of how Stevenson "actively modifies the romance form" to generate a critique of British globalization and its logic of spatial differentiation (2015: 344).

CONCLUSION

1. The return in Victorian studies to such values as distance, omniscience, and agency in criticism of liberalism after 2001—against what was represented, in internecine disciplinary polemics, as a shopworn or otherwise exhausted Marxist and postcolonial critique—is perhaps best seen as the ideological forward wing (in the admittedly highly mediated arena of professionalized literary studies) of the militarized neoliberalism soon to be in the ascendant. From this angle, the polemical reanimation of the Enlightenment's conceptual legacies, and the consequent depoliticization of literary criticism in favor of (neo-Kantian) ethics, showed how fully critical practice could be coopted by what Edward Said calls "the realities of power and

authority" that it is the office of criticism to contest (1983: 5). At the level of intellectual practice no less than in material fact, however, the notion that a reworked liberal ideology might secure for the world a peaceful equilibrium could not be sustained.

2. As Jameson observes, any historical structure-concept or "periodizing hypothesis" (Jameson, quoted in Brown 2006: 311) need not be true so much as operative: a periodizing rubric is not an ontology of history so much as a representation of it. For a more extended discussion of these determinist frameworks, see Hensley (2012).

References

Ackrill, J. L. (1980). "Aristotle on Action." In Amélie Oksenberg Rorty (ed.), *Essays on Aristotle's Ethics*, 93–102. Berkeley: University of California Press.

Adams, Edward (2011). *Liberal Epic: The Victorian Practice of History from Gibbon to Churchill*. Charlottesville: University of Virginia Press.

Adorno, Theodor and Max Horkheimer (2002). *Dialectic of Enlightenment: Philosophical Fragments*, trans. Edmund Jephcott. Stanford: Stanford University Press.

Agamben, Giorgio (1998). *Homo Sacer: Sovereign Power and Bare Life*, trans. Daniel Heller-Roazen. Stanford: Stanford University Press.

Agamben, Giorgio (1999). "The Messiah and the Sovereign: The Problem of Law in Walter Benjamin." In *Potentialities: Collected Essays in Philosophy*, trans. and ed. Daniel Heller-Roazen, 160–76. Stanford: Stanford University Press.

Agamben, Giorgio (2002). *Remnants of Auschwitz: The Witness and the Archive*, trans. Daniel Heller-Roazen. New York: Zone Books.

Agamben, Giorgio (2005). *State of Exception*, trans. Kevin Attell. Chicago: University of Chicago Press.

Allott, Kenneth (1959). "Matthew Arnold's Reading-Lists in Three Early Diaries." *Victorian Studies* 2(3): 254–66.

Anderson, Amanda (2001). *The Powers of Distance: Cosmopolitanism and the Cultivation of Detachment*. Princeton: Princeton University Press.

Anderson, Benedict (1991). *Imagined Communities: Reflections on the Origin and Spread of Nationalism*. New York: Verso.

Anderson, Olive (1967). *A Liberal State at War: English Politics and Economics During the Crimean War*. New York: St. Martin's Press.

Anghie, Antony (1999). "Finding the Peripheries: Sovereignty and Colonialism in Nineteenth Century International Law." *Harvard International Law Journal* 40(1): 1–80.

Arac, Jonathan (1979). "Rhetoric and Realism in Nineteenth Century Fiction: Hyperbole in *The Mill on the Floss*." *ELH* 46(4): 673–92.

Arendt, Hannah (1970). *On Violence*. New York: Harvest.

Arendt, Hannah (1973). *The Origins of Totalitarianism*. New York: Harcourt.

Arendt, Hannah (1991). *On Revolution*. New York: Penguin.

Aristotle (1951). *Poetics*, trans. S. H. Butcher. 1911. New York: Dover. Available at: www.classics.mit.edu/Aristotle/poetics.1.1.html.

Armstrong, Isobel (1993). *Victorian Poetry: Poetry, Poetics, and Politics*. London: Routledge.

Armstrong, Nancy (2002). *Fiction in the Age of Photography: The Legacy of British Realism*. Cambridge, Mass.: Harvard University Press.

Armstrong, Nancy (2005). *How Novels Think: The Limits of Individualism 1719–1900*. New York: Columbia University Press.

Armstrong, W. A. (1978). "The Census' Enumerators Books: A Commentary." In Richard Lawton (ed.), *The Census and Social Structure: An Interpretive Guide to the Nineteenth Century Censuses for England and Wales*, 28–81. Totoma: Frank Cass.

Arnold, Matthew (1861). *On Translating Homer: Three Lectures Given at Oxford. 1855*. London: Longman's. Web. 7 Oct. 2008.

Arnold, Matthew (1993). *Culture and Anarchy and Other Writings*, ed. Stefan Collini. New York: Cambridge University Press.

Arnold, Matthew ([1855] 1995). "Stanzas from the Grande Chartreuse." In *The Selected Poems of Matthew Arnold*, ed. Timothy Peltason. New York: Penguin.

Arrighi, Giovanni (2007). *Adam Smith in Beijing: Lineages of the Twenty-First Century*. London: Verso.

Arrighi, Giovanni (2010). *The Long Twentieth Century: Money, Power, and the Origins of Our Times*. London: Verso.

Auerbach, Erich (2003). *Mimesis: The Representation of Reality in Western Literature*. Princeton: Princeton University Press.

Azoulay, Ariella (2008). *The Civil Contract of Photography*. Cambridge, Mass.: MIT Press.

Badiou, Alain (2005). *Metapolitics*, trans. Jason Barker. London: Verso.

Badiou, Alain (2006). *Being and Event*, trans. Oliver Feltham. New York: Continuum.

Bagehot, Walter (1872). *Physics and Politics; or Thoughts on the Application of the Principles of Natural Selection and Inheritance to Political Society*. London: Henry King.

Bain, William (2013). "Vitoria: The Law of War, Saving the Innocent, and the Image of God." In Stefano Recchia and Jennifer M. Welsh (eds), *Just and Unjust Military Intervention: European Thinkers from Vitoria to Mill*, 70–95. Cambridge: Cambridge University Press.

Bakhtin, Mikhail (1981). "Forms of Time and of the Chronotope in the Novel." In *The Dialogic Imagination: Four Essays*, 84–258. Austin: University of Texas Press.

Balibar, Etienne (2014). *Equaliberty: Political Essays*, trans. James Ingram. Durham, NC: Duke University Press.

Banerjee, Sukanya (2010). *Becoming Imperial Citizens: Indians in the Late-Victorian Empire*. Durham, NC: Duke University Press.

Barrett, Dorothea (1993). "The Politics of Sado-Masochism: Swinburne and George Eliot." In Rikky Rooksby and Nicholas Shrimpton (eds), *The Whole Music of Passion: New Essays on Swinburne*, 107–19. Aldershot: Scolar Press.

Barthes, Roland (1982). *Camera Lucida: Reflections on Photography*, trans. Richard Howard. New York: Hill & Wang.

Bataille, Georges (1985). *Visions of Excess: Selected Writings, 1927–1939*, ed. Allan Stoekl. Minneapolis: University of Minnesota Press.

Baucom, Ian (1999). *Out of Place: Englishness, Empire, and the Locations of Identity*. Princeton: Princeton University Press.

Baucom, Ian (2005). *Specters of the Atlantic: Finance Capital, Slavery, and the Philosophy of History*. Durham, NC: Duke University Press.

Baucom, Ian (2009). "Cicero's Ghost: The Atlantic, the Enemy, and the Laws of War." In Russ Castronovo and Susan Kay Gilman (eds), *States of Emergency: The Objects of American Studies*, 124–42. Chapel Hill: University of North Carolina Press.

Bayly, C. A. (1990). *Indian Society and the Making of the British Empire*. Cambridge: Cambridge University Press.

Beer, Gillian (1986). *George Eliot*. Bloomington: Indiana University Press.

Belich, James (2011). *Replenishing the Earth: The Settler Revolution and the Rise of the Anglo-World, 1783–1939*. Oxford: Oxford University Press.

Bell, Duncan (ed.) (2007). *Victorian Visions of Global Order: Empire and International Relations in Nineteenth-Century Political Thought*. Cambridge: Cambridge University Press.

Bell, Duncan (2014). "What is Liberalism?" *Political Theory* 42(6): 682–715.

Bell, Duncan (2015). "Desolation Goes Before Us (on John Darwin, *The Empire Project*)." *Journal of British Studies* 54(4): 987–93.

Bell, Duncan (2016). "The Dream Machine: On Liberalism and Empire." In *Reordering the World: Essays on Liberalism and Empire*. Princeton: Princeton University Press.

Benjamin, Walter (1977). *The Origin of German Tragic Drama*. London: Verso.

Benjamin, Walter (1978). "Critique of Violence." In *Reflections: Essays, Aphorisms, Autobiographical Writings*, ed. Peter Demetz, 277–300. New York: Schocken.

Benjamin, Walter (1999). *The Arcades Project*. Cambridge, Mass.: Harvard University Press.

Berlant, Lauren (2007). "On the Case." *Critical Inquiry* 33(4): 663–72.

Bersani, Leo (1977). *Baudelaire and Freud*. Berkeley: University of California Press.

Best, Stephen, and Sharon Marcus (2009). "Surface Reading: an Introduction." *Representations* 108(1): 1–21.

Bevington, Merle Mowbray (1941). *The Saturday Review, 1855–1868: Representative Educated Opinion in Victorian England*. New York: Columbia University Press.

Bigelow, Gordon (2013). "Form and Violence in Trollope's *The Macdermots of Ballycloran*." *Novel: A Forum on Fiction* 46(3): 386–405.

Blanchot, Maurice (1965). "Sade." In [Marquis de Sade,] *Justine, Philosophy in the Bedroom, and other Writings*, trans. Richard Seaver and Austryn Wainhouse. New York: Grove.

Bleby, Henry (1868). *The Reign of Terror: A Narrative of Facts Concerning Ex-Governor Eyre, George William Gordon, and the Jamaica Atrocities*. London: William Nichols. Web. 9 Jan. 2016.

Booth, William (1890). *In Darkest England and the Way Out*. London: Funk & Wagnalls.

Bowden, Brett (1997). "Civilization and Savagery in the Crucible of War." *Global Change, Peace & Security* 19(1): 3–16.

Braddon, Mary Elizabeth (1998). *Lady Audley's Secret* [1862]. New York: Penguin.

Brantlinger, Patrick (1988). *Rule of Darkness: British Literature and Imperialism, 1830–1914*. Ithaca, NY: Cornell University Press.

Brantlinger, Patrick (1998). *The Reading Lesson: The Threat of Mass Literacy in Nineteenth Century British Fiction*. Bloomington: Indiana University Press.

Briggs, Asa (1953). *Victorian People: A Reassessment of Persons and Themes, 1851–67*. New York: Harper.

Brooks, Peter (1976). *The Melodramatic Imagination: Balzac, Henry James, Melodrama, and the Mode of Excess*. New Haven: Yale University Press.

Brown, Wendy (2006). *Regulating Aversion: Tolerance in the Age of Identity and Empire*. Princeton: Princeton University Press.

Browning, Elizabeth Barrett (1995). "The Cry of the Children." In *Aurora Leigh and Other Poems*, ed. John Robert Glorney Bolton and Julia Bolton Holloway, 315–19. New York: Penguin.

Buckland, Adelene (2013). *Novel Science: Fiction and the Invention of the Nineteenth-Century Geology*. Chicago: University of Chicago Press.

Buckley, Jerome (1974). *Season of Youth: The Bildungsroman from Dickens to Golding*. Cambridge, Mass.: Harvard University Press.

Burke, Edmund (1987). *Reflections on the Revolution in France* [1790], ed. J. G. A. Pocock. Indianapolis: Hackett.

Burn, W. L. (1964). *The Age of Equipoise: A Study of the Mid-Victorian Generation*. New York: Norton.

Burroughs, Peter (1999). "Imperial Institutions and the Government of Empire." In Andrew Porter (ed.), *The Oxford History of the British Empire*, vol. 3: *The Nineteenth Century*, 170–97. Oxford: Oxford University Press.

Burrow, J. W. (1966). *Evolution and Society: A Study in Victorian Social Theory*. Cambridge: Cambridge University Press.

Burrow, J. W. (1991). "Henry Maine and Mid-Victorian Ideas of Progress." In Alan Diamond (ed.), *The Victorian Achievement of Sir Henry Maine*, 55–69. Cambridge: Cambridge University Press.

Cain, P. J. and A. G. Hopkins (2001). *British Imperialism: 1688–2000*. London: Longman.

Callwell, C. E. (1906). *Small Wars: Their Principles and Practice*, 3rd edn. London: Harrison.

Carlyle, Thomas (1897). "Shooting Niagara, and After?" In *The Works of Thomas Carlyle*, vol. 16, 589–633. New York: Collier.

Carroll, David (ed.) (1971). *George Eliot: The Critical Heritage*. London: Routledge & Kegan Paul.

Chadwick, Edwin (1842). *Report to Her Majesty's Principal Secretary of State for the Home Department, From the Poor Law Commissioners, On an Inquiry into the Sanitary Condition of the Labouring Population of Great Britain; With Appendices*. London: W. Clowes & Sons.

Chakrabarty, Dipesh (2000). *Provincializing Europe: Postcolonial Thought and Historical Difference*. Princeton: Princeton University Press.

Chandler, James (1998). *England in 1819: The Politics of Literary Culture and the Case of Romantic Historicism*. Chicago: University of Chicago Press.

Chare, Nicholas (2006). "The Gap in Context: Giorgio Agamben's *Remnants of Auschwitz*." *Cultural Critique* 64: 40–68.

Chaudhari, Sashi Bhutan (1979). *English Historical Writings on the Indian Mutiny, 1857–1859*. Kolkata: World Press.

Chaudhary, Zahid (2012). *Afterimages of Empire: Photography in Nineteenth-Century India*. Minneapolis: University of Minnesota Press.

Chrisman, Laura (2000). *Rereading the Imperial Romance: British Imperialism and South African Resistance in Haggard, Schreiner, and Plaatje*. Oxford: Clarendon Press.

Claeys, Gregory (2012). *Imperial Sceptics: British Critics of Empire, 1850–1920*. Oxford: Oxford University Press.

Cohen, Morton (1960). *Rider Haggard: His Life and Works*. London: Hutchinson.

Colby, Robert A. (1990). "Harnessing Pegasus: Walter Besant, 'The Author,' and the Profession of Authorship." *Victorian Periodicals Review* 23(3): 111–20.

Cole, Sarah Rose (2012). *At the Violet Hour: Modernism and Violence in England and Ireland*. Oxford: Oxford University Press.

Collini, Stefan (1991). *Public Moralists: Political Thought and Intellectual Life in Britain, 1850–1930*. New York: Oxford University Press.

Collins, Wilkie (1862). *No Name*. Repr. New York: Oxford University Press, 1998.

Collins, Wilkie (1871). *Poor Miss Finch*. Repr. New York: Oxford University Press, 2000.

Collins, Wilkie (1859–60). *The Woman in White*. Repr. New York: Penguin, 2003.

Collins, Wilkie (1866). *Armadale*. Repr. New York: Penguin, 2004.

Crosby, Christina (1991). *The Ends of History: Victorians and the Woman Question*. New York: Routledge.

Cruikshank, George et al. (1844–53). *The Comic Almanack; An Ephemeris in Jest and Earnest, Containing Merry Tales, Humorous Poetry, Quips, and Oddities*, 2nd series. Repr. London: Chatto & Windus, 1912.

Cuvier, Jean Léopold Nicolas Frédéric (Baron) (1825). *Discours sur les révolutions de la surface du globe*. Paris: G. DuFour. Web. 12 Jan. 2016.

Cvetkovich, Ann (1989). "Ghostlier Determinations: The Economy of Sensation and *The Woman in White*." *NOVEL: A Forum on Fiction* 23(1): 24–43.

Daly, Nicholas (2000). *Modernism, Romance, and the Fin de Siècle: Popular Fiction and British Culture, 1880–1914*. Cambridge: Cambridge University Press.

Darwin, John (1997). "Imperialism and the Victorians: The Dynamics of Territorial Expansion." *English Historical Review* 112(447): 614–42.

Darwin, John (2011). *The Empire Project: The Rise and Fall of the British World-System, 1830–1970*. Cambridge: Cambridge University Press.

Davis, Thomas S. (2015). *The Extinct Scene: Late Modernism and Everyday Life*. New York: Columbia University Press.

de Man, Paul (1979). *Allegories of Reading: Figural Language in Rousseau, Nietzsche, Rilke, and Proust*. New Haven: Yale University Press.

de Man, Paul (1983a). "The Rhetoric of Blindness." In *Blindness and Insight: Essays in the Rhetoric of Contemporary Criticism*. Minneapolis: University of Minnesota Press.

de Man, Paul (1983b). "The Rhetoric of Temporality." In *Blindness and Insight: Essays in the Rhetoric of Contemporary Criticism*. Minneapolis: University of Minnesota Press.

de Man, Paul (1984). "Autobiography as De-Facement." In *The Rhetoric of Romanticism*. New York: Columbia University Press.

de Man, Paul (1996). "The Epistemology of Metaphor." In *Aesthetic Ideology*, ed. Andrzej Warminski. Minneapolis: University of Minnesota Press.

de Vitoria, Francisco (1991). "On the Law of War." In *Political Writings*, 293–328. Cambridge: Cambridge University Press.

Deane, Bradley (2014). *Masculinity and the New Imperialism: Rewriting Manhood in British Popular Literature, 1870–1914*. New York: Cambridge University Press.

Deleuze, Gilles and Felix Guattari (1987). *A Thousand Plateaus: Capitalism and Schizophrenia*, trans. Brian Massumi. Minneapolis: University of Minnesota Press.

Demoor, Marysa (1987a). "Andrew Lang versus W. D. Howells: A Late-Victorian Literary Duel." *Journal of American Studies* 21(3): 416–22.

Demoor, Marysa (1987b). "Andrew Lang's Letters to H. Rider Haggard: The Record of a Harmonious Friendship." *Études anglaises* 40(3): 313–22.

Demoor, Marysa (ed.) (1990). *Dear Stevenson: Letters from Andrew Lang to Robert Louis Stevenson with Five Letters from Stevenson to Lang*. Leuven: Peeters.

Dentith, Simon (2006). *Epic and Empire in Nineteenth-Century Britain*. Cambridge: Cambridge University Press.

Derrida, Jacques (1980). "The Law of Genre," trans. Avital Ronell. *Critical Inquiry* 7(1): 55–81.

Derrida, Jacques (1982). "Différance" [1968]. In *The Margins of Philosophy*, trans. Alan Bass, 1–28. Chicago: University of Chicago Press.

Derrida, Jacques (1992). "The Force of Law: The 'Mystical Foundation of Authority'," trans. Mary Quaintance. In *Deconstruction and the Possibility of Justice*, ed. Drucilla Cornell et al., 3–67. New York: Routledge.

Derrida, Jacques (1997). *Of Grammatology*. Trans. Gayatri Chakravorty Spivak. Baltimore: Johns Hopkins University Press.

Derrida, Jacques ([1967] 2005). "Violence and Metaphysics." In *Writing and Difference*, trans. and ed. Alan Bass. London: Routledge.

"Dianoia" (2001). *Strong's Online Greek Dictionary*. Available at: http://bibleapps.com/greek/1271.htm

Dickens, Charles (1853). *Bleak House*. Repr. New York: Book of the Month, 1998.

Dickens, Charles (1865). *Our Mutual Friend*. Repr. New York: Penguin, 1998.

Dickens, Charles (1999). *The Letters of Charles Dickens*, vol. 11. New York: Oxford University Press.

Dickens, Charles (1859). *A Tale of Two Cities*. Repr. New York: Penguin, 2003.

Dickens, Charles (1854). *Hard Times*. Repr. New York: Oxford University Press, 2008.

Dolin, Kieran (1999). *Fiction and the Law: Legal Discourse in Victorian and Modernist Literature*. Cambridge: Cambridge University Press.

Dorson, Richard M. (1968). *The British Folklorists: A History*. Chicago: University of Chicago Press.

Dunn, Richard S. (2000). *Sugar and Slaves: The Rise of the Planter Class in the English West Indies, 1624–1713*. 1972. Chapel Hill: University of North Carolina Press.

Eagleton, Terry (1996). *Literary Theory: An Introduction*. Minneapolis: University of Minnesota Press.

Edel, Leon (1962). *Henry James: The Middle Years, 1882–1895*. New York: Lippincott.

Eliot, George (n.d.). *The Mill on the Floss*. British Library Add MS 34023–34025. Manuscript.

Eliot, George (1958–78). *The George Eliot Letters*, ed. Gordon Haight. 9 vols. New Haven: Yale University Press.

Eliot, George (1860). *The Mill on the Floss*. Repr. New York: Penguin, 2003.

Eliot, George (1963). *Essays of George Eliot*, ed. Thomas Pinney. New York: Columbia University Press.

Eliot, George (1979). *George Eliot's Middlemarch Notebooks: A Transcription*, ed. John Clark Pratt and Victor A. Neufeldt. Berkeley: University of California Press.

Eliot, George (1981). *A Writer's Notebook, 1854–1879, and Uncollected Writings*, ed. Joseph Wiesenfarth. Charlottesville: University of Virginia Press.

Eliot, George (1991). *Selected Essays, Poems, and Other Writings*, ed. A. S. Byatt. New York: Penguin.

Elshtain, Jean Bethke (2003). *Just War Against Terror: The Burden Of American Power in A Violent World*. New York: Basic Books.

Elwin, Malcolm (1939). *Old Gods Falling*. New York: Macmillan.

Empson, William (1974). *Some Versions of Pastoral*. New York: Norton.

Engels, Friedrich (1987). *The Condition of the Working Class in England*. New York: Penguin.

Esty, Jed (2012). *Unseasonable Youth: Modernism, Colonialism, and the Fiction of Development*. New York: Oxford University Press.

Etherington, Norman (1984). *Rider Haggard*. Boston: Twayne.

Evans, Eric J. (1983). *The Forging of the Modern State: Early Industrial Britain, 1783–1870*. Repr. New York: Longman, 2001.

Fabian, Johannes (1982). *Time and the Other: How Anthropology Makes its Object*. New York: Columbia University Press.

Fairman, Charles (1930). *The Law of Martial Rule*. Chicago: Callaghan.

Fanon, Frantz (1963). *The Wretched of the Earth*, trans. Constance Farrington. New York: Grove.

Farwell, Byron (1972). *Queen Victoria's Little Wars*. New York: Harper.

Faverty, Frederic E. (1968). *The Victorian Poets: A Guide to Research*. Cambridge: Harvard University Press.

Favret, Mary (2009). *War at a Distance: Romanticism and the Making of Modern Wartime*. Princeton: Princeton University Press.

Felski, Rita (2015). *The Limits of Critique*. Chicago: University of Chicago Press.

Ferejohn, John and Pasquale Pasquino (2004). "The Law of the Exception: A Typology of Emergency Powers." *I.CON* 2.2: 210–39. Web. 12 Jan. 2016.

Ferguson, Niall (2004). *Empire: How Britain Made the Modern World*. New York: Penguin.

Fish, Stanley (1980). "Interpreting the Variorum." In *Reader Response Criticism: From Formalism to Post-Structuralism*, ed. Jane Tomkins. 164–84. Baltimore: Johns Hopkins University Press.

Flikschuh, Katrin (2000). *Kant and Modern Political Philosophy*. New York: Cambridge University Press.

Fludernik, Monika (1995). "The Linguistic Illusion of Alterity: The Free Indirect as Paradigm." *Diacritics* 25(4): 89–115.

Forrester, John (1996). "If *p*, Then What? Thinking in Cases." *History of the Human Sciences* 9(1): 1–25. Web. 12 Jan. 2016.

Forster, John (1911). *The Life of Charles Dickens*, vol. 2. New York: Baker & Taylor.

Foucault, Michel (1976). *The History of Sexuality*, vol. 1: *An Introduction*, trans. Robert Hurley. Repr. New York: Vintage, 1990.

Foucault, Michel (1984). "Truth and Power." In *The Foucault Reader*, ed. Paul Rabinow, 51–75. New York: Pantheon.

Foucault, Michel (1994). *Critique and Power: Recasting the Foucault/Habermas Debate*, ed. Michael Kelley. Cambridge, Mass.: MIT Press.

Foucault, Michel (2003). *"Society Must Be Defended": Lectures at the Collège de France, 1975–1976*, trans. David Macey. New York: Picador.

Foucault, Michel (2007). *Security, Territory, Population: Lectures at the Collège de France, 1977–1978*, trans. Graham Burchell. New York: Picador.

Fraiman, Susan (1993). "*The Mill on the Floss*, the Critics, and the Bildungs-roman." *PMLA* 108(1): 136–50.

Fraser, Nancy (2005). "Reframing Justice in a Globalizing World." *New Left Review* 36: 69–88.

Freud, Sigmund (1989). "Mourning and Melancholia" [1917]. In *The Freud Reader*, ed. Peter Gay, 584–9. New York: Norton.

Frye, Northrop (1957). *The Anatomy of Criticism: Four Essays*. Princeton: Princeton University Press.

Gallagher, Catherine (1985). *The Industrial Reformation of English Fiction: Social Discourse and Narrative Form, 1832–1867*. Chicago: University of Chicago Press.

Gitelman, Lisa (2014). *Paper Knowledge: Toward a Media History of Documents*. Durham, NC: Duke University Press.

Glass, D. V. (1973). *Numbering the People: The Eighteenth Century Population Controversy and the Development of Census and Vital Statistics in Britain*. Westmead: D. C. Heath.

Goodlad, Lauren M. E. (2003). *Victorian Literature and the Victorian State: Character and Governance in a Liberal Society*. Baltimore: Johns Hopkins University Press.

Goodlad, Lauren M. E. (2015a). "Liberalism and Literature." Unpublished MS.

Goodlad, Lauren M. E. (2015b). *The Victorian Geopolitical Aesthetic: Realism, Sovereignty, and Transnational Experience.* New York: Oxford University Press.

Gottlieb, Paula (2014). "Aristotle on Non-contradiction." In *The Stanford Encyclopedia of Philosophy.* Web. 29 July 2014.

Graver, Suzanne (1984). *George Eliot and Community: A Study in Social Theory and Fictional Form.* Berkeley: University of California Press.

Green, Martin Burgess (1979). *Dreams of Adventure, Deeds of Empire.* New York: Basic Books.

Green-Lewis, Jennifer (1996). *Framing the Victorians: Photography and the Culture of Realism.* Ithaca, NY: Cornell University Press.

Grosz, Elizabeth (2004). *The Nick of Time: Politics, Evolution, and the Untimely.* Durham, NC: Duke University Press.

Guillory, John (2010). "Enlightening Mediation." In Clifford Siskin and William Warner (eds), *This is Enlightenment*, 37–63. Chicago: University of Chicago Press.

Gunn, Simon and James Vernon (eds) (2011). *The Peculiarities of Liberal Modernity in Imperial Britain.* Berkeley: University of California Press.

Guth, Deborah (2003). *George Eliot and Schiller: Intertextuality and Cross-Cultural Discourse.* Aldershot: Ashgate.

Hack, Daniel (2006). "Revenge Stories of Modern Life." *Victorian Studies* 48(2): 277–86.

Hadley, Elaine (1995). *Melodramatic Tactics: Theatricalized Dissent in the English Marketplace, 1800–1885.* Stanford: Stanford University Press.

Haggard, H. Rider (1881). "Unpublished Letter to Ella Doveton Haggard," 2 Mar. 1881. Henry Rider Haggard Papers, David M. Rubenstein Rare Book & Manuscript Library, Duke University.

Haggard, H. Rider (1892). *Cetywayo and His White Neighbors; or Remarks on Recent Events in Zululand, Natal, and the Transvaal.* London: Trübner.

Haggard, H. Rider (1912). *The Days of My Life: An Autobiography.* 2 vols. Repr. online Feb. 2003 by Project Gutenberg of Australia.

Haggard, H. Rider (2007). *King Solomon's Mines* [1885]. New York: Penguin.

Haight, Gordon Sherman (1968). *George Eliot: A Biography.* New York: Oxford University Press.

Hall, Catherine (2002). *Civilising Subjects: Colony and Metropole in the English Imagination, 1830–1867.* Chicago: University of Chicago Press.

Hall, Catherine, Keith McClelland, and Jane Rendall (2000). *Defining the Victorian Nation: Class, Race, Gender, and the British Reform Act of 1867.* New York: Cambridge University Press.

Hall, Douglas (1959). *Free Jamaica, 1838–1865: An Economic History.* New Haven: Yale University Press.

Hall, E. W. (1880). *Treatise on International Law.* Repr. Oxford: Clarendon Press, 1895.

Hallward, Peter (2003). *Badiou: A Subject to Truth*. Minneapolis: University of Minnesota Press.

Hamer, D. A. (1968). *John Morley: Liberal Intellectual in Politics*. Oxford: Clarendon Press.

Harrison, Frederic (1885). "The Life of George Eliot." *Littell's Living Age* 165: 23–31.

Harvey, David (2003). *The New Imperialism*. Oxford: Oxford University Press.

Hayes, Kevin J. (ed.) (1996). *Henry James: The Contemporary Reviews*. Cambridge: Cambridge University Press.

Henry, Nancy (2001). "George Eliot and Politics." In George Levine (ed.), *The Cambridge Companion to George Eliot*, 138–58. New York: Cambridge University Press.

Henry, Nancy (2006). *George Eliot and the British Empire*. New York: Cambridge University Press.

Hensley, Nathan K. (2012). "Allegories of the Contemporary." *NOVEL: A Forum on Fiction* 45(2): 276–300.

Hensley, Nathan K. (2013). "What is a Network (And Who is Andrew Lang)?" *RaVoN: Romanticism and Victorianism on the Net* 64: https://www.erudit.org/revue/ravon/2013/v/n64/1025668ar.html.

Hensley, Nathan K. (2015). "Empire." In Dino Felluga, Linda K. Hughes, and Pamela K. Gilbert (eds), *The Blackwell Encyclopedia of Victorian Literature*. Oxford: Wiley-Blackwell. Available at: http://www.literatureencyclopedia.com/public/victorian_about

Herbert, Christopher (2009). *War of No Pity: The Indian Mutiny and Victorian Trauma*. Princeton: Princeton University Press.

Hertz, Neil (2003). *George Eliot's Pulse*. Stanford: Stanford University Press.

Heuman, Gad (1994). *The Killing Time: The Morant Bay Rebellion in Jamaica*. London: Macmillan.

Hobbes, Thomas (1982). *Leviathan*. New York: Penguin.

Hobsbawm, Eric (1968). *Industry and Empire: An Economic History of Britain since 1750*. London: Weidenfeld & Nicolson.

Hobsbawm, Eric (1989). *The Age of Empire: 1875–1914*. New York: Vintage.

Homer (1928). *The Odyssey of Homer, Done into English Prose*, trans. S. H. Butcher and Andrew Lang. 1878. London: Macmillan.

Homer (1939). *The Iliad of Homer, Done into English Prose*, trans. Andrew Lang, Walter Leaf, and Ernest Myers. 1883. London: Macmillan.

Homer (1990). *The Iliad*, trans. Robert Fagles. New York: Penguin.

Horowitz, Evan (2006). "George Eliot: The Conservative." *Victorian Studies* 49(1): 7–32.

Howe, Anthony (2007). "Free Trade and Global Order: The Rise and Fall of a Victorian Vision." In Duncan Bell (ed.), *Victorian Visions of Global Order: Empire and International Relations in Nineteenth-Century Political Thought*, 26–46. New York: Cambridge University Press.

Howells, William Dean (1882). "Henry James, Jr." *The Century* 25(1): 24–9.

Howells, William Dean (1892). *Criticism and Fiction*. New York: Harper & Brothers.

Howells, William Dean (1993). *Selected Criticism*, vols 1 and 2. Bloomington: Indiana University Press.

Hultgren, Neil (2014). *Melodramatic Imperial Writing: From the Sepoy Rebellion to Cecil Rhodes*. Columbus: Ohio University Press.

Hussain, Nasser (2003). *The Jurisprudence of Emergency: Colonialism and the Rule of Law*. Ann Arbor: University of Michigan Press.

Hutchins, W. John (1977). "The Problem of 'Aboutness' in Document Analysis." *Journal of Informatics* 1(1): 17–35.

Hyder, Clyde K. (1933). *Swinburne's Literary Career and Fame*. Durham, NC: Duke University Press.

Hyder, Clyde K. (ed.) (1970). *Swinburne: The Critical Heritage*. London: Routledge & Kegan Paul.

Jaffe, Audrey (2000). *Scenes of Sympathy: Identity and Representation in Victorian Fiction*. Ithaca, NY: Cornell University Press.

Jakobson, Roman (1956). "Two Aspects of Language and Two Types of Aphasic Disturbance." In Roman Jakobson and Morris Halle (eds), *Fundamentals of Language*, 53–83. The Hague: Mouton.

Jakobson, Roman (1987). "Linguistics and Poetics." In Krystyna Pomorska and Stephen Rudy (eds), *Language in Literature*, 62–94. Cambridge, Mass.: Harvard University Press.

Jamaica Papers No. 1 (1866). *Facts and Documents Relating to the Alleged Rebellion in Jamaica, and the Measures of Repression; Including Notes of the Trial of Mr. Gordon*. London: Jamaica Committee.

Jamaica Papers No. 6 (1867). *Illustrations of Martial Law in Jamaica, Compiled from the Report of the Royal Commissioner, and Other Blue Books Laid Before Parliament*, ed. John Gordie. London: Jamaica Committee.

James, Henry (1884). "The Art of Fiction." *Longman's Magazine* 4(23): 502–21. Available at: http://public.wsu.edu/~campbelld/amlit/artfiction.html.

James, Henry (1907). "Preface to Volume 2 of the New York Edition, Containing *The American*." Repr. in *Prefaces to Volumes of the New York Edition, 1907–1909*: henryjames.org.uk.

James, Henry (1968). "The Novels of George Eliot." *Atlantic Monthly* 18, 'Views and Reviews' [1866]. Repr. Freeport: Books for Libraries.

James, Henry (1980). *The Letters of Henry James*, vol. 3: *1883–1895*, ed. Leon Edel. 4 vols. Cambridge, Mass.: Belknap Press of Harvard University Press.

James, Henry (1987). *The Princess Casamassima*. 1886. New York: Penguin.

Jameson, Fredric (1974). *Marxism and Form*. Princeton: Princeton University Press.

Jameson, Fredric (1981). *The Political Unconscious: Narrative as a Socially Symbolic Act*. Ithaca, NY: Cornell University Press.

Jameson, Fredric (1992). *Postmodernism; Or, the Cultural Logic of Late Capitalism*. Durham, NC: Duke University Press.

Jameson, Fredric (1998). "Periodizing the '60s." In *The Ideologies of Theory*, 178–208. Minneapolis: University of Minnesota Press.

Jameson, Fredric (2002). *A Singular Modernity: Essay on the Ontology of the Present*. London: Verso.

References

Jameson, Fredric (2007). *Late Marxism: Adorno; or the Persistence of the Dialectic.* London: Verso.

Jones, Anna Maria (2007). *Problem Novels: Victorian Fiction Theorizes the Sensational Self.* Columbus: Ohio State University Press.

Jones, J. Mervyn (1947). *British Nationality Law and Practice.* Oxford: Clarendon Press.

Joshi, Priti (2007). "Mutiny Echoes: India, Britons, and Charles Dickens's *A Tale of Two Cities.*" *Nineteenth-Century Literature* 62(1): 48–87.

Joyce, Patrick (2003). *The Rule of Freedom: Liberalism and the Modern City.* London: Verso.

Kahn, Victoria (2004). *Wayward Contracts: The Crisis of Political Obligation in England, 1640–1674.* Princeton: Princeton University Press.

Kant, Immanuel (1881). *The Critique of Pure Reason*, trans. Max Müller. London: Macmillan.

Kant, Immanuel (1991a). "An Answer to the Question: What is Enlightenment?" In *Political Writings*, ed. H. R. Reiss, 54–60. New York: Cambridge University Press.

Kant, Immanuel (1991b). "Perpetual Peace: A Philosophical Sketch." In *Political Writings*, ed. H. R. Reiss, 93–130. New York: Cambridge University Press.

Kant, Immanuel (1996). *The Metaphysics of Morals*, trans. Mary Gregor. New York: Cambridge University Press.

Kant, Immanuel (2000). *Critique of the Power of Judgment*, trans. Paul Guyer and Eric Matthews. Cambridge: Cambridge University Press.

Kaplan, Amy (1988). *The Social Construction of American Realism.* Chicago: University of Chicago Press.

Kaplan, Lindsay (2015). "Figures of Slavery: Jewish Hereditary Inferiority and the Emergence of Race." Unpublished MS.

Kenner, Hugh (1971). *The Pound Era.* Berkeley: University of California Press.

Ker, W. P. (1931). *Epic and Romance: Essays on Medieval Literature.* London: Macmillan.

Kipling, Rudyard (1994). "The White Man's Burden." *In The Collected Poems of Rudyard Kipling.* Ware: Wordsworth Editions.

Kirshenbaum, Matthew (2012). *Mechanisms: New Media and the Forensic Imagination.* Cambridge, Mass.: MIT Press.

Kostal, R. W. (2005). *A Jurisprudence of Power: Victorian Empire and the Rule of Law.* New York: Oxford University Press.

Kubitz, Oskar Alfred (1932). *Development of John Stuart Mill's System of Logic*, vol. 18. Urbana: University of Illinois Press.

Lacan, Jacques (2006). "Kant with Sade." In *Écrits*, trans. Bruce Fink, 645–68. New York: Norton.

Lacoste, Anne (2010). *Felice Beato: A Photographer on the Eastern Road.* Los Angeles: Getty.

Lafourcade, Georges (1928). *La Jeunesse de Swinburne.* Paris: Les Belles-Lettres.

Lang, Andrew (1887). "Realism and Romance." *Contemporary Review* 52: 683–93.

Lang, Andrew (1893). *Homer and the Epic*. London: Longmans, Green.

Lang, Andrew (1910). *The World of Homer*. London: Longmans, Green.

Lang, Andrew and H. Rider Haggard (1890). *The World's Desire*. London: Longmans, Green.

Larsen, Neil (2001). *Determinations: Essays on Theory, Narrative and Nation in the Americas*. London: Verso.

Lasourdo, Dominic (2014). *Liberalism: A Counter-History*. London: Verso.

Latour, Bruno (2004). "Why Has Critique Run Out of Steam? From Matters of Fact to Matters of Concern." *Critical Inquiry* 30(2): 225–48. Web. 12 Nov. 2015.

Leavis, F. R. (1948). *The Great Tradition: George Eliot, Henry James, Joseph Conrad*. New York: Stewart.

Levine, George (ed.) (2001). *The Cambridge Companion to George Eliot*. New York: Cambridge University Press.

Levine, Caroline (2015). *Forms: Whole, Rhythm, Hierarchy, Network*. Princeton: Princeton University Press.

Li, Hao (2000). *Memory and History in George Eliot: Transfiguring the Past*. New York: St. Martin's.

Liu, Alan (2008). *Local Transcendence: Essays on Postmodern Historicism and the Database*. Chicago: University of Chicago Press.

Locke, John (1988). *Two Treatises of Government*, ed. Peter Laslett. New York: Cambridge University Press.

Loesberg, Jonathan (1986). "The Ideology of Narrative Form in Sensation Fiction." *Representations* 13: 115–38.

Lorimer, James (1883). *The Institutes of the Laws of Nations*. Edinburgh: Blackwood.

Lukács, Georg (1971). *The Theory of the Novel: A Historico-Philosophical Essay on the Forms of Great Epic Literature*. [1920], trans. Anna Bostock. Cambridge, Mass.: MIT Press.

Lukács, Georg (1983). *The Historical Novel* [1962], trans. Hannah Mitchell and Stanley Mitchell. Lincoln: University of Nebraska Press.

Lyell, Charles (1860). *Principles of Geology; or, The Modern Changes of the Earth and its Inhabitants* [1830]. Repr. New York: Appleton.

Lynch, Deirdre Shauna (1998). *The Economy of Character: Novels, Market Culture, and the Business of Inner Meaning*. Chicago: University of Chicago Press.

Lynn, Martin (2009). "British Policy, Trade, and Informal Empire in the Mid-Nineteenth Century." In Andrew Porter (ed.), *The Oxford History of the British Empire*, vol. 3: *The Nineteenth Century*, 101–21. Oxford: Oxford University Press.

Magee, Gary and Andrew Thompson (2010). *Empire and Globalization: Networks of People, Goods, and Capital in the British World, c.1850–1914*. Cambridge: Cambridge University Press.

Maine, Henry Sumner (1873). *Ancient Law: Its Connection with the Family History of Society, and its Relation to Modern Ideas* [1861]. Repr. New York: Henry Holt.

Maine, Henry Sumner (1888). *Lectures on the Early History of Institutions* [1874]. Repr. New York: Henry Holt.

Maixner, Paul (ed.) (1998). *Robert Louis Stevenson: The Critical Heritage*. London: Routledge.

Makdisi, Saree (2002). *William Blake and the Impossible History of the 1790s*. Chicago: University of Chicago Press.

Mantena, Karuna (2010). *Alibis of Empire: Henry Maine and the Ends of Liberal Imperialism*. Princeton: Princeton University Press.

Marcus, Steven (1975). *The Other Victorians: A Study of Sexuality and Pornography in Mid-Nineteenth Century England*. New York: Basic Books.

Marcuse, Herbert (1968). "The Affirmative Character of Culture," trans. Jeremy J. Shapiro. In *Negations: Essays in Critical Theory*, 88–133. Boston: Beacon.

Markovits, Stefanie (2006). *The Crisis of Action in Nineteenth Century English Literature*. Columbus: Ohio State University Press.

Martin, Meredith (2012). *The Rise and Fall of Meter: Poetry and English National Culture 1860–1930*. Princeton: Princeton University Press.

Marx, Karl (1852). *The Eighteenth Brumaire of Louis Bonaparte*. Reprinted 2006, trans. Saul K. Padover. Available at: https://www.marxists.org/archive/marx/works/1852/18th-brumaire/

Marx, Karl (1857). "The Revolt in India." *New-York Daily Tribune*, 4 Aug. Accessed 24 Nov. 2015 at: https://www.marxists.org/archive/marx/works/1857/07/17.htm.

Marx, Karl (1974). *The Enthnological Notebooks of Karl Marx*, ed. Lawrence Krader. Assen: Van Gorcum.

Marx, Karl (1990). *Capital: A Critique of Political Economy*, vol. 1 [1867], trans. Ben Fowkes. New York: Penguin.

Marx, Karl (1993). *Grundrisse: Foundations of the Critique of Political Economy*, trans. Martin Nicolaus. New York: Penguin.

Mayhew, Henry (1861). *London Labour and the London Poor*. 1851. Repr. London: Griffin, Bohn.

Mazower, Mark (2006). "An International Civilization? Empire, Internationalism, and the Crisis of the Mid-Twentieth Century." *International Affairs* 82(3): 553–66.

Mbembe, Achille (2001). *On the Postcolony*. Berkeley: University of California Press, 2001.

Mbembe, Achille (2003). "Necropolitics." *Public Culture* 15(1): 11–40.

McCaw, Neil (2000). *George Eliot and Victorian Historiography: Imagining the National Past*. London: Macmillan.

McClintock, Anne (1995). *Imperial Leather: Race, Gender, and Sexuality in the Colonial Contest*. London: Routledge.

McClure, Kristie (2015). "Figuring Authority, Authorizing Statistics." In Dvora Yanow and Peregrine Shwartz-Shea (eds), *Interpretation and Method: Empirical Research Methods and the Interpretive Turn*, 50–63. London: Routledge.

McGann, Jerome (1972). *Swinburne: An Experiment in Criticism*. Chicago: University of Chicago Press.

McGann, Jerome (1983). *The Romantic Ideology: A Critical Investigation*. Chicago: University of Chicago Press.

McGurl, Mark (2001). *The Novel Art: Elevations of American Fiction After Henry James*. Princeton: Princeton University Press.

McKeon, Michael (ed.) (2000). *The Theory of the Novel: A Historical Approach*. Baltimore: Johns Hopkins University Press.

Mehta, Uday Singh (1999). *Liberalism and Empire: A Study in Nineteenth Century British Liberal Thought*. Chicago: University of Chicago Press.

Menke, Richard (2007). *Telegraphic Realism: Victorian Fiction and Other Information Systems*. Stanford: Stanford University Press.

Meredith, Martin (2007). *Diamonds, Gold, and War: The British, the Boers, and the Making of South Africa*. New York: Public Affairs.

Michalski, Robert (1995). "Towards a Popular Culture: Andrew Lang's Anthropological and Literary Criticism." *Journal of American Culture* 18(3): 13–17.

Mill, John Stuart (1963–91). *The Collected Works of John Stuart Mill*. ed. J. M. Robson, Harold Bohme, J. C. Cairns, J. B. Conacher, D. P. Dryer, Marion Filipiuk, Frances Halpenny, Samuel Hollander, R. F. McRae, Ian Montagnes, Ann P. Robson, and F. E. Sparshott. Toronto: University of Toronto Press and London: Routledge & Kegan Paul. 33 vols. Available at: http://oll.libertyfund.org/titles/mill-collected-works-of-john-stuart-mill-in-33-vols.

Mitchell, W. J. T. (2005). *What Do Pictures Want? The Lives and Loves of Images*. Chicago: University of Chicago Press.

Monsman, Gerald (2000). "Of Diamonds and Deities: Social Anthropology in H. Rider Haggard's King Solomon's Mines." *English Literature in Transition (1880–1920)* 43(3): 280–97.

Morley, John (1866). "Felix Holt." *Saturday Review*, 16 June: 723.

Morley, John (1897). *Machiavelli*. London: Macmillan.

Mufti, Aamir R. (2007). *Enlightenment in the Colony: The Jewish Question and the Crisis of Postcolonial Culture*. Princeton: Princeton University Press.

Muirhead, John H. (1930). *Coleridge as Philosopher*. London: Allen & Unwin.

Muthu, Sankar (2003). *Enlightenment Against Empire*. Princeton: Princeton University Press.

Nancy, Jean-Luc (2000). *Being Singular Plural*, trans. Anne O'Byrne and Robert Richardson. Stanford: Stanford University Press.

Nietzsche, Friedrich (1967). *On the Genealogy of Morals and Ecce Homo*, trans. Walter Kaufmann. New York: Vintage.

Nissel, Muriel (1987). *People Count: A History of the General Register Office*. London: Stationery Office.

Norman, E. Herbert (2000). *Japan's Emergence as a Modern State: Political and Economic Problems of the Meiji Period*. Vancouver: University of British Columbia Press.

"Norwich Castle Museum Catalogue of the Holograph Manuscripts of Novels, Romances, and Works on Agriculture and Sociology by Sir H. Rider Haggard, K.B.E." (1920). Pamphlet in Henry Rider Haggard Papers, David M. Rubenstein Rare Book & Manuscript Library, Duke University.

Noyes, Alfred (1968). *A Pageant of Letters*. New York: Ayer.

Nussbaum, Arthur (1947). *A Concise History of the Law of Nations*. New York: Macmillan.

Page, Norman (ed.) (1974). *Wilkie Collins: The Critical Heritage*. London: Routledge & Kegan Paul.

Parry, Jonathan P. (1993). *The Rise and Fall of Liberal Government in Britain*. New Haven: Yale University Press.

Pashukanis, Evgeny B. (1978). *Law and Marxism: A General Theory* [1924]. Repr. New York: Pluto.

Pateman, Carole (1988). *The Sexual Contract*. Stanford: Stanford University Press.

Patmore, Coventry (1961). *Coventry Patmore's "Essay on English Metrical Law"*, ed. Sister Mary Augustine Roth. Washington, DC: Catholic University of America Press.

Patterson, Orlando (1982). *Slavery and Social Death: A Comparative Study*. Cambridge, Mass.: Harvard University Press.

Patteson, Richard (1978). "*King Solomon's Mines*: Imperialism and Narrative Structure." *Journal of Narrative Technique* 8(2): 112–23.

Paxton, Nancy L. (1991). *George Eliot and Herbert Spencer: Feminism, Evolutionism, and the Reconstruction of Gender*. Princeton: Princeton University Press.

Pease, Allison (2000). *Modernism, Mass Culture, and the Aesthetics of Obscenity*. New York: Cambridge University Press.

Peters, Catherine (1991). *The King of Inventors: A Life of Wilkie Collins*. Princeton: Princeton University Press.

Pitts, Jennifer (2005). *A Turn to Empire: The Rise of Imperial Liberalism in Britain and France*. Princeton: Princeton University Press.

Poovey, Mary (1995). *Making a Social Body: British Cultural Formation, 1830–1864*. Chicago: University of Chicago Press.

Poovey, Mary (1998). *A History of the Modern Fact: Problems of Knowledge in the Sciences of Wealth and Society*. Chicago: University of Chicago Press.

Poovey, Mary (2008). *Genres of the Credit Economy: Mediating Value in Eighteenth and Nineteenth Century Britain*. Chicago: University of Chicago Press.

Pope, Alexander (1899). *The Iliad*, by Homer. Available at: https://www.gutenberg.org/files/6130/6130-h/6130-h.html.

Porter, Theodore M. (1986). *The Rise of Statistical Thinking, 1820–1900*. Princeton: Princeton University Press.

Povinelli, Elizabeth (2011). *Economies of Abandonment: Social Belonging and Endurance in Late Liberalism*. Durham, NC: Duke University Press.

Prasch, Tom (2012). "After the Slaughter: Felice Beato and the Possibilities of Victorian War Photography." Paper presented at Midwest Conference on British Studies. University of Toronto, 12–14 Oct.

Prins, Yopie (1999). *Victorian Sappho*. Princeton: Princeton University Press.

Prins, Yopie (2000). "Victorian Meters." In Joseph Bristow (ed.), *The Cambridge Companion to Victorian Poetry*, 89–113. Cambridge: Cambridge University Press.

Prins, Yopie (2013). "Metrical Discipline: Algernon Swinburne on 'The Flogging-Block.'" In *Algernon Charles Swinburne: Unofficial Laureate*, ed. Catherine Maxwell and Stefano Evangelista, 95–124. Manchester: Manchester University Press.

Psomiades, Kathy A. (1997). *Beauty's Body: Femininity and Representation in British Aestheticism*. Stanford: Stanford University Press.

Psomiades, Kathy A. (2009). "He Knew He Was Right: The Sensational Tyranny of the Sexual Contract and the Problem of Liberal Progress." In Regenia Gagnier, Margaret Markwick, and Deborah Morse (eds), *The Politics of Gender in Anthony Trollope's Novels: New Readings for the Twenty First Century*, 31–44. Farnham: Ashgate.

Psomiades, Kathy (2013). "Hidden Meaning: Andrew Lang, H. Rider Haggard, Sigmund Freud, and Interpretation." *Romanticism and Victorianism on the Net* 64. http://www.erudit.org/revue/ravon/2013/v/n64/1025669ar.html?vue=resume.

Psomiades, Kathy A. (n.d.) "Primitive Marriage: Victorian Anthropology and the Novel." Unpublished MS.

Pug's Tour Through Europe; or, The travell'd monkey, containing his wonderful adventures in the principal capitals of the greatest empires, kingdoms, and states. London: John Harris, *c*.1825.

Pykett, Lyn (2005). *Authors in Context: Wilkie Collins*. New York: Oxford University Press.

Pyle, Forest (2015). "'I give my dreams as dreams': The *Grammatology* Effect." Conference presentation, MLA.

Rancière, Jacques (1993). *Dis-Agreement: Politics and Philosophy*, trans. Julie Rose. Minneapolis: University of Minnesota Press.

Randall, John H. Jr. (1965). "John Stuart Mill and the Working-Out of Empiricism." *Journal of the History of Ideas* 26(1): 59–88.

"Reign of Terror Legislation in Jamaica" (1866). *The Anti-Slavery Reporter*, 15 Jan.: 26.

Reimer, Marga and Eliot Michaelson (2014). "Reference." In *The Stanford Encyclopedia of Philosophy*, Winter 2014 edn. Accessed 10 June 2016.

Rignall, John (ed.) (2000). *Oxford Reader's Companion to George Eliot*. New York: Oxford University Press.

Ritchin, Fred (2010). "Felice Beato and the Photography of War." In Anne Lacoste (ed.), *Felice Beato: Photographer on the Eastern Road*, 119–33. Los Angeles: Getty.

Rizzuto, Nicole (2015). *Insurgent Testimonies: Witnessing Colonial Trauma in Modern and Anglophone Literature*. New York: Fordham University Press.

Robbins, Bruce (1999). *Feeling Global: Internationalism in Distress*. New York: New York University Press.

Roberts, Frederick (1924). *Letters Written During the Indian Mutiny*. London: Macmillan.

Robinson, Kenneth (1952). *Wilkie Collins: A Biography*. New York: Macmillan.

Rooksby, Rikky (1997). *A. C. Swinburne: A Poet's Life*. Farnham: Ashgate.

Rosen, Frederick (2006). "The Philosophy of Error and Liberty of Thought: J. S. Mill on Logical Fallacies." *Informal Logic* 26(2): 121–47.

Rosenberg, John D. (1968). "Introduction." In *Swinburne: Selected Poetry and Prose*, xii–xiv. New York: Modern Library.

Rossiter, Clinton L. (1948). *Constitutional Dictatorship: Crisis Government in the Modern Democracies.* Princeton: Princeton University Press.

Rubin, Larry (1956). "River Imagery as a Means of Foreshadowing in *The Mill on the Floss*." *Modern Language Notes* 71(1): 18–22.

Rudwick, Martin J. S. (2008). *Worlds Before Adam: The Reconstruction of Geohistory in the Age of Reform.* Chicago: University of Chicago Press.

Rudwick, Martin J. S. (2014). *Earth's Deep History: How It Was Discovered and Why It Matters.* Chicago: University of Chicago Press.

Ruskin, John (1890). "Fiction—Fair and Foul." In *The Ethics of Dust; Fiction, Fair and Foul; The Elements of Drawing*, 153–219. Boston: Dana Estes.

Russell, David (2013). "Aesthetic Liberalism: John Stuart Mill as Essayist." *Victorian Studies* 56(1): 7–30.

Russell, William Howard (1860). *My Diary in India, In the Year 1858–9*, vol. 1. London: Routledge, Warne, & Routledge.

Said, Edward W. (1983). *The World, the Text, and the Critic.* Cambridge, Mass.: Harvard University Press.

Said, Edward (1994). *Culture and Imperialism.* New York: Vintage.

Saint-Amour, Paul (2005). "Air War Prophecy and Interwar Modernism." *Comparative Literature Studies* 42(2): 130–61.

Saint-Amour, Paul (2015). *Tense Future: Modernism, Total War, Encyclopedic Form.* New York: Oxford University Press.

Saintsbury, George ([1910]1961). *A History of English Prosody.* New York: Russell & Russell.

Samalin, Zach (2015). "Plumbing the Depths, Scouring the Surface: Henry Mayhew's Scavenger Hermeneutics." Unpublished MS.

Sanyal, Debarati (2006). *The Violence of Modernity: Baudelaire, Irony, and the Politics of Form.* Baltimore: Johns Hopkins University Press.

Sartori, Andrew (2014). *Liberalism in Empire: An Alternative History.* Berkeley: University of California Press.

Schiller, Friedrich (1998). "On Naïve and Sentimental Poetry" [1795], trans. Daniel O. Dahlstrom. In *Essays*, ed. Walter Hinderer and Daniel O. Dahlstrom, 179–260. New York: Continuum.

Schmitt, Carl (1996). *The Crisis of Parliamentary Democracy* [1923, 1926], trans. Ellen Kennedy. Cambridge, Mass.: MIT Press.

Schmitt, Carl (2003). *The Nomos of the Earth in the International Law of the Jus Publicum Europaeum*, trans. G. L. Ulmen. New York: Telos.

Schmitt, Carl (2005). *Political Theology: Four Chapters on the Concept of Sovereignty* [1922], trans. G. Schwab. Chicago: University of Chicago Press.

Secord, James (1986). *Controversy in Victorian Geology: The Cambrian–Silurian Dispute.* Princeton: Princeton University Press.

Sedgwick, Eve Kosofsky (1986). *The Coherence of Gothic Conventions*. London: Routledge & Kegan.

Sedgwick, Eve Kosofsky (2002). "Paranoid Reading and Reparative Reading, or, You're So Paranoid, You Probably Think This Essay is About You." In *Touching Feeling*, 124–51. Durham, NC: Duke University Press.

Semmel, Bernard (1963). *Jamaican Blood and Victorian Conscience: The Governor Eyre Controversy*. New York: Houghton Mifflin.

The Sepoy's Daughter: A True Tale of the Indian War (1860).

Sheller, Mimi (2012). *Citizenship from Below: Erotic Agency and Carribbean Freedom*. Durham, NC: Duke University Press.

Shelley, Percy Bysshe (1920). *A Philosophical View of Reform*, ed. T. W. Rolleston. Oxford: Oxford University Press. Web. 18 Jan. 2016.

Smith, Adam (1982). *The Theory of Moral Sentiments* [1759]. Repr. Indianapolis: Liberty Fund.

Smith, Daniel W. (1998). "'A Life of Pure Immanence': Deleuze's 'Critique et Clinique' Project." Introduction to *Gilles Deleuze, Essays Critical and Clinical*, trans. Daniel W. Smith and Michael A. Greco. London: Verso.

Smith, Janet Adam (1948). *Henry James and Robert Louis Stevenson: A Record of Friendship and Criticism*. London: Rupert Hart-Davis.

Smith, Shawn Michelle (2007). "The Evidence of Lynching Photographs." In Dora Apel and Shawn Michelle Smith (eds), *Lynching Photographs*, 11–41. Berkeley: University of California Press.

Snyder, Laura J. (2006). *Reforming Philosophy: A Victorian Debate on Science and Society*. Chicago: University of Chicago Press.

Sontag, Susan (1967). "Against Interpretation." In *Against Interpretation and Other Essays*, 3–14. London: Eyre & Spottiswoode.

Sontag, Susan (2002). *Regarding the Pain of Others*. New York: Farrar, Straus & Giroux.

Spencer, Herbert ([1874] 1897). *The Principles of Sociology*, vol. 1. New York: D. Appleton & Co.

Stedman Jones, Gareth (1971). *Outcast London: A Study in the Relationship Between Classes in Victorian Society*. Oxford: Oxford University Press.

Steer, Philip (2015). "Romances of Uneven Development: Spatiality, Trade, and Form in Robert Louis Stevenson's Pacific Novels." *Victorian Literature and Culture* 43: 343–56.

Steiner, George (1996). *Homer in English*. New York: Penguin.

Steiner, George (2004). "Homer in English Translation." In Robert Fowler (ed.), *The Cambridge Companion to Homer*, 363–75. New York: Cambridge University Press.

Steinlight, Emily (2010). "Dickens's 'Supernumeraries' and the Biopolitical Imagination of Victorian Fiction." *NOVEL: A Forum on Fiction* 43(2): 227–50.

Stephen, James Fitzjames (1865). "Hobbes on Government." *Saturday Review*, 26 Aug.: 271–3.

Stephen, James Fitzjames (1866). "Sovereignty." *Saturday Review*, 10 Nov.: 570–2.

Stephen, James Fitzjames (1892). *Horae Sabbaticae: A Reprint of Articles Contributed to the Saturday Review.* 2 vols. London: Macmillan.

Stephen, James Fitzjames (1967). *Liberty, Equality, Fraternity* [1873]. Repr. Cambridge: Cambridge University Press.

Stephen, Leslie (1895). *The Life of Sir James Fitzjames Stephen, Bart., K.C.S.I., a Judge of the High Court of Justice.* London: Smith, Elder.

Stevenson, Robert Louis (1882). "A Gossip on Romance." *Longman's Magazine* 1(1): 69–79.

Stevenson, Robert Louis (1906). *The Dynamiter; New Arabian Nights*, ed. Charles C. Curtis and Temple Scott. New York: Bigelow.

Stevenson, Robert Louis (1994). *The Letters of Robert Louis Stevenson*, ed. Bradford A. Booth and Ernest Mehew. New Haven: Yale University Press.

Stevenson, Robert Louis (2002). *The Strange Case of Dr. Jekyll and Mr. Hyde and Other Tales of Terror.* New York: Penguin.

Stevenson, Robert Louis (2004). *Treasure Island* [1883]. Repr. New York: Bantam.

Stevenson, Robert Louis (2007). *Kidnapped* [1886]. Repr. New York: Penguin.

Stewart, Garrett (1984). *Death Sentences: Styles of Dying in British Fiction.* Cambridge, Mass.: Harvard University Press.

Stewart, Garrett (2009). *Novel Violence: A Narratography of Victorian Fiction.* Chicago: University of Chicago Press.

Stoler, Ann Laura (1995). *Race and the Education of Desire: Foucault's History of Sexuality and the Colonial Order of Things.* Durham, NC: Duke University Press.

Stoler, Ann Laura (2010). *Along the Archival Grain: Epistemic Anxieties and Colonial Common Sense.* Princeton: Princeton University Press.

Swinburne, Algernon Charles (1866a). *Poems and Ballads.* London: Edward Moxon.

Swinburne, Algernon Charles (1866b). *Poems and Ballads.* London: John Camden Hotten.

Swinburne, Algernon Charles (1866c). Preface. In *A Selection from the Works of Lord Byron.* London: Edward Moxon.

Swinburne, Algernon Charles (1868). *William Blake: A Critical Essay.* London: John Camden Hotten. Available at: https://archive.org/stream/williamblakecrit00swinrich#page/n5/mode/2up.

Swinburne, Algernon Charles (1875). "Byron." In *Essays and Studies*, 238–58. London: Chatto & Windus.

Swinburne, Algernon Charles (1876). Letter to Theodore Watts-Dunton, 12 Dec. 1876. British Library, Ashley MS, 1887.

Swinburne, Algernon Charles (1959). *The Swinburne Letters*, vol. 1: *1854–1869*, ed. Cecil Y. Lang. New Haven: Yale University Press.

Swinburne, Algernon Charles (1968a). *Selected Poetry and Prose*, ed. John D. Rosenberg. New York: Modern Library.

Swinburne, Algernon Charles (2000). *Poems and Ballads & Atalanta and Calydon*, ed. Kenneth Haynes. New York: Penguin.

Swinburne, Algernon Charles (2004). "Emily Brontë." In *Major Poems and Selected Prose*, ed. Jerome McGann and Charles L. Sligh, 395–9. New Haven: Yale University Press.

"Swinburne's William Blake" (1868). *New York Times*, 29 March: 3. Web. 20 Oct. 2007.

Tadiar, Neferti (2009). *Things Fall Away: Philippine Historical Experience and the Makings of Globalization*. Durham, NC: Duke University Press.

Thomas, David Wayne (2003). *Cultivating Victorians: Liberal Culture and the Aesthetic*. Philadelphia: University of Pennsylvania Press.

Tickell, Alex (2013). *Terrorism, Insurgency, and Indian-English Literature, 1830–1947*. London: Routledge.

Tillyard, E. M. W. (1948). *Five Poems, 1470–1870*. London: Chatto & Windus.

Tonnies, Ferdinand (1957). *Community and Society: Gemeinschaft and Gesellschaft* [1887], trans. Charles P. Loomis. New York: Harper.

Tremenheere, Henry (1858). "How is India to be Governed?" *Bentley's Miscellany A3*: 111–23.

Trollope, Anthony (1973). *Phineas Redux* [1869]. Repr. New York: Oxford University Press.

Trollope, Anthony (2003). *Australia and New Zealand*, vol. 1. New York: Cambridge University Press.

Tucker, Herbert (2008). *Epic: Britain's Heroic Muse, 1790–1910*. New York: Oxford University Press.

Tucker, Irene (2000). *A Probable State: The Novel, the Contract, and the Jews*. Chicago: University of Chicago Press.

V21 Collective. "Manifesto of the V21 Collective." Accessed 15 June 2016 at: http://v21collective.org/manifesto-of-the-v21-collective-ten-theses/

Vernon, James (2005). "Historians and the Victorian Studies Question: Response." *Victorian Studies* 47(2): 272–80.

Weber, Max (1994). "The Profession and Vocation of Politics," trans. Ronald Speirs. In *Political Writings*, ed. Peter Lassman and Ronald Speirs, 309–69. New York: Cambridge University Press.

Weintraub, Joseph (1975). "Andrew Lang: Critic of Romance." *English Literature in Transition (1880–1920)* 18(1): 5–15.

Whitaker, J. K. (1975). "John Stuart Mill's Methodology." *Journal of Political Economy* 83(5): 1033–49.

White, R. J. (1967). "Introduction." In James Fitzjames Stephen, *Liberty, Equality, Fraternity* [1873]. Repr. Cambridge: Cambridge University Press.

Williams, Raymond (1977). *Marxism and Literature*. Oxford: Oxford University Press.

Winter, Sarah (2016). "On the Morant Bay Rebellion in Jamaica and the Governor Eyre-George William Gordon Controversy, 1865–70." *BRANCH: Britain, Representation, and Nineteenth-Century History*, http://www.branchcollective.org/?ps_articles=sarah-winter-on-the-morant-bay-rebellion-in-jamaica-and-the-governor-eyre-george-william-gordon-controversy-1865-70, accessed 18 Jan. 2016.

Woloch, Alex (2003). *The One vs. the Many: Minor Characters and the Space of the Protagonist in the Novel*. Princeton: Princeton University Press.

Woodward, Llewellyn (1962). *The Age of Reform: 1815–1870*. 1938. Repr. Oxford: Oxford University Press.

Wordsworth, William (2000). "Lines Written a Few Miles Above Tintern Abbey." In *The Major Works*, ed. Stephen Gill, 131–5. New York: Oxford University Press.

Workman, Gillian (1974). "Thomas Carlyle and the Governor Eyre Controversy: An Account With Some New Material." *Victorian Studies* 14(1): 77–102.

Yeazell, Ruth (2009). *Art of the Everyday: Dutch Painting and the Realist Novel*. Princeton: Princeton University Press.

Index

1841 Census 85–9, 99–100, 112, 258 n. 1
1880s as transitional moment in Victorian
    global rule

abandonment 6, 34, 88, 90, 101–2,
    104–7, 113, 125–6, 131, 139, 217,
    260 n. 16
abstraction 93, 95–8, 111, 113, 121
  aesthetic 122
  circuit or system of 109, 260 n. 11
  human 89
  inductive 88
  particulars converted to 128
  process of 91–2
  universal 99
  violence of 125–6. *See also* Jameson,
    Fredric; Mill, John Stuart; Collins,
    Wilkie; Marx, Karl
accumulation
  capital 124, 246, 249 n. 16
  geological 48, 160
  historical 62
  logic of 156–7
  metaphors of 45, 70
  slave-based 113, 123, 125
action
  as an aesthetic 193
  cognition or deliberation versus 196,
    198, 202–3, 219, 238
  diegetic 44, 81
  novelistic category of 18, 35, 193, 200,
    205–6, 234, 269 n. 11
  and objects 250 n. 25
  political problem of 205
  role in literature 269 n. 11
  romance 200
  second-generation 115–16
  theory of 204. *See also* Haggard, H. Rider;
    James, Henry; Lang, Andrew
Acts of War 179
Adams, Edward 225, 230, 236, 273 n. 38
Adorno, Theodor 30, 97, 122, 126, 192,
    257 n. 46, 264–5 n. 22
aestheticism 162, 245
aesthetics
  anti-commercial 204–5
  ethical 78
  and geopolitical dynamics 19
  and imperialism 86

mechanical 121
  and modernization 199
  neo-Kantian 178
  neo-Romantic ideology of 18
  philosophical 77
  practice 88, 121, 249 n. 15
  progressivism 198
  Sadean 190
  of temporal sentimentalism 81
  and violence 65. *See also* art
affect
  dichotomy of reflection and 262 n. 5
  embodied 181, 198, 200, 235
  of enchantment 20
  Kant on 154, 262 n. 6
  readerly 27
affordances 18–19, 22, 34, 42, 74, 84,
    184, 250 n. 26
Africa 6, 35, 200, 212, 220, 230,
    270 n. 18
Agamben, Giorgio 12, 42, 106, 147,
    181–3, 263 n. 15
Age of Discussion 3, 9, 149, 174. *See also*
    Bagehot, Walter
agency 8, 32, 53, 116, 123, 243, 245,
    273 n. 1
allegory
  of antagonism 109
  anti-cosmopolitan 255 n. 24
  of pain 175
  ruptured 192
  of sublime rhythm 154
  temporal-political 59
anarchy 142, 155, 170, 179, 187
Anderson, Amanda 47, 56, 112, 166,
    252 n. 5, 253 n. 12, 254 n. 17,
    259 n. 6
Anderson, Benedict 252 n. 7
Arendt, Hannah
  on the 1880s 194–5
  and law 107–8
  on revolutionary transition 68–9,
    256 n. 33
  rights 111, 224
  on social death 124
  on violence 199
Aristotle 8, 106, 203–4
Armstrong, Isobel 185, 264 n. 20,
    265–6 n. 28

Armstrong, Nancy 55
Arnold, Matthew
  on character 112, 209
  chart of commitments 189
  on democracy 93, 122, 179
  distinction between Swinburne
    and 261–2 n. 4
  on Homer 206
  on Kant 141–2, 155, 188, 265 n. 24
  preference for culture over
    anarchy 187
  treatment of Philomela 175
  two ages 59
Arrighi, Giovanni 11, 211, 241, 245,
  268 nn. 1, 5
art
  bureaucratic and journalistic accounts
    of Morant Bay as 138
  and commercialism 204
  and liberal state 141
  as mode of defusing anarchy 155
  pour l'art 188
  and realism 201
  restorative powers of literary 129
  as technology 18
  and temporality 77. *See also* aesthetics
Auerbach, Erich 196–8, 234–5
Austin, John 4–5, 169
Azoulay, Ariella 251 n. 30

Badiou, Alain 50, 65, 68, 70, 183,
  255 n. 32, 256 n. 33
Bagehot, Walter 3, 149, 174, 263 n. 12
Baker, E. A. 255 n. 31
Bakhtin, Mikhail 212–14, 235
Balibar, Etienne 94, 99
Banerjee, Sukanya 7, 248 n. 9, 271 n. 27
Barbados 114, 119, 122, 125, 172
Barthes, Roland 31, 83, 258 n. 51
Bataille, Georges 265 n. 25, 266 n. 36
Baucom, Ian 101, 262 n. 8, 271 n. 28
Baudelaire, Charles 140, 149, 163–4,
  261 n. 3
Bayly, C. A. 1, 247 n. 1
Beato, Felice 20–1, 23, 32, 172,
  250–1 n. 27, 251 nn. 32, 33
  "British Naval Landing Party at the
    Maedamura Battery,
    Shimonoseki" 21–2
  "The Hanging of Two Rebels" 24–6
  "Interior of the Secundra Bagh" 26–31.
    See also Lucknow
Beauvoir, Simone de 264 n. 22
Belich, James 11
Bell, Duncan 7, 247 n. 4, 248 nn. 8, 11

belonging
  Derrida on 267 n. 43
  globalized system of 20
  and imperial modernity 34
  law and 5, 145, 147, 267 n. 43
  Mill on 95
  national 144
  in the novels of Collins 105–6, 108, 111
  political 111, 124, 148, 221
Benjamin, Walter 4, 71–2, 130–1, 176,
  183, 256 n. 38, 257 n. 40, 261 n. 21
Bentham, Jeremy 94, 99
Bentley's Miscellany 3
Berlant, Lauren 261 n. 20
Berlin Conference (1885) 33
Berlin Wall 42
Bersani, Leo 163–4
Bevington, Merle Mowbray 266 n. 31
Bibighar Massacre 247 n. 3
Bigelow, Gordon 250 n. 23
Bildungsroman 33, 39, 65, 187, 212–13,
  214, 251 n. 1
#BlackLivesMatter 262 n. 10
Blackwood, John 44, 251 n. 2
Blackwood's 75, 80–1
Blake, William. *See* Swinburne, Algernon
  Charles
Blanchot, Maurice 264–5 n. 22
Bleby, Henry 183–4
Bodin, Jean 229
Boer Wars 2
Boers 195–6, 216–17
Braddon, Elizabeth 102–3
Brady, Matthew 23
Brantlinger, Patrick 238
Briggs, Asa 41, 49, 74, 256 n. 33
Bright, John 9, 110, 146
Britain. *See* England
Brontë, Emily 175, 188
Brooks, Cleanth 250 n. 23
Brooks, Peter 272–3 n. 37
Brown, Wendy 249 n. 16, 258 n. 49
Browning, Elizabeth Barrett 100, 185
Buchanan, Robert 164, 266 n. 29
Buckley, Jerome 69, 251 n. 1
Bulwer-Lytton, Edward 63
Burke, Edmund 46, 64, 183, 255 n. 30,
  256 n. 37
Burrow, W. L. 60, 251–2 n. 3, 254 n. 21
Butcher, S. H. 234
Byron, Lord. *See* Swinburne, Algernon

Cain, P. J. 6, 11, 122, 241, 249 nn. 17, 18,
  268 n. 1, 270 n. 15
Callwell, C. E. 224–6

formalism 184, 188
  new 187
  poetic 185
  political 19
Forster, John 131
Foucault, Michel 12–13, 89–90, 170,
    218–19, 249 nn. 19, 20, 259 n. 9,
    264 n. 17, 267 n. 46
  History of Sexuality 12
  Society Must be Defended 147. *See also*
    sovereignty
free indirect discourse 33, 112, 204, 208,
    235, 237, 260 n. 15
freedom 14, 65, 94, 178–9, 182, 187,
    205, 209, 222
  bourgeois 115
  individualized 53
  intellectual 93
  liberal 208, 230
Frye, Northrop 213

Gallagher, Catherine 100, 104
Gemeinschaft and *Gesellschaft* 40, 59,
    255 n. 26
General Register Office 89
geology 33, 41–2, 45–6, 50, 59, 74,
    252–3 n. 8, 253 n. 9
Gitelman, Lisa 18–19
Goodlad, Lauren 7, 12, 103, 109, 112–13,
    116–17, 250 n. 26
Gordon, William 144–6, 167, 202, 263 nn.
    12, 14
Government of India Act (1858) 3
Governor Eyre Defence Committee. *See*
    Carlyle, Thomas
Graver, Suzanne 59, 83, 255 n. 26
Great Exhibition of 1851 41, 115, 125
Green-Lewis, Jennifer 29
Green, Martin 268 n. 4
Green, T. H. 92
Greiner, Rae 82
Guattari, Felix 265 n. 26
Guillory, John 17
Gunn, Simon 7, 10, 248 n. 11

Habermas, Jürgen 247 n. 4, 252 n. 5,
    253 n. 14
Hadley, Elaine 116
Haggard, H. Rider
  anti-deliberative aesthetic of 200–1,
    204, 219, 230, 239
  *Cetywayo and His White
    Neighbors* 216–18, 220, 223–4,
    226, 270–1 n. 21, 272 n. 33
  The Days of My Life 216

and imperialism 210
  interventions in novel theory 202
  Jess 273 n. 37
  and just war doctrine 230
  King Solomon's Mines 35, 60, 198–202,
    205, 210–11, 213–17, 222, 226,
    229, 234, 236, 238, 270–1 nn. 21–2
  law and 219, 221–3, 227
  liberal idealism and 9, 215, 225
  military service in Africa 195–6,
    270 n. 18
  mock-epic form of 35, 199, 206, 209
  narrative structure of 208
  neo-Homeric idiom of 228, 235, 237
  positioned by Lang as realism's savage
    other 205
  reconception of action and event in
    context of British small wars 34–5
  romances of 11, 193, 197–8, 211
  relation to melodrama 268 n. 4
  and science 270 n. 16
  and sovereignty 218, 226, 229
  violence and 224
  The World's Desire 269 n. 10. *See also*
    Lang, Andrew; realism
Hall, Catherine 12, 262 n. 11
Hall, E. W. 222
Hallward, Peter 256 nn. 34, 36
Harcourt, Vernon 42, 45
Hardy, Thomas 64
Harrison, Frederic 54, 84, 146, 171–2
Harvey, David 211
Hegel, G. F. W. 58
hegemony 11, 33, 35, 40, 113, 193,
    195, 231, 241, 243, 245, 268 nn.
    1, 5
Henry VII 179
Henry VIII 179
heroic couplet 18, 34
Hertz, Neil 58
historicism 43–4, 48, 50, 56, 63, 91, 93,
    101, 103, 123–5, 169, 187, 209
  new 17, 22, 149, 191–2
Hobbes, Thomas 58, 170–1, 176, 229
Hobsbawm, Eric 119, 193
Homer 198, 202, 205–6, 209–11, 233–7,
    272 n. 36, 272–3 n. 37
  The Odyssey 206, 208, 234–6,
    272 n. 36
Hopkins, A. G. 6, 11, 249 n. 17, 268 n. 1,
    270 n. 15
Hotten, James Camden 142
Howells, William Dean
  and American realism 199, 207
  attack on H. Rider Haggard by 237

on *The Mill on the Floss* 33, 64–5, 69, 71, 255 n. 31
post-Jamesian critical tradition 199, 236, 268 n. 6
The Princess Casamassima 204
The Portrait of a Lady 204
rationality 235
realist probability 72, 212
surface and depth 201, 209. *See also* Howells, William Dean; Lang, Andrew; realism
Jameson, Fredric 19, 26, 30, 40, 46, 51, 61–3, 97, 126, 192, 210, 250 n. 26, 253 n. 10, 255 nn. 28, 29, 265 n. 25, 269 n. 14, 274 n. 2
Japan 20–3
jingoism 11, 27, 35, 210, 216
Jones, Anna Maria 8
Jones, Gareth Stedman 88
Joubert, Joseph 179
Joyce, James 272 n. 36
Joyce, Patrick 86–7
justice
    control of 266 n. 30
    equal 40, 51
    military 26
    poetic 122
    procedural 144
    and ruination 224
    transactional dispensation of 101
    universal 217, 222, 224
    war for 228

Kant, Immanuel
    affects and 174, 262 n. 6
    Critique of the Power of Judgment 154, 267 n. 39
    dynamical sublime of 155
    international law and 221, 225
    and liberal political tradition 48, 265 n. 24
    links beauty and moderation 141–2, 265 n. 23
    on self-regulating power 228
    on the unjust enemy 224, 227, 271 n. 28
    "What is Enlightenment?" 48
Kaplan, Amy 207, 263 n. 15
Keats, John 141, 164, 175
Kenner, Hugh 272 n. 36
killing
    distinction between murder and 145
    and empire 202
    extrajudicial 2, 190

persistence of in modernity 4, 243
and power 12
racialized 25
in service of peace 230
sovereign 24
by the state 13, 226, 244–5
world structured by 156. *See also* sovereignty
Kingsley, Charles 146
Kipling, Rudyard 2, 6, 269 n. 13
Kirshenbaum, Matthew 250 n. 25
Kostal, R. W. 5, 9, 144, 180, 247 n. 5

Lacan, Jacques 264 n. 22
Lacoste, Anne 250–1 n. 27
Lafourcade, George 261 n. 1, 264 n. 21
Lang, Andrew
    action-oriented mode of 206, 209, 238
    as champion of Haggard 197–8, 201, 205, 210, 231, 236–7, 269 n. 10
    coterie of 34–5, 200
    on epic life 235
    Homeric scholarship of 35, 206, 208–9, 233–4, 236–7, 272 n. 36
    meets Tylor 269 n. 12
    writing practices of 269 n. 9. *See also* Haggard, H. Rider; Howells, William Dean; James, Henry; realism
Larsen, Neil 116
Latour, Bruno 31–2, 130
law
    civil 144
    colonial 1, 3, 262 n. 8, 263 n. 13
    as counting apparatus 107
    common 167
    custom and 77–8, 257 n. 41
    English 43, 117
    of exchangeability 51
    extension of category of 103
    force and 7
    and free trade 41
    history as process of progressive societies emerging into 54, 188
    Hobbesian thesis of 5
    idealist visions of 142
    imperial 16, 147
    international 220–3, 225, 227, 230, 272 n. 30
    of liberal choice 52
    martial 9, 13, 34, 131, 138, 143, 146, 148, 167, 172, 178–85, 266 n. 32, 267 n. 39, 267 nn. 40, 41
    modern 144, 170, 211
    and its other 218

Victorian 5–6, 113
welfare 252 n. 4. *See also* sovereignty;
  statelessness; violence
statelessness 108, 124, 263 n. 15. *See also*
  state
status
  civil 263 n. 15
  as counted citizen 98
  force as central feature of the state of
    58, 74
  racial 263 n. 14
  strictures of 66
  succeeded by contract 4, 11, 42, 52–4,
    60–1, 63, 73, 102, 115–17, 169,
    187, 197, 207
  as tool for administering colonial
    zones 171–2. *See also* Maine,
    Henry Sumner; Mill, John Stuart
  vendetta of 56
Steiner, George 235
Steinlight, Emily 90, 110, 258–9 n. 3
Stephen, James Fitzjames 4, 50–1,
  167–72, 180, 183
Stephen, Leslie 93–4
Stevenson, Robert Louis 9
  and British masculinity 219
  and critique of British globalization
    273 n. 41
  Kidnapped 231
  and small wars 35
  *The Strange Case of Dr. Jekyll and
    Mr. Hyde* 200, 238–42
Stewart, Garrett 18, 58, 67–9, 71
Stoler, Ann Laura 147, 250 n. 22,
  264 n. 17
struggle, anticolonial 1, 248 n. 9
sublime 154, 163, 256 n. 37, 265 n. 23,
  267 n. 39
surface and depth 20, 22, 25, 30, 69, 112,
  199, 201–2, 209, 237, 253 n. 10,
  260 n. 15, 268–9 n. 7,
  272–3 n. 37
Swinburne, Algernon Charles
  affect in 140
  "Anactoria" 34, 150, 153–9, 161–4,
    175, 185–6, 191, 265 n. 26
  anti-liberalism of 160, 162
  "A Ballad of Death" 140
  "A Ballad of Life" 140–2, 261 n. 2
  "The Birch" 150–3
  on Blake 174–6, 267 n. 37
  on Byron 172–4
  dialectic strategy of 185, 188–9
  "Dolores" 164, 175
  and excess 160

and fascism 160–1, 175
formal devices of poetry 154
genealogy of 267 n. 46
influence by Marquis de Sade 150, 264
  n. 21, 264–5 n. 22
"Itylus" 175–7
"Laus Veneris" 156, 162–4, 176–7, 224
"The Leper" 164
Lesbia Brandon 164
metaphoric procedure of 163, 192,
  265 n. 25
metonymic juxtaposition with Morant
  Bay 139
personification of poetry 141
Poems and Ballads 9, 34, 137, 139–40,
  142, 148–50, 156, 162–6, 170,
  173, 175, 177, 184, 187–91
poems lodge surplus within
  formalism 184
political logic of poetry of 34, 162, 190
questions universalist vocabulary
  148, 224
Republicanism of 149, 190, 264 n. 20,
  265 n. 25
"The Roundel" 186
on Shelley 173–4
similarity between restraint and
  violence 165
Songs Before Sunrise 149
totality of 193. *See also* Morant Bay
  Rebellion; poetry
sympathy 50, 57–8, 78, 80, 82, 206–8,
  263 n. 16

Tadiar, Neferti 105
telegrams and telegraphy 1–4, 13–14, 19
temporality 43–4, 49, 70, 77, 115
Tennyson, Alfred, Lord 142, 156,
  185, 187
theory 32–3
  analytic 94
  design 18
  distinction between ideology and 8
  legal 5, 52, 59, 224
  liberal 7, 113, 115, 138, 145, 149, 178,
    188, 208
  modernization 59, 252 n. 4
  poetic 34
  political 8, 10, 33, 40, 50, 59, 88, 103,
    139, 149, 159, 165
Tillyard, E. M. W. 156, 159–62, 164, 175
time
  of colonial law 3
  developmental 8, 172
  empty 52, 196, 212

Printed and bound by CPI Group (UK) Ltd, Croydon, CR0 4YY